Oracle 10g Developing Media Rich Applications

Oracle Database Related Book Titles:

Oracle 9iR2 Data Warehousing, Hobbs, et al,
ISBN: 1-55558-287-7, 2004

Oracle 10g Data Warehousing, Hobbs, et al,
ISBN 1-55558-322-9, 2004

Oracle High Performance Tuning for 9i and 10g, Gavin Powell,
ISBN: 1-55558-305-9, 2004

Oracle SQL Jumpstart with Examples, Gavin Powell,
ISBN: 1-55558-323-7, 2005

Oracle Performance Tuning for 10gR2 Second Edition, Gavin Powell,
ISBN: 1-55558-345-8, 2006

Implementing Database Security and Auditing, Ben Natan,
ISBN 1-55558-334-2, 2005

Oracle Real Applications Clusters, Murali Vallath,
ISBN: 1-55558-288-5, 2004

Oracle 10g RAC Grid, Services & Clustering, Murali Vallath,
ISBN 1-55558-321-0, 2006

Oracle Database Programming Using Java and Web Services, Kuassi Mensah
ISBN 1-55558-329-6, 2006

For more information or to order these and other Digital Press
titles, please visit our website at www.books.elsevier.com/digitalpress!
At www.books.elsevier.com/digitalpress you can:
•Join the Digital Press Email Service and have news about
our books delivered right to your desktop
•Read the latest news on titles
•Sample chapters on featured titles for free
•Question our expert authors and editors
•Download free software to accompany select texts

Oracle 10g Developing Media Rich Applications

Larry Guros
Lynne Dunckley

ELSEVIER

DIGITAL
PRESS

Amsterdam · Boston · Heidelberg · London · New York · Oxford
Paris · San Diego· San Francisco · Singapore · Sydney · Tokyo

Elsevier Digital Press
30 Corporate Drive, Suite 400, Burlington, MA 01803, USA
Linacre House, Jordan Hill, Oxford OX2 8DP, UK

Library of Congress Cataloging-in-Publication Data
Application Submitted.

British Library Cataloguing-in-Publication Data
A catalogue record for this book is available from the British Library.

ISBN-10: 1-55558-331-8

ISBN-13: 978-1-55558-331-6

For information on all Elsevier Digital Press publications visit our Web site at www.books.elsevier.com

Transferred to Digital Printing 2009

Lynne Dunckley

To Matt and Chris

Larry Guros

To Family and Friends

Table of Contents

Acknowledgments   **xv**

1   Introduction   **1**

    1.1   Uses for Digital Media   1
    1.2   The Challenge of Digital Media   3
    1.3   The Evolution of Digital Media Storage and Management   3
    1.4   The Value Proposition for the Full Use of a Database for Digital Media   4
    1.5   The Value Proposition for Using Media Types   5
    1.6   Summary   6

2   Multimedia Basics   **7**

    2.1   Introduction   7
    2.2   What Is Different about Multimedia Data?   8
    2.3   Multimedia Metadata   9
    2.4   Image Data   11
        2.4.1 History of the Pixel and Digital Images   11
    2.5   Multimedia Data Acquisition   12
    2.6   Multimedia Data Transformation   13
        2.6.1 Resolution   15
        2.6.2 Delivery   18
        2.6.3 Compression   22
    2.7   Color Perception   29
        2.7.1 CIE_XYZ Color-space   30
        2.7.2 RGB Additive Color from Glowing Bodies, Lights, TVs, and Monitors   30
        2.7.3 CMYK: Subtractive Color from Reflecting Objects—Color Printing   31

2.7.4   HSB System (Hue, Saturation, and Brightness)   31
2.7.5   RYB (Red, Yellow, and Blue)   32
2.7.6   Comparing the Four Models   32
2.8   Real-time Media   34
2.8.1   Seeing Video   34
2.8.2   Audio   37
2.8.3   Video and Audio Streaming   37
2.8.4   What Is Available?   38
2.8.5   3GP Standards   41
2.9   What Is Metadata?   42
2.9.1   Generating and Extracting Metadata   42
2.9.2   Image Metadata   43
2.9.3   Image Metadata Format   45
2.10 Summary   47

3   Introduction to interMedia Storage   49

3.1   Introduction   49
3.2   Object-relational and Relational Features   50
3.3   Using Large Object Data Types   50
3.4   Using LOB Locators   51
3.5   Using BFILES   51
3.5.1   The Disadvantages of Using BFILES   53
3.6   Using the Relational Approach   55
3.6.1   The Disadvantages of Using BLOBS and BFILES   58
3.7   Using the Object-relational Approach   58
3.8   Using Oracle interMedia   59
3.8.1   Manipulating Image Data Using interMedia   64
3.8.2   New Formats Supported   67
3.8.3   ORDImage   68
3.8.4   Using PL/SQL Stored Procedures   70
3.8.5   ORDAudio   74
3.8.6   ORDDoc   76
3.8.7   ORDVideo   77
3.9   Using SQL/MM Still Image Standard (ISO/IEC 13249-5:2001
       SQL/MM)   78
3.10 Using interMedia to Create Your Own Object Types   83
3.10.1   The Disadvantages of Using Your Own Object Types   85
3.11 Summary   86

4   Introduction to Web Delivery of interMedia
Multimedia Data   **87**

    4.1   HTTP Delivery   87
        4.1.1   How Browsers Handle Media   87
        4.1.2   Image   88
        4.1.3   Arbitrary MIME Types   88
        4.1.4   Browser Plug-ins   89
        4.1.5   HTTP Caching   90
    4.2   Servlets   92
    4.3   interMedia HTTP Classes   93
    4.4   The mod_plsql Module   100
    4.5   interMedia JSP Tag Library   105
    4.6   Oracle Portal   105
    4.7   Oracle Data Provider for .NET (ODP.NET)   110
        4.7.1   ODP.NET Media Delivery to Browser   112
        4.7.2   ODP.NET Media Delivery from Browser   118
    4.8   PHP: Hypertext Preprocessor with OCI8 extension   125
        4.8.1   PHP Media delivery to browser   125
        4.8.2   PHP Media delivery from browser to database   129
    4.9   Streaming Server Delivery   133
        4.9.1   Real/Helix Server   133
        4.9.2   Microsoft Streaming Server   136
    4.10 Oracle Wireless   139
        4.10.1 Media Image Adaptation   140
    4.11 Oracle interMedia OraDAV Driver   143
        4.11.1 Install OraDAV Database Infrastructure in ORDSYS   144
        4.11.2 Define the OraDAV Endpoint in the Webdav
                Configuration File   148
        4.11.3 Using the OraDAV Endpoint   149
    4.12 Summary   151

5   Introduction to interMedia APIs   **153**

    5.1   PL/SQL   153
        5.1.1   Preparation   153
        5.1.2   Place the Images into the Database   154
        5.1.3   Processing the Image, Creating a JPEG Thumbnail   155
        5.1.4   Obtaining the Thumbnail in a File—Exporting the Image 156
        5.1.5   Putting It All Together   157
    5.2   interMedia Java Proxy Classes   157

5.2.1   Overview of ORDSYS.ORDImage (Oracle Database) and OrdImage (Java) Objects   157
5.2.2   Setting Up the Required Java Environment—Imports and CLASSPATH   159
5.2.3   Creating the JDBC Connection   161
5.2.4   Uploading Images from Files into Tables   162
5.2.5   Creating the JDBC Connection, Uploading Images from Files into Tables, and Retrieving Image Properties   164
5.2.6   Creating Thumbnails and Changing Formats   164
5.2.7   Downloading Image Data from Tables into Files   165
5.3   Oracle C++ Call Interface   166
5.3.1   Includes and C++ Namespaces   166
5.3.2   Creating the Connection   167
5.3.3   Populating the Image Row from a File   167
5.3.4   Extracting the Thumbnail from the Database into a File 170
5.4   C# Using Oracle Data Provider for .NET (ODP.NET)   172
5.4.1   Prerequisites for Using Oracle with Visual Studio .NET 172
5.4.2   Preparing the Visual Studio Project to Use ODP.NET   172
5.4.3   Object References   172
5.4.4   Creating the Connection   173
5.4.5   Creating the Database Commands to Insert a Row   173
5.4.6   Populating the Image Row   175
5.4.7   Extracting the Thumbnail from the Database into a File 178
5.5   Java Advanced Imaging interMedia APIs   180
5.5.1   JAI Includes   181
5.5.2   Creating the Database Row   181
5.5.3   Get the Thumbnail Image, Put a Logo on the Image, and Put the Image into a File   185
5.5.4   Running the Sample   188
5.6   Summary   190

6   Loading Media   191
6.1   PL/SQL   191
6.1.1   Loading from Local Files   192
6.1.2   Loading from an HTTP Source   194
6.1.3   Loading from a User Written Source   195
6.1.4   Unrecognized Formats   195
6.1.5   PL/SQL Loading Methods Performance Considerations   200
6.2   SQL*Loader   201
6.3   External Tables   203
6.4   Transportable Tablespaces   207

6.5   HTTP Form Load   210
6.6   Thick Client Loading   211
6.7   Summary   212

7   Planning interMedia Applications   213

7.1   Introduction   213
7.2   Gathering Requirements   215
        7.2.1   Functional Requirements   217
        7.2.2   Data Requirements   217
        7.2.3   Environmental Requirements—Context of Use   217
        7.2.4   User Requirements   218
        7.2.5   Usability Requirements   218
        7.2.6   Tools and Techniques   220
7.3   Define Architecture   227
        7.3.1   Technical Architecture   230
        7.3.2   Client-server Architecture   231
        7.3.3   Alternative Architectures   232
7.4   Data Modeling   235
        7.4.1   Define Schema   235
7.5   Prototyping   240
        7.5.1   Why Prototype?   240
        7.5.2   What Is Prototyping?   242
        7.5.3   Low-fidelity Prototypes   243
        7.5.4   High-fidelity Prototypes   245
7.6   Refine Requirements   252
7.7   Test Infrastructure   253
7.8   References   257

8   Media in Object Types   259

8.1   Media Objects   259
8.2   Methods Available for ORDImage Object Type   263
        8.2.1   Dealing with Image Metadata   274
8.3   Methods Available for ORDAudio Object Type   281
8.4   Methods Available for ORDVideo Object Type   284
8.5   Methods Available for ORDDoc Object Type   290
8.6   SI_StillImage Object Type   296
        8.6.1   SI_StillImage Methods   297
        8.6.2   Methods for Image Processing   305
8.7   Object Tables   309
8.8   Summary   310

9   J2EE/ADF Application Development   **311**

 9.1 Introduction   311
 9.2 Application Development Framework   312
   9.2.1 Creating the Model Component   313
   9.2.2 Creating the Controller and View Components   316
 9.3 interMedia Java Server Pages Tag Library   324
   9.3.1 Retrieving Multimedia Data Using the interMedia
      JSP Tag Library   324
   9.3.2 Uploading Multimedia Data Using the interMedia
      JSP Tag Library   329
 9.4 interMedia Java Proxy Classes   334
   9.4.1 A Note on the Context Parameter   335
   9.4.2 Preparing to Use the Proxy Classes   335
   9.4.3 OrdAudio, OrdImage, OrdAudio, and OrdDoc   339
   9.4.4 OrdImageSignature Methods   350
 9.5 interMedia Java Classes for Servlets   351
   9.5.1 Media Delivery   352
   9.5.2 Media Upload Classes for Servlets   361
 9.6 Summary   372

10   Image Metadata Support   **373**

 10.1 Introduction   373
 10.2 Metadata Schemas   375
 10.3 Extracting Image Metadata   380
 10.4 Inserting Image Metadata   384
 10.5 Indexing Image Metadata   387
   10.5.1 Oracle Text Indexing   392
 10.6 DICOM Metadata   393
 10.7 Summary   395

11   Query Mode   **397**

 11.1 Introduction   397
 11.2 Querying Media Data   398
 11.3 Attribute-based Retrieval   400
 11.4 How Is Metadata Used in Query Processing?   401
 11.5 Using SQL   401
 11.6 Content-based Retrieval   404
 11.7 PL/SQL Application Development   405
   11.7.1 Developing PL/SQL Web Applications   409

	11.7.2	Optimizing PL/SQL	412
	11.7.3	Make Loops as Efficient as Possible	414
11.8	Server-side SQL		416
11.9	Text-based Retrieval		420

12   interMedia Application Performance   421

12.1	Identify Performance Needs and Goals		421
12.2	Tuning the Database		422
12.3	Creating Tables with Media Data		430
12.4	Distributing the I/O Load		432
12.5	Load Performance		433
12.6	Performance Tools		436
12.7	Delivery on the Web		436
12.8	Backup		437
12.9	Summary		438

13   Advanced Queries   439

13.1	Introduction		439
13.2	Content-based Image Retrieval in interMedia		439
13.3	Retrieval Process—Precision and Recall		444
13.4	Using SQL/MM StillImage for CBIR		448
	13.4.1	Image Matching	451
	13.4.2	For Color Matching—Using SI_ColorHistogram Object Type	453
13.5	Summary		459

14   Streaming Audio and Video   461

14.1	Introduction		461
14.2	Microsoft Media Services		462
	14.2.1	Background	462
	14.2.2	Integration with Oracle	464
	14.2.3	Creating a Mount Point	465
	14.2.4	Creating a Publishing Point	465
	14.2.5	File Types Supported by the interMedia MMS Data Source Plug-in	467
14.3	Real/Helix Server		469
	14.3.1	Background	469
	14.3.2	Integration with Oracle	469
	14.3.3	Creating a Mount Point	470

14.4   Creating an interMedia Streaming Server Plug-in Procedure   473
14.5   Summary   476

Appendix   **477**

Where to get more information   477

Index   **481**

Acknowledgments

This book would not have been possible without the contribution of many people who were involved directly or indirectly in the production of the book.

Firstly, we would like to thank the Oracle *inter*Media engineering team in Nashua, New Hampshire USA, especially the Engineering manager, Susan Mavris, for her extensive review and comments on the manuscript, and Mike Turnill, Oracle UK, and Thames Valley University, and Dr. Samia Oussena for very thoroughly reviewing large sections of the manuscript. Also, thanks to Professor Andy Smith for his support and encouragement.

Finally, we are grateful to everyone at Digital Press for all their encouragement and work.

—Larry Guros
—Lynne Dunckley

Introduction

1.1 Uses for Digital Media

Digital media is becoming an ever more prevalent aspect of our lives. The uses for digital media include entertainment, financial, document management, security, marketing, medical, research, art, and personal use. Digital media includes:

- Digital images
- Digital audio
- Digital video

Most people are familiar with using digital media for personal uses. Digital media is popularly used for:

- Family pictures
- Family videos
- Movies
- Songs

Digital media is all around us. The proliferation of digital devices such as MP3 players, digital cameras, digital video recorders, video playback devices, and other devices is increasing. The amount of media available in digital form is also increasing. Today most media is created using digital devices, but also images, songs, and videos that were once available only in analog form, such as magnetic tape, photographs, and movie reels, are being digitized so that they can be archived, shared, and used by a larger number of people anywhere in the world.

Since the era of the World Wide Web (WWW) is upon us, digital media is being used more often than ever before—it is all around us. People save, share, buy, and use digital media every day. Digital images are nearly required to sell products over the Internet. Many people share their family pictures with online photo albums or put media on the Web to inform or entertain the general public.

Other equally important uses of digital media are used every day. Security is enhanced with the use of digital media. Images of missing people or criminal suspects can be sent around the world in a matter of seconds. Images from security cameras can be used to identify criminals. Media from a crime scene can be used to prosecute, defend, or solve a crime.

Digital satellite images are used to measure environmental impact, such as the shrinking of the rain forest. They can also be used for crop predictions and other kinds of research. Images from space are expanding our knowledge of the universe.

Medical information is now routinely digitized, including waveforms (such as audio), images, and video. This allows for recordkeeping, perhaps to judge the progression of a condition to enhance patient care. This digital media information can also be sent to specialists around the world to improve and expedite diagnoses.

Media related to news and current events are created and stored in digital form for broadcasting around the world and for archiving for future use.

Photographers are increasingly making their stock photography available on the Web. Stock photography can be used for advertising, editorial, and the entertainment industries, as well as for Internet use.

Financial institutions store images of important documents, such as checks for check clearing purposes and customer inspection.

Pattern images, such as those used for fabrics, wallpaper, and carpeting and other flooring are stored in image databases. Image content–based retrieval is particularly useful for searching these kinds of pattern images for color, texture, and shape from thousands of pattern images.

Entire collections of art, history, and archeology are being digitized and made available. This process makes this information available to anyone in the world. Because of this, we are more aware of our own history and culture, as well as the history and culture of others.

1.2   The Challenge of Digital Media

The challenge of this proliferation of digital media, in what it is used for and the amount and size of media, is how to make it available to the people who can, and should, use it. Making this media easily available includes the following challenges:

- How to store the media

- How to find the media

- How to secure the media

- How to manage the media

- How the media is previewed

- How to deliver the media

1.3   The Evolution of Digital Media Storage and Management

Perhaps the first and simplest digital media management solution is a set of files in an individual computer directory, which can be called directory managed media. This kind of storage and management needs the knowledge of the users to find and access the media. This kind of storage and access is, and will be, used to store digital media, even today, for small collections of media. This kind of storage depends on the individual users and computer operators to manage the data correctly, such as backing up the data. This kind of storage is typically used for temporary storage or work in progress.

This simple kind of storage was moved to networked computers so that the media could be stored or accessed by a number of users. In time these computers were increasingly managed by operators rather than individual users.

One obvious limitation of directory managed media is the limitation of information about the image, or image metadata, that is available. The only metadata available is the directory structure, the file name, and file date/time. Other metadata might be available in the media itself, but it could not be used to locate the media.

Indexes were created to overcome the metadata limitations of directory managed media. These indexes help users find media. These indexes could include as much metadata as needed for the particular application the user has in mind. These indexes are stored in individual files and may include metadata information from the media itself. In fact, many popular desktop search engines, such as those supplied by Google, use media metadata to find media on a desktop. Indexed solutions allow for descriptions and keyword searches.

The separation of metadata indexes and actual media data continued for a long time. The metadata indexes moved from flat files (heap, hash, B+-tree, and so on) to databases. These media metadata indexes were eventually put into purpose-built databases such as indexed sequential access method (ISAM) databases and relational databases.

This kind of management had different storage for index and media. For example, the media might be stored on a laser disk farm and the index on a magnetic disk. Many times different tools were needed to manage the media and index. Digital media management applications were built. Sometimes these were custom applications and other times these were special-purpose media applications. These kinds of systems are binary systems, where index and content are separated.

Eventually, the management of digital media was achieved using a single database infrastructure. This infrastructure is a database where both the media metadata and content itself is stored and managed.

1.4   The Value Proposition for the Full Use of a Database for Digital Media

Having a single infrastructure for both digital media indexes and digital media content means having one set of management tools to deal with. In a binary system, the data must be managed separately. The media index as well as the content must be managed. For example, the content is backed up using one tool and the index is backed up separately.

Along with unifying management of the digital media database, the database has access to the set of features offered by the database. These database features include features for performance, security, integrity, and loss prevention of the data.

Performance features include many techniques to automatically distribute the physical input/output (I/O) load among a set of physical disks. This can be very important for a media database since the amount of data that is moved from disk to the application can be large. Database indexes are well suited to finding data quickly.

A database is also especially well suited to securing data. Access can be blocked to only the users who have the privilege to access the data. This can be either on the database as a whole or individual items of media within the database itself. For integrity of the data, transactions can be used so that there is not a mismatch between what is in the index and the content in the digital media database. The database also has a plethora of techniques for loss prevention of data, from mirroring data to backing up data to real-time transfer of database updates to a remote site.

1.5   The Value Proposition for Using Media Types

Initially there was only one type of data that was stored in a database—the text type. Soon there were other types introduced, such as a number type and date type. These date and number types could be stored in the text type as well. However, by using different types for date and number types they can be better understood and better managed. For example, a number or a date could be converted to binary for efficient storage. Also, these types suggest operations that can be performed on them. For example, numbers can have arithmetic operations and dates can be output in different national standards.

The types also have the advantage that database tools and applications implicitly know how to deal with the data—how it can be represented, how it can be output, how it can be used, etc. For example, a simple image browsing application could be written to scan all the tables that belong to a user. Using the table metadata, the application can determine the tables that have an image stored in one of the columns because the table metadata indicates the column is an image type. The application can then use the image metadata stored in the image type to display the image (MIME type, width, height, etc.).

In initial unified media databases, image content was stored in simple binary large objects (BLOB) data types. These data types could be used to store any kind of data, including text, but were traditionally used for binary data items, such as every media type or large binary documents. The BLOB does not suggest what it holds and what metadata can be associated with it.

By using a type to store media data, applications can deal with the type automatically. For example, it is known that media has a MIME (multipurpose Internet mail extensions) type. The type gives a standard way to access this MIME type. Other metadata is also implicit, for example, there is a height and width for an image, so accessors are available in the type to allow access to this information as well.

As well as being able to implicitly understand what a database column holds, a media type also has operations that can be performed on that data type. For example, the image data type has methods to do things such as making a smaller version of the image (a thumbnail image). These media operations are close to the data so that the cost of data transfer from and to the database is minimized.

1.6   Summary

The infrastructure for handling Digital Media has evolved from storage in simple filesystems to being managed by databases. The database infrastructure has likewise evolved, increasing functionality especially for managing Digital Media. The database centralizes the management of digital media, and various other technologies are provided to access the media in the database. Any system designed to deal with Digital Media should strongly consider the advantages of managing the media within a database.

2

Multimedia Basics

2.1   Introduction

One of the first issues facing the application developer working with rich media data is the sheer size of the objects—image, audio, video, mapping data, and documents (in binary or XML format). The second problem is that the application may not need to store just one version of the media. For example, in the case of images we may need replica images of different sizes and quality for different purposes. Media data can be stored in many different file types—data formats—that meet various user requirements so decisions need to be made about replication and storage options. In this chapter we will start by looking at the characteristics of the rich media itself and how some of these characteristics are stored as metadata. Then we will look at the relationship between file format and compression using images as the main example.

The richness of information stored in a media file, such as an image, provides many more opportunities for change. If we were dealing with a text string such as

Yosemite National Park

the potential changes are strictly limited:

- Change style (e.g., font, bold, or italics).
- Change text (e.g., uppercase, lowercase, or initial capitals).

Also we would not store these different formats because transforming the data can be achieved simply and efficiently by using standard SQL functions. But if we were dealing with an image from Yosemite, we would need to use a format with as small a size as possible for delivery and display on the Web but a much larger file of dense information for printing. In the next section we look at the differences between multimedia data and normal "database" data.

2.2   What Is Different about Multimedia Data?

There are several challenges to using multimedia data:

- The first challenge is size—one colored image could require 24 Mb. In traditional SQL databases the data types used for storing data are of strictly limited size. The format might be very restricted as well (e.g., DATE). Even for string data the limit for VARCHAR2 is currently 32,768 bytes. This can cause difficulties for storing rich media within the database.

- The second challenge is time—called "real time nature" (e.g., in video, the frame sequence). The components of a video have to be maintained in the right order even if they have been processed separately.

- The third challenge is that the semantic nature of multimedia is much more complex. Data retrieval is much more complex with rich media. With traditional structured data, we can search for a specific value in a straightforward manner using SQL and retrieve exact matches or use BOOLEAN operators. With rich media there can be a great deal of information, but that information if described in words would be different for different people. This causes a great deal of confusion in retrieval and indexing rich media and means we may be looking at near matches instead of exact matches.

Despite these challenges electronic multimedia can offer the users a richer experience. Multimedia can engage the senses to inform, persuade, and entertain, but, used poorly, multimedia can annoy and confuse an audience. The reduction in hardware cost and the increase in hardware performance have enabled the assembly of large heterogeneous collections of raw image and video data. Initially, applications have been driving the development almost entirely so that although an application "works," its functionality is not transferable to any other domain. Examples of this type of development are interactive games and WWW encyclopaedias.

Multimedia refers to the combination of two or more media. For the Web this would include:

- Spoken word
- Text
- Music
- Audio
- Images
- Video
- Animation

Therefore, we will need to deal with a range of multimedia file formats:

- Specific for different media types—image, audio, video
    - Audio such as file formats, .wav, .mp3
    - Video such as file formats, .avi, .mov, .mpg
- Specific for different compressions algorithms
    - MPEG, JPEG, LZW

2.3 Multimedia Metadata

Metadata literally means data about data. It has always been an essential component of databases. For example, in a relational database there is metadata relating to every table that stores its structure in the data dictionary. There is information about every user and their access rights to data within the database. Therefore, metadata is any data that is required to interpret other data as meaningful information and it is an extremely important aspect of multimedia databases since it is used for retrieving and manipulating the data. It can be based on the interpretation of information held within the media, or alternatively, it can be based on the interpretation of multiple media and their relationships. In the case of multimedia, metadata deals with the content, structure, and semantics of the data. In a straightforward relational database we would have metadata about the table, associated views, and indexes. In a rich media database we would need metadata

Table 2.1   *Example of Metadata*

	Metadata	
	File Name	Graduation.jpg
	File Format	JFIF
	Compression	JPEG
	MIME Type	Image/JPEG
	Size	73,874
	Image Height	360
	Image Width	564

about each row of the table and certainly for every media object. For example, in Table 2.1 we can see an image and the metadata associated with it.

In the next sections we are going to look at digital data attributes in detail, such as the metadata shown in Table 2.1:

- File format

- Size

- Compression

- Ownership

- Content

In terms of rich media databases we are virtually always dealing with the storage of digital data, although an image created with *vector graphics* consists of mathematical formulas or equations that represent lines and curves, but these would also be stored in a digital file. We will start by using image data as an example of the general features of rich media. We are going to look first at general image properties, then at image features and resolution. We will digress to look at the way the Internet has influenced image processing requirements before looking in more detail at compression. Then we will look at MIME types and metadata so that we can interpret the data shown in Table 2.1.

2.4   Image Data

We will nearly always be storing image data for later use by humans so that human capabilities and preferences are going to have to be considered in the design of the system. Human vision is fast, high resolution, and detects a large range of colors. Images used in information and communication technology (ICT) are now displayed on a wide range of hardware, such as:

- Computer monitors
- LCD screens
- Mobile phones
- PDA
- Printers
- Data projectors
- Plasma screens
- Interactive TVs

These devices deal with digital images. However, many of the instruments that capture images are analog. These analog signals are continuously variable in their description of color, brightness, or loudness. Digital images result from a process called sampling, which results in the conversion of analog data into digital data. The resulting digital image, often called a raster graphic image, is a mosaiclike grid of picture elements known as pixels. In the process of sampling the image a measurement is taken at a given position that records the color and brightness of the image. A binary number holds the information for specifying a pixel.

2.4.1   History of the Pixel and Digital Images

The pixel first appeared in New Jersey in 1954 when mathematicians and engineers created the first computer graphic at Princeton's Institute for Advanced Study.

This was the first instance of digital typography and required a computer the size of a Manhattan apartment to generate the digital image. This produced a primitive graphic—a small matrix of glowing vacuum tubes that was used to spell out letters in the first-ever instance of computer memory being mapped directly to dots in a display.

A number of technologies contributed to the development of digital images. Medical staff started working with images from X-ray machines from 1900 and ultrasound scanners were invented in the 1950s with the display of images on cathode ray tubes. At the same time printers were being used to display digital images. Peterson of Control Data Corporation (CDC) utilized a CDC 3200 computer and a "flying-spot" scanner to create a digital transposition/representation of da Vinci's *Mona Lisa* in 1964. This can be seen at http://www.digitalmonalisa.com/. The production process took 14 hours to complete the image, which contained 100,000 pixels that were plotted using numerals, sometimes overprinted, to approximate the required density. In the thirtieth year of the pixel, the Macintosh arrived, the first commercially successful personal computer that used a graphical user interface that treated on-screen text as just another graphic.

2.5   Multimedia Data Acquisition

Digital media is created by a diverse range of processes, but there are common stages that are carried out, summarized as:

- Capture the multimedia data (e.g., by exposing a photographic film).
- Sample the analog signal at double the bandwidth and convert to a digital value (e.g., scanner).
- Predict how much redundant data is present that can be removed.
- Transform the raw data by compression to reduce size.

The more sampling that takes place the more information will be held about the image so that more storage space will be required for the image. Analog sources could be photographic film, prints, sketches, etc. The whole sampling process can be carried out by an analog-to-digital converter (ADC), which could be hardware or software based.

Look at a simple application such as the Family Picture Book described in Chapter 3. Users may want to store images with as high a resolution as possible to ensure no details are lost, later the images may need to be displayed on a website so that an efficient compressed image is needed. If we want the image printed we will need a high-resolution image. In addition, media-specific applications have been developed that require data in their own format, such as Adobe Photoshop. The diversity of media devices—digital cameras, inkjet printers, etc.—has led to a minefield of compatibility problems.

2.6 Multimedia Data Transformation

Manipulating multimedia involves some operations that would never arise in traditional applications. Most of these operations can be summarized as concerned with

- Manipulation (editing and modifying data)
- Presentation
- Analysis (indexing and searching)

Table 2.2 shows the range of operations supported by different media types in digital form grouped by the concepts of manipulation, presentation, and analysis. Many of these operations could in theory be carried out within the database as an alternative to retrieving the media data from the database and then manipulating it with specialist software. The operations shown in bold are currently supported by Oracle *inter*Media. The operations connected with presentations tend not to be supported for obvious reasons.

Table 2.2 *Multimedia Operations*

Text	Audio	Image	Animation	Video
Manipulation				
Character manipulation	Sample manipulation	Geometric manipulation	Primitive editing	Frame manipulation
String manipulation	Waveform Manipulation	Pixel operations	Structural editing	Pixel operations
Editing	Audio editing	Filtering		
Presentation				
Formatting	Synchronization	Compositing	Synchronization	Synchronization
Encryption	Compression	**Compression**	Compression	Compression
				Video effects

Table 2.2 *Multimedia Operations (continued)*

Text	Audio	Image	Animation	Video
			Rendering	Mixing
Sorting	Conversion	**Conversion**		Conversion
Analysis				
Indexing	Indexing	**Indexing**	Indexing	Indexing
Searching	**Searching**	**Searching**	Searching	**Searching**

Multimedia data introduce different kinds of relationships between data. For example, the relationships between the data items may be both spatial and temporal. Temporal relationships describe

- When an object should be presented.
- How long an object is presented.
- How one object presentation relates to others (audio with video).

Image data can be stored in many different file types known as formats. These formats allow the user to prepare and store the data in specific ways for future use in specialized applications. In Table 2.3 we can see a brief comparison of common file formats, some of which are described in more detail later. This information can help us decide which format should be the main vehicle for the media storage.

Table 2.3 *File Formats*

File Type	Data Compression	DTP Use	Internet Use	Layers	Saved Selections	Saved Paths
Adobe Photoshop (.psd)	X	X	X	√	√	√
GIF (.gif)	√	X	√	X	X	√
PNG (.png)	√	X	√	X	√	√
JPEG (.jpg)	√	X	√	X	X	√
JPEG2000	√		√		X	

→

Table 2.3   *File Formats (continued)*

File Type	Data Compression	DTP Use	Internet Use	Layers	Saved Selections	Saved Paths
Photoshop EPS (.eps)	X	√	X	X	X	√
PICT (.pct)	X	X	X	X	X	√
TIFF (.tiff)	√	√	√	X	√	√

Here are three common reasons for wanting to change media

- Resolution
- Delivery
- Compression

2.6.1   **Resolution**

Digital image resolution refers to the quantity of visible information and the number of colors present. The quality of a digital image is described by two independent measurements:

- The pixel dimension (e.g., 640 × 480—number of pixels).
- The color depth from 1 bit to 48 bits, but most devices operate with either 8 bits (grayscale of 256 tones) or 24 bits (16 million colors).

Pixels are approximately square in shape and a grid of pixels is called a *bitmap*. Digital images are therefore bitmapped to square or rectangular shapes. The exact position of each pixel in the grid can be mapped using x (horizontal) and y (vertical) coordinates. This gives the specific address of each pixel. Black-and-white images, which are known as *grayscale*, are created from a limited palette of 256 tones that range from black (0) to white (255). These files are much smaller than red, green, and blue (RGB) images.

We have said that we may need to store images of different quality. Resolution is a way of assessing image quality but it can be measured in different ways by different technologies. One way of comparing this quality in digital images is *pixel count* resolution. The higher the resolution, the more pixels in the image. Higher resolution allows for more detail and subtle color transitions in an image. A printed image that has a low resolution may look pixelated or made up of small squares, with jagged edges and without smoothness. Image *spatial resolution* refers to the spacing of pixels in an image within a physical measurement range and is measured in pixels per inch (ppi), sometimes called dots per inch (dpi). Therefore it is not a property of the image itself and is variable—it only becomes fixed when the image takes physical form (e.g., when it is printed). Size versus resolution is often an issue of compromise. In Figure 2.1(a) it is possible to see the individual pixels that give the image a jagged appearance, while Figure 2.1(b) would be the normal resolution.

Figure 2.1
Resolution and pixels.

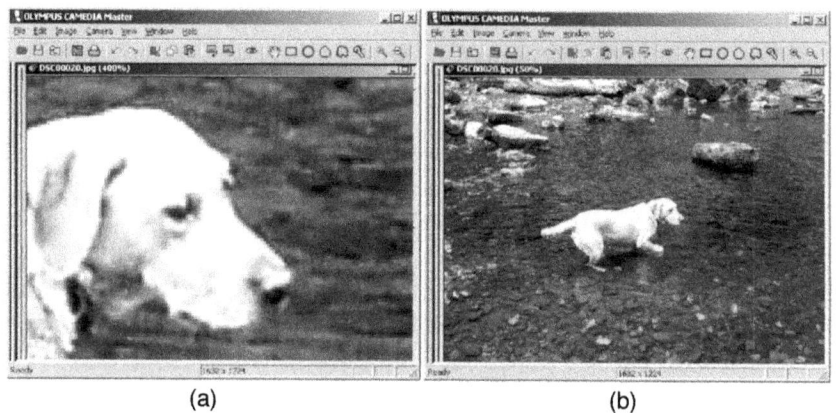

(a)   (b)

Monitors have a smaller dynamic range than printers and are not able to display the deepest tones. The term *dynamic range* refers to the variations that can exist between the brightest and darkest parts of an image. Analog devices—cameras with photographic film, human visual system—will produce much wider dynamic range than most digital scanners and display devices. The spatial resolution of a monitor is usually 72 to 75 dots per inch (dpi). The pixel dimension of a monitor is also often quoted as the number of horizontal pixels, x dimensions, versus the number of vertical pixels, y dimensions (e.g., 1152×870). LCD screens have less dynamic range than cathode ray tube (CRT) monitors. A letter-size, 300-dpi RGB image will be about 24 MB while a 200-dpi image will require about 10 MB of storage. The digital image file would contain three color values for every RGB pixel, or location, in the image grid of rows and columns. The data is also organized in the file in rows and columns. File formats vary, but the beginning of the file contains numbers specifying the number of rows and columns (which is the image size, like 800×600 pixels) and this is followed by huge strings of data representing the RGB color of every pixel.

Color Depth

The computer monitor is the oldest device for displaying digital images. Therefore, it was an important technology for setting the original standards and methods for digital images. The computer monitor is based on a flat cathode ray tube that is coated with phosphors that glow and produce light of different colors when hit by an electron beam. Three color phosphors are present, red, green, and blue (RGB). These are arranged in triads—clusters of three—with each triad corresponding to a pixel on the screen. The effect of the color is to change the pixel from the original black. Each pixel's color sample has three numerical RGB components to represent the color. These three RGB components are three 8-bit numbers for each pixel. Three 8-bit bytes (one byte for each of RGB) are called 24-bit color. If all three values are equal, the result is white. 24-bit RGB color images use 3 bytes of storage, and can have 256 shades of red, 256 shades of green, and 256 shades of blue. This is $256 \times 256 \times 256 = 16.7$ million possible combinations or colors for 24-bit RGB color images. Screen images are seen as transmitted light (radiating from the surface). This is completely different from a printed image that is reflected light from the surface. The visible color gamat, which is the range the eye can see, includes many more colors than the RGB gamut.

In the SI_StillImage set of objects described in Chapter 8 there is an object type, SI_Color, that encapsulates color values of an image in terms of its RGB values as integers in range 0 to 255.

Image Channels

Each separate pixel in the RGB color image derives its color from a combination of three separate values. The separate colors are often called *channels*, each with a brightness value from 0 to 255. At present the 24-bit RGB is the most common image type but 30-, 36-, and 48-bit color are available.

Using individual image channels with a large image file could be an important option if the main image is too large to be processed in memory. As pixel dimensions are set when a digital image is captured, enlarging or reducing an image means adding new pixels to the mosaic. This process is known as *interpolation* or *resampling*. It makes the pixel grid larger but does not add any detail. New pixels that are added are assigned a color value that is derived from their nearest neighbors. This can result in a loss of the sharpness of the image and produce a jagged-edge effect. Reducing an image is the opposite and means taking pixels away. Cropping is an operation that reduces image size and it is beneficial as it makes for efficient storage. In this way unnecessary background information can be removed from the image.

Contrast Correction

This is an operation that is used to manipulate digital images. We could simply brighten an image by adding an adjustment to every pixel. *Gamma* is a term used for the extent of contrast in the midtone gray areas of an image. In Chapter 8 we cover the way *inter*Media object types include operators to carry out this kind of image processing, including cropping and gamma correction.

Dithering

A problem arose with displaying images on the Web because the originator has no idea what hardware/software combination a user will be employing. There is a standard system for color reproduction on the Internet but Mac and PC operating systems use two different sets of 256 colors with only 216 common values. The 216 colors form the browser-safe palette. If there are unsafe colors in the image they can be converted to an approximate value by a process called *dithering*, which breaks up complex colors into a pattern of dots but can create disappointing results with bright colors.

Layers

Layers have become increasingly important for some media applications for animated and digital images. *Layers* are individual overlay cells in an animated sequence. Different source images can be floated over each other and combined. A designer may want to store an image in layers so that he can easily backtrack from a change and make finite alterations to the image until the desired effect is achieved. Some image software, such as Photoshop, permit the use of layers. Different source images can be floated over each other and set down as required. Digital image creators find it easier to maintain and manage images stored as layers. As well as original developers, third-party developers produce software plug-ins (see later) that add extra features and functions.

2.6.2 Delivery

Internet and ICT Applications

Most Web pages do not consist of a single file, but often contain embedded images and graphics in specific formats. The Web browser needs to know what to do with these specialist files if the Web page is to be displayed correctly. This may involve the use of a plug-in, which we can look upon as a helper application that can deal with files of a specified format. The plug-in tends to be deployed either

- Incorporated within the browser so that the media data will be displayed in the same browser window (e.g., SVG graphic image), or

- Called so that the media data is displayed in a separate window opened by the plug-in application with a separate set of controls (e.g., Real Player).

For example, IE5 supports GIF, PNG, and JPEG (see Table 2.3) while SVG, Acrobat, shockwave, flash graphics, and CGM require plug-ins. The current version of Firefox supports SVG without a plug-in. Currently WBMP is not that widely supported because it is a very limited file format.

If the digital data is then used in an ICT system, other processes are needed to send the media data as packets across a network, deal with packet loss, reorder packets, receive media data, restore redundant data, and display data using required output technology.

These processes may involve several transformations of the data. It is worth noting the bandwidth issue. We already appreciate that the accuracy of the digital representation of the analog original depends on the rate at which it is sampled. The term *bandwidth* originally meant the difference between the minimum and maximum frequencies in the analog signal. If the signal varies a lot then we need to take more samples—music is much more variable than human speech. Nyquist's theorem tells us the signal must be sampled at double the bandwidth. Bandwidth will influence factors such as buffer size and real-time delay.

MIME Types

MIME types are very important in terms of any transmission of files across the Internet. MIME stands for multipurpose Internet mail extensions, a protocol which was developed in the early 1990s. It was devised to provide a way for specifying and describing the format of Internet messages. The original MIME Request for Comments (RFC) defined a message representation protocol that specified considerable detail about message headers, but which left the message content, or message body, as a flat ASCII text. This was then amended by later RFCs to specify the format of the message body to allow multipart textual and nontextual message bodies to be represented and exchanged without loss of information. In particular, this was designed to provide facilities to include multiple objects in a single message, to represent body text in character sets other than US-ASCII, to represent formatted multifont text messages, and to represent nontextual material such as images and audio fragments. Generally the intention was

to facilitate later extensions for new types of Internet mail for use by coop-
erating mail agents. As explained previously, a browser will look for a plug-
in to display the component files of a Web page, especially the rich media
files. This is where the MIME type is vital as this information is provided
by the HTTP protocol as illustrated for the following fragment of HTML:

```
<image width="600" height = "400" data ="mygraphic.svg"
type="image/svg+xml">
<img src=-"mygraphic.png" width ="600" height = "400"/>
</image>
```

The type element gives the MIME type of the document requested. The
MIME type consists of a major type and a minor type. A particular MIME
type is a pair of elements delimited by a slash (/). The first element describes
the "type" of data, for example, text or image. Examples include, but are
not limited to:

- Application
- Audio
- Image
- Text
- Video

The second element describes the format of the type such as:

- msword
- GIF
- JPEG

WWW server applications come configured to handle most MIME types.

The browser looks at the MIME type and decides what to do. If the
browser supports the MIME type it can download the document file and
process it. If it does not support the MIME type the browser can try to load
the appropriate plug-in into memory and hand the data over to it. If the
plug-in required in this instance is not available it can look for the other

alternative file "mygraphic.png." The file extension can also be used by the browser to deduce the MIME type. When a file is downloaded from a Web server the MIME type is downloaded automatically in the HTTP file. If the image file is located in the local file system the MIME type is not available. Plug-ins will have a number of file extensions registered, as shown in Table 2.4. The MIME standard was flexible enough that it could be easily incorporated into HTTP. Consequently, MIME provides the mechanism for seemlessly transferring nontext data easily to the browser.

The format indicates which plug-in is required for the registered format type.

When the browser (or e-mail application) receives a MIME type in the form application/msword it is expected to know what application to run (Microsoft Word) and handle it accordingly. Similarly, when your browser receives data of type text/html (the most common WWW MIME type), then the browser knows to interpret the incoming data as HTML and display it accordingly.

Table 2.4   *MIME Type Plug-ins*

MIME Type	Extensions	Plug-in
application/asf	.asf	Media Player
application/pdf	.pdf	Acrobat
application/windowsmedia	.wma	Media Player
application/x-pn-realaudio	.ram, .rm, .rpm	RealPlayer
application/x-shockwaveflash	.spl, .swf	Flash
Audio/mp3	.mp3	Crescendo, Koan, Liquid MusicPlayer, Media Player
Audio/wav	.wav	Apple Quicktime, Beatnik, Liquid MusicPlayer, Media Player
image/bmp	.bmp	Innomage, Prizm
image/jpeg	.jpg, .jpeg	Innomage, Prizm, RapidVue
image/gif	.gif	Innomage, Prizm

Table 2.4   *MIME Type Plug-ins (continued)*

MIME Type	Extensions	Plug-in
image/png	.png, .ptng	Apple Quicktime, Innomage
image/tiff	.tif, .tiff	Apple Quicktime, Innomage, Prizm, RapidVue
video/avi	.avi	Apple Quicktime, Media Player, NET TOOB Stream
video/mpeg	.mpe, .mpeg	Apple Quicktime, Media Player, NET TOOB Stream
video/x-pn-realvideo	.ram, .rm, .rpm	RealPlayer
x-world/x-svr	.svr, .vrt, .xvr	Superscape e-Visualizer
x-world/x-vrt	.svr, .vrt, .xvr	Superscape e-Visualizer
audio/x-pn-RealAudio	.ram	Real Player
video/mpg	.mpg	Real Player, Media Player
video/mp4	.mp4	Real Player, Media Player

2.6.3   Compression

The most significant media transformations are those involving compression. The main issues associated with compression can be summarized as:

- Remove any redundant data in the media, particularly before transmission.

- Lossless compression can be restored.

- Lossy compression will permanently lose data.

- Lossy compression will reduce media size more than lossless compression.

Computer engineers are always trying to develop better compression methods but these methods may have different objectives, for example:

- Reduce bandwidth
- Ability to restore to original
- Robustness
- Scalability
- Extensibility

Compression allows the image to be reduced in size for efficient transport and storage. JPEG, TIFF, and GIF files can be used to reduce storage size. There are hundreds of different ways of compressing images, called *compression algorithms*, which have been developed by computer scientists. Compression methods for video and audio are performed by codecs. The compression ratio is the number of bytes in the original image compared with the number of bytes after compression. The first stage is to estimate how much redundant data exists that could be removed in this way and select the best compression algorithm. Although there are many different ways in which this can be achieved the principles are the same—removing information that is duplicated and abbreviating information whenever possible. For example, one way of compressing an image is by abbreviating any repeated information in the image and eliminating information that is difficult for the human eye to see. MP3 compression, for example, does not keep information about sound outside of what is audible by humans. When the digital data is restored this is called *decompression*. If it can be decompressed in such a way that none of the original information is lost, this is known as *lossless* compression. However, if some information is lost by the process, it is known as *lossy* compression.

Even lossy compression can be applied to images of text documents without any significant loss and may result in a much smaller binary object. However, when the object cannot be restored to the original, lossy compression may not be appropriate for some applications such as medical imaging. Lossless compression techniques typically result in ratios of 2:1 or 3:1 in medical images. Lossy compression can accomplish 10:1 to 80:1 compression ratios. In the case of text, this could be achieved by building up a dictionary or look-up table where frequently used words were mapped to a symbol. The file would then be coded so that its size would be very much reduced. This is called the *dictionary method*, which can also be applied to image and audio files. For example, a group of pixels with the same color values can be replaced by a single symbol as shown in Table 2.5, which demonstrates run-length encoding. Fortunately we will not be concerned with the details of how this is achieved. For image, audio, and video there are devices that encode, decode, compress, and decompress all together, called *codecs* (coder/decoders). However, we will be concerned with the results of the process. Run-length encoding is based on long runs of identical symbols. For example, LZW compression would be more suitable for data files with similar sequences (e.g., graphics) while Huffman coding would suit data sets where some symbols have higher frequencies than others (e.g., text). Most images will have sequential pixel patterns that occur frequently throughout the file, which is particularly suitable for LZW compression.

Table 2.5   *Example of Run-length Encoding*

Original Pixels	Compressed Pixels
2211333334333222 (16 characters)	22 21 53 14 33 32 (i.e., two 2s, two 1s, five 3s, etc.) (12 characters)

The amount of abbreviation can be significant. With voice coding, a codec system can just send differences in adjacent speech samples, reducing the size by 50%. This can be very effective because even if information were lost, humans would interpolate speech to make gaps comprehensible. However, because musical input is much more varied than speech this can be more of a problem as significant loss of information can be very noticeable. TIFF files are generally better at preserving information than JPEG format. To some extent there is a minefield of incompatibility at present with many applications that require specific format and compression. Therefore, there is a good reason for incorporating common software codecs within the Database Management System (DBMS).

Let's look at some common file types and contrast the way they deal with compression and MIME type.

Computer graphics metafile (CGM) is the main vector drawing format available before SVG. It is an ISO standard for transmitting 2D-vector graphics data, widely used in engineering. Vector graphics images have a number of advantages for Web use. They are smaller and download faster. They can be interacted with and zoomed without losing quality unlike images. The main problem is that there are many different implementation profiles. One Web profile has been agreed WebCGM based on the original profile for Air Transport. *inter*Media does not have codecs for this format.

Graphic interchange format (GIF) can display 255 colors for Web use and is particularly useful as separate frames can be stored together to provide a simple animation. These files are produced with lossless compression processes. The format was based on LZW compression, which was subject to a patent held by Unisys. Creating a GIF encoder required the payment of a royalty fee. Therefore, although this is a very popular format, others have been developed that are free from patents. The image consists of a set of LZW compressed blocks. GIF images can be interlaced; this means that the GIF image need not be transmitted row by row in order but instead rows of the image are output so that the image is gradually built up on the screen. However, for images less than 10 Kbytes, interlacing will not improve performance. There are two specific variants of the GIF format, called 87a and 89a; *inter*Media reads both variants but writes the 87a variant. All GIF images are compressed using a GIF-specific LZW compression scheme, which *inter*Media calls GIFLZW. *inter*Media can read GIF images that include animations and transparency effects but only the first frame of an animated GIF image is made available, and there is no support for writing animated GIF images. The MIME type is image/gif.

Encapsulated postscript (EPS) image files are specialized for desktop publishing applications and can be used to create irregular shapes or cutouts. A related file format is DCS, desktop color separation. *inter*Media does not have codecs for this format.

Joint Photographic Experts Group (JPEG) created ISO standard in 1993. It was designed to transmit continuous-tone still images efficiently. JPEG users can trade quality against compression ratio and the standard includes 29 different coding methods to achieve compression. JPEG is based on a 24-bit palette. It can be used to compress photographic images without causing them to posterize, a distortion that tends to make the image look less natural (i.e., more like a poster). JPEG uses a lossy compression process that assigns a compromise color to a block of 9×9 pixels. This produces a deterioration in image quality that is most noticeable in images with smooth gradient areas. Sequential storage processes can actually cause further deterioration. The main compression method is based on using a transform, which means the inverse process does not result in the same image. A process called *quantization* reduces the accuracy of some terms, reducing the information that needs to be transmitted. However, quantization can cause errors in the image, such as 2–3%, which in a photograph would not be noticed by the average viewer. The high compression ratios are achieved by the transform function picking out major features in the image distinct from the noise, and the quantizer reducing the accuracy of the less important values. This results in an image that is similar but not identical with the original. Hard edges are likely to become fuzzy. For these reasons PNG is a viable alternative. The JPEG-compression format is very complex, but most images belong to a class called "baseline JPEG," which is a much simpler subset. Oracle *inter*Media supports only baseline JPEG compression. The MIME type is image/jpg.

JPEG-Progressive is a variation of the JPEG-compression format in which image scanlines are interlaced, or stored in several passes, all of which must be decoded to compute the complete image. This variant is intended to be used in low-bandwidth environments where users can watch the image take form as intermediate passes are decoded, and terminate the image display if desired. While the low-bandwidth requirement is not typically relevant anymore, this variant sometimes results in a smaller encoded image and is still popular. Oracle *inter*Media provides read, but not write, support for this encoding.

JPEG2000 is a new version of JPEG intended to provide an image coding system using state-of-the-art compression based on wavelets, especially for digital cameras, mobile phones, and medical imaging. It is ideal for processes where the main characteristics of the image are transmitted followed by successive refinements. This can appear similar to interlacing, but in this case fundamental parts of the image can be transformed and transmitted. A low-resolution image can be delivered to the user first, followed by successively higher resolution images. JPEG2000 also allows the user to add encrypted copyright information. Though JPEG2000 is a new format that is not yet widely supported by image-editing and Web-browsing applications, it can already be of major benefit to photographers who learn to incorporate it into their workflow routines. JPEG2000 offers

- Completely lossless image compression.

- Transparency preservation in images.

- Use of masks (alpha channels) to specify an area of the image that should be saved at a lower rate of data compression (loss of image information) than other areas of the image that are of less interest to the viewer.

- EXIF (exchangeable image file format) data preservation in images. EXIF is a standard for storing interchange information in image files, especially those using JPEG compression. Most digital cameras now use the EXIF format to support interoperability.

- User options as to the size, quality, and number of image-preview thumbnails on a website.

PICT is Apple's own high-quality compressed image file. The Macintosh PICT format was developed by Apple Computer, Inc., as part of the Quick-Draw toolkit built into the Macintosh ROM. It provides the ability to "record" and "playback" QuickDraw sequences, including both vector and raster graphics painting. Oracle *inter*Media supports only the raster elements of PICT files. Both Packbits and JPEG-compressed PICT images are supported. The MIME type is image/pict.

The *portable network graphics (PNG)* format was the result of an industry-based working group who was seeking an alternative to GIF that would not be bound by patents. It is aimed at the transmission of computer graphics images but improves GIF, including better support for color, transparency, and interlacing. This combines the sharpness of GIF with the subtle color reproduction of JPEG with lossless compression of natural images. File sizes are larger than JPEG for 24-bit and 8-bit but the PNG process involves massaging the image to achieve as much compression as possible. PNG refers to samples of a particular type (e.g., green as a channel). PNG images can be used for progressive display as the original image is converted to a sequence of smaller images so that the first image in the sequence defines a coarse view until the last image completes the original source image. The set of reduced images is called an interlaced PNG image. This allows the image to be seen more quickly but may make it more difficult to compress. PNGF is the Oracle *inter*Media designation for the portable network graphics (PNG) format. All PNG images are compressed using the DEFLATE scheme. The MIME type is image/png.

PSD, PSP, etc. are proprietary formats used by graphics programs. Adobe Photoshop's files have the PSD extension, while PaintShop Pro files use PSP. These are the preferred working formats since these are used to edit images in the software, because only the proprietary formats retain all the editing power of the programs. These packages use layers, for example, to build complex images, and layer information may be lost in the nonproprietary formats such as TIFF and JPEG. However, these are not wise choices for long-time storage and you may not be able to view the image in a few years when the software has changed. Therefore, these should be saved as standard TIFF or JPEG.

RAW is an image output option available on some digital cameras. RAW images are extremely high-quality images that are not degraded by compression algorithms when recorded. However, they are not currently supported by most image-editing programs in their native format, so they must be converted before use. Though lossless, it is a factor of three of four smaller than TIFF files of the same image. Even though the TIFF file only retains 8 bits/channels of information, it will take up twice the storage space because it has three 8-bit color channels versus one 12-bit RAW channel. It is popular with professional photographers since RAW preserves the original color bit depth and image quality and saves storage space compared to TIFF. Some cameras offer nearly lossless compressed RAW. The disadvantage is that there is a different RAW format for each manufacturer, and so you may have to use the manufacturer's software to view the images.

RPIX, or Raw Pixel, is a format developed by Oracle for storing simple raw pixel data without compression and using a simple well-described header structure. It was designed to be used by applications whose native image format is not supported by *inter*Media but for which an external translation might be available. It flexibly supports N-banded image data (8 bits per sample) where N is less than 256 bands, and can handle data that is encoded in a variety of channel orders (such as RGB, BGR, BRG, and so forth); a variety of pixel orders (left-to-right and right-to-left); a variety of scanline orders (top-down or bottom-up); and a variety of band orders (band interleaved by pixel, scanline, and plane). The flexibility of the format includes a data offset capability, which can allow an RPIX header to be prepended to other image data, thus allowing the RPIX decoder to read an otherwise compliant image format. The extension is .rpx, and the MIME type is image/x-ora-rpix.

Tag image format file (TIFF) is used for bit-mapped images and provides lossless compression. It is often used for printing. TIFF is a flexible and adaptable file format. It can handle multiple images and data in a single file through the inclusion of "tags" in the file header. Tags can indicate the basic geometry of the image, such as its size, or define how the image data is arranged and whether various options are used. Unlike standard JPEG, TIFF files can be edited and resaved without suffering a compression loss. Other TIFF file options include multiple layers or pages.

Oracle *inter*Media supports the "baseline TIFF" specification and also includes support for some TIFF "extensions," including tiled images and certain compression formats not included as part of the baseline TIFF specification. "Planar" TIFF images are not supported. TIFF images in either big-endian or little-endian format can be read, but *inter*Media always writes big-endian TIFFs. (Note this refers to the type of computer system—in a big-endian system, the most significant value in the sequence is stored at the lowest address of the computer memory; in a little-endian system, the least significant value in the sequence is stored first. Most PCs are little endians.)

One final important difference between TIFF and most other image file formats is that TIFF defines support for multiple images in a single file. In Chapter 8 when we deal with image-processing methods of ORDImage we need to note that although the TIFF decoder in *inter*Media includes support for page selection using the "page" verb in the process() and processCopy() methods, the setProperties() method always returns the properties of the initial page in the file. It is important to note that this initial page is accessed by setting `page=0` in the process command string. Oracle *inter*Media currently does not support writing multiple page TIFF files.

Wireless bitmap (WBMP) format is a simple image format used in the context of WAP and mobile phones. (WAP is an open international standard for applications that use wireless communication, e.g., Internet access from a mobile phone.) Currently, the only type of WBMP file defined is a simple black-and-white image file with one bit per pixel and no compression.

For a list of *inter*Media file formats see Oracle *inter*Media Reference 10*g* Release 2 (10.2).

2.7   **Color Perception**

In the human visual system cells called cones found at the center of the retina perceive three colors. There are about six million cones that can distinguish eight million colors. Color sensations arise because there are three types of color receptors:

1.   Blue cones peak at 445 nm.

2.   Green cones peak at 535 nm.

3.   Red cones peak at 570 nm.

The different cones cover three overlapping portions of the visual spectrum. The spectral sensitivity of the human vision varies. Eyes are most sensitive to green range and least sensitive to blue range. All the other two million colors are perceived because of the tristimulus theory of color mixing, which is covered in more detail later in this chapter. The average person can distinguish one to two million colors. However, color perception is very individual with about 8% of the population being color blind. It is impossible to consistently describe a particular color without using a color model. A color model is a representative system and there are a number of different ones in use.

2.7.1 CIE_XYZ Color-space

CIE (Commission Internationale de l'Eclairage) created the CIE_XYZ color-space as early as 1931. The color vision of a group of people was tested and a model for human visual perception called the *CIE Standard Observer* was created based on those tests. The CIE_XYZ color-space was then created by combining

- Well-known physical properties of light, and
- The characteristics and restrictions/boundaries of the human visual perception according to the *CIE Standard Observer.*

In other words the CIE_XYZ color-space

- Defines the light radiation exactly as it appears in real life.
- Is weighted by the color-matching abilities of the average human eye.
- Is restricted to the radiation spectrum that is visible for the average human eye.
- Is a physical axis system that closely simulates the human visual perception.

For these reasons, CIE_XYZ is the fundamental basis of all color management, such as calibration, color-space conversions, and color matching. It is also the foundation for all other color-spaces. CIE is different from the RGB standard and needs to be converted by using a formula.

2.7.2 RGB Additive Color from Glowing Bodies, Lights, TVs, and Monitors

This color model describes colors as a mixture of red, green, and blue (RGB).

This is an additive color model so adding all three colors gives white. If we look at a computer screen with a magnifying glass we can see separate pixels of only one of these three colors. At a distance the human eye blends the colors to mix all the different colors. Colors on monitors look brighter in a darkened room and vice versa.

RED + GREEN = YELLOW.

2.7.3 CMYK: Subtractive Color from Reflecting Objects—Color Printing

Most objects reflect light. A blue shirt will have absorbed the other light colors—they have been subtracted so blue is left. In a subtractive system, mixing two colors gives a darker color (e.g., painting and printing). CMYK derives from cyan, which is the complement of red; magenta, which is the complement of green; yellow, which is the complement of blue; and the K in CMYK confusingly stands for black because originally this was called the *key* color.

If we printed cyan and yellow on top of each other, the result would be green.

```
CYAN + YELLOW = GREEN.
```

If we printed cyan and magenta on top of each other, the result would be blue.

```
CYAN subtracts RED, YELLOW subtracts BLUE, leaving GREEN.
```

These are the standard links used in the lithographic printing industry to reproduce color images. Photographic images are divided into four channels, one for each print ink color. This is why the printed image will look different from the screen display. The conversion of RGB images into CMYK involves the storage of extra data corresponding to the fourth channel so the image file could increase by 25%.

2.7.4 HSB System (Hue, Saturation, and Brightness)

This is similar to traditional paint-based systems for describing color.

Hue—the name of the color (e.g., red). The numeric value for hue is given in the degrees around a circle, so that, for example, 120 is green, 240 is blue, while red is zero.

Saturation—the purity of the color (e.g., pure green, 120, is fully saturated while pale green has a lot of white so it has low saturation). White, black, and grey all have zero saturation. Numeric values vary from 0 to 100% for pure colors.

Brightness—white has the highest brightness, black the lowest. Again there is a numeric scale from 0 to 100%. As brightness decreases there is a smaller range in saturation values because humans are less able to sense differences in hue and saturation in darker colors. This leads to the system being presented as a cone.

2.7.5   RYB (Red, Yellow, and Blue)

This is the system used traditionally by artists to understand color and it is often presented as a color wheel:

- *Primary* colors are red, yellow, and blue.
- *Secondary* colors are made by mixing equal quantities of primary colors to give orange, violet, and green.
- *Tertiary* colors are the result from mixing equal quantities of a primary color with a secondary color to give six colors: red-violet, blue-violet, yellow-green, yellow-orange, blue-green, and red-orange.

These 12 colors are the basis of color harmony design.

2.7.6   Comparing the Four Models

Not all colors can be expressed in all color systems. The designer needs to be aware that

- RGB is hardware-oriented but is also used by CBIR methods (see Chapter 11).
- CMYK is technology-oriented (i.e., printers). It is a system that cannot produce colors of high saturation and brightness.

- HSB is an attempt to be more usable for users to describe the color they want.

- HSB and RYB use a circular arrangement of colors that is useful for creating and analyzing color harmonies.

For example, a bright red on a screen would have values (255, 0, 0) in RGB and (0, 100, 10) in HSB, but will be outside the range for description by CMYK.

However, although we know roughly the frequencies of the red, green, and blue color receptors in the human visual system, we may not be sure what "red," "green," and "blue" mean for different computer hardware. What frequency should we consider to be pure red, pure green, and pure blue? A cheaper monitor with less range will generally use slightly different frequencies for red, green, and blue than a more expensive model. To get truly accurate color on devices that define their color differently, we need to refer to the ICC/ICM profiles that describe the characteristics of how an image or device reproduces color using primaries. The ICC/ICM profile is a set of measurements that describes the colors of a particular imaging device. It contains:

- Transfer function of the device. It is either a measured or mathematical function by which the particular device codes the intensities, in the simplest form a single gamma value.

- Trichromatic coordinates of the device. It describes the device's color gamut in the CIE_XYZ color-space.

- The white-point coordinates of the device. It is the description of this hue that is considered to be colorless (gray, achromatic).

These together fully describe the colors that a digital imaging device uses and allows accurate color conversion from device to device. Color conversion is more of an issue with printers than for monitors.

Color gamut is another term used for a subset of CIE_XYZ color-space, in other words color gamut describes the variety or range of colors that the device is able to reproduce. Another sense, less frequently used but not less correct, refers to the complete set of colors found within an image at a given time. In this context, digitizing a photograph, converting a digitized image to a different color space, or outputting a digitized image to a given medium using a certain output device generally alters its gamut, in the sense that some of the colors in the original are lost in the process. Note that the generic traditional photography and film term for the complete range of colors that can be captured on a particular medium is *dynamic range*.

2.8   Real-time Media

Most of the previous discussion has focused on image media. When we consider video and audio we need to deal with what is termed their real-time nature. This usually refers to the need for synchronization and order. Since digital images are specified by the coordinates of pixels, there is no need to be concerned about the order of delivery of the pixels to the display device. With audio and video samples, the order is crucial.

2.8.1   Seeing Video

Temporal and spatial attributes will be important. Other cells in the retina called rods react to light in 25 ms, significantly faster than cones. Our ability to fuse images into a continuum depends on the image size and brightness. Cinema displays at 24 frames per second (fps) while TV is refreshed at 60 Hz in the United States and 50 Hz in the United Kingdom

Brightness is a subjective reaction to levels of light. It is affected by the luminance of an object, which in turn is a physical property, the result of the amount of light falling on an object and its reflective properties. Visual acuity increases with brightness but flicker also increases. The eye will perceive a light turned rapidly on and off as continuous as long as the speed of switching is more than 50 Hz, otherwise it will be seen to flicker.

Video can be processed to extract audiovisual features, such as

- Image-based features
- Motion-based features
- Object detection and tracking
- Speech recognition
- Speaker identification
- Word spotting
- Audio classification

There is no single best format for delivering audio and video at present. The choice of format is related to the way the media is going to be delivered to the users. There are three alternatives:

1.   Download. The materials must be downloaded and can only be played once these are fully loaded. The media data would continue to be available stored on the user's computer for replaying whenever they wish, sharing with others, or transfer to other devices.

2.   Progressive download. This is similar in all ways to download, except that the user's download software is set up to start playing the materials when enough has been downloaded to ensure a continuous listening/viewing experience. The media is stored on the local computer.

3.   Streaming. The user does not actually download any materials to his or her computer; rather, the streaming software on his or her computer makes a semi-real-time connection to a streaming server, which sends a stream of "moving images" of compressed audio/video over the Internet that are displayed as they arrive. Once playing is completed, no materials are available on the user's computer, so if he or she wishes to play the material again, he or she must repeat the streaming process. No media is stored on the local computer.

To take an example, the RealVideo delivery system can download or stream media. A RealVideo clip is a file or live broadcast containing sound and video encoded in RealVideo format. These formats are highly compressed to deliver good quality sound and video over a limited-bandwidth connection. The RealVideo system provides several formats that are optimized differently for different kinds of content. For example, you would use a different format to deliver speech over a 14.4 Kbps modem than you would to deliver a music video over an ISDN connection.

The .rm files can contain multiple streams, including audio, video, image maps, and events. If we want the user to download the file from the Web, we would insert into the HTML file a reference to a video file for format type .rm:

```
<a href="video01.rm">Click here to download video</a>
```

However, if we want the user to stream the same video, we actually need to create another file, a simple text file with a .ram extension. This is known as a *metafile*—a file that contains data about another file. The metafile is a simple text file that includes the URL of the media data source, such as

```
http://www.mycollege.com/media/video/video01.rm
```

We would then change the HTML reference to the video metafile with the extension .ram:

```
<a href="video01.ram">Click here to view streaming video</a>
```

When the user clicks this hyperlink, the metafile opens and in turn opens the video file at the specified URL. This time the video will be streamed instead of downloaded. This process is transparent to the user, as far as he or she is concerned the hyperlink just starts the streaming.

There are two metafile formats, .ram and .rpm (RealPlayer Plug-in metafile). This is the same as a metafile, but used with RealPlayer Plug-in for Netscape Navigator and Internet Explorer 3.0 and later:

.ram file—browser launches RealPlayer

.rpm file—browser launches RealPlayer Plug-in (see below)

For files with .rpm file extension (RealPlayer Plug-in), the Web server sets the MIME type of the file to audio/x-pn-RealAudio-plugin.

In order for RealMedia files to stream from the website the user's host server must recognize the .ra, .ram, .rm, and .rpm MIME types. The Web server delivers the RealVideo metafile to the Web browser. Based on the .ram file extension, the Web server sets the MIME type of the file.

The Web browser looks up the MIME type of the RealVideo metafile. Based on the MIME type, the Web browser starts RealPlayer as a helper application and passes it the metafile.

RealPlayer reads the first URL from the metafile and requests it from RealServer.

RealServer begins streaming the requested RealVideo or RealAudio clip to RealPlayer.

A related concept is a container data type, such as RealMedia File Format (RMFF) or ASF, that can contain other data types. Each container data type is identified by a unique MIME type. *inter*Media supports RMFF data format for file extension .rm with MIME type video/x-pn-realvideo.

Table 2.6 outlines common video file formats.

Table 2.6 *Common Video File Formats*

Video Format	File Extension	Originator	Streaming	Additional Player
AVI	.avi	Microsoft	Yes	No
QuickTime	.qt	Apple	Yes	No
MPEG-4	.mpg	MPEG	Yes	No
RealVideo	.rm	RealNetworks	Yes	Yes

2.8.2 Audio

There are two categories for audio, streaming and nonstreaming. In the case of nonstreaming, the entire file is downloaded and saved to disk before playing. In the case of streaming, the file is not saved to disk. The advantages of streaming are that the user can listen during the download process. The formats for nonstreaming audio files include .wav, .au, or .midi. Formats for streaming audio include .ra, .mps. However, streaming audio may not be displayed by the Web browser without a plug-in being available, such as RealAudio, and may require a helper application, such as RealPlayer. Compression is available for MP3 and RealAudio formats.

Another issue with audio is that it is considered good practice to include a transcript of any spoken audio files so that users can read as an alternative to listening. This can be catered to in the ORDAudio object type (see Chapter 3).

2.8.3 Video and Audio Streaming

It has been possible to download and play back high-quality audio and video files from the Internet for some years. This was achieved by full-file transfer but it meant very long, unacceptable transfer times and playback latency. Ideally, video and audio should be streamed across the Internet from the server to the client in response to a client request for a Web page containing embedded videos. The client plays the incoming multimedia stream in real time as the data is received.

The most important video codec standards for streaming video are H.261 and MPEG-1, MPEG-2, and MPEG-4. Codecs designed for the Internet are more complex because of the problems of latency. In addition, the codecs must be tightly linked to network delivery software to achieve the highest possible frame rates and picture quality. None of the existing codecs are ideal for Internet video.

2.8.4 What Is Available?

H.261 was targeted at teleconferencing applications and is intended for carrying video over ISDN—in particular for face-to-face videophone applications and for videoconferencing. H.261 needs substantially less CPU power for real-time encoding than MPEG. However, because of the nature of the application it does not usually involve database storage so the format is not supported by *inter*Media.

MPEG-1, -2, and -4 are standards for the bandwidth efficient transmission of video and audio. MPEG-1 does not offer resolution scalability and the video quality is highly susceptible to packet losses. MPEG-2 extends MPEG-1 by including support for higher resolution video and increased audio capabilities. The targeted bit rate for MPEG-2 is 4–15Mbits/sec, providing broadcast-quality full-screen video. For the same reasons as MPEG-1, it is also prone to poor video quality in the presence of packet losses. However, both MPEG-1 and MPEG-2 are well suited to the purposes for which they were originally developed. For example, MPEG-1 works well for playback from CD-ROM, and MPEG-2 is fine for high-quality archiving applications and for TV broadcast applications. However, for existing computer and Internet infrastructures, MPEG-based solutions are too expensive and require too much bandwidth; they were not designed with the Internet in mind. *inter*Media supports video MPEG formats—MPEG-1, MPEG-2, and MPEG-4—with the MIME types given in Table 2.4.

MPEG-7 has not yet been widely implemented but it has been promoted as a standard with the objective to provide a common interface for audiovisual content description in multimedia environments. This would easily provide interoperability for different MPEG-7 systems or modules. The standard is based on the previous MPEG standards but in addition includes the notion of descriptors (D) and description schemes (DS). The former (D) represents a model for specific high- or low-level features that can be annotated for a given media object. The latter (DS) just represents a grouping of a series of descriptors or further description schemes in a particular functional area.

The definition of the MPEG-7 standard relies on further standards of the MPEG family and heavily on the XML language and XML-schema that are used in its representation and its definition. MPEG-7 itself is provided in the form of an extensible XML-schema defining an object-oriented type hierarchy that delivers a set of predefined descriptors grouped into its functional description schemes. For example, the standard defines an Agent DS that can represent data for persons, groups, or organizations.

However, from a database viewpoint the MPEG-7 standard does not define how searching or indexing should be implemented on the media data. It also does not make any assumptions about the internal storage format. The terms used in the standard include the following:

- FileFormat (MPEG-7 FileFormat CS or MIME)
    - System (MPEG-7 System CS)
    - Bandwidth (Hz)
    - BitRate (attributes: minimum, average, maximum)
- VisualCoding
    - Format (MPEG-7 VisualCoding CS; attribute: color domain)
    - Pixel (attributes: resolution, aspectRatio, bitPer [accuracy])
    - Frame (attributes: height, width, aspectRatio, rate)
- AudioCoding
    - Format (MPEG-7 AudioCoding CS)
- AudioChannels
    - Sample (attributes: rate, bitPer)
    - Presentation (MPEG-7 AudioPresentation CS)
- Classification DS
    - Form (recommend LC's migfg)
    - Genre (recommend LC's migfg)
    - Subject (recommend LCSH or other)
    - Language (also SubtitleLanguage, ClosedCaptionLanguage, etc.)
    - Release (country and date)
    - Target (market, age [e.g., audience, such as higher education])
- 9.1.4 RelatedMaterial DS

- PublicationType (MPEG-7 PublicationType CS)
- MaterialType (recommend Ruth Bogan list of MaterialTypes)
- MediaLocator
- MediaInformation
- CreationInformation
- UsageInformation

Some MPEG-7 implementations have been achieved, such as an implementation of an MPEG-7 database that was reported by Wust & Celma in 2004, for the content-based retrieval of music using Oracle 9. In addition *Fedora* (flexible extensible digital object and repository architecture; http://www.fedora.info/) was created to implement the sharing and preservation of digital library objects using a profile of the METS metadata scheme. This has also been based on Oracle Database.

Another evolving standard is MPEG-21. As noted in *ISO/IEC*, "The vision for MPEG-21 is to define a multimedia framework to enable transparent and augmented use of multimedia resources across a wide range of networks and devices used by different communities" (2001, p. 5).

Work on the new standard MPEG-21, "Multimedia Framework," started in June 2000 with the aims of defining a normative open framework for multimedia delivery and consumption for use by all the players in the delivery and consumption chain. This open framework is intended to provide content creators, producers, distributors, and service providers with equal opportunities in an MPEG-21 enabled open market. This will also benefit the content consumer in providing them with access to a large variety of content in an interoperable manner. MPEG-21 is based on two essential concepts: the definition of a fundamental unit of distribution and transaction (the digital item) and the concept of users interacting with digital items. The digital items can be considered the "what" of the Multimedia Framework (e.g., a video collection, a music album), and the users can be considered the "who." The goal of MPEG-21 can be rephrased as defining the technology needed to support users to exchange, access, consume, trade, and otherwise manipulate digital items in an efficient, transparent, and interoperable way.

However, as of yet, MPEG-21 has even fewer current implementations but there is one in development at Los Alamos National Laboratory (Bekaert, 2004). It has been estimated from previous experience that it takes about ten years for a new MPEG standard to be fully adopted.

Despite the open standards of MPEG most people use one of the big three proprietary formats. These are *RealMedia*, *Quicktime*, and *Windows Media*. All three have specific advantages that have allowed them to gain ground in the market, mainly because they are free and support the Real-Time Streaming Protocol (RTSP).

New solutions are appearing that use Java to eliminate the need to download and install plug-ins or players. Such an approach will become standard once the Java Media Player APIs being developed by Sun, Silicon Graphics, and Intel are available. This approach will also ensure client platform independence.

2.8.5   3GP Standards

3G stands for third generation, a generic wireless industry term for high-speed mobile data delivery over cellular networks. 3G networks allow users to send and receive bandwidth-intensive information, such as video, video conferencing, high-quality audio, and Web data on demand, virtually anytime and anyplace.

3GPP and 3GPP2 are the new worldwide standards for the creation, delivery, and playback of multimedia over third-generation, high-speed wireless networks. Defined by the 3rd Generation Partnership Project and 3rd Generation Partnership Project 2, respectively, these standards seek to provide uniform delivery of rich multimedia over newly evolved, broadband mobile networks (third-generation networks) to the latest multimedia-enabled wireless devices. 3GPP and 3GPP2 take advantage of MPEG-4, the standard for delivery of video and audio over the Internet, but are tailored to the unique requirements of mobile devices. These formats are supported by *inter*Media and the MIME types are audio/3gpp or video/3gpp. The extensions are as follows:

.3gp 3GPP standard, GSM network

Video: MPEG-4, H.263

Audio: AAC, AMR

.3g2 3GPP2 standard, CDMA2000 network

Video: MPEG-4, H.263

Audio: AAC, AMR, QCELP

2.9   What Is Metadata?

In the earlier sections of the chapter we introduced a number of different forms of metadata:

- In database schema and constraints, setting up value sets and domain.
- In distributed DBMS, the location and distribution of data.
- In multimedia databases, descriptions of the individual objects (data about data) and descriptive data about each stored object.
- On the Web, provenance (i.e., origin), quality, and integration of data.

We have already met several examples of both metadata and its use. For example the RealVideo metafiles needed to stream video. There are many uses of metadata, including:

- Administrative: managing data collection process.
- Descriptive: describing for retrieval purposes and creating indexes.
- Preservation: managing data refreshing and migration.
- Technical: used to describe a media object in a technical sense (formats, compression, scaling, encryption, authentication, and security).
- Usage: users, users' level and type of use, and user tracking.

2.9.1   Generating and Extracting Metadata

The generation of metadata can be achieved in a number of ways, for example:

- Analysis of raw media data
- Implicit metadata generation
- Semi-automatic generation
- Manual augmentation

The creation and management of metadata can become a complex issue when we wish to provide metadata for text and content-based retrieval. Unlike text documents, images make no attempt to tell us what they are about and often they are used for purposes not anticipated by their originators. In terms of manual augmentation, it is very difficult to express in words what a work of art is about when it is based on a wordless medium. Annotating digital images with additional metadata is a common practice in photographic and news-gathering applications, for image archiving usages, and at the consumer level. However, metadata based on the manual addition of keywords to image objects is very time-consuming.

Multimedia objects may acquire layers of metadata as they move through their lifecycle so when we design the structure of the metadata we need to consider how it would be updated. Where will the metadata be stored in the database? There are a range of ways in which metadata can be associated with the media object:

- Contained within the same envelope as the media, for example, through the header of an image file, as part of the object definition in Oracle *inter*Media.

- Bundled with the media object, for example, universal preservation format (UPF).

- Attached to the information object through bidirectional pointers and hyperlinks.

- Stored separately in a metadata registry, which is a special kind of data dictionary for metadata.

2.9.2 Image Metadata

Storing metadata together with image data in the same container provides encapsulation. With encapsulation, both types of data can be shared and exchanged reliably as one unit. Metadata that is stored in the image file format is referred to as *embedded metadata*. Metadata can be stored in image files using a variety of mechanisms. Digital cameras and scanners automatically insert metadata into the images as they are created. Digital photograph processing applications like Adobe Photoshop allow users to add or edit metadata to be stored with the image.

For a large number of image file formats, Oracle *inter*Media can extract and manage a limited set of metadata attributes. These attributes include height, width, contentLength, fileFormat, contentFormat, compressionFormat, and MIME type. All these are included in the ORDImage data type described in Chapter 3.

For a limited number of image file formats, *inter*Media can also extract a rich set of metadata attributes. This metadata is represented in schema-based XML documents. These XML documents can be stored in a database, indexed, searched, updated, and made available to applications using the standard mechanisms of Oracle database.

*inter*Media supports metadata embedding for the GIF, TIFF, and JPEG file formats using the methods described in Chapters 8. The application provides the metadata as a schema-based XML document. Then *inter*Media processes the XML document and writes the metadata into the image file. The metadata must conform to the Adobe XMP format and may also be required to conform to one of the standards for the interoperability of systems, such as the data shown in Table 2.7.

Table 2.7   *ISO/IEC 11179 Attributes*

Attribute	Description
Name	The label assigned to the data element
Identifier	The unique identifier assigned to the data element
Version	The version of the data element
Registration authority	The entity authorized to register the data element
Language	The language in which the data element is specified
Definition	A statement that clearly represents the concept and essential nature of the data element
Obligation	Indicates if the data element is required to always or sometimes be present (contains a value)
Data type	Indicates the type of data that can be represented in the value of the data element
Maximum occurrence	Indicates any limit to the repeatability of the data element
Comment	A remark concerning the application of the data element

- ISO/IEC 11179: for the exchange of data between organizations (Table 2.7).

- The Dublin Core Metadata Set (http://purl.org/metadata/dublin_core): online libraries.

■ Resource Description_Framework (RDF): Web documents.

Resource Description_Framework (RDF)

The World Wide Web Consortium is developing a standard, the Resource Description Framework (RDF) for metadata. RDF allows multiple metadata schemes to be read by humans as well as parsed by machines. RDF is a foundation for processing metadata; it provides interoperability between applications that exchange machine-understandable information on the Web.

RDF will specify a framework for detailed descriptions of all kinds of objects stored on the Web, allowing search engines to identify relevant content with much greater precision than is at present possible. The specification allows users to define attribute types and values relevant to their own needs, with the objective of providing sufficient extensibility to meet a whole range of specialist needs. RDF uses XML to express structure thereby allowing metadata communities to define the actual semantics.

2.9.3 Image Metadata Format

The term *image metadata format* refers to the standard protocols and techniques used to store image metadata within an image file. The embedded image metadata formats supported by *inter*Media are:

■ EXIF. The standard for image metadata storage for digital still cameras. It can be stored in TIFF, JPEG, and JPEG2000 format images. *inter*Media supports the extraction of EXIF metadata from TIFF, JPEG, and JPEG2000 file formats.

■ IPTC-IIM. The International Press Telecommunications Council—Information Interchange Model (IPTC-IIM) Version 4 is a standard developed jointly by the International Press Telecommunications Council and the Newspaper Association of America. This metadata standard is designed to capture information that is important to the activities of news gathering, reporting, and publishing. These information records are commonly referred to as IPTC tags. IPTC metadata can be stored in TIFF, JPEG, and JPEG2000 format images. The use of embedded IPTC tags in image file formats became widespread with the use of Adobe Photoshop's tool for image editing. *inter*Media supports the extraction of IPTC metadata from TIFF, JPEG, and JPEG2000 file formats.

- XMP. The extensible metadata platform (XMP) is a standard metadata format, developed by Adobe, for the creation, processing, and interchange of metadata in a variety of applications. XMP uses Resource Description Framework (RDF) technology for data modeling. XMP also defines how the data model is serialized (converted to a byte stream), and embedded within an image file. *inter*Media supports the extraction of XMP metadata from GIF, TIFF, JPEG, and JPEG2000 file formats. *inter*Media also supports writing XMP data packets into GIF, TIFF, JPEG, and JPEG2000 file formats.

Once metadata has been extracted from the binary image file, the next step is to represent the metadata in a form that can be easily stored, indexed, queried, updated, and presented. *inter*Media returns image metadata in XML documents. These documents are based on XML schemas that *inter*Media registers with the database, the XML schemas used by the metadata methods of the ORDImage object type. Each type of image metadata has a separate XML schema. These XML schemas are used by the metadata methods of the ORDImage object type. These schemas are registered in Oracle Database when Oracle *inter*Media is installed. The schemas may be examined by querying the dictionary view ALL_XML_SCHEMAS.

The following XML schemas are available:

- XML schema for DICOM metadata
- XML schema for EXIF metadata
- XML schema for IPTC-IIM metadata
- XML schema for ORDImage attributes
- XML schema for XMP metadata

Users may store the returned metadata documents in metadata columns of type XMLType, which are bound to the corresponding metadata XML schemas that *inter*Media provides. An example of an XML instance document follows.

```
/*

<xmpMetadata xmlns="http://xmlns.oracle.com/ord/meta/xmp"
    xsi:schemaLocation="http://xmlns.oracle.com/ord/meta/xmp
```

```
        http://xmlns.oracle.com/ord/meta/xmp"
        xmlns:xsi="http://www.w3.org/2001/XMLSchema-instance">

<rdf:RDF xmlns:rdf="http://www.w3.org/1999/02/22-rdf-syntax-
ns#">
<rdf:Description about="" xmlns:dc="http://purl.org/dc/
elements/1.1/">
        <dc:title>A Winter Day<dc:title>
        <dc:creator>Frosty S. Man</dc:creator>
        <dc:date>21-Dec-2004</dc:date>
        <dc:description>a sleigh ride</dc:description>
        <dc:copyright>North Pole Inc.</dc:copyright>
    </rdf:Description>
  </rdf:RDF>
</xmpMetadata>

*/
```

There are specialized ORDImage methods available for dealing with image metadata. ORDImage has methods to get and write the metadata into special XML documents as described in Chapter 8.

We claim DICOM is indeed a file format as well as a communcation protocol. Midway in this paragraph I asked you to add the following sentence "It specifies a file format as well as a communication protocol." I also asked you to remove some earlier text, including this sentence "It does not specify a separate file format; rather, it assumes a media environment using industry standard media." This earlier sentence directly contradicts the later sentence. It does not specify a file format. It specifies a file format. We cannot say both. I would like to remove the sentence that says, "It does not specify a separate file format; rather, it assumes a media environment using industry standard media." We do have a member of the team on the DICOM standards committee and I believe it is accurate to say DICOM is a file format and a communications protocol.

2.10 **Summary**

In this chapter we have looked at the format, compression, and delivery requirements for rich media. It was clear that the standards for interoperability, quality, and metadata are vital. In the next chapter we will look at the options for storing rich media in a database.

3

Introduction to inter*Media Storage*

3.1   Introduction

Many enterprises expend tremendous resources on the acquisition, storage, and management of collections of images, including graphics, video, and audio. While acquiring such data can be time-consuming and expensive, it has tremendous business value and represents a large investment. Therefore, storage and processing this media is one of the fastest growing applications.

In this chapter we look at the options for storing media within a database. We also learn how to create a multimedia database using relational and object-relational concepts. We will introduce a simple information systems case study to illustrate the issues and see how the different approaches could work out in practice. To summarize, in this chapter we will cover how

- Object-relational and relational features of Oracle can contribute to the development of media rich databases.

- Standard SQL data types, BLOB and BFILE, can be used to store media data.

- Oracle *inter*Media data types provide advantages for developers.

- SQL/MM can be used to store media data.

- Object types and object tables can be developed to store media data.

This chapter focuses on the storage options for media data that have arisen through the recent developments of object-relational databases and media technologies. First, we will focus on the relational approach and the standard data types available for media storage based on LOBS and BFILES, since these data types are at the basis of the object types described later in this chapter, and it is important to have a sound grasp of their functions and capabilities. This way we will understand the limitations of this approach, particularly in terms of storage of metadata and retrieval before we look at the more complex alternatives.

3.2 Object-relational and Relational Features

We can use a relational or object-relational approach to developing databases for media-rich applications. What this means is that we can follow the relational approach based on the standard SQL data types and those implemented in Oracle, or we can use object types as specified in SQL:1999.

As a first option we can choose to restrict the database to the standard media data types specified in SQL:1999 for large object (LOB) data types. These LOB data types include binary large object (BLOB), which is used for image, video, and audio data. In addition there are CLOBs for character data, which we will not be particularly interested in but they can hold large documents and are manipulated by Oracle Text and BFILES, which can be used for any type of data but have certain limitations.

However, SQL:1999 provided a framework for creating object types (also called user-defined, UDT) types that can be used for media databases. There are several advantages to adopting this approach. In the next section we will first briefly explain how to use the SQL types BLOB and BFILE and their advantages and disadvantages. This is important to understand even if we decide to use object types because, from time to time in the development, we will need to know about the properties of BLOBS and BFILES and be able to manipulate them.

3.3 Using Large Object Data Types

Large object (LOB) data types in Oracle10g have the advantage of being able to accommodate large size files and to support random access. In Oracle10g there is support for terabyte-size LOB values (maximum size limit for LOBS is 8–128 terabytes, depending on the database block size) in such a way that they can be stored in the database and manipulated in the following programmatic environments:

- Java (JDBC)

- OCI

- PL/SQL (particularly through the package DBMS_LOB)

This means we can store and manipulate LOB (BLOB, CLOB, and NCLOB) data types larger than 4 GB, which was the limit in previous versions of the database, stored in the database tablespaces in a way that optimizes space and provides efficient access. A column of a table can be specified with any LOB data type in the normal way. Incidently Oracle *inter*Media uses LOB data types to create data types for use in multimedia applications such as *inter*Media-specialized object types ORDAudio, ORDDoc, ORDImage, and ORDVideo.

3.4   Using LOB Locators

When a LOB data type is declared for a column in a table, the values stored are references, known as the LOB locators, that specify the location of the large stored object. If the LOB is small (up to 4 KB) it can be stored with its locator but otherwise it will be moved to a different physical location in the database tablespaces. This is referred to as inline storage but obviously large BLOBS may not be stored inline with other row data. In that case, a locator is stored in the row and the actual BLOB is stored in other tablespaces. The locator can be considered a pointer to the actual location of the BLOB value. When you select a BLOB, you are selecting the locator instead of the actual value, although this is done transparently. An advantage of this design is that multiple BLOB locators can exist in a single row. For example, you might want to store a short video clip of a training tape, an audio recording containing a brief description of its contents, a syllabus of the course, a picture of the instructor, and a set of maps and directions to each training center all in the same row.

LOB data types are restricted in terms of their storage options and standard SQL operations, as shown in Table 3.1. For example they are restricted from primary and foreign key constraints and from use in comparisons other than pure equality tests. However, there are several operations for BLOBs including concatenation, substring, overlay, and trim that are executed through the LOB locator.

3.5   Using BFILES

The BFILE data type is a special external LOB data type. These are useful for data objects stored in operating system files, outside the database tablespaces. The database accesses external LOBS using the SQL data type, BFILE. BFILES are read-only data types. The database allows read-only byte stream access to data stored in BFILES and therefore we cannot write

Table 3.1   *Oracle10g Large Object Data Types*

Name	Data Type	Size Limitations	Characteristics
BLOB	Binary	8–128 TB	Random access Transaction support Needs LOB locator
CLOB	Character	8–128 TB	Random access Transaction support Needs LOB locator
BFILE	Binary	4 GB	Read-only External file

to a BFILE from within an application. This obviously makes their use very limited and we would not normally use them. However, we need to know about them as they provide a means of getting data from the external file system into a BLOB.

Any storage device accessed by your operating system can hold BFILE data, including hard-disk drives, CD-ROMs, PhotoCDs, and DVDs. The database can access BFILES provided that the operating system supports stream-mode access to the operating system files. A summary of characteristics of LOB data types are:

- Media objects with data types BLOB and CLOB can be stored in the database.

- BLOB and CLOB are described as internal LOBS stored within the database tablespaces.

- BFILE data type is used for objects stored externally as operating system files.

- BFILE objects are called external LOBS stored outside the database tablespaces.

- External LOBS (BFILES) could be located in another part of the network or on CD-ROMs or DVDs that are accessible to the database.

- BFILE data type allows read-only access to these large files and they cannot participate in transactions.

In Oracle10g, small LOBS (up to 4 KB) can be stored inline with the rest of your row data:

- All types of LOBS are manipulated through a LOB locator.

- A locator is a unique binary value that acts as a surrogate for the actual binary object held in the database. It can be used to identify either a binary large object or a character large object.

3.5.1 The Disadvantages of Using BFILES

Storing the media data within the database gives a number of advantages that cannot be applied to BFILES, such as

- Database security

- Transaction control

- Database backup and recovery, etc.

When we use a BFILE, the media is stored in files outside the database, and file location and attributes are stored inside the database. Although media functionality, such as image processing, can still be supported by moving the data to a temporary BLOB, the advantages listed above will be lacking.

When we develop an application for media data using an object-relational database there are several options available that would not have been possible with a basic relational database. In order to illustrate the different approaches we will use the following Picture Book case study to develop different solutions.

Family and Friends Picture Book Case Study

The Family and Friends Picture Book database should be capable of storing a wide variety of images obtained from different sources, including digital cameras and scanners. The family mentioned here intends to access the images through a website and to be able to browse through the images to select and retrieve different images. The application should support the following scenarios:

Jo, who is 11 years old, wants to be able to produce greeting cards, especially birthday cards, for her friends using photos of her pets that she takes with her point-and-shoot digital camera.

Jason would like to produce some sports greetings cards but also posters to support and promote the local tennis club events. He will particularly need to locate shots of sporting events and activities.

Marie needs to produce a calendar and a magazine cover for the charity she works for. She needs to locate photos of different seasons of the year.

In addition Marie has an interest in family history and has collected and scanned old black-and-white photographs from the nineteenth century from various older relatives. She wants to link these to the family tree that she is researching.

Matt is interested in astronomy, and his set of photos is mainly focused on the solar system. He captures images from his telescope as well as gets them from various sources, including the Internet. He needs to identify images from the night sky at different locations and times of the year.

In addition, the family records videos and images of their holidays and audio recordings of special family celebrations and music.

As far as possible, the family wants one generic photo database that will support this range of requirements. In this chapter we will focus particularly on the storage requirements and options for the Picture Book. In later chapters we will look at how to retrieve and display the media data. The scenarios above lead to the following functional requirements:

- Storage of photographic images with a variety of file formats, including application-specific formats.

- Availability of thumbnail images (lower-resolution images used for quick display) as a means of browsing the database and displaying the result sets from queries.

- Availability of images of different resolutions, including print levels.

- Storage of image subjects for future searching and compilation of collections of images.

3.6   Using the Relational Approach

First, just using BLOB and BFILE data types, for example, we could specify the main table as follows:

```
CREATE TABLE photos (
        id            NUMBER PRIMARY KEY,
        description   VARCHAR2(40) NOT NULL,
        location      VARCHAR2(40),
        image         blob,
        thumb         blob
);
```

In this way we would store both the main image and the thumbnail image within the database as they would be used for random access, transactions, image-processing, and indexing purposes. This is basically a relational approach to the problem and the database would be manipulated mainly through SQL. Consider the following data for rows for the Picture Book photos table that identify the two image files (Figure 3.1) we want to insert into the database.

id	4310
description	Graduates entering Senate House, 2004
location	C:\PICTURES
image	Graduation.jpg
thumb	Small_grad.jpg

The family will probably want to add single images and generate thumbnails to store in the database. This is quite complicated with the relational approach. It involves the following processes for adding a row for a single image:

- Initialize the image columns so that they can receive data using the EMPTY_BLOB() function.

- Create a directory object for the corresponding directory, external to the database, that holds the images.

Figure 3.1
*Storing media
data.*

Graduation.jpg   Isaac.tiff

- Create a temporary storage for the images by using a BFILE and initialize it as well using the BFILENAME() function.

- Store the image in a BFILE and then transfer this to the image column with the BLOB data type by using the DBMS_LOB package.

This process is sufficiently complex to put many users off from developing a media database. Why is this necessary?

Before media data can be entered into the image column, we must ensure the LOB locator must be non-NULL. Instead of using NULL when the BLOB is missing from a row, the BLOB value is set to EMPTY by using the EMPTY_BLOB() function in the INSERT statement. A column containing a LOB value set to NULL has no locator. By contrast, an empty LOB is a LOB of zero length that has a LOB locator. So, if we select from an empty LOB column or attribute, we get back a locator, which we can use to fill the LOB with data using the OCI or DBMS_LOB routines or an appropriate import method. This initialization requirement will arise whenever a BLOB occurs, even with the *inter*Media data types described later in this chapter.

This can also be done for initializing the locator of the BFILE column by using the BFILENAME() function. Oracle provides a special function BFILENAME() to associate the external file with the database locator. To associate the BFILE objects with a directory in the external file system that will hold the actual data, we would need to create a DIRECTORY object. We must be connected as dba/system to do this unless, as users, we have been granted the create directory privilege, such as:

```
GRANT CREATE ANY DIRECTORY TO SCOTT;
```

This directory association is done by giving the subdirectory holding the image a logical name, using a statement, such as, for Windows,

```
CREATE DIRECTORY "PHOTO_DIR" AS 'C:\PICTURES';
```

or, for Unix or Linux,

```
CREATE DIRECTORY "PHOTO_DIR" AS 'home/images'
```

We must then grant the users access to the directory object. A directory object has thus been created to hold the external files, called "PHOTO_DIR," and then access rights can be given to the users as:

```
GRANT READ ON DIRECTORY PHOTO_DIR TO SCOTT
```

As we have seen already it is difficult to manipulate LOBS in SQL because the standard functions do not exist and often SQL editors cannot cope with the display of media data. However, there are often reasons why using SQL to update LOBS or extract segments of data without necessarily displaying the data to the user would be an advantage. There are three approaches to manipulating a LOB in Oracle;

1. Using Oracle API, such as Oracle Objects, for OLE and JDBC API.

2. Using DBMS_LOB package.

3. Using Oracle Call Interface (OCI).

We can use the special package DBMS_LOB provided for manipulating LOBS and BFILES. DBMS_LOB is a package that is based on working with LOB locators. It consists of a number of routines for manipulating LOBS. The DBMS_LOB package routines would normally be used within a PL/SQL procedure but some of the DBMS_LOB functions that deal with LOBS can be used directly in SQL. More details are given in Chapters 8 and 11.

3.6.1   The Disadvantages of Using BLOBS and BFILES

In addition to the problems we have already encountered, when we look at the Picture Book scenarios there are some data items that need to be stored that are associated with the media, for example:

- The type of media file.

- The name of the external source file.

- The time when the media was captured or altered.

- The height and width of the images when displayed.

It would be much better if the media metadata could be bundled together with the media data so they could not get separated or confused. To do this we will need to create object types. The storage approaches we will consider in the rest of the chapter all use object types. The ways in which we can manipulate LOBS using the relational approach is very limited. As an alternative approach, we can use the Oracle *inter*Media data types that include LOBS as attributes but provide classes with methods that give the required multimedia functionality. For example, in the Picture Book system we need a method to generate a thumbnail. Oracle *inter*Media can store the actual multimedia data as an internal source within the database, under transactional control as a BLOB. This is the recommended approach. It can also deal with multimedia data stored as an external source in an operating system–specific file in a local file system, as a URL on an HTTP server, or as a user-defined source on other servers, such as media servers. Although these external storage mechanisms are particularly convenient for integrating existing sets of multimedia data with a database, the multimedia data will not be under transactional control if it is not stored in the database. This would mean that when we wanted to carry out any database processing or image processing, we would need to copy the external BFILE into a temporary LOB within the database before we could process it.

3.7   Using the Object-relational Approach

With an object-relational database (ORDBMS) it is possible to create *object types* that are more complex than the simple data types in SQL. User-defined data types make it easier for applications developers to work with complex data. This approach also gives the developer maximum flexibility in their design because both the relational and object properties can be exploited. This means that we would be able to create object types with more complex structures, for example if we stored a video object we could hold both media data and the related metadata. These object types can then be used in a number of ways. In Oracle an object type is equivalent in concept to a class in UML and would have three kinds of components (Figure 3.2): it must have a *name* that uniquely identifies it within the database schema; it can have *attributes* that are either built-in types or object types; and *methods* that describe the operations that can be applied to the object type. This facility has given the developer the ability to introduce the concepts of object-oriented development into databases, giving the basis for the development of object-relational databases.

Figure 3.2
An object type's components.

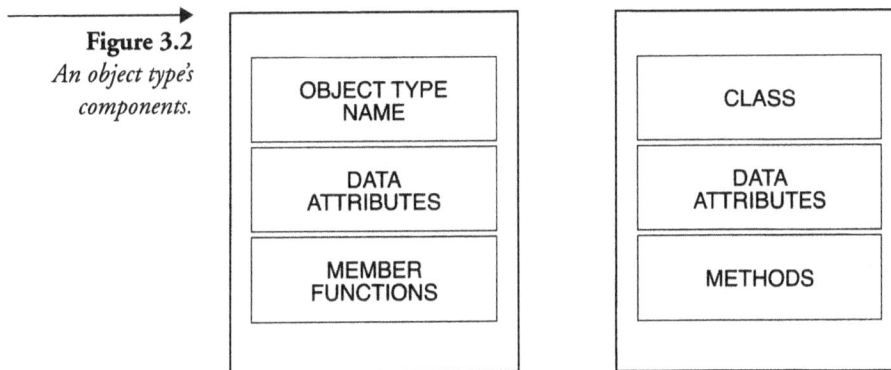

In the next section we will look at the object types available in *inter*Media that integrate data types based on BLOBS and BFILES with other useful data and methods. We will illustrate their application by seeing how these could be used to develop the Picture Book database.

3.8   Using Oracle *inter*Media

First, we will look at the way media data is stored in Oracle *inter*Media and what other attributes are included.

- Is the recommended approach to using BLOB or BFILE data types for reasons we will learn as we go along.

- Is a way of building multimedia applications rather than providing an end-user application.

- Is a way of supporting existing media standards.

- Supports a base set of popular multimedia data characteristics.

- Can be extended to cope with new codecs, data sources, and even specialized data-processing algorithms for audio and video data.

- Provides a set of multimedia user-defined types to make it easier for the database designer to create multimedia applications.

There are four object types available in *inter*Media for different kinds of media:

1.   ORDAudio for storing audio data characteristics.

2.   ORDImage for storing image data characteristics.

3.   ORDVideo for storing video data characteristics.

4.   ORDDoc for storing heterogeneous data characteristics.

*inter*Media provides an object-relational type, known as *ORDDoc*, that allows a column to hold a mixture of image, audio, and video data, or other heterogeneous media data. All these types belong to the ORDSYS schema and store data source information in an object-relational type, known as ORDSource, that holds the actual digital media data. In addition to specific attributes for the different kind of media (Table 3.2), another advantage is that the object types include a number of data manipulation methods, for example, for image media using ORDImage:

- Format and compression conversion
- Scaling
- Cropping
- Copying

Although *inter*Media includes object types for the different media (i.e., ORDAudio, ORDImage, ORDVideo, and ORDDoc), these all have a common data storage model. The media data could be stored as a BLOB under transaction control or outside the database as a BFILE. In that case a pointer is stored in the database and the media itself stored in a BFILE or HTTP server-based URL, or the source may be located on a special external media server. This data can be imported into a BLOB in the database when it is required for transaction processing. However, with new developments it would always be recommended to store the data as a BLOB. We can also process the *inter*Media data types by using the DBMS_LOB package in the same way as conventional BLOBS but this is usually unnecessary as more extensive methods are provided by *inter*Media.

Table 3.2 *ORDSource Attributes*

ORDSource Attribute	Data Type	Purpose
LocalData	BLOB	Locally stored multimedia data
SrcType	VARCHAR2(4000)	Type of data source for nonlocal data (e.g., FILE, HTTP)
SrcLocation	VARCHAR2(4000)	Location of data Directory for FILE URL for HTTP
SrcName	VARCHAR2(4000)	Name of object or file
UpdateTime	DATE	Last modified timestamp
Local	NUMBER	Flag that indicates whether the data is local (1 or NULL) = BLOB or external (0)

Before we consider the separate object types, we will briefly look at the attributes of ORDSource because occasionally we may need to access its attributes. This base type can accommodate media data as a BLOB or a BFILE, in which case the location and name of the data file is stored. Although ORDSource has object methods, these should not be called directly. Instead, we should invoke a wrapper method of the media object corresponding to the ORDSource method. We can think of the wrapper as a software adapter or shell that isolates the ORDSource component from other components and provides a cleaner or more specific way of using complicated classes. All the *inter*Media object types provide wrapper methods to do the following:

- Set the source of the data as local or external.

- Modify the time an object was last updated.

- Set information about the external source type, location, and name of the data.

- Transfer data into or out of the database.

- Obtain information about the local data content, such as its length, location, or handle to the BLOB; put the content into a temporary BLOB; or delete it.

- Access source data by opening it, reading it, writing to it, trimming it, and closing it.

The ORDSource object is embedded within the other *inter*Media object types and we do not deal with it directly since Oracle Corporation does not recommend that we use this object type. We would normally use the multimedia data types; for example, we could specify the photos table so that it contains *inter*Media objects. Recall that we defined a table

```
CREATE TABLE photos
(id            NUMBER PRIMARY KEY,
 description   VARCHAR2(40) NOT NULL,
 location      VARCHAR2(40),
 image         blob,
 thumb         blob);
```

that could be specified instead as

```
CREATE TABLE photos
(id            NUMBER PRIMARY KEY,
 description VARCHAR2(40) NOT NULL,
 location      VARCHAR2(40),
 image         ORDSYS.ORDIMAGE,
 thumb         ORDSYS.ORDIMAGE);
```

Since Oracle *inter*Media uses object types, an instance of these object types will consist of the media data itself, the methods associated with it, and metadata about the instance, which makes it much easier to develop media applications. We can insert an image into this table using INIT() methods for the *inter*Media type ORDIMAGE as follows:

```
INSERT INTO photos
VALUES
(1234, 'Outside Senate House - Graduation 2004', 'Cambridge',
```

```
ORDSYS.ORDIMAGE.INIT('FILE', 'PHOTO_DIR', 'graduation.jpg'),
ORDSYS.ORDIMAGE.INIT());
```

When this row is added to the table, the ORDImage INIT() method inserts a LOB locator into the image column to specify the external target file in the PHOTO_DIR directory and initializes the thumb column as empty rather than NULL. We discuss this method in more detail later.

In *inter*Media, Oracle has used object-relational concepts to create a set of multimedia object types to make it easier for the database designer to create multimedia applications. The object types have associated methods that cover common media requirements and image processing; for example, it provides methods getContent() and process(), which will already be available so we will not need to develop them specially for the application. This also has another advantage in that it allows databases to be developed in a generic style so that media data can be exchanged between applications. Another advantage is that the data types can still be accessed through a relational approach using PL/SQL and OCI or an object approach can be used based, for example, on C++ or JAVA. A database designer can also use *inter*Media to

- Create new object types or composite object types based on the basic *inter*Media types.

- Create specialized plug-ins to support new external sources of media data, such as new data formats, using a special ORDPLUGINS schema.

- Process audio or video data in new ways.

By using these *inter*Media data types we can then use the methods for

- Manipulating data about the source and comment attributes.

- Getting and managing data from Web servers and other servers.

- Performing file operations (open, close, trim, read, and write) for audio and video only.

- Extracting metadata attributes from media data.

When we deal with a conventional SQL data type, such as CHAR, we are not conscious that the CHAR data type has methods associated with it. In fact SQLPLUS provides about 15 methods that we know as built-in functions for this data type (UPPER, LOWER, SOUNDEX, SUBSTR, and so on). The *inter*Media object types also have a useful set of methods. In Chapter 8 we look at these methods in greater detail.

Recall that if using *inter*Media, we would treat the Picture Book table differently.

```
CREATE TABLE photos
(id           NUMBER PRIMARY KEY,
 description VARCHAR2(40) NOT NULL,
 location     VARCHAR2(40),
 image        ORDSYS.ORDIMAGE,
 thumb        ORDSYS.ORDIMAGE);
```

This structure would allow us to include data relevant to the application, such as the description and location of the images, separately from data about the images, such as height, width, and MIME type, which would be encapsulated in the ORDIMAGE data type.

3.8.1 Manipulating Image Data Using *inter*Media

Oracle *inter*Media uses instances of object types that consist of the media data itself, the methods associated with it, and metadata about the instance. The methods will be the special procedures needed to manage the object and will be the same for all instances of the object. The metadata might include information about the object's size, compression, or format. The metadata are always stored in the database even if the media data is externally located. The metadata includes the information about the source of the media data, source type, location, source name, and whether the media data is stored locally (in the database) or externally. Examples of metadata used by the different types of media are included in Table 3.3. It also shows what kind of media data it applies to and the purpose of the metadata in separate attributes. *inter*Media manages the metadata for all the media types and may automatically extract it for audio, image, and video processing.

The metadata described in Table 3.3 (e.g., relating to size) is often called content- or format-related metadata. The object types ORDAudio, ORD-Doc, ORDImage, and ORDVideo contain specific attributes (see Table

Table 3.3   *Metadata and* inter*Media*

Media Data	Metadata	Purpose/Comment/Note
Audio, video	Description	Needed for semantic nature
Audio, doc, image, video	MIME type	Needed for real-time nature, so that browser knows how to display/play media. When MIME is used, all the media is retrieved and then played using a single local clock.
Audio, doc, video	Comments	Semantic nature, text-based retrieval
Audio	Encoding type, number of channels, sampling rate, sample size, compression type, play time (duration) format	Size—needed for issues related to performance for delivery across networked systems. This is particularly important because poor performance will result in distortions that are not acceptable to the user.
Doc	Source, format, content length	Size—needed for issues related to performance for delivery across networked systems as this type could include image, audio, or video.
Image	Height and width, image content length, format, compression type	Size—needed for issues related to performance for delivery across networked systems.
Video	Frame width and height, frame resolution, frame rate, play time (duration), number of frames, compression type, number of colors, bit rate	Size—needed for issues related to performance for delivery across networked systems where jitter becomes a problem.

3.4) and methods for their kind of media. In addition to specific attributes, another advantage is that the package includes a number of data manipulation methods, for example for image media:

- checkProperties()
- getCompressionFormat()
- getContentFormat()
- getHeight()
- getWidth()

Table 3.4   *Attributes of interMedia Types*

Attribute	Data Type	Purpose
ORDAudio		
Description	VARCHAR2(4000)	Free form description
Source	ORDSource	Source storing data
Format	VARCHAR2(31)	e.g., WAV
mimeType	VARCHAR2(4000)	MIME type of stored data (e.g., audio/x-aiff)
Comments	CLOB	Extracted metadata as XML
Encoding	VARCHAR2(256)	Encoding type that will be the same as the compression type
numberofChannels	INTEGER	Audio channel number form 1–6
samplingRate	INTEGER	Rate data recorded in samples per second, range 5500–48,000
sampleSize	INTEGER	Width 8–16 bits
compressionType	VARCHAR2(4000)	For audio it is the same as encoding
audioDuration	INTEGER	Time to play whole object
ORDImage		
Source	ORDSource	Source storing data
mimeType	VARCHAR2(4000)	MIME type of stored data (e.g., image/tiff)
Height	INTEGER	Height in pixels
Width	INTEGER	Width in pixels
contentLength	INTEGER	Size in bytes
fileFormat	VARCHAR2(4000)	File type (e.g., tiff)
contentFormat	VARCHAR2(4000)	Type of image (e.g., grayscale)
compressionFormat	VARCHAR2(4000)	Image compression format (e.g., JPEG)
ORDVideo		
Description	VARCHAR2(4000)	Free form description
Source	ORDSource	Source storing data

Table 3.4 *Attributes of* inter*Media Types (continued)*

MIME type	VARCHAR2(4000)	MIME type of stored data (e.g., video/x-msvideo)
Comments	CLOB	Extracted metadata as XML
compressionType	VARCHAR2(4000)	Compression type
Height	INTEGER	Height of frame in pixels
Width	INTEGER	Width of frame in pixels
frameResolution	INTEGER	Number of pixels per inch
frameRate	INTEGER	Number of frames per second
videoDuration	INTEGER	Time to play entire clip
ORDDoc		
Source	**ORDSource**	**Source storing data**
Format	VARCHAR(80)	Format of the media data
mimeType	VARCHAR(80)	MIME type information
contentLength	INTEGER	Length of the media data
Comments	CLOB	Extracted metadata as XML

3.8.2 New Formats Supported

Another advantage of using *inter*Media is that the object types are updated to include new formats and methods as multimedia technology changes and new standards are set up. This makes maintenance of multimedia applications much more straightforward. For example, *inter*Media now supports the MPEG-2 and MPEG-4 file formats and new methods are also incorporated as required. It also includes DICM as the *inter*Media designation for the digital imaging and communications in medicine (DICOM) format. FPIX, or FlashPix, is a format developed by Kodak, Microsoft Corporation, Hewlett-Packard Company, and Live Picture, Inc., for storing digital photography. Oracle *inter*Media does not write FlashPix images. The MIME type is image/x-fpx. The ORDVideo and ORDDoc object types now support the setProperties() method for extracting metadata information from MPEG-2 video streams. The ORDVideo, ORDAudio, and ORDDoc object types now support the setProperties() method for extracting metadata from MPEG-4 (.MP4) files.

Oracle *inter*Media also supports the ASF file format for ORDAudio, ORDVideo, and ORDDoc objects. Windows Media files from Microsoft (.WMV, .WMA, and .ASF) use the ASF file format. With this feature, the setProperties() method can extract metadata from ASF files. New image processing features are also now available through *inter*Media, as discussed in Chapter 9.

In the following sections we will show how to use each of the *inter*Media object types for storage of the different media.

3.8.3 ORDImage

In this section we will find out how to intialize the ORDImage object type (set the encapsulated BLOB to EMPTY_BLOB()), locate the data in the external source, and then import into the database when required. This process involves using several ORDImage methods. There are two ORDImage initialization methods available:

- INIT()
- INIT (srcType, srcLocation, srcName)

The fact that *inter*Media object types can evolve as technology changes brings many benefits. However, there are potential compatibility issues with client-side applications that were developed with previous releases, even after a server upgrade that includes evolved object types. The recommended approach, therefore, is to always use the INIT() method provided for all ORDSYS types, which initalizes all attributes before inserting data. INSERT statements left unchanged using the default constructor, which initializes each object attribute, and may fail if *inter*Media object types evolve.

```
INSERT INTO photos(id, description, image)
VALUES (1255, 'my image', ORDSYS.ORDImage.init());
```

The INIT() method is a static method that initializes all the ORDImage attributes to NULL with the following exceptions:

- source.updateTime is set to SYSDATE
- source.local is set to 1 (local)

- source.localData is set to EMPTY BLOB

The alternative signature, INIT(srcType, srcLocation, srcName), is a static method that initializes all the ORDImage attributes to NULL with the following exceptions:

- source.updateTime is set to SYSDATE
- source.local is set to 0
- source.localData is set to EMPTY BLOB
- source.srcType is set to the input value
- source.srcLocation is set to the input value
- source.srcName is set to the input value

To initialize an ORDImage object, we can use a PL/SQL procedure:

```
CREATE OR REPLACE PROCEDURE init_image_type
AS
BEGIN
  INSERT INTO photos (id,description, image)
    VALUES (1235, 'graduates in Cambridge',
ORDSYS.ORDImage.INIT('FILE', 'PHOTO_DIR','graduation.jpg'));
  COMMIT;
END;
```

This procedure will link the row identified as 1235 with the external file graduation.jpg in the directory called PHOTO_DIR. The media data is still outside the database.

Note that when we use the INIT() method, then 'FILE' could be 'HTTP' if the media file were read from a Web server and then the directory object for the file, in this case 'PHOTO_DIR', would be a URL instead. As we mentioned before, this will add the data in such a way that the actual source is not local to the database.

3.8.4 Using PL/SQL Stored Procedures

This section gives a brief reminder of PL/SQL stored procedures, if you were not familiar with these. The procedures are useful for accessing data stored in tables and combining this with variables created to hold data for processing within the procedure. PL/SQL variables can have a wide range of data types, such as scalar, object types, and LOBS. The procedure begins with a specification of its name, `init_image_type`. The inclusion of the keyword IS or AS is essential, since the declaration of variables needed by the stored procedure is placed between the words AS and BEGIN. The second part, between BEGIN and END, forms the *body* of the procedure in the form of a *compound statement* that expresses step-by-step how the procedure processes the data. Although the compound statement may consist of a number of SQL statements separated by semicolons, it is essential that the definition of the body of the procedure is treated as a complete unit, and not as a series of individual SQL statements.

EXCEPTION is an important section that is not included in this example but is executed whenever an error occurs based on a group of predefined PL/SQL errors. Using the EXCEPTION clause, which is an optional part of the COMPOUND statement, is a way of clearly separating error-processing from normal-processing statements. Predefined internal exceptions are provided by Oracle to cater for common problems, such as when no data is retrieved or a statement attempts to divide by zero.

A procedure is defined with a list of parameters. Each parameter for a procedure must have a name that is unique for that procedure, a data type, and a mode of use. The purpose of the three modes of parameter and the way parameters of the different modes can be used are listed here.

IN   Provides an input value; an argument for this kind of parameter can be a literal (i.e., an actual) value, a variable, or an expression. It cannot be assigned a different value by the procedure and so cannot be placed on the left-hand side of an assignment statement or receive data through either a SELECT...INTO statement or FETCH statement.

INOUT   Can either provide an input value or return an output value; an argument for this kind of parameter must be a variable so that its value can be changed by the procedure.

OUT   Returns an output value; an argument for this kind of parameter must be a variable.

If a mode is not specified for a parameter, it is assumed to be an IN parameter. An IN parameter for a procedure can never be changed within the procedure. It must have the same value after an invocation call as before it.

An OUT or INOUT parameter does not have these restrictions and can be used much more freely in a procedure. You should note, however, that an OUT parameter does not have an initial value (and an INOUT parameter may not have one) so initialization is required if it is used to provide a value.

Since we have inserted the media data we can then process the data to transfer it to the internal source as follows using one of the methods of the ORDImage type as

```
obj.importFrom(ctx,'file','PHOTO_DIR','Graduation.jpg');
```

This statement would be used within a PL/SQL procedure, such as the one below, which copies the existing image with id 1235 from the table into the variable obj that is a temporary variable defined as an ORDSYS.ORDImage object type containing a BLOB that can then be used with the importFrom method. We can see that the procedure also outputs a number of useful messages about the source and checks that it is now local to the database.

```
CREATE OR REPLACE PROCEDURE import_ext_image
AS
 obj ORDSYS.ORDImage;
 ctx RAW(64) :=NULL;
BEGIN
 SELECT p.image INTO obj FROM photos p
  WHERE p.id  = 1235 FOR UPDATE;
 -- set source to a file
 -- import data
 obj.importFrom(ctx,'file','PHOTO_DIR','Graduation.jpg');
 -- check size
 DBMS_OUTPUT.PUT_LINE('Length is ' || obj.getContentLength);
 DBMS_OUTPUT.PUT_LINE('Source is ' || obj.getSource());
 UPDATE photos p SET p.image = obj WHERE p.id = 1235;
 COMMIT;
SELECT p.image INTO obj FROM photos p
  WHERE p.id  = 1235 FOR UPDATE;
```

```
IF (obj.isLocal()= True ) THEN DBMS_OUTPUT.PUT_LINE('Local is
set true');
ELSE DBMS_OUTPUT.PUT_LINE('Local is set FALSE');
END IF;
END;
```

In this procedure there is a SELECT statement that selects a single image value from a table and places it INTO the variable obj. This procedure works by selecting the row that has the initalized image column (ID 1235) for update. The importFrom method is called to import the actual media data into the variable obj and to check some details such as its content length and source. Then the data from obj is written into the database itself with the update statement. Finally, we check if the local attribute is true to check the data is inside the database.

In the procedure we used a ctx variable. This is a parameter used by a source plug-in, if it exists. If not used, as in this case, it should be set to NULL.

The recommended declaration for the ctx variable when not used is as follows:

```
ctx raw(64) := NULL;
```

If a source plug-in were developed and used, then the ctx variable would be used to initialize context information for the client. Until the execution of the `importFrom()  method`, the image object content is a FILE, but importFrom(ctx) moves the data into the database and makes it reside in the database, making the image object contain the media content in the BLOB attribute of the object.

The UPDATE statement makes the actual changes to the table row.

When we execute the procedure we obtain the following information showing the image has been imported as local data

```
SQL> EXECUTE import_ext_image;
Length is 73874
Source is file://PHOTO_DIR/Graduation.jpg
Local is set true

PL/SQL procedure successfully completed.
```

The advantage of using the object type is that we can now manipulate the media data in ways that would have been very difficult with a simple BLOB. There are several operators that alter the scale of an image, so simplify the creation of images with a specific size such as thumbnail images. The maxScale and **fixedScale** operators are especially useful for creating thumbnail images from various-sized originals. The *fixedScale* operator specifies scaling values in pixels. The two integer values supplied to the fixedScale operator are the desired dimensions (width and height) of the destination image. The supplied dimensions may be larger or smaller (or one larger and one smaller) than the dimensions of the source image.

The *maxScale* operator as well preserves the aspect ratio (relative width and height) of the source image and also accepts two integer dimensions, but these values represent the maximum value of the appropriate dimension after scaling. The final dimension may actually be less than the supplied value. We can use these ORDImage methods to generate a thumbnail image and store this in the thumb column, as in the following example that creates, at most, a 32 × 32 pixel thumbnail image, preserving the original aspect ratio.

```
CREATE OR REPLACE PROCEDURE image_thumb
  (img_id IN NUMBER)
 AS
    timage ORDSYS.ORDImage;
 BEGIN
  SELECT image INTO timage FROM photos
    WHERE id = img_id FOR UPDATE;
  timage.process('maxScale=32 32');
  UPDATE photos p SET thumb = timage
    WHERE id = img_id;
  COMMIT;
  EXCEPTION
    WHEN ORDSYS.ORDImageExceptions.DATA_NOT_LOCAL THEN
      DBMS_OUTPUT.PUT_LINE('Data is not local');
 END;

SQL> execute image_thumb(1235);
```

We deal with the development of PL/SQL applications in Chapter 8 but the example above illustrates how the image is selected and then how the thumbnail is generated. The statement

```
DBMS_OUTPUT.PUT_LINE('Data is not local');
```

is used to display messages and data values from PL/SQL.

Another useful method is setProperties(), which can be used in a procedure to extract the metadata of the image in id 1235:

```
image width = 1407
image height = 1320
image size = 309128
image file type = JFIF
image type = 24BITRGB
image compression = JPEG-PROGRESSIVE
image mime type = image/jpeg
```

3.8.5 **ORDAudio**

The family wanted to store their audio files in the database, perhaps by using a table with the following structure.

```
CREATE TABLE audio_ord
(id      NUMBER PRIMARY KEY,
 description VARCHAR2(40) NOT NULL,
 audio       ORDSYS.ORDAudio,);
```

We can initialize the ORDAudio object attribute in the usual way, as follows.

```
BEGIN
INSERT INTO audio_ord(id,description, audio)
VALUES (1729, 'School String Festival Beethovens 9th ',
ORDSYS.ORDAudio.init());
  COMMIT;
END;
```

We can also update using the INIT method, as follows.

```
UPDATE audio_ord
  SET
audio=ORDSYS.ORDAUDIO.INIT('FILE','AUDIO_DIR','BEETHOVEN.WAV'
);
```

SetProperties() is a useful method that reads the audio data to get the values of the object attributes and then stores them in the object attributes. This method sets the properties for each of the following attributes of the audio data for which values are available: compression type, duration, encoding type, format, MIME type, number of channels, sampling rate, and sample size. It also populates the comments field of the object with a rich set of format and application properties in XML form if the value of the setComments parameter is TRUE as illustrated by the following procedure.

```
CREATE OR REPLACE PROCEDURE get_audio_props
AS
 obj ORDSYS.ORDAudio;
 ctx RAW(64) :=NULL;
BEGIN
 SELECT p.audio INTO obj FROM audio_ord p
  WHERE p.id = 1729 FOR UPDATE;
 obj.setProperties(ctx,TRUE);
 DBMS_OUTPUT.PUT_LINE('format: ' || obj.getformat);
 DBMS_OUTPUT.PUT_LINE('encoding: ' || obj.getEncoding);
 DBMS_OUTPUT.PUT_LINE(
                'numberOfChannels: ' ||
TO_CHAR(obj.getNumberOfChannels));
 DBMS_OUTPUT.PUT_LINE('samplingRate: ' ||
TO_CHAR(obj.getSamplingRate));
 DBMS_OUTPUT.PUT_LINE('sampleSize: ' ||
TO_CHAR(obj.getSampleSize));
 UPDATE   audio_ord p set p.audio = obj
   WHERE   p.id = 1729;
 COMMIT;
 EXCEPTION
  WHEN ORDSYS.ORDAudioExceptions.METHOD_NOT_SUPPORTED THEN

DBMS_OUTPUT.PUT_LINE('ORDAudioExceptions.METHOD_NOT_SUPPORTED
caught');
  WHEN OTHERS THEN
   DBMS_OUTPUT.PUT_LINE('EXCEPTION caught');
END;
```

3.8.6 ORDDoc

The ORDDoc object type supports the storage and management of any media data including image, audio, and video. This object type is defined as follows.

```
CREATE OR REPLACE TYPE ORDDoc
AS OBJECT
(
  -- ATTRIBUTES
source              ORDSource,
format              VARCHAR(80),
mimeType            VARCHAR(80),
contentLength       INTEGER,
comments            CLOB,
```

We could create a table for the Family Picture Book that could hold any type of multimedia data and then insert using the following statements.

```
CREATE TABLE doc_ord
  (id                 NUMBER PRIMARY KEY,
   description VARCHAR2(40) NOT NULL,
   my_doc       ORDSYS.ORDDoc)

INSERT INTO doc_ord VALUES
  ('1241','the grape in many wines such as Chablis',
ORDSYS.ORDdoc.INIT('FILE', 'PHOTO_DIR','CHARDONNAY.JPEG'));

INSERT INTO doc_ord VALUES
  ('1242','A recipe for Hungarian Goulash',
ORDSYS.ORDdoc.INIT('FILE', 'PHOTO_DIR','recipe.doc'))
```

This object type also has a setProperties() method that reads the media data to get the values of the object attributes and then stores them in the object attributes. This method understands all supported image, audio, and video format. This method sets the properties for the following attributes of the media data: format, MIME type, and content length. It populates the comments field of the object with an extensive set of format and application properties in XML form if the value of the setComments parameter is TRUE. The next procedure illustrates how this is done in the case where the comments field of the object remains unpopulated. The default value is FALSE.

```
create OR REPLACE PROCEDURE set_doc_prop
  AS
    obj ORDSYS.ORDDoc;
    ctx RAW(64) :=NULL;
  BEGIN
    SELECT my_doc INTO obj FROM doc_ord
      WHERE id = 1242 FOR UPDATE;
    obj.setProperties(ctx,FALSE);
    DBMS_OUTPUT.put_line('format: ' || obj.getformat());
    UPDATE  doc_ord SET my_doc = obj
      WHERE  id=1242;
    COMMIT;
    EXCEPTION
     WHEN ORDSYS.ORDDocExceptions.DOC_PLUGIN_EXCEPTION THEN
       DBMS_OUTPUT.put_line('DOC PLUGIN EXCEPTION caught');
     WHEN OTHERS THEN
       DBMS_OUTPUT.put_line('EXCEPTION caught');
  END;
```

3.8.7 **ORDVideo**

The family could create a separate table to store their family videos in the database, perhaps with the following structure.

```
CREATE TABLE video_ord
(       id           NUMBER PRIMARY KEY,
        description VARCHAR2(40) NOT NULL,
        video        ORDSYS.ORDVideo);

INSERT INTO video_ord VALUES
  ('1234','some pond life', ORDSYS.ORDVIDEO.INIT('FILE',
 'VIDEO_DIR','CYCLIDIUM_GLAUCOMA.MOV'))
COMMIT;
```

Now we can use a procedure to capture the properties of the video. The video that has been stored as a BFILE in the ORDVideo column is selected and copied to a temporary BLOB within the database to get its attributes, which are then displayed.

```
CREATE OR REPLACE PROCEDURE get_video_props
AS
 obj ORDSYS.ORDVideo;
 tempLob    CLOB;
 ctx RAW(64) :=NULL;
BEGIN
 SELECT p.video INTO obj FROM video_ord p
  WHERE p.id  = 1234;
 DBMS_OUTPUT.PUT_LINE('getting comma separated list of all
attributes');
 DBMS_OUTPUT.PUT_LINE('-------------------------------------
-------');
 DBMS_LOB.CREATETEMPORARY(tempLob, FALSE, DBMS_LOB.CALL);
 obj.getAllAttributes(ctx,tempLob);
 DBMS_OUTPUT.PUT_LINE(DBMS_LOB.substr(tempLob,
DBMS_LOB.getLength(tempLob),1));
 COMMIT;
 EXCEPTION
  WHEN ORDSYS.ORDVideoExceptions.METHOD_NOT_SUPPORTED THEN
   DBMS_OUTPUT.PUT_LINE('VIDEO METHOD_NOT_SUPPORTED EXCEPTION
caught');
  WHEN OTHERS THEN
   DBMS_OUTPUT.PUT_LINE('EXCEPTION CAUGHT');
END;
```

We have seen how it is possible to use these *inter*Media object types to store and manipulate actual media data. In the case of an object type, methods can be functions or procedures written in PL/SQL or written in an external language, such as C++ or Java, and stored externally to the database. The methods are all called *member functions*.

3.9   Using SQL/MM Still Image Standard (ISO/IEC 13249-5:2001 SQL/MM)

This ISO/IEC standard defines object-relational types for images and image characteristics. It was developed in response to requests to deal with multimedia applications and issues of interoperability that had emerged with the popularity of Web-based user interfaces and multimedia delivery systems. The proposed standard was initially known as *SQL/MM* (MM for multimedia). It was originally intended to cover a number of different application domains such as full-text data, spatial data, and image data (still and moving). Later, data mining was added to the standard.

In addition, it was intended that the media data should be accessed through ordinary SQL:1999 facilities or by expressions that invoke SQL stored routines. SQL/MM is a multipart standard, however, unlike SQL itself, the various parts of SQL/MM are quite independent from one another. There is one common part known as the Framework that is found in Part 1. This provides definitions of common concepts used in all the other parts and the relationship between them. In particular, it describes the manner in which the other parts use SQL's structured user-defined types to define the types required by the subject matter of each part.

Since the parts of the standard that deal with full-text, spatial data and data mining do not concern us here, we will focus on the standard for images.

SQL/MM Still Image is the part of the SQL/MM standard that provides structured user-defined types that would allow you to store new images into a database, retrieve them, modify them in various ways, and—most importantly—locate them by applying various "visual" predicates to collections of images. In SQL/MM Still Image, images are represented using an SQL:1999 structured type called SI_StillImage. This type can be used to store collections of picture elements (pixels) representing two-dimensional images.

The images can be stored in several formats, depending on what the underlying implementation supports—for example, formats such as JPEG, TIFF, and GIF are commonly supported as input and output formats, as well as formats in which images are stored and manipulated. The SI_StillImage type also encapsulates metadata information about each image, such as its format, its dimensions (height and width in pixels), its color space, and so forth. Methods applied to SI_StillImage instances include routines to scale an image (change its size proportionally); to crop an image (remove pixels both horizontally and vertically); and to create a thumbnail image.

A related set of object types is included in the standard to describe various features of images, for example:

- SI_AverageColor type is used to represent the "average" color of a given image. The idea is that we can describe or match an image on the basis of its average color. This value may be used in locating images in collections (seeking an image of the sea by finding an image that is primarily blue).

- SI_ColorHistogram type provides information about the colors in an image at a finer level of granularity than the image's average color; it indicates *how much* of each color is found in an image (see Chapter 2).

- SI_PositionalColor type represents the location of specific colors in an image, supporting queries such as "sunsets at sea" provided this was expressed as "has red and orange above dark blue"; such images could be located using those color characteristics. The idea is that we can divide an image into a number of rectangular areas and then describe the image by the most significant color in each area.

- SI_Texture type allows the recording of information such as coarseness, contrast, and direction of granularity.

- SI_FeatureList type permits recording all of the features described in the above list for each image.

These object types are provided within Oracle *inter*Media for interoperability purposes. A developer needs to consider whether to use it or ORDImage in an application. Some features that are available through ORDImage are not specified by the SQL/MM Still Image standard, and therefore are not available for StillImage objects:

- Storing image data outside the database

- Image processing operations (such as scaling up, compressing, and so on) that are specific to ORDImage

- Java client API

In addition, the following image-matching features are not specified by the SQL/MM Still Image standard, and therefore are not available for StillImage objects:

- Image matching based on shape

- Indexing (average color, texture, positional color, and color histogram)

One of the ideas behind the SQL/MM standard was that SQL should be used to query the rich media data in as straightforward a way as possible.

By combining several features of an image, it is possible to write queries that can retrieve from a very large image base a much smaller collection of images from which we can quickly select the exact image we want. It is also possible to *screen* collections of images to find images of potential interest for various reasons. For example, checking whether a new logo might conflict with other logos that have already been copyrighted, using an SQL statement like this one:

```
SELECT id
FROM photo_table
WHERE SI_findTexture(new_image).
SI_Score(image) > 1.2
```

Additional challenges are posed by moving images, such as digitized video. That sort of data is not addressed by SQL/MM Still Image, but it is possible that some future part of SQL/MM will be oriented toward moving images.

Oracle *inter*Media provides support for the first edition of the ISO/IEC 13249-5:2001 SQL/MM Part 5: Still Image Standard through the SI_StillImage object type. This is a complex object type. The media data within the object type is held as the ORDSource object type that was described in detail earlier. Each object type includes attributes, methods, and associated SQL functions and procedures. In addition, Oracle has added some extra attributes. Although the SQL/MM standard does not provide support for all the features currently offered by the ORDImage object type in *inter*Media described next, the use of the SQL/MM standard interface may make some applications more portable across various vendor databases.

The SI_StillImage object type represents digital images with inherent image characteristics such as height, width, format, and so on. It is created in the ORDSYS schema with invoker rights and it is declared as INSTANTIABLE and NOT FINAL (see Chapter 8).

We can see from Table 3.5 that the SI_StillImage type is a complex type where a number of attributes are themselves object types known as collection types (e.g., colorsList). These are explained in greater detail in Chapter 8. You can obtain a full description by typing in SQL*PLUS, "DESCRIBE SI_StillImage."

These attributes are listed to help understanding of the object type, however, it is recommended to access the properties of SI_StillImage type through its methods as the attributes are subject to change since a revised

Table 3.5   *SI_StillImage Data Attributes*

Attribute Name	Data Type	Purpose
Content_SI	ORDSYS.ORDSOURCE	Holds binary image as BLOB
contentLength_SI	INTEGER	Length of the image in bytes
Format_SI	VARCHAR2(4000)	Image format
height_SI	INTEGER	Number of image lines
width_SI	INTEGER	Number of image columns
Oracle Attribute Extensions		
mimeType_ora	VARCHAR2(4000)	MIME type information
contentFormat_ora	VARCHAR2(4000)	Type of image (e.g., black-and-white)
compressionFormat_ora	VARCHAR2(4000)	Compression algorithm
retainFeatures_SI	INTEGER	A flag that indicates whether or not image features will be extracted and cached
averageColorSpec_ora	SI_Color	The cached SI_Color object
colorsList_ora	colorsList	Cached array of colors
frequenciesList_ora	colorFrequenciesList	Cached array of color frequencies
colorPositions_ora	colorPositions	Cached array of color positions
textureEncoding_ora	textureEncoding	Cached array of textures

version of the SQL/MM standard is expected soon. To illustrate its use we could use the SI_StillImage object type to define the images in a Photo Store table, as follows.

```
CREATE TABLE photos_SI
(     id          NUMBER PRIMARY KEY,
      description VARCHAR2(40) NOT NULL,
      location    VARCHAR2(40),
      image       SI_StillImage,
      thumb       SI_StillImage)
```

The following example demonstrates how to insert a StillImage object into a database table. This example uses the PL/SQL package DBMS_LOB.LOADFROM FILE to load a BFILE into a temporary

BLOB, which is then inserted into the column attribute. Alternatively, it would be possible to use SQL*Loader. Typically, you would use the PL/SQL package if you were inserting objects one-by-one, and you would use SQL*Loader to insert objects in a batch job.

```
CREATE OR REPLACE PROCEDURE still_insert
AS
    lobd blob;
    fils BFILE := BFILENAME('PHOTO_DIR','cats.jpg');
BEGIN
    DBMS_LOB.CREATETEMPORARY(lobd, TRUE);
    DBMS_LOB.fileopen(fils, DBMS_LOB.file_readonly);
    DBMS_LOB.LOADFROMFILE(lobd, fils,
    DBMS_LOB.GETLENGTH(fils));
    DBMS_LOB.FILECLOSE(fils);
    INSERT INTO photos_si (id,description,location, image)
        VALUES(1239, 'Two Siamese cats - Ben and Emma',
            'Buckinghamshire',new ORDSYS.SI_StillImage(lobd));
    DBMS_LOB.FREETEMPORARY(lobd);
    COMMIT;
END;
```

3.10 Using *inter*Media to Create Your Own Object Types

An object type is a simple definition of the class that will be stored in the data dictionary. For example, we could define a *person* object type. An example of a full specification of object and attributes would be:

```
CREATE TYPE person_t AS OBJECT
(       first_name      CHAR(20),
        second_name     CHAR(20),
        d_o_b           DATE);
```

The advantage of this approach would be that we could have a standard definition of a person that can be incorporated into any relational table of our database ensuring consistency throughout the enterprise. Alternatively, object types can be used to create object tables. Let us look again at the first table definition for the Photo Book:

```
CREATE TABLE photos
(       id              NUMBER PRIMARY KEY,
```

```
description VARCHAR2(40) NOT NULL,
location    VARCHAR2(40),
image       BLOB,
thumb       blob);
```

Instead we could create a simple object consisting of the same SQL data types:

```
CREATE TYPE photo_t AS OBJECT
(     id          NUMBER,
      description VARCHAR2(40),
      image       BLOB,
      thumb       BLOB);
```

We can use object types in two ways: to specify an attribute in a relational table or to generate an object table of the same type. The object type can then be used to set up an object table for the photo_table type with a primary key based in the id column:

```
CREATE TABLE photo_table OF photo_t
(CONSTRAINT PK_photo_tab PRIMARY KEY(id))
```

This has the advantage of avoiding the storage and performance overhead of maintaining the 16-byte OID column and its index. Instead of using the system-generated OIDs, we used a CREATE TABLE statement to specify that the system use the primary key column(s) as the OIDs of the objects in the table. This can appear to be like a normal relational table so we can DESCRIBE, SELECT, INSERT, and UPDATE.

```
SELECT description FROM photo_table;
```

A system-defined constructor method is generated automatically for every object type. The name of the constructor method is the same as the name of the object type. We can INSERT into the `photo_table` using the constructor method:

```
INSERT INTO photo_table
VALUES
```

```
(photo_t(1234, 'Outside Senate House - Graduation 2004',
'Cambridge', EMPTY_BLOB(),EMPTY_BLOB()))
```

The advantage of this development approach is that it would give a standardized table for images that could be used to meet many requirements. This object type, just like a class, can be used to specify the structure of the data and the ways of operating on it. An instance of data that is structured according to the object type and stored in the database is an object. Since an object type is a concept or a template, when it is defined in the database it does not result in any allocation of storage. Since Oracle is following an object-relational paradigm instead of storing the objects in the database, we can create an object table that is defined for the purpose of holding object instances of a particular type.

3.10.1   The Disadvantages of Using Your Own Object Types

There are several disadvantages to using your own object types:

- Problems of inconsistency and interoperability can arise.
- Object types consist of attributes and methods so we would need to develop our own methods for each object type.
- Maintenance problems are also increased as media devices change.

These problems make it sensible for developers to consider the advantages of using the standard *inter*Media types provided by Oracle, the SI_StillImage object type and the ORD types described previously.

There is, however, one advantage for developers who are familiar with object-relational concepts in that it is possible to develop an object type that contains the *inter*Media object types combined with metadata for specific application areas. For example, if we were developing an application that was related to the Dublin Core metadata standards (http://purl.org/metadata/dublin_core; see Chapter 2), we could create a type as an alternative to a purely relational approach, which would ensure the metadata was encapsulated with the *inter*Media attributes and methods.

```
CREATE TYPE dublin_core_t     AS OBJECT
(       identifier            CHAR(10),
        subject               VARCHAR2(80),
```

```
      title              VARCHAR2(80),
      creator            VARCHAR2(80),
      publisher          VARCHAR2(60),
      description        ORDSYS.ORDDOC,
      contributor        VARCHAR2(80),
      subject_date       DATE,
      resource           VARCHAR2(100),
      format             VARCHAR2(30),
      relation           VARCHAR2(100),
      source             VARCHAR2(100),
      language           CHAR(10),
      coverage           VARCHAR2(100),
      rights             VARCHAR2(100))
```

Then create the object table for that type setting the primary key:

```
CREATE TABLE dublin_core_table OF dublin_core_t
(CONSTRAINT PK_dublin_core PRIMARY KEY(identifier))
```

3.11 Summary

This chapter has introduced the storage options for the developer of rich-media databases. We started by considering the SQL:1999 large binary object use in databases. However, when we deal with media it is essential to know the source of the data and who owns the data and issues, such as compression, file type, etc. This metadata needs to be stored in such a way that it is integrated as much as possible with the media data and cannot be separated from it. For these reasons an object-relational approach is preferable.

Therefore, the chapter introduced object types and looked at the implications of designing user-defined types and using SQL/MM data types such as SI_StillImage as well as the *inter*Media data types.

4

Introduction to Web Delivery of interMedia *Multimedia Data*

Multimedia data must be delivered to a program that is capable of exhibiting it since this data cannot be exhibited in text. The most used technology for computer-based multimedia data is the Web. In this chapter we will introduce various techniques to get your multimedia onto the Web from the database. We will also explain how multimedia data is handled by standard programs over the Web.

4.1   HTTP Delivery

Web browsers use HTTP (hyper text transfer protocol) to communicate with Web servers. This protocol is used to deliver text, multimedia data, and other information to and from the browser on request. HTTP is also used in other programs to obtain data, for example, a Java program can use the HTTP protocol to display an image in a thick-client program. Multimedia data that is delivered to browsers are referenced by URLs.

4.1.1   How Browsers Handle Media

It is important to understand how a browser delivers Web pages with multimedia included on the page. A common misconception is that a Web page with multimedia is delivered as one piece of information. This is not the case. A Web page first gets the text of the page in HTML format. The Web browser then parses the page to see what else besides the text is to be displayed. The Web browser then fetches each multimedia object, using HTTP, until the page is complete.

In many browsers, you can turn off the display of multimedia data like images. In this case, only the text in the HTML is displayed and the bandwidth used for the large multimedia data is never asked for by the browser.

In developing multimedia applications, it is useful to know how browsers handle multimedia data.

4.1.2   Image

In the case of an "inline" image, the Web browser will find an <img> tag that describes the image. This tag will have an SRC attribute that indicates the location of the image. This attribute is also in the form of a URL. The URL is a relative URL if there is no path information included, that is an image on the page located at http://webServer.com/aPath/webPage.html might be specified as <img src="myImage.png" />.

The SRC attribute would be translated by the browser into http://web-Server.com/aPath/myImage.png. Since the image is indicated in the form of a URL, the image itself can be located anywhere on the Web, not just on the HTML server machine. If you look closely, you will see that many popular websites will have image servers; that is, the HTML will be delivered from one server and the images from another.

The SRC attribute in traditional applications is often in the form of a reference to a simple filename as in the previous example, but can also specify a program. This program might deliver images from the database where the location of the image in the database is indicated within the URL. Other programs may actually generate images, for example, an up-to-the-minute stock chart might be generated as an image on request.

Since image data is delivered from a URL endpoint, there is great flexibility in who and where the data is obtained or generated.

4.1.3   Arbitrary MIME Types

The browser can handle all multimedia data (and other types of data) by using an <a> (anchor) tag. In the case of an image, the <a> tag can be used to allow a user to click on a thumbnail image and get back a display of a larger image by using the HREF attribute to specify the location of the file. For example:

```
<a href="http://server.com/bigImage.png"> <img src="http://
smallImage.png"> </a>
```

It is important to note that the server delivering the data in this case must be configured to indicate the MIME type of the data in the HTTP header. For files, this is typically accomplished by mapping the file extension to a MIME type from a table. In the case of a program, the MIME type should be set in the header before the data is delivered. The anchor tag itself can give a hint of the MIME type of the data using the "type" attribute. For example:

```
<a href="http://server.com/bigImage.png" type="image/png">
<img src="http://smallImage.png"> </a>
```

The "type" attribute is an advisory content type that will be overridden by the content type of the data returned in the HTTP response packet. It allows the browser to know what kind of data is being delivered before it requests it.

If the browser can handle, either with a built-in decoder or a plug-in, the MIME type of the multimedia data, the multimedia is displayed or played within the browser. The browser can be configured to use helper applications to display or play multimedia data in the case that it cannot handle the multimedia data returned. In the case that there is no such helper application configured, the browser will typically ask if it should use the operating system default for the data or save the content to a file.

The browser will inspect the MIME type of the data. It will attempt to handle it in the following order:

- A built-in decoder
- A browser plug-in
- A helper application
- Allow the user to download data to a file

For all data that uses the <a> tag, the approach is to completely download the data and then display or play it. Download and play can be used for all types of multimedia. This approach, which can be contrasted to streaming for time-based media (video and audio), will be covered later in this chapter.

4.1.4 Browser Plug-ins

Browser plug-ins extend the capability of browsers to handle MIME types that are not handled by the browser natively. For multimedia, plug-ins are used to display images, video, and audio that do not have native browser support.

Plug-in tags for browsers use the <embed> or <object> tag. Samples are:

```
<embed src="myVideo.rpm" width=320 height=240 />
<object data="svgSample.svgz" type="image/svg+xml"
    width="240" height="160" name="svgSamp">
</object>
```

Usage of either <embed> or <object> depends on the plug-in used and the kind of browser you are using. Many times the <embed> tag is used within the <object> tag and is picked up by whichever the browser you are using prefers. For example:

```
<object data="mySample.svgz" type="image/svg+xml"
    width="240" height="160">
    <embed src="mySample.svgz" type="image/svg+xml"
            width="240" height="160" />
</object>
```

Again, the "type" attribute hints at the MIME type being used on the Web page, it does not dictate it.

4.1.5 HTTP Caching

Perhaps one of the most important performance considerations with delivering media on the Web is to reduce the number of times that media actually has to be delivered. The most efficient media delivery is one that is not done. Caching controls in HTTP are extensive, so this is a simplified description.

Caching can occur anywhere between the browser and the server. The browser itself will cache information, many ISPs will cache information, firewalls cache information, HTTP proxies cache information, and there are some caching servers that front-end applications, like Oracle Web Cache. Some caches will have caching policies that differ from the HTTP standard to increase performance, sometimes at the risk of delivering stale data, for example, a policy that states that server data is fresh for at least 10 minutes.

HTTP caching falls into two categories:

1. Eliminate the need for a request–response.

2. Eliminate the need to deliver media.

The first category—to eliminate the need for a request–response—depends on the original content being delivered with an expiration time. This expiration time is used along the HTTP pipeline, in caching servers and firewalls, to store the data until the expiration time. This kind of caching requires the server to set appropriate HTTP headers. This includes the HTTP "Expires" header, which gives an explicit expiration time, when a cache should consider this content stale:

```
Expires: Fri, 1 Oct 2005 13:29:31 GMT
```

Another HTTP header that can be used to eliminate unnecessary requests is the "Cache-Control" header. Since computer clocks do sometimes differ from each other, Cache-Control specifies a "max-age." For example,

```
Cache-Control: max-age=3600, must-revalidate
```

Cache-Control also includes many other caching parameters, too many to go over here, but using either, or both, parameter "Cache-Control" or "Expires" HTTP headers can reduce media requests and increase performance.

The other caching mechanism is to eliminate the need to deliver media. This mechanism requires the media server to set information in a media response. The most commonly used is the "Last-Modified" HTTP header on the media HTTP response. For example:

```
Last-Modified: Fri, 11 Oct 2005 14:37:08 GMT
```

This parameter tells the client the modification time of the content. The client, any caching mechanism along the path, can then make an HTTP "Conditional Get" to get the media only if it has changed since the last time it was requested. The "Conditional Get" returns the "Last-Modified" date in the "If-Modified-Since" HTTP request field. The presence of "If-Modified-Since" makes an HTTP "Get" an HTTP "Conditional Get." For example:

```
If-Modified-Since: Sat, 02 Oct 2005 15:39:20 GMT
```

Another mechanism for "Conditional Get" was introduced with HTTP 1.1. This is the *entity tag*. These entity tags, in the "Etag" response header, are server-generated identifiers that change when the server representation of the media does, for example, a version number. For example, on static files, the Apache Server typically generates an Etag based on update time, file size, and filesystem inode. These entity tags can then be returned in an "If-None-Match" request field and the server can see if the resource identifier, for example, version number, has changed or not. These Etags have the advantage that the server can create their own content change data, independent of sometimes messy date-time mismatches.

If, on an HTTP "Conditional Request," a server finds the content has not changed, an HTTP status 304 (not modified) status response is returned to the request without the media. This indicates that the cached media is still fresh and should be used.

*inter*Media HTTP classes, *inter*Media JSP tags, and the *inter*Media PL/SQL Gateway Wizard–generated procedures use the "Last-Modified" and "If-Modified-Since" mechanisms using the "Update Time" of the media object in the database (part of the media object metadata) to reduce unnecessary movement of media to increase performance.

Most, if not all, HTTP servers use the "Conditional Get" features by default. This is typically done transparently. For database operations, not using the *inter*Media-supplied mechanisms, the programmer must set and check the appropriate HTTP header fields for efficiently serving media from the database.

An application may also decide that certain media can have a longer age to avoid any request–response cycle. Setting of the age policies can typically be done by the programmer or by system administration settings. These are application dependent and must be considered on a case-by-case basis.

4.2 Servlets

Servlets can serve as an endpoint for URLs to deliver HTTP data. This data can be of any MIME type. For *inter*Media, we are mostly concerned with servlets delivering multimedia data. Where this media is stored, or generated, is of no particular concern to the browser as long as it is delivered with the HTTP response.

For serving multimedia from the database, the following generalized steps occur:

- HTTP request is received by the servlet
- The servlet makes a JDBC request to the database
- The servlet creates an HTTP response
- The servlet populates the HTTP response header with the MIME type of the multimedia
- The servlet sends the HTTP response

There are java classes supplied by *inter*Media to make the process above easier to accomplish.

4.3   *inter*Media HTTP Classes

*inter*Media HTTP classes are a convenience to send media data from the database or to store media data sent from the database. These are in addition to the Java proxy classes that represent the database media in a Java program.

The best way to explain how the *inter*Media HTTP classes work is to give the simplest retrieval of an image from the database. In this example, the URL is of the form http://server/servlets/pictureServlet?id=number where number is the key to the image in the database. Typically the HTML that includes this URL is created dynamically using database information, for example, a list of image names and alongside the image names an <img> tag is used to obtain the picture on the Web page.

The following code is a simple "doGet" method of a standard servlet, the *inter*Media HTTP class section is in bold.

```
public void doGet( HttpServletRequest request,
                   HttpServletResponse response )
    throws ServletException, IOException
{
    Connection conn = null;

    //
    // Use a try-block to ensure that JDBC connections are always returned
    // to the pool.
```

```
    //
    try
    {
        //
        // Get a JDBC connection from the pool
        //
        conn = myPooledConnection.getConnection();

        //
        // Perform a SQL query for the media
        //
        PreparedStatement stmt =
            conn.prepareStatement( "select " + media +
                            " from photos where id = ?" );
            stmt.setString( 1, request.getParameter( "id" ) );
         OracleResultSet rset = (OracleResultSet)stmt.executeQuery();

        //
        // Fetch the row from the result set.
        //
        if ( rset.next() )
        {
            //
            // Get the OrdImage object from the result set.
            //
            OrdImage img =
                (OrdImage)rset.getORAData(1, OrdImage.getORADataFactory());

            //
            // Create an OrdHttpResponseHandler object,
            // then use it to retrieve
            // the image from the database and deliver it to the browser.
            //
            OrdHttpResponseHandler handler =
                new OrdHttpResponseHandler( request, response );
            handler.sendImage( img );
        }
        else
        {
            //
            // Row not found, return a suitable error.
```

```
            //
            response.setStatus( response.SC_NOT_FOUND );
        }
    }
    catch ( SQLException e )
    {
        //
        // Log what went wrong.
        //
        e.printStackTrace( System.out );

        //
        // Turn SQL exceptions into ServletExceptions.
        //
        throw new ServletException( e.toString() );
    }
    finally
    {
        //
        // If we have a JDBC connection, implicitly return it to the pool.
        //
        if (conn != null) conn.close();
    }
}
```

In general, we get a connection, select the *inter*Media object into a Java proxy class, create an OrdHttpResponseHandler object, and tell this object to send the image. Quite simple.

Note that in this example we are using an implicit JDBC cached connection managed by Oracle Application Server Containers for J2EE Services (OC4J). We use cached, or pooled, connections for performance reasons. Creating a new JDBC connection every time an image is requested would be expensive. The connection caching is done implicitly through a JDBC DataSource, so the programmer does not need to code differently than a noncached connection. This connection is defined in the OC4J data-sources.xml file and can be managed with an editor or Oracle Enterprise Manager. The entry to this XML file is as follows.

```
<data-source
    class="oracle.jdbc.pool.OracleConnectionCacheImpl"
```

```
          name="OracleMediaPoolDS"
          location="jdbc/cache/OracleMediaCacheDS"
          connection-driver="oracle.jdbc.driver.OracleDriver"
          username="scott"
          password="tiger"
          url="jdbc:oracle:thin:@lguros-us.us.oracle.com:1521:orcl2"
          inactivity-timeout="30">
          <property name="cacheScheme" value="1" />
```

The implementation of myGetPooledDataSource() uses this data source defined in data-sources.xml.

```
    /*
     * Get a Pooled database connection
     */
    private void myGetPooledConnection()
              throws SQLException, NamingException
    {
        javax.naming.InitialContext ic =
              new javax.naming.InitialContext();
        OracleDataSource ds = (OracleDataSource)
              ic.lookup("jdbc/cache/OracleMediaCacheDS");
        conn = (OracleConnection)ds.getConnection();
    }
```

The *inter*Media HTTP classes can also be used to upload media data to the database. This case is a bit more complicated, as is the case with uploading a file to the server. The SQL used is similar to the SQL used to load an image from PL/SQL. The following is a simple example of an HTTP servlet's doPost method:

```
public void doPost( HttpServletRequest request,
                HttpServletResponse response )
    throws ServletException, IOException
{
    Connection conn = null;

    //
    // Use a try-block to ensure that JDBC connections are always returned
    // to the pool.
```

```
//
try
{
    //
    // Get a JDBC connection from the pool
    //
    conn = myPooledConnection.getConnection();

    //
    // Create an OrdHttpUploadFormData object.
    //
    OrdHttpUploadFormData formData =
                    new OrdHttpUploadFormData( request );

    //
    // Nothing to do if this is not an upload request
    //
    if ( !formData.isUploadRequest() )
    {
        throw new ServletException( "Not a media upload request" );
        conn.close()
        return;
    }

    //
    // Parse the multipart/form-data message.
    //
    formData.parseFormData();

    //
    // Get the description, location and photo.
    //
    String description = formData.getParameter( "description" );
    String location = formData.getParameter( "location" );
    OrdHttpUploadFile photo = formData.getFileParameter( "photo" );

    //
    // Make sure a valid image file was provided.
    //
    if ( photo == null ||
        photo.getOriginalFileName() == null ||
```

```
            photo.getOriginalFileName().length() == 0
        )
    {
        // In a real application, go back to the upload form
        // with an error msg
        throw new ServletException( "A file was not provided." );
        return;
    }

    if ( photo.getContentLength() == 0 )
    {
        // In a real application, go back to the upload form with
        // an error msg
        throw new ServletException( "Please supply a valid image file."
);
        return;
    }

    //
    // Use the file name if there's no description.
    //
    if ( description == null || description.length() == 0 )
    {
        description = "Image from file: " + photo.getSimpleFileName() +
        ".";
        description = description.substring(0, 40);
    }

    //
    // We're going to be updating the database and writing to LOBS, so
    // make sure auto-commit is disabled.
    //
    conn.setAutoCommit( false );

    //
    // Get a value for the ID column of the new row
    //
    OraclePreparedStatement stmt =
        (OraclePreparedStatement)conn.prepareStatement(
            "select photos_sequence.nextval from dual" );
    OracleResultSet rset = (OracleResultSet)stmt.executeQuery();
    if ( !rset.next() )
```

```
{
    throw new ServletException( "new ID not found" );
}
String id = rset.getString( 1 );
rset.close();
stmt.close();

//
// Prepare and execute a SQL statement to insert the new row.
//
stmt = (OraclePreparedStatement)conn.prepareStatement(
        "insert into photos (id,description,location,image,thumb) " +
        " values (?,?,?," + EMPTY_IMAGE ")" );
stmt.setString( 1, id );
stmt.setString( 2, description );
stmt.setString( 3, location );

stmt.executeUpdate();
stmt.close();

//
// Prepare and execute a SQL statement to fetch the initialized
//  image object from the table.
//
stmt = (OraclePreparedStatement)conn.prepareStatement(
            "select image from photos where id = ? for update" );
stmt.setString( 1, id );
rset = (OracleResultSet)stmt.executeQuery();
if ( !rset.next() )
{
    throw new ServletException( "new row not found in table" );
}
OrdImage image =
    (OrdImage)rset.getORAData( 1, OrdImage.getORADataFactory());
rset.close();
stmt.close();

//
// Load the photo into the database and set the properties.
//
photo.loadImage( image );
```

```
    }
    catch ( SQLException e )
    {
        //
        // Log what went wrong.
        //
        e.printStackTrace( System.out );

        //
        // Turn SQL exceptions into ServletExceptions.
        //
        throw new ServletException( e.toString() );
    }
    finally
    {
        //
        // If we have a JDBC connection, then return it to the pool.
        //
        if (conn != null) conn.close();
    }
}
```

4.4   The mod_plsql Module

mod_plsql is an Apache module that is shipped with Oracle Database and Application Server products. This module supports efficient HTTP access to the Oracle Database through PL/SQL stored procedures. This module is installed by default on Oracle's Application Server and the Apache Server shipped with Oracle Database.

Typically, as far as *inter*Media data is concerned, you would want to use the *inter*Media Code Wizard for the PL/SQL Gateway with mod_plsql to write PL/SQL procedures to display or load *inter*Media data from a Web page. Here, the use of only mod_plsql to deal with *inter*Media data is described. Again, typically you would not want to write this code when there is a tool that will write it for you, but this section is included to further your understanding of mod_plsql. You may need to modify the code produced by the Code Wizard for the PL/SQL Gateway to customize it for your application, for example, creating thumbnail images when loading an image, but it is easier to insert this code into a procedure that does most of what you need.

mod_plsql funnels HTTP requests to a PL/SQL procedure. These procedures can handle GET, PUT, POST, or other HTTP request messages. Inside the procedure, the request is processed, and the results are passed back in an HTTP response message. mod_plsql procedures require a DAD (database access descriptor) and also a document table must be created if media data is to be uploaded to the database. For *inter*Media, these procedures will query, insert, or update media. The results of the operation, either the media or status, will be returned to the browser. To illustrate what a mod_plsql procedure does, we will examine two procedures, one to deliver media data and one to insert data.

First, we look at a simple procedure to deliver an image to a browser. These images are assumed to be stored in the database rather than on the file system or on the Web. We don't check to see if the image in the browser cache is up to date, as the procedures produced by the *inter*Media PL/SQL wizard do.

```
CREATE OR REPLACE PROCEDURE GET_IMG ( IMG_ID IN VARCHAR2 )
AS
  img ORDSYS.ORDIMAGE;
  rid UROWID;
  etag VARCHAR2(50);
  etag_gen VARCHAR2(50);
  b BLOB;
BEGIN
  --
  -- Retrieve the object from the database.
  --
  BEGIN
    SELECT imgtbl.img,rowid INTO img, rid FROM IMG_TABLE
imgtbl
      WHERE imgtbl.ID = IMG_ID;
  EXCEPTION
    WHEN NO_DATA_FOUND THEN
        owa_util.status_line( 404, 'Not Found', FALSE );
        owa_util.mime_header( 'text/html' );
        owa_util.http_header_close;
        htp.print( '<h1>Not Found</h1> The requested image' ||
        '<tt>' ||
            owa_util.get_cgi_env( 'SCRIPT_NAME' ) ||
            owa_util.get_cgi_env( 'PATH_INFO' ) ||
            '?img_id=' || IMG_ID ||
```

```
                             '</tt> was not found.' );
          RETURN;
      END;


      --
      -- Check if the browser has the latest media
      --
      etag_gen := to_char(img.getUpdateTime(),'ssmihh24ddmmyyyy')
                  || rid || img.getContentLength();
      --
      -- NOTE: Getting this value depends on the
      -- following entry in
      -- dads.conf for the DAD that this routine is used through.
      --
      --     PlsqlCGIEnvironmentList HTTP_IF_NONE_MATCH
      --
      etag := owa_util.get_cgi_env ('HTTP_IF_NONE_MATCH');
      IF etag IS NOT NULL THEN
          IF etag = etag_gen THEN
              owa_util.status_line( 304, 'Not Modified', TRUE );
              RETURN; -- Don't send image again, requester has
                      -- latest media.
          END IF;
      END IF;


      --
      -- First, set the HTTP header fields.
      --
      owa_util.mime_header( img.getMimeType(), FALSE );
      htp.p('Content-Length: ' || img.getContentLength());
      htp.p('ETag: ' || etag_gen);
      owa_util.http_header_close();


      --
      -- Now, deliver the data
      --
      IF owa_util.get_cgi_env( 'REQUEST_METHOD' ) <> 'HEAD' THEN
        b := img.getContent();
        wpg_docload.download_file( b );
      END IF;
    END GET_IMG;
```

This procedure simply does a select on the data using IMG_ID query expression from the URL. The mod_plsql URL would be in the form:

```
http://<server>:<port>/<mod_plsql_dad>/get_img?IMG_ID=<SELECT_STRING>
```

Uploading images to the database requires the creation of a *document table*. This document table receives the input before the insert procedure is called. The *inter*Media PL/SQL wizard can create a document table for you if you like.

```
CREATE OR REPLACE PROCEDURE UPLOAD_IMG
  ( in_ID IN VARCHAR2,
    in_IMG IN VARCHAR2 DEFAULT NULL,
    in_DESCRIPTION IN VARCHAR2 DEFAULT NULL )
AS
  IMG ORDSYS.ORDIMAGE := ORDSYS.ORDIMAGE.init();
  ID IMG_TABLE.ID%TYPE := NULL;
  upload_size     INTEGER;
  upload_mimetype VARCHAR2( 128 );
  upload_blob     BLOB;
BEGIN
  --
  -- Try an update, in case the row already exists.
  -- In that case, we will update it.
  --
  UPDATE IMG_TABLE imgtbl
    SET imgtbl.IMG = IMG,
        imgtbl.DESCRIPTION = in_DESCRIPTION
    WHERE imgtbl.ID = in_ID
    RETURN imgtbl.ID INTO ID;


  --
  -- If the ID is null, we need to insert a new row.
  --
  IF ID IS NULL
  THEN
    --
    -- Insert new row into table
    --
    INSERT INTO IMG_TABLE ( ID, IMG, DESCRIPTION )
```

```
        VALUES ( in_ID, IMG, in_DESCRIPTION );
END IF;


--
-- Select interMedia object(s) for update
-- (necessary for storing BLOBS)
--
SELECT mtbl.IMG INTO IMG
  FROM IMG_TABLE imgtbl WHERE imgtbl.ID = in_ID FOR UPDATE;


--
-- Store media data for column in_IMG, getting data from the

-- document table associated with the DAD that was created.
-- The KEY is passed to this procedure by mod_plsql
-- in in_IMG
--
IF in_PICTURE IS NOT NULL
THEN
    SELECT dtbl.doc_size, dtbl.mime_type, dtbl.blob_content
INTO
        upload_size, upload_mimetype, upload_blob
      FROM DOCUMENT_TABLE dtbl WHERE dtbl.name = in_IMG;
   IF upload_size > 0
   THEN
     dbms_lob.copy( img.source.localData,
                    upload_blob,
                    upload_size );
     img.setLocal();
     BEGIN
       img.setProperties();
     EXCEPTION
       WHEN OTHERS THEN
         --
         -- setproperties failed! Set the Object to
         -- what we know from the web parameters.
         --
         img.contentLength := upload_size;
         img.mimeType := upload_mimetype;
     END;
   END IF;
   --
```

```
        -- Clean up document table
        --
        DELETE FROM WPG_DOCUMENT dtbl WHERE dtbl.name =
            in_PICTURE;
    END IF;


    --
    -- Update interMedia objects in table
    --
    UPDATE IMG_TABLE imgtbl
      SET imgtbl.PICTURE = img
      WHERE imgtbl.ID = in_ID;


    --
    -- Redirect to main menu
    --
    owa_util.redirect_url('/myMenu.html');

END UPLOAD_IMG;
```

As you can see, the upload procedure is quite a bit more complicated. This is due to finding out if we must update or insert the row, and the necessity of inserting a BLOB (within the object) in the database before we can populate it.

4.5 *inter*Media JSP Tag Library

*inter*Media provides a set of JSP tags to make developing JSP pages with media content from the database easier for the JSP developer. The support is provided by the *inter*Media JSP tag library that includes custom JSP tags for *inter*Media data. The JSP tag library is best supported through Jdeveloper. The JSP tag library will be covered in Chapter 9.

4.6 Oracle Portal

OracleAS Portal natively supports *inter*Media in forms and reports. This support can be achieved because Portal recognizes *inter*Media data types, and thus can handle rich-media columns. For reports, Portal allows you to display media either embedded in the report or by a linked icon.

Portal Forms allow for the upload of *inter*Media data. To insert *inter*Media data into the database the following general steps are necessary:

- Create a table with an *inter*Media type.

- Create a database provider.

- Use the Oracle Portal Forms Wizard to create a media input form.

The Forms Wizard is accessed through the Portal Builder. First select Navigator and then the Providers tab to see a screen similar to the one in Figure 4.1.

Figure 4.1
Oracle Portal
Providers

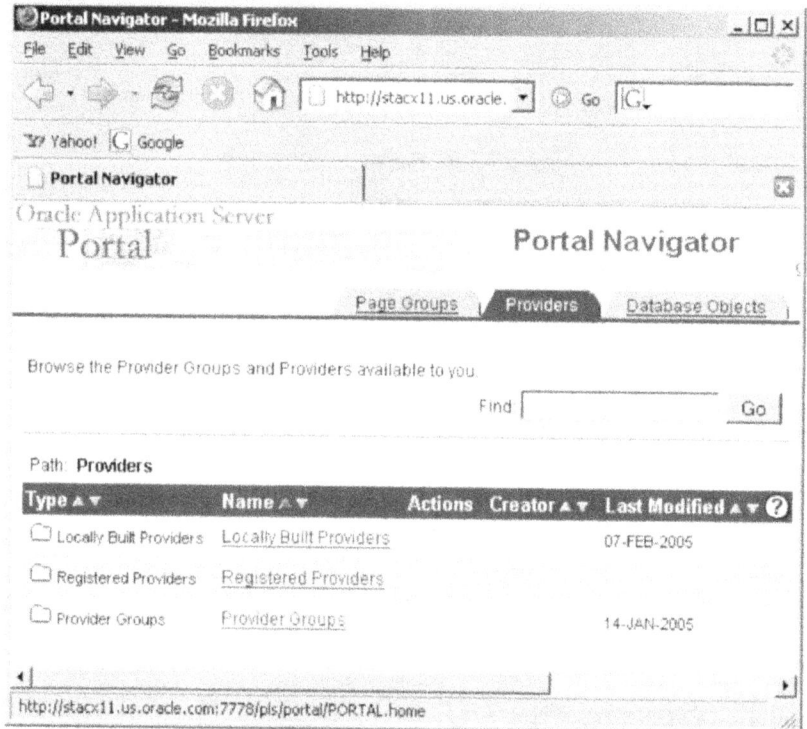

Click on Locally Built Providers. At the top of the screen, there will be a Create Database Provider. The first screen will allow for entry of general information about the provider, as shown in Figure 4.2. Once the provider is created, you can click on the provider and select the Forms Wizard.

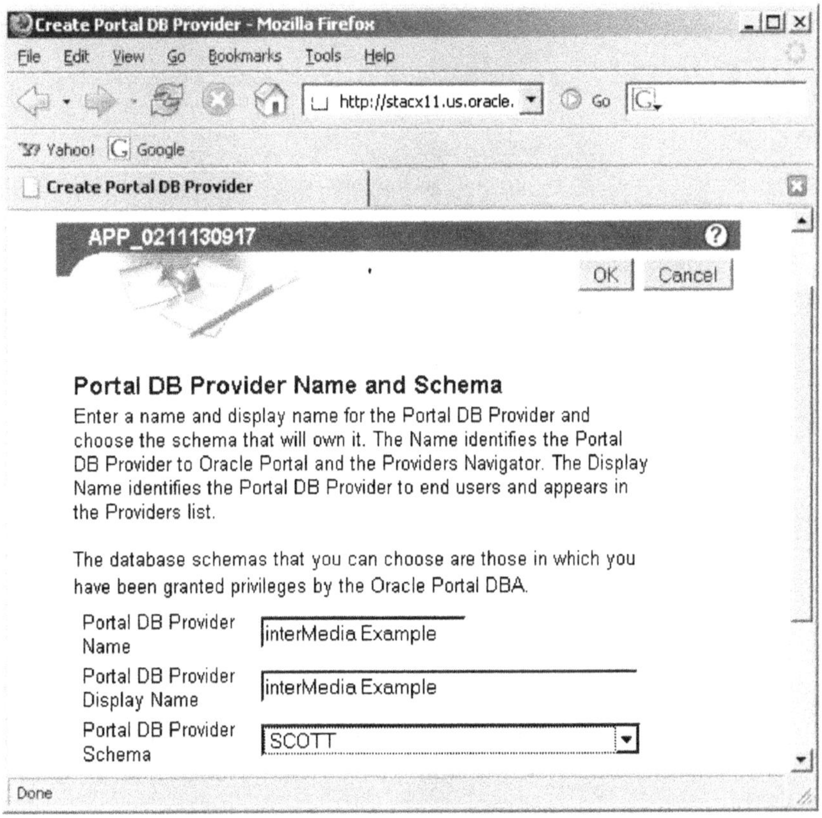

Figure 4.2
Oracle Portal
CREATE
DATABASE
Provider

At this point, you must have a table that includes an *inter*Media type defined within it. It must be in the schema indicated in the form above, in this case the *inter*Media table will be in the SCOTT schema. Select the form based on the table or view to enter the Forms Wizard.

The second step in the Forms Wizard prompts for the table to be used for the form, in this case a table with *inter*Media image types. We select the PHOTOS table (Figure 4.3) and go to the next steps.

From here, we take all the default values until step 5 where we can specify what information we want the form to collect. All the columns are selected for us, and in this case we will remove the thumbnail column from the form since thumbnail creation is not part of form's functionality. To have thumbnails created, a database job running in the background can create thumbnails where there are IMAGE columns where the THUMBNAIL column is null, or has an update time earlier than the IMAGE column. Figure 4.4 is an example of what the Forms Wizard looks like at this point.

Figure 4.3
*Oracle Portal
Forms Wizard*

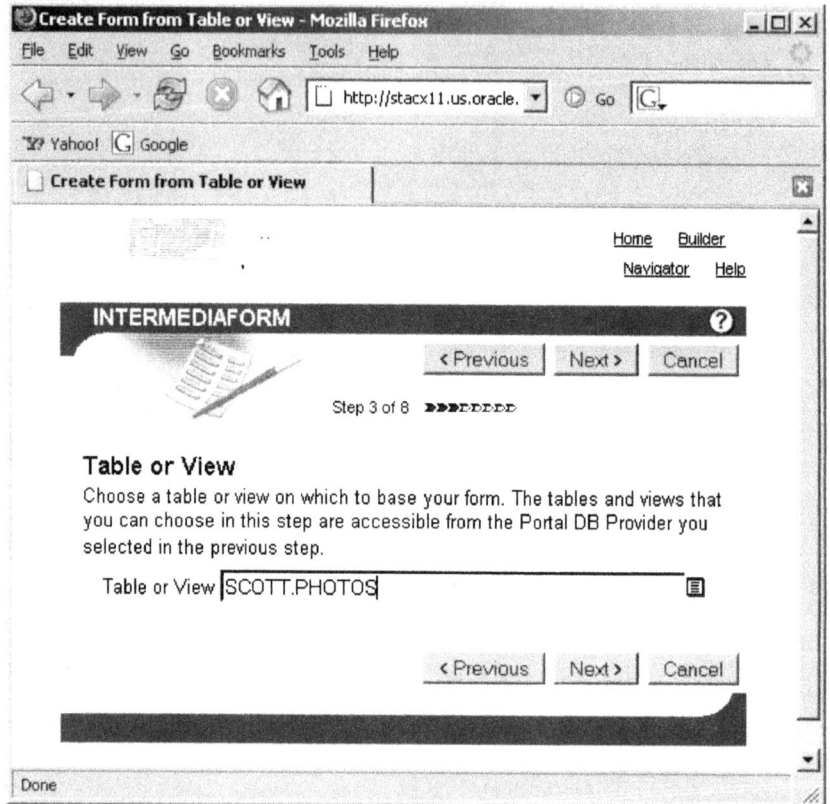

At this point, we can finish to accept the rest of the form's defaults, and run and test the form. From this form you can now insert images into the database using Oracle Portal and use them in portlets (see Figure 4.5).

You can then insert an image, and if you want to query the table through this portlet, you can see a screen similar to Figure 4.6.

After playing with the form, you can now use the Oracle Portal Report's wizard to see the images you have placed into the database. From the locations where we chose Create New Form, we can choose to create a new report. To create a Portal Report on the form, you create a new provider from the Provider tab in Portal Navigator. Choose Create New Report. Select Reports from Query Wizard. In this example the preceding form's examples are used to create the table.

First, enter the report name and properties using the *inter*Media portal DB provider used for the *inter*Media portal form. At this point your screen will look like Figure 4.7.

Figure 4.4
Oracle Portal Forms Wizard

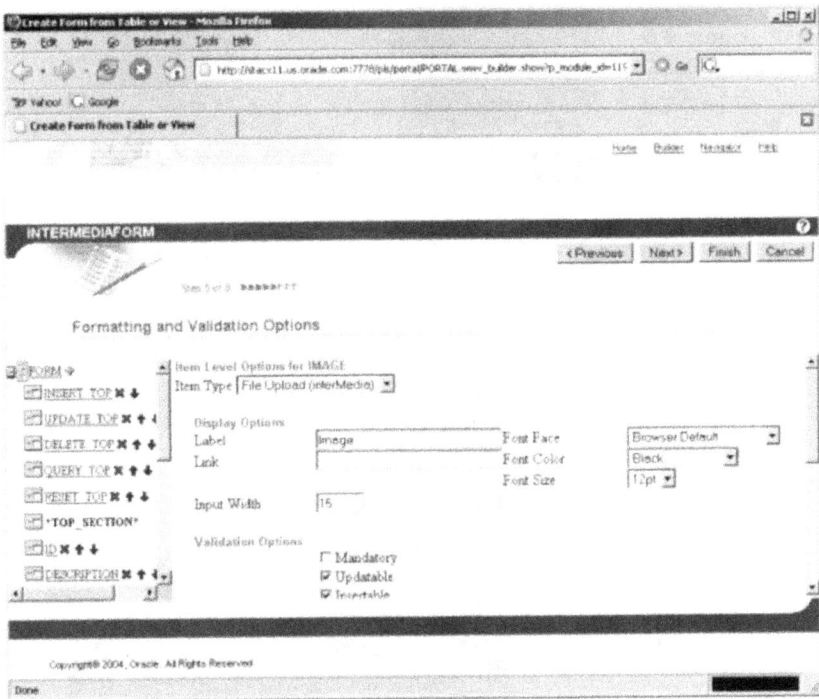

Figure 4.5
Created Oracle Portal Form

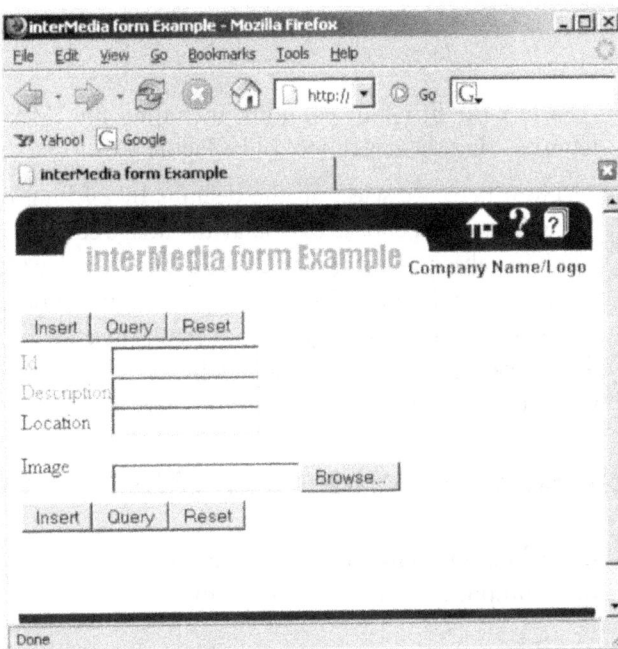

Figure 4.6
Using Oracle
Portal Form

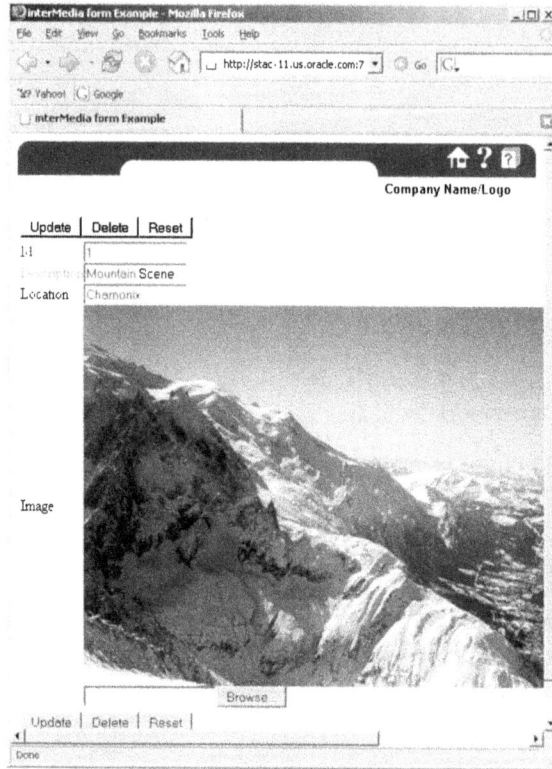

Select the first four columns, including the IMAGE column, into the report so that the screen looks like Figure 4.8.

From here, we select all the defaults by clicking on the Finish button. Note that we can choose to display the image column inline, or by means of a link in subsequent pages when we choose Display Options. The default is to display a link to *inter*Media content, but it can be changed to embed the image in a report. Running a report results in a portlet that looks like Figure 4.9. Clicking on the picture icon will result in the page showing the image in the table.

4.7   Oracle Data Provider for .NET (ODP.NET)

In the Windows environment, using Microsoft .NET, media delivery is easily accomplished. This includes media delivery to and from the Web.

Figure 4.7
Oracle Portal Reports Wizard Step 3

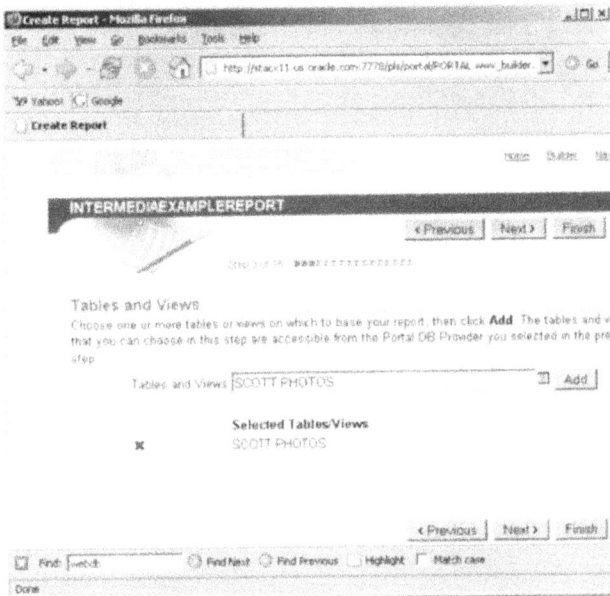

Figure 4.8
Oracle Portal Reports Wizard Step 5

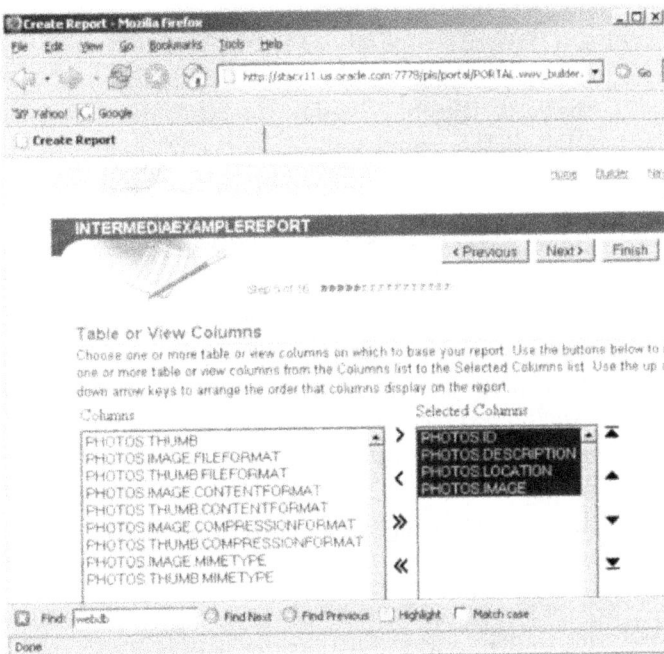

The prerequisite for developing ODP.NET applications is to install ODP.NET onto the system where such applications will be developed.

Figure 4.9
Oracle Portal
Report

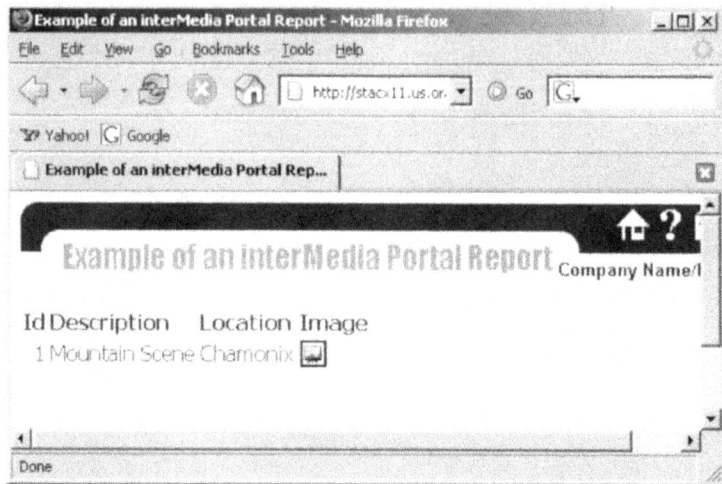

Since these applications require a Web server, a server version of Microsoft Windows will be required. It is also a great convenience to use Visual Studio to develop these applications with the Oracle Developer Tools for Visual Studio .NET add-in.

ODP.NET applications for the Web include an .aspx script component and programmed components. The programmed components can be in C Sharp, a Java or C++-like object-oriented language, or Visual Basic. ODP.NET supports both C Sharp and Visual Basic. In the following examples in this section, the C Sharp language is used.

4.7.1 ODP.NET Media Delivery to Browser

In ODP.NET, the first component to be defined is the .aspx file. These files are scripting languages that define browser display and define how the application reacts to events. In the case of delivery of binary media data, no text data, like HTML, is used. But in our example, we deliver the media with an .aspx front end. In the case of an error, we can deliver error text in the label. This error message would only be displayed when directly interfacing with the media URL, not embedded URLs, like image or plug-in tags.

If there is no error, we take over the .NET HTTP Response Stream, set the content type to what the media is, and copy the binary media data from the *inter*Media BLOB to the .NET HTTP Response Stream. The ASP file contains the following code.

```
<%@ Page language="c#" Codebehind="getMedia.aspx.cs"
  AutoEventWireup="false" Inherits="SmilDemo.getMedia" %>
<!DOCTYPE HTML PUBLIC
                    "-//W3C//DTD HTML 4.0 Transitional//EN" >
<html>
   <head>
      <title>getMedia</title>
      <meta name="GENERATOR"
   Content="Microsoft Visual Studio 7.0">
      <meta name="CODE_LANGUAGE" Content="C#">
      <meta name="vs_defaultClientScript"
       content="JavaScript">
      <meta name="vs_targetSchema"
    content="http://schemas.microsoft.com/intellisense/ie5">
   </head>
   <body MS_POSITIONING="GridLayout">
      <form id="getMedia" method="get" runat="server">
      <P>
           <asp:Label id="getMediaLabel" runat="server"
         Visible="False"></asp:Label>
      </P>
      </form>
   </body>
</html>
```

In the preceding ASPX, any error message would be delivered within the Label tag, otherwise the ASPX will be ignored.

The code to deliver media will use a URL of the form:

```
http://<SERVER>:<PORT>/<PATH>/
getMedia.aspx?tbl=<TABLE>&col=<COLUMN>&keycol=<KEY
COLUMN>&key=<KEY>
```

For example:

```
http://myserver.myco.com/getMedia/
getMedia.aspx?tbl=photos&col=thumb&keycol=id&key=1
```

The code to actually supply the image to the browser from the database follows; it simply does a database query and returns the binary data and MIME type to the response stream of the .NET application (in the normal case):

```
using System;
using System.Collections;
using System.ComponentModel;
using System.Configuration;
using System.Data;
using System.Drawing;
using System.Web;
using System.Web.SessionState;
using System.Web.UI;
using System.Web.UI.WebControls;
using System.Web.UI.HtmlControls;

using Oracle.DataAccess.Client;
using Oracle.DataAccess.Types;

namespace getMedia
{
  /// <summary>
  /// This code delivers Media from Oracle database interMedia
  /// objects.
  /// It takes URL requests of the form:
  /// http://{SERVER}:{PORT}/getMedia/
  /// getMedia.aspx?tbl={TABLE}&col={COLUMN}&keycol={KEY
  /// COLUMN}&key={KEY}
  /// where:
  /// {TABLE} is the datbase table name where the media
  /// resides
  /// {COLUMN} is the datbase column name where the media
  /// resides
  /// {KEY COLUMN} is the selection key column for the where
  /// clause
  /// {KEY} is the selection key to be used in the where
  /// clause as in
  ///       where {KEY COLUMN} = {KEY}
  /// for Example:
  /// http://localhost/getMedia/getMedia.aspx?tbl=photos&
  /// col=image&keycol=id&key=1
  ///
```

```
/// Database connection parameter is a configuration
/// setting in Web.config
///
/// This code sets an Etag based upon update time
/// and content length.
/// The Etag is checked against the If-None-Match
/// request HTTP
/// header field to only deliver media if necessary.
/// </summary>
public class getMediaForm : System.Web.UI.Page
{
  protected System.Web.UI.WebControls.Label getMediaLabel;

  protected static readonly string dbConnectionString =

ConfigurationSettings.AppSettings["OracleConnectionString"];

  private void Page_Load(object sender, System.EventArgs e)
  {
    // Get connection (from pool)
    OracleConnection dbConn =
        newOracleConnection(dbConnectionString);
    dbConn.Open();

    string tbl = Request.QueryString["tbl"];
    string col = Request.QueryString["col"];
    string keycol = Request.QueryString["keycol"];
    string key = Request.QueryString["key"];

    if (tbl == null || col == null || keycol == null || key
        == null)
    {
      getMediaLabel.Text = "404 - Media not found." +
                             " Missing Request Parameters.";
      getMediaLabel.Visible = true;
      Response.StatusCode = 404;
      return;
    }

    try
    {
      // Create command
```

```
OracleCommand cmd = new OracleCommand
  ("select t."+col+".getContent(), " +
  " t."+col+".getMimeType(), " +
  " to_char(t."+col+".getUpdateTime(),||
    || 'ssmihh24ddmmyy'), " +
  " t."+col+".getContentLength() " +
  "from " + tbl + " t " +
  "where t." + keycol + " = " + key,
  dbConn);

OracleDataReader reader = cmd.ExecuteReader();
if (!reader.Read() || reader.IsDBNull(0))
{
  getMediaLabel.Text = "404 - Media not found!";
  getMediaLabel.Visible = true;
  Response.StatusCode = 404;
  return;
}

//
// If this is a conditional Request, see if media
// has changed.
// If we can't let requester use cache, set ETag.
//
if (!reader.IsDBNull(2))
{
  String myTimeStamp = reader.GetString(2);
  Decimal len = reader.GetDecimal(3);
  String Etag = myTimeStamp + ":" + len.ToString();
  string ifNoneMatch =
    Request.Headers["If-None-Match"];
  if (ifNoneMatch != null &&
    ifNoneMatch.IndexOf(Etag) != -1)
  {
    Response.StatusCode = 304; // Return not-modified
    return;
  }

  // Set the ETAG (like Last-Modified-Time) so
  // we can cache.
  Response.Cache.SetETag(Etag);
}
```

```csharp
      // Return the data
      OracleBlob bLob = reader.GetOracleBlob(0);
      Response.ContentType = reader.GetString(1);
      Response.AddHeader("Content-Length", ||
          || bLob.Length.ToString());
      // Indicate this is not session private media
      Response.Cache.SetCacheability
         (HttpCacheability.Public);

      int bufsiz = bLob.OptimumChunkSize * 8;
      int readLen;
      byte[] buf = new byte[bufsiz];
      do
      {
        readLen = bLob.Read(buf, 0, buf.Length);
        Response.OutputStream.Write(buf,0,readLen);
      } while (readLen > 0);
      Response.Flush();
    }
    catch(OracleException ex)
    {
      getMediaLabel.Text = ex.Message;
      getMediaLabel.Visible = true;
    }
    finally
    {
      // Close DB connection (return to pool)
      dbConn.Close();
    }
  }

  #region Web Form Designer generated code
  override protected void OnInit(EventArgs e)
  {
    //
    // CODEGEN: This call is required by the ASP.NET Web
    // Form Designer.
    //
    InitializeComponent();
    base.OnInit(e);
  }
```

```
/// <summary>
/// Required method for Designer support - do not modify
/// the contents of this method with the code editor.
/// </summary>
private void InitializeComponent()
{
  this.Load += new System.EventHandler(this.Page_Load);

}
#endregion
}
}
```

4.7.2   **ODP.NET Media Delivery from Browser**

In the case that it is necessary to deliver media data from a user to the database, this is accomplished in a somewhat similar manner to delivery of data to the browser. The complicating factors are the creation of a database row and the processing of the data from the browser.

The .aspx file will also be a bit more complicated, since it will be used to supply the data for the new media database row. An .aspx file to upload media to the database that was generated by Visual Studio follows.

```
<%@ Page language="c#" Codebehind="WebForm1.aspx.cs"
    AutoEventWireup="false" Inherits="uploadDB.WebForm1" %>
<!DOCTYPE HTML PUBLIC
                    "-//W3C//DTD HTML 4.0 Transitional//EN" >
<HTML>
  <HEAD>
    <title>WebForm1</title>
    <meta content="Microsoft Visual Studio 7.0"
        name="GENERATOR">
    <meta content="C#" name="CODE_LANGUAGE">
    <meta content="JavaScript"
                              name="vs_defaultClientScript">
    <meta content=
      "http://schemas.microsoft.com/intellisense/ie3-2nav3-0"
        name="vs_targetSchema">
  </HEAD>
  <body>
    <form id="Form1" method="post"
```

```
                    encType="multipart/form-data" runat="server">
                <P> </P>
                <P>
            <TABLE id="Table1" height="119" cellSpacing="1"
                    cellPadding="1" width="744" border="1">
                <TR>
                  <TD width="141">
                    <asp:label id="Label1"
                    runat="server">Description of Picture:
                    </asp:label>
                  </TD>
                <TD>
                    <asp:textbox id="Description" runat="server"
                     Columns="50"></asp:textbox>
                    <asp:requiredfieldvalidator
                     id="RequiredFieldValidator1"
                     runat="server" Width="237px"
                     ControlToValidate="Description"
                  ErrorMessage="You must Enter a picture description">
                    </asp:requiredfieldvalidator>
                  </TD>
                </TR>
                <TR></TR>
              <TR>
                <TD width="141">
                    <asp:label id="Label2"
                     runat="server">Location of Picture:
                    </asp:label>
                  </TD>
                  <TD>
                    <asp:textbox id="Location" runat="server"
                      Columns="50">
                    </asp:textbox>
                    <asp:requiredfieldvalidator
                     id="RequiredFieldValidator2" runat="server"
                     ControlToValidate="Location"
                     ErrorMessage="You must enter a picture Location">
                    </asp:requiredfieldvalidator>
                  </TD>
                </TR>
                <TR>
```

```
            <TD width="141"><asp:label id="Label3"
             runat="server">Picture File</asp:label>
            </TD>
            <TD>
              <INPUT id="mediaFile" type="file" size="50"
               runat="server">
              <asp:requiredfieldvalidator
                 id="RequiredFieldValidator3" runat="server"
                 Width="136px" ControlToValidate="mediaFile"
                 ErrorMessage="File must be entered"
                 Height="15px">
              </asp:requiredfieldvalidator>
            </TD>
          </TR>
        </TABLE>
        </P>
        <P>
        <asp:button id="Button1" runat="server"
         Text="Upload Picture"></asp:button>
        </P>
        <P>
          <asp:label id="StatusLabel" runat="server"
             Visible="False"></asp:label></P>
      </form>
      </body>
    </HTML>
```

The code behind this .aspx form inserts a new row into the database, populates the *inter*Media BLOB, populates the metadata of the *inter*Media type using setProperties(), and creates a thumbnail if possible (the image is a popular format that *inter*Media can process).

Also note that this code takes the content type, or MIME type, of the media from the sending Web browser. This value is used in case the image itself is a nonpopular image format, or not even an image. In this case, we will still preserve the content type of the data. We could check to see if the content type began with "image/" to make certain that the data is an image type, at least according to the sending Web browser, but in the following example we accept any file delivered over the Web.

```
using System;
using System.Configuration;
```

```
using System.IO;
using System.Collections;
using System.ComponentModel;
using System.Data;
using System.Drawing;
using System.Web;
using System.Web.SessionState;
using System.Web.UI;
using System.Web.UI.WebControls;
using System.Web.UI.HtmlControls;

using Oracle.DataAccess.Client;
using Oracle.DataAccess.Types;

namespace uploadDB
{
  /// <summary>
  /// Summary description for WebForm1.
  /// </summary>
  public class WebForm1 : System.Web.UI.Page
  {
    protected System.Web.UI.WebControls.TextBox Description;
    protected System.Web.UI.WebControls.Label Label2;
    protected System.Web.UI.WebControls.TextBox Location;
    protected System.Web.UI.WebControls.Label Label3;
    protected System.Web.UI.HtmlControls.HtmlInputFile
              mediaFile;
    protected
            System.Web.UI.WebControls.RequiredFieldValidator
              RequiredFieldValidator1;
    protected
            System.Web.UI.WebControls.RequiredFieldValidator
              RequiredFieldValidator2;
    protected
            System.Web.UI.WebControls.RequiredFieldValidator
              RequiredFieldValidator3;
    protected System.Web.UI.WebControls.Button Button1;
    protected System.Web.UI.WebControls.Label Label1;
    protected System.Web.UI.WebControls.Label StatusLabel;
    protected static readonly string dbConnectionString =
            ConfigurationSettings.AppSettings["dbConnString"];
```

```
              private void Page_Load(object sender,
                            System.EventArgs e)
      {
      // Put user code to initialize the page here
      }


      #region Web Form Designer generated code
      override protected void OnInit(EventArgs e)
      {
        //
        // CODEGEN: This call is required by the ASP.NET
        // Web Form Designer.
        //
        InitializeComponent();
        base.OnInit(e);
      }

      /// <summary>
      /// Required method for Designer support - do not modify
      /// the contents of this method with the code editor.
      /// </summary>
      private void InitializeComponent()
      {
        this.Button1.Click +=
            new System.EventHandler(this.Button1_Click);
        this.Load += new System.EventHandler(this.Page_Load);


      }
      #endregion

      private void Button1_Click(object sender,
                              System.EventArgs e)
      {
        bool success = false;
        OracleConnection dbConn =
                new OracleConnection(dbConnectionString);
        dbConn.Open();

        // Start transaction
        OracleTransaction trans = dbConn.BeginTransaction();
```

```
// Get image characteristics
Stream imgStream = mediaFile.PostedFile.InputStream;
int imgLength = mediaFile.PostedFile.ContentLength;
string imgContentType =
                        mediaFile.PostedFile.ContentType;
string imgFileName = mediaFile.PostedFile.FileName;
try
{
  OracleCommand cmd =
    new OracleCommand(
      "  insert into photos t values " +
      "    (photosSeq.nextval, '" +
      "      Description.Text + "', " +
      "      '" + Location.Text + "',   " +
      "      ordImage.init(), ordImage.init()) " +
  " returning rowid, t.image.getContent() " +

      "    into :rwid, :image",
      dbConn);
  cmd.Parameters.Add("rwid", OracleDbType.Varchar2,
                     80).Direction =
          ParameterDirection.Output;
  cmd.Parameters.Add("image",
                     OracleDbType.Blob).Direction =
          ParameterDirection.Output;

  cmd.ExecuteNonQuery();
  OracleString rowid =
        (OracleString)cmd.Parameters["rwid"].Value;
  OracleBlob imageBlob =
        (OracleBlob)cmd.Parameters["image"].Value;

  //
  // Copy the blob from the net (max 2 gig, due to
  // .NET interface using int as length)
  //
  byte[] buf = new byte[imageBlob.OptimumChunkSize*8];
  int num;
  int total = 0;
  do
  {
    num = imgStream.Read(buf, 0, buf.Length);
```

```
        imageBlob.Write(buf, 0, num);
        total += num;
    } while (total < imgLength);

    OracleCommand procCmd =
        new OracleCommand(
          "Declare " +
          "   img ordImage; " +
          "   thumbnail ordImage; " +
          "Begin " +
          "   Select image, thumb into img, thumbnail " +
          "       from photos where rowid = :rowid " +
          "       for update; "+
          "   img.setMimeType(:mimetype); " +
          "   Begin " +
          "     img.setProperties(); " +
          "     img.processcopy('fileformat=JFIF " +
          "         maxscale=128 128', thumbnail);" +
          "   Exception " +
          "     when others then thumbnail := null;" +
          "   End; " +
          "   update photos set image=img, " +
          "     thumb=thumbnail where rowid = :rowid; " +
          "End; ", dbConn);
    procCmd.Parameters.Add("rowid",
        OracleDbType.Varchar2,ParameterDirection.Input)
        .Value=rowid;
    procCmd.Parameters.Add("mimetype",
        OracleDbType.Varchar2,ParameterDirection.Input)
        .Value=imgContentType;

    procCmd.ExecuteNonQuery();

    trans.Commit();
    StatusLabel.Text = "Upload sucessful";
    StatusLabel.Visible = true;
    success = true;
}
catch(OracleException ex)
{
    trans.Rollback();
```

```
                StatusLabel.Text = "Upload failed. <br>" +
                                ex.Message;
                StatusLabel.Visible = true;
            }
            finally
            {
              // Close connection (release connection to pool)
              dbConn.Close();
            }
            // Make it that the fields are cleared on suceess
            if (success)
            {
              Response.Redirect("webform1.aspx");
            }
        }
      }
    }
```

This example shows how to use an anonymous PL/SQL block, but can also be performed by calling a precompiled PL/SQL procedure, which would be somewhat more efficient.

4.8   PHP: Hypertext Preprocessor with OCI8 extension

PHP is a general scripting language suited for use in web servers, especially HTML. It is supported by many web server environments. It is probably used mostly with the Apache web server as an Apache module.

As with the other scripting languages, it is an easy chore to create a PHP script to upload media to the database or deliver media from the database.

The prerequisite for developing PHP applications that will interface with *inter*Media is to install PHP onto your web server, and to activate the OCI8 PHP extension. This extension is used by PHP to communicate with an Oracle database.

4.8.1   PHP Media delivery to browser

In PHP, as in ODP.NET, there are no proxy objects that represent the database *inter*Media objects, therefore, the objects must be handled within SQL statements or PL/SQL procedures or blocks.

This script again uses the flexible URL of the form:

```
http://webserver.co.com/getMedia.php?
tbl=<TABLE NAME>&keycol=<KEY COLUMN NAME>
&key=<KEY>&col=<MEDIA COLUMN>
```

Where:

- <TABLE NAME> is the table name to query for media (for example: PHOTOS)
- <KEY COLUMN NAME> is the name of the column that is used to search for a single entry (for example: ID)
- <KEY> is the singleton search key used to locate the appropriate row.
- <MEDIA COLUMN> is the column where an *inter*Media object resides, for example: IMAGE)

An example URL would be:

```
http://my.svr.com/getMedia.php?tbl=photos&
keycol=id&key=1&col=image
```

The PHP script to accomplish getting media is as follows:

```php
<?php

    // Call procedure to get media
    getMedia();


    function getMedia()
    {

      // this procedure requires PHP5 and OCI extension
      if (!isset($_GET['tbl']) || !isset($_GET['col']) ||
          !isset($_GET['keycol']) || !isset($_GET['key'])) {
        header("HTTP/1.0 404 Not Found");
        return;
      }

      $tbl = $_GET['tbl'];
      $col = $_GET['col'];
```

```php
$keycol = $_GET['keycol'];
$key = $_GET['key'];

// Connect to the DB. Using EZCONNECT (QuickConnect)
syntax
// (must have EZCONNECT configured)
$conn = oci_connect('scott', 'tiger',
              '//my.server.com:1521/orcl2');

if (!$conn) {
  header("HTTP/1.0 500 Internal Error");
  echo "500 Internal Error on connection";
  return;
}

// Create SQL statement
$query =
  "SELECT t." . $col . ".getContent(),
        t." . $col . ".getMimeType(),
    to_char(t." . $col .
          ".getUpdateTime(), 'ssmihh24ddmmyyyy'),
        t." . $col . ".getContentLength()
    FROM   " . $tbl . " t
    WHERE  " . $keycol . " = :key";

$stid = oci_parse($conn, $query);

// Bind key
$r = oci_bind_by_name($stid, ":key", $key, -1);
if (!$r) {
  header("HTTP/1.0 500 Internal Error");
  echo "500 Internale Error on bind";
  return;
}
// Execute SQL statement.
$r = oci_execute($stid, OCI_DEFAULT);
if (!$r) {
  header("HTTP/1.0 500 Internal Error");
  echo "500 Internal Error on SQL execute";
  return;
}
```

```php
// Fetch row.
$arr = oci_fetch_row($stid);
if (!$arr) {
  header("HTTP/1.0 404 Not Found");
  echo "Not Found";
  return;
}

$lob = $arr[0];
$mime = $arr[1];
$timstamp = $arr[2];
$medialen = $arr[3];

//
// If this is a conditional Request,
// see if media has changed or not.
//
if ($timstamp != '') {
    // Create the Etag we will use for caching
    $Etag = $timstamp . ":" . $medialen;
    $headers =  Apache_Request_Headers();

    $ifNoneMatch = '';
    if (isset($headers["If-None-Match"]))
$ifNoneMatch = $headers["If-None-Match"];

    // If this is a conditional request, and the Etag
    // matches, we don't have to deliver media.
    if ($ifNoneMatch == $Etag){
        header("HTTP/1.0 304 Not Modified");
        oci_free_statement($stid);
        $lob->free();
        return;
    }
    // Set the ETAG (like Last-Modified-Time)
    //so we can cache.
    header("ETag: " . $Etag);
}

// set media mimetype
header("Content-type: " . $mime);
```

```
// write media
while (!$lob->eof()) echo $lob->read(65534);

// Free resources
oci_free_statement($stid);
$lob->free();
}

?>
```

As with our other examples, we set an Etag in the header so that if the browser, or a caching system, has the media cached locally, and the cache is correct (by media size and update time) it will not be delivered. Instead an HTTP response will tell the browser (or caching firewall or caching server) to use the media in it's cache.

4.8.2 PHP Media delivery from browser to database

In the case that it is necessary to deliver media data from a user to the database, this is accomplished in a somewhat similar manner to delivery of data to the browser. The complicating factors are the creation of a database row, and the processing of the data from the browser.

This PHP script looks for the necessary inputs to create a new row in the HTTP request. If the HTTP request does not have these fields, a user form is displayed to collect the necessary information. It is done in this manner as an example only, so there is only a single script, most applications will have a form created by one script, and then sent the results to a PHP script to accept the form inputs and put the information into the database.

As in the other examples, inserting a BLOB into the database is a multi step process. The first step is to populate a row and create a BLOB to receive the binary data from the application, the second step is for the application to populate the blob, and the third step is to create a database procedure to process the uploaded image.

```
<?php

if (!isset($_POST['description']) ||
    !isset($_POST['location']) ||
    !isset($_FILES['photo'])) {
?>
```

```
<HTML>
  <BODY>
    <FORM name="uploadForm"
          method="post"
          enctype="multipart/form-data">
      <P>
        Location?    <INPUT type="text"
                            name="location"/><BR/>
        Description? <INPUT type="text"
                            name="description"/><BR/>
        Image File?  <INPUT type="file"
                             name="photo"/><BR/>
        <INPUT type="submit" value="Submit" />
      </P>
    </FORM>
  </BODY>
</HTML>
<?php
    }
else{
    // Connect to the DB. Using EZCONNECT
    //(QuickConnect) syntax
    // (must have EZCONNECT configured)
    $conn = oci_connect('scott', 'tiger',
                        '//my.srvr.com:1521/orcl2');
    // Call procedure to put photo
    $r = db_put_photo($conn, $_POST['description'],
                      $_POST['location'],
                      $_FILES['photo']['tmp_name'],
                      $_FILES['photo']['type']);
    $here = $_SERVER['PHP_SELF'];
    if ($r) echo "Upload Successful.
                 <a href=\"$here\"> Again? </a>";
    else echo "Upload Failed.
              <a href=\"$here\"> Try Again? </a>";
    }

    //
    // Function to put photo into database
    //
    function db_put_photo($conn, $description,
```

```
                              $location,
                              $imgfile, $defaultmime)
    {
      $stmttxt =
        "INSERT INTO photos t
          (id, description, location, image, thumb)
          VALUES(photos_tbl_seq.nextval,:descr,:loc,
                 ordimage.init(), ordimage.init())
          RETURNING t.image.getcontent(), rowid into
                 :lob, :rid";

      $stmt = oci_parse($conn, $stmttxt);

      // Fill in text filelds
      oci_bind_by_name($stmt, ':descr',
                       $description, -1);
      oci_bind_by_name($stmt, ':loc',
                       $location, -1);

      // Get lob descriptor
      $lob = oci_new_descriptor($conn, OCI_D_LOB);
      oci_bind_by_name($stmt, ':lob', $lob,
                       -1, OCI_B_BLOB);

      // Get rowid
      oci_bind_by_name($stmt, ':rid', $rid, 64);

      // Execute the statement
      oci_execute($stmt, OCI_DEFAULT);

      $handle = fopen($imgfile, "r");
      while ( !feof($handle) )
          $lob->write(fread($handle, 65534));

      // Update the photo and create a
      // thumbnail image. If we can't figure
      // out the mimetype, use the mimetype
      // passed into the webserver.
      $stmttxt =
    "DECLARE
          img ordimage;
```

```
                          th  ordimage;
                        BEGIN
                          select image, thumb into
                                 img,   th from photos
                              where rowid = :rid;
                          begin
                            img.setproperties();
                            img.processcopy
                             ('fileFormat=JFIF maxScale=128 128',
                               th);
                          exception
                            when others then
                              img.setMimeType(:mt);
                              th := null;
                          end;
                          update photos set
                                 image=img, thumb=th
                                 where rowid=:rid;
                          commit;
                        END;";
                    $stmt = oci_parse($conn, $stmttxt);

                    oci_bind_by_name($stmt, ':rid',
                                  $rid, -1);
                    oci_bind_by_name($stmt, ':mt',
                                  $defaultmime, -1);
                    oci_execute($stmt, OCI_DEFAULT);

                    // Free up resources
                    oci_free_statement($stmt);
                    $lob->free();

                    return true;
                  }
                ?>
```

This example shows how to use an anonymous PL/SQL block, but can also be performed by calling a pre-compiled PL/SQL procedure, which would be somewhat more efficient.

4.9   Streaming Server Delivery

Media, including video, audio, images, and XML documents, can also be delivered from streaming servers directly from the database. Streaming servers do not generally use HTTP, but use their own streaming protocols. RTSP (real-time streaming protocol) is used by a number of streaming servers, including Helix server and Real server. Microsoft uses both RTSP and Microsoft Media Server (MMS) protocols. These protocols can handle many multimedia types.

Aside from simply serving content from the database, the database can be used to deliver custom media based on a SQL query; for example, the request may be to play the most popular song for the day rather than a particular song.

If the streaming client supports other types of media, like the XML standard SMIL (synchronized multimedia integration language), a more complex presentation may be crafted; for example, play a sample of the top ten most popular songs of the day while displaying their album covers. The XML can be created from SQL queries and delivered to the client, and the client would then request the actual contents of media from the streaming server.

4.9.1   Real/Helix Server

*inter*Media supports the Real server or the Helix server, which is based on the streaming server from Real Networks through a plug-in. This plug-in can be downloaded through the OTN website at http://www.oracle.com/technology/products/intermedia.

After following the installation procedure, an Oracle Filesystem mount point can be configured from the Helix administration Web page, as shown in Figure 4.10.

Once the mount point has been defined, you can then define a procedure to play media. Note that the Helix or Real server can play or display many kinds of streaming and nonstreaming media (e.g., images), so the procedure may have to be modified for the kind of media displayed. Here is an example of a PL/SQL procedure that plays video on the Helix server.

```
CREATE OR REPLACE PROCEDURE getVideo(IdIn     IN VARCHAR2,
                            data     OUT BLOB,
                            mimetype OUT VARCHAR2)

    AS
```

Figure 4.10

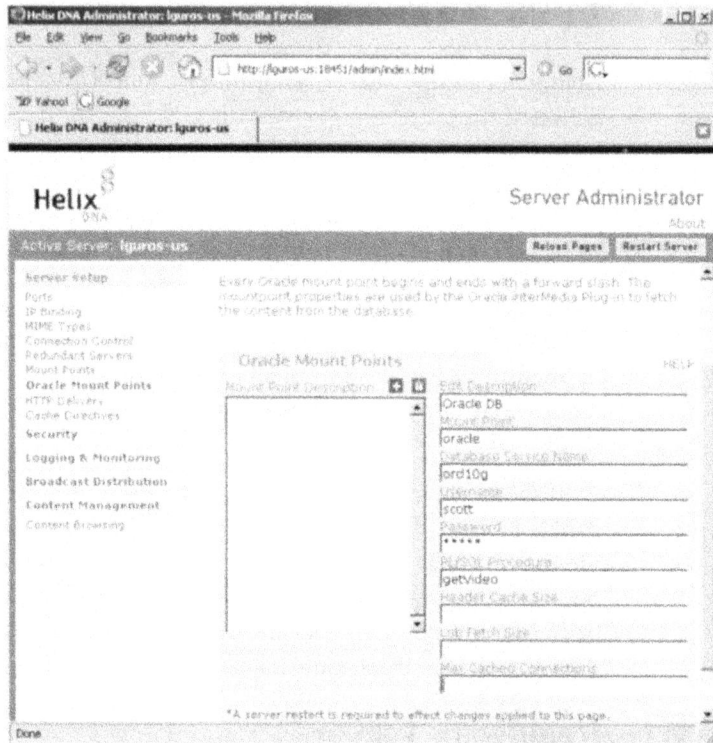

```
        mt varchar2(200);
        BEGIN
          SELECT t.video.getcontent(),
                 t.video.getmimetype()
          INTO   data,
                 mt
          FROM videos t
          WHERE t.item_id   = IdIn;
          if (mt like '%real%') then
             mt := 'audio/x-pn-realaudio';
          end if;
          mimetype := mt;
        END;
```

Note that the MIME type may have to be modified. This is because the Real/Helix server maps file extensions to one particular MIME type, which may not be an intuitive MIME type, and only uses this MIME type to play the streaming media. In this particular case, the video must be presented to

Real/Helix server as an audio MIME type for the server to recognize the media as valid. Other MIME types, such as Quicktime, must be represented as the exact one that Real/Helix expects.

Using a URL of the form RTSP://<HOST>:<PORT>/oracle/5 will retrieve the video in row five within a video player as Figure 4.11 shows.

Figure 4.11
Video from
Database

This video can also be embedded into a Web page. The following HTML is a simple example of how this can be achieved. Note that we use an HTTP protocol to the Helix server to a ramgen mount point. This produces a metafile for the plug-in (so all the video is not downloaded) that references the RTSP streaming protocol.

```
HTML>
  <HEAD>
     <TITLE>Very Simple embeded Video page</TITLE>
  </HEAD>
  <BODY>
     <EMBED name="realvideoax"
        src="http://server.company.com:1234/ramgen/oracle/5"
        type="audio/x-pn-realaudio-plugin">
```

Figure 4.12
Real Video on
Web Page

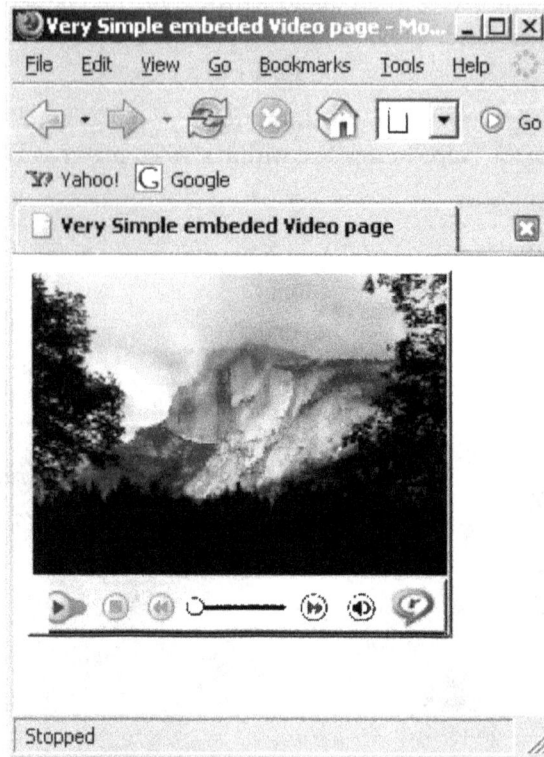

```
      </EMBED>
    </BODY>
  </HTML>
```

The above code results in the Web video presentation shown in Figure 4.12.

4.9.2   Microsoft Streaming Server

*inter*Media offers a data source plug-in for Microsoft Windows Media Streaming Services to obtain its media directly from an Oracle database. The *inter*Media Plug-in feature is installed in a similar manner to other Microsoft Windows products. Because Microsoft Media Services are only available on Microsoft Windows server, the *inter*Media Plug-in for Microsoft Windows Media Streaming Services can only be installed on a Windows server machine. One thing to note is that this plug-in must be installed by a Windows user who has administrator privileges. Figure 4.13 shows the Media Services administration screen.

Figure 4.13
*Microsoft
Media Server
Configuration*

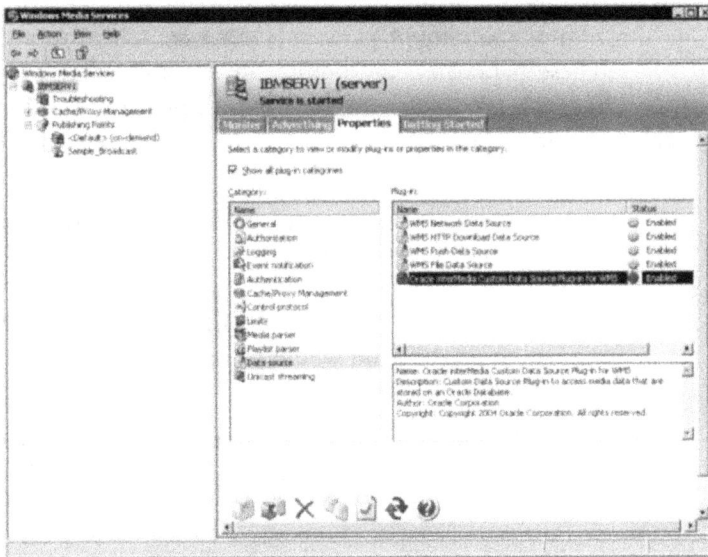

Once the installation wizard is finished, a mount point must be defined, similar to the mount point in Helix server, except the Microsoft mount point is not included as a part of the Media URL.

From the Media Services page, select the server you are managing, then select the Properties tab and click on the box Show All Plug-in Categories. Click on the Data Source category and find the Oracle *inter*Media custom source plug-in for WMS. Enable this plug-in and double click on the plug-in to display the plug-in properties. On this screen, you will be able to add mount points.

The mount point specifies an Oracle database and PL/SQL procedure to obtain the media. The PL/SQL procedure must define an output parameter

Table 4.1 *Streaming Server Procedure Parameter.*

Name	Type	Description
Data (required)	BFILE or BLOB	Media data to be streamed
MIME type (optional)	Varchar2	MIME type of media data

named DATA of type BLOB or BFILE. The output parameters must use the names and data types shown in Table 4.1.

Like the Real/Helix server plug-in, the PL/SQL procedure can have zero or more input parameters that are taken from the requesting URL. These parameters are bound, in the order they appear in the URL, to available parameters in the PL/SQL procedure. For example, if you have the procedure:

```
myGetVid (id IN Number, name IN Varchar2, Data OUT blob,
MIMEtype Out varchar2);
```

the URL could be mms://<SERVER>/<PUBLISHING POINT>/1/ George. In this case, id would be passed the value one and name would be passed the value "George."

As the procedure that we defined in the Helix server example follows these conventions, we can use the procedure from the preceding section to obtain the media.

Please note that to fully support metadata extraction from Windows Media files, you must install *inter*Media Support into your database for the Windows Media file format from OTN (Oracle Technology Network). You will want to do this if you deal with Windows Media formats. Figure 4.14 shows a mount point being defined for Microsoft Media Services.

Figure 4.14

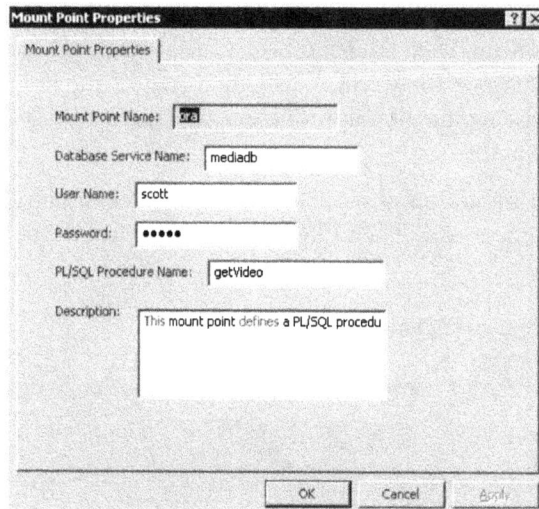

Once the mount point is defined and the plug-in is enabled, you must define a publishing point. This publishing point will define the URL used to access media. Figure 4.15 shows a publishing point being defined.

Figure 4.15
*Adding
Media Server
Publishing Point*

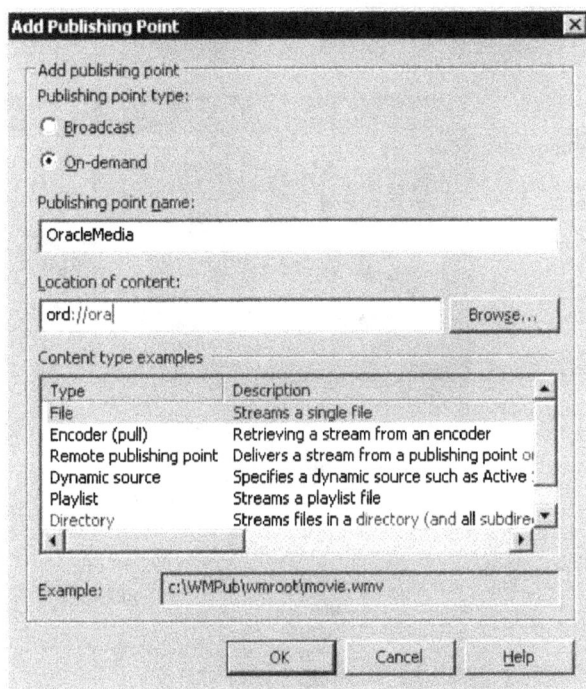

After the mount point and publishing point have been defined, media can be streamed from the database. The URL is of the form mms://<WINDOWS SERVER>/<ORACLE PUBLISHING POINT>/<SELECTION KEY>. For example, the URL might look like mms://server1.oracle.com/OracleMedia/8.

Figure 4.16 is an example of a video in the playlist streamed from Oracle.

4.10 Oracle Wireless

Oracle Wireless gives diverse user devices the ability to see content that is customized for their device, for example, a laptop using HTML versus a cellular telephone using WML. One of the things necessary for adapting content to specific devices is to supply a device with images that are tailored to it. For instance, a laptop may be able to display JPEG images at a large size where a cell phone may only be able to display WBMP images on a small screen. *inter*Media provides these adaptation services.

Figure 4.16
*Playing Audio
From Database*

4.10.1   Media Image Adaptation

*inter*Media has a module within OracleAS Wireless that adapts images to a
size, color depth, and format that is viewable on the device in question. In
developing Oracle Wireless applications, a language called Mobile XML or
XHTML/XForms is used. Since XHTML/XForms is currently the recommended language, our samples will be in this language. The Oracle Wireless
Multi Channel Server takes XHTML/XForms, or applications that produce
XHTML/XForms are used, and converts it into a representation that can be
used for the target device.

Images are adapted using the Object tag. The following is an example of
XHTML/XForms that will convert an image to a format, color depth, and
size that is defined by the device's profile in the Multi Channel Server.

```
<?xml version="1.0" encoding="UTF-8" standalone="yes"?>
<%@ page import="java.util.*" %>
<%@ page session="false" %>
<html xmlns="http://www.w3.org/1999/xhtml"
      style="_orcl-aural-props: fetchtimeout(180s)"
      profile="http://xmlns.oracle.com/ias/dtds/xhtml+xforms/
0.9.0/1.0">
```

```
<head>
    <title>Adapting images using the OBJECT tag in XHTML </
title>
  </head>
  <body>
    <h3>Simple Image Adaptation</h3>
    <div>
      <object id="myid"
        data="http://www.oracle.com/admin/images/oralogo.gif"
         type="image/gif" />
    </div>
  </body>
</html>
```

As you can see, to adapt images to the best format your device can handle is easy and automatic. Images that can be used by the requesting device unmodified by image adaptation are simply passed through unchanged. Figure 4.17 is how the screen would look on a standard Web browser.

Figure 4.17

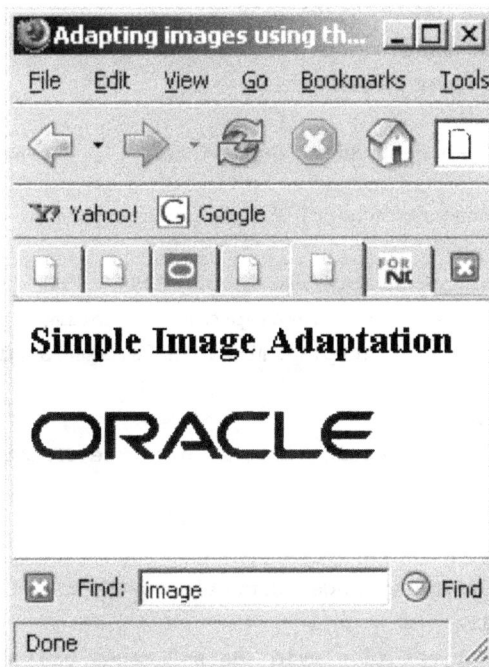

However, image adaptation typically makes little sense for static images such as a logo. Although adapted images are cached using Oracle Web Cache so the logo would not be adapted for every request, image adaptation is much more useful for images that are dynamically produced from temporal data, such as stock graphs.

For static images that are used frequently, Oracle Wireless provides a command line tool to convert images to particular formats. Following is an example of using the command line tool to convert a color JPEG file to a smaller monochrome GIF.

```
ImageGenerate -inFile stock_600_450.jpg -outFile
stock_240_180.gif -outW 240 -outH 180 -outContent monochrome
-outFormat giff
```

If we want to use these static images produced with the command line tool, we will have to change our above example:

```
<?xml version="1.0" encoding="UTF-8" standalone="yes"?>
<%@ page import="java.util.*" %>
<%@ page session="false" %>
<%-- Prevent Page Caching --%>
<%
  response.setHeader("Cache-Control", "no-store"); // HTTP
1.1
  response.setHeader("Pragma", "no-cache"); // HTTP 1.0
%>
<html xmlns="http://www.w3.org/1999/xhtml"
      style="_orcl-aural-props: fetchtimeout(180s)"
      profile="http://xmlns.oracle.com/ias/dtds/xhtml+xforms/
0.9.0/1.0">
  <head>
    <title>Adapting images using the OBJECT tag in XHTML </
title>
  </head>
  <body>
    <h3>Simple Image Adaptation with pre-formatted Logos</h3>
    <div>
      <object id ="myid" data="images/oralogo.gif"
        type="image/gif">
        <object id="myid2" data="images/logo.wbmp"
                    type="image/vnd.wap.wbmp"/>
```

```
          </object>
        </div>
      </body>
    </html>
```

In this case, the nested object tag can deliver a GIF or a WBMP image. Depending on device support, we have left image adaptation on in this example in case a device that does not support these two formats requests this image.

For temporal data, such as stock graphs, we would use tags to prevent the optimization of caching the image before the <html> tag:

```
<%-- Prevent Page Caching --%>
<%
  response.setHeader("Cache-Control", "no-store"); // HTTP
1.1
  response.setHeader("Pragma", "no-cache"); // HTTP 1.0
  response.setHeader("Expires", "0"); // prevents caching at
the proxy server
%>
```

4.11 Oracle *inter*Media OraDAV Driver

Another way to access *inter*Media data is to use Webdav access. Webdav (Web-based distributed authoring and versioning) is an HTTP standard that allows use of a remote Web server like a file system. This technology is also known as Web Folders. Webdav allows for download and upload of files in the server's file system to the Webdav endpoint that is defined with a URL.

OraDAV (Apache module for Oracle distributed authoring and versioning) is an extension to Apache Webdav. OraDAV extends Webdav access to/from files in the file system to data within the Oracle database. The data is exposed from a URL that eventually retrieves and/or uploads data from the database. OraDAV ships with OracleAS 10g.

The OraDAV module allows for media to be uploaded and downloaded from OraDAV containers stored in tablespaces on the database server machine. The Oracle *inter*Media OraDAV driver adds functionality to the OraDAV module to add functionality for multimedia data. This allows the media to be managed by Oracle rather than a file system.

Along with media managed in the OraDAV containers, the Oracle *inter*Media OraDAV driver can expose *inter*Media data that resides in exiting tables, and OracleAS 10g must be installed with the Apache module for Oracle distributed authoring and versioning option. You will also need to download the Oracle *inter*Media OraDAV driver available on OTN.

To make OraDAV expose *inter*Media media in a table, the following steps must be taken:

1.   Install OracleAS 10g with Apache module for Oracle distributed authoring and versioning.

2.   Download the Oracle *inter*Media OraDAV Driver from OTN.

3.   Install the OraDAV infrastructure in ORDSYS.

4.   Create an OraDAV container in the database.

5.   Expose the *inter*Media data in a table through the container.

6.   Define the OraDAV endpoint in the Webdav configuration file.

4.11.1   Install OraDAV Database Infrastructure in ORDSYS

To install the necessary OraDAV infrastructure within the database, which includes packages, procedures, types, and granting of privileges, the following, which is documented in the INSTALL instructions, is performed:

1.   Find the admin directory within the downloaded and expanded Oracle *inter*Media OraDAV driver and change to that directory.

2.   Log into SQL/PLUS as a sysdba user.

3.   Load a Java stored procedure to adjust GMT time, for example:

```
$ loadjava -force -grant PUBLIC -resolve -schema ordsys
  OraGMTOffset.class
```

4.   Log in as an SYSDBA privileged user, set the schema to the ordsys schema and install the infrastructure packages, for example:

```
SQL> connect sys/welcome1 as sysdba
SQL> alter session set current_schema = "ORDSYS";
SQL> @orddavin.sql
```

A container is a set of housekeeping tables that OraDAV uses to find content in an Oracle database as well as a place to store content uploaded to the container from the Web. The SQL file oradavcc.sql from the Oracle *inter*Media OraDAV driver is used to create a container. The following steps are taken to create a container:

1. Create a user to contain the OraDAV containers. This user should have CONNECT, RESOURCE, DROP TABLESPACE, CREATE TABLESPACE, and CREATE ANY TRIGGER privileges granted to it. For example:

```
SQL> create user oradavcontainers identified by
     oradavcontainers;
SQL> grant CONNECT, RESOURCE, CREATE VIEW, DROP TABLESPACE,
     CREATE TABLESPACE, CREATE ANY TRIGGER to
     oradavcontainers;
```

2. Log into a SYSDBA privileged user: `SQL> connect sys/ welcome1 as sysdba`.

3. Grant access to the media table to the container user, for example, `SQL> grant select, insert on scott.photos to oradavcontainers`.

   Still logged in as a SYSDBA user, set the schema to the container user: SQL> alter session set current_schema = "ORADAV-CONTAINERS".

4. Invoke orddavcc.sql and enter appropriate values, for example:

```
SQL> set serveroutput on; -- To see errors
SQL> @orddavcc
-- Enter a Container Name (<= 20 characters).  This will
-- serve as a prefix for tables, views, triggers,
-- indices, and tablespaces created for the container.
-- Default: oradav

Container Name: photos

-- Enter a Container Size in megabytes (e.g. 100) that
-- you want for the two tablespaces created for the
-- container.  Currently twenty percent of this
```

```
-- number will be used to create a tablespace
-- for the OraDAV housekeeping tables created for the
-- container.  The other 80 percent will be used for
-- the tablespace that owns the default storage
-- for BLOBS.
-- Default: 1000 Minimum:100


Container Size: 100


-- Enter Y if you want to not execute the create
-- container logic but simply only want to generate
-- a script (i.e. Logfile which can be later executed
-- directly in SQL*Plus.
-- Default: n


NoExecute    : n


-- Enter a LogFileDir if you want to log the output of
-- all DDL that is generated to create the container.
-- Note that the LogFileDir MUST BE a directory
-- owned and known
-- by the Oracle Server to which you are connected.  The
-- server must have a UTL_FILE_DIR=<LogFileDir> set
-- in its INIT.ORA file.
-- Default:


LogFileDirectory:
-- Enter a LogFile name if LogFileDir is set.
-- Default: oradav_schema.sql


LogFile       :
-- Enter Y if you want tracing enabled.  This means
-- that DDL gets generated to go to serveroutput.
-- Note that to enable this option you need to issue
-- the following command in SQL*Plus:
-- SET SERVEROUTPUT ON
-- Default: n


Trace Output    :


-- Enter Y if you would like a small index.html file to
```

```
-- be added to the container being created.
-- This index.htm can later be deleted or
-- overwritten with any DAV client.
-- It serves as an easy way to visually
-- verify successful container creation via a browser.
-- Default: y

Add index.html  :

-- Enter Y if you would like the multimedia file
-- to be stored in three separate tables of ORDImage,
-- ORDAudio, and ORDVideo objects.
-- Otherwise, all files will be stored as BLOBS.
-- Default: y

Use interMedia objects  :

-- Enter the server directory (including the
-- trailing slash if appropriate) where tablespace
-- data files for the container should be created. If
-- you wish you can just hit enter the
-- default location for your database will be used.
-- Default: <DATABASE DEFAULT>
Tablespace datafile directory :

PL/SQL procedure successfully completed.
```

Expose the media columns through the container.

To expose *inter*Media content (ORDImage, ORDAudio, ORDVideo, and ORDDoc), a procedure is called when logged in as the container user. The following is an example of how the *inter*Media data in the PHOTOS table is exposed:

```
DECLARE
BEGIN
  ORDSYS.DAV_PUBLIC.expose_interMedia_column(
    ORDSYS.DAV_PUBLIC.Generate_Ctx('PHOTOS'),
    -- For Container 'photos'
    'SCOTT',
    'PHOTOS',
```

```
     'IMAGE', -- Media column
     'ID', -- Primary key of table
     NULL, -- No Prefix
     NULL, -- No suffix
     '/image', -- Use image as path.
     1, -- Add triggers
     ORDSYS.DAV_PUBLIC.DUPE_MODE_FAIL);
        -- Fail if duplicate would result
  COMMIT;
END;
/
```

4.11.2   Define the OraDAV Endpoint in the Webdav Configuration File

After the previous steps, an OraDAV container has been built into the database. The next step is to let the Apache Web server, through OraDAV, know about it. The following entry is added to the file moddav.conf in the <AS_HOME>/Apache/oradav/conf/ directory.

```
<Location /photos>
  DAV Oracle
  DAVParam OraService              ORCL10g
  DAVParam ORAUSER                 oradavcontainers
  DAVParam ORAPASSWORD             oradavcontainers
  DAVParam ORAContainerName        PHOTOS
  DAVParam ORAPackageName          ORDSYS.DAV_API_DRIVER
  DAVParam OraLockExpirationPad    0
  DAVParam OraException            NORAISE
  DAVParam OraTraceLevel           0
  DAVDepthInfinity                 ON
  DAVMinTimeout                    5
  Options                          Indexes
</Location>
```

The Apache Web server must be restarted to reload its configuration files. This can be done with the following command:

```
opmnctl restartproc ias-component=HTTP_Server
```

4.11.3 Using the OraDAV Endpoint

Now you can get a list of images in a Web browser that are stored in the database with a URL of the following form: http://<SERVER>:<PORT>/ photos/image.

As you can see from the list, the file names are given the form <PRIMARY KEY>.<FILE EXTENSION FOR MIMETYPE>, for example, http://server:7777/photos/image/1.jpg.

You can also now browse through the images, as well as upload images using Webdav clients such as Windows Explorer. To browse using Windows Explorer, click on Add a Network Place. In the wizard, specify the DAV location you just created (see Figure 4.18).

Figure 4.18
Adding Network Place in Windows Explorer Step 1

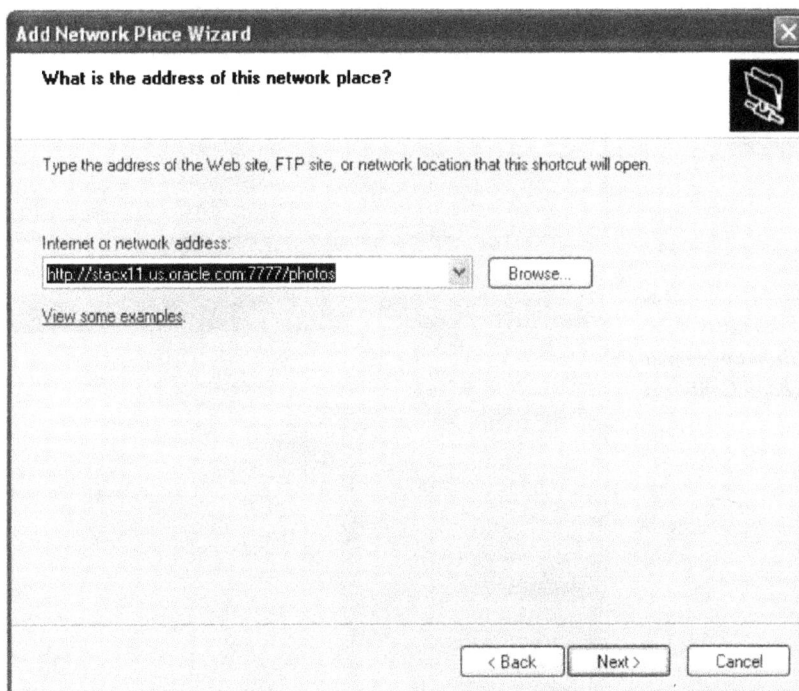

After this step, specify a name for the network place as shown in Figure 4.19.

At this point, you can browse the container, upload to it, and treat it as a normal WebDAV server, as shown in Figure 4.20.

Figure 4.19
Adding Network
Place to Windows
Explorer Step 2

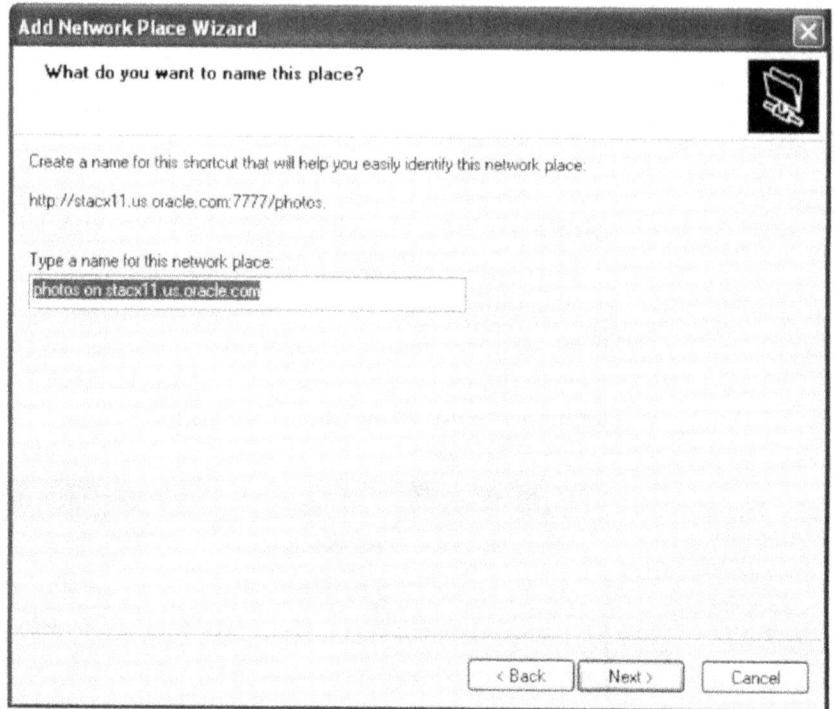

Figure 4.20
Browsing Oracle
Webdav Container

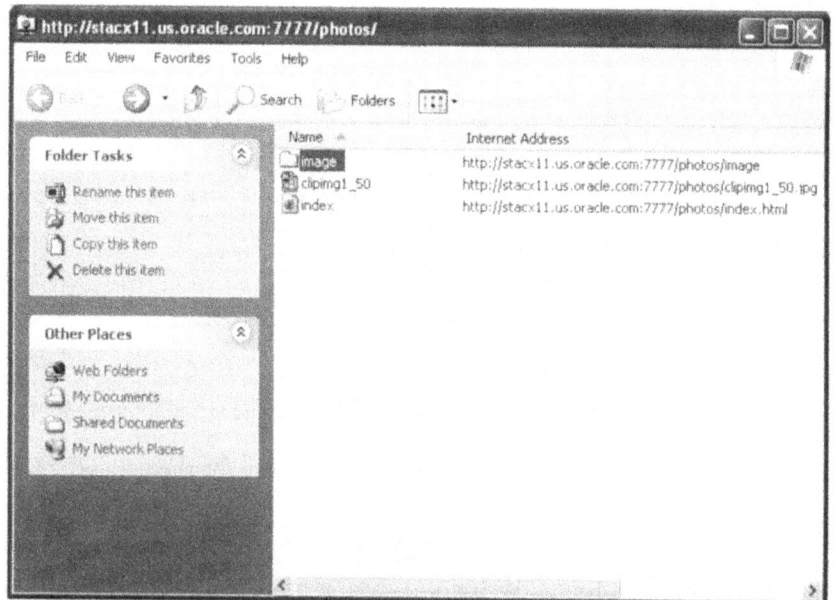

4.12 Summary

For media applications, it is important to be able to move the media over the Web. *inter*Media data can be delivered onto the Web from or to the database in many ways. This chapter described a few of these methods, but by no means is this an exclusive list. Other Web-programming environments and languages can also access and deliver *inter*Media data, the only requirement is that they are able to perform a SELECT statement and access database BLOBS. For putting data into the database, the ability to call database procedures is required to set the media properties or process the media.

5

Introduction to inter*Media APIs*

In this chapter we will introduce *inter*Media APIs with simple examples. We will use the various APIs to load an image, convert that image to a smaller size image and store the thumbnail in the database, and retrieve the image and store it in a local file.

5.1   PL/SQL

5.1.1   Preparation

To prepare the database for *inter*Media file operations, the user schema must be assigned the privileges to access files and create files. Before a file can be accessed, a database directory object must be created, and access to that directory object must be granted to the database user. From a system administrator account, the following PL/SQL steps are used to prepare the user Scott for file input and output operations:

- Create or replace directory IMAGEDIR as 'c:\Images'

- Allow Scott to import images from IMAGEDIR

- Grant READ on directory IMAGEDIR to Scott

- Allow Scott to export images to IMAGEDIR

- Grant WRITE on directory IMAGEDIR to Scott

- Grant Java file permission to ORDSYS (only needed for Oracle9); call dbms_java.grant_permission ('ORDSYS','java.io.FilePermission', 'c:\plsql*','write')

- Grant to user Java file permission to ORDSYS; call dbms_java.grant_permission('SCOTT','java.io.FilePermission', 'c:\ plsql*','write');

Please note that directory object names are case sensitive. The database, by default, uppercases a directory name unless the name is encased in double quotes. If you tried to specify the directory object as 'imagedir,', rather than 'IMAGEDIR,' the directory would not be found.

5.1.2 Place the Images into the Database

After we have prepared the database security environment, we can log into the database and create a PL/SQL procedure to upload images into the database, as follows.

```
create or replace procedure upload_image(file_name varchar2,
                                         prikey_id number,
                                         descr varchar2,
                                         loc varchar2)
as
    imgobj         ORDSYS.ORDImage;
    ctx        raw(64):=null;
    thisrowid urowid;

BEGIN
    insert into photos (id, description, location, image, thumb)
        values (prikey_id, descr, loc,
                ORDSYS.ORDImage.init(), ORDSYS.ORDImage.init())
        returning rowid, t.image into thisrowid, imgobj;

    imgobj.importFrom(ctx, 'FILE', 'IMAGEDIR', file_name);

    update photos t set t.image=imgobj where rowid = thisrowid;

    EXCEPTION
      WHEN OTHERS THEN
        DBMS_OUTPUT.put_line('EXCEPTION caught '||sqlcode||
        ' '||sqlerrm);
END;
/
```

There are three important things to note:

1. An empty media object must be inserted into the database before the media can be imported into it. This is necessary to create an empty BLOB to receive the raw binary data.

2. An object-relational method called Import or ImportFrom is used to load the image into the database. By default, this method will also populate the image metadata in the image object.

3. After importation, the uploaded image object column must be updated.

This procedure does not fully commit the image into the database; we are saving that operation for after we create the thumbnail for efficiency.

5.1.3 Processing the Image, Creating a JPEG Thumbnail

Now that the original image is in the database, we can create a thumbnail. Typically, most applications that use thumbnails avoid the costly nature of repeatedly creating the thumbnail by creating a thumbnail once and storing it. The size of the thumbnail is typically much smaller than the original, much more than the reduction of the width and height. The following procedure creates the thumbnail.

```
create or replace procedure make_thumbnail(prikey_id number)
as

    imgobj        ORDSYS.ORDImage;
    th            Ordsys.OrdImage;
    thisrowid urowid;

BEGIN

    select t.image, t.thumb, rowid into imgobj, th, thisrowid from
      photos t
          where id = prikey_id for update;
    imgobj.processCopy('fileFormat=JFIF maxScale=128 128', th);
    update photos t set t.thumb=th where rowid = thisrowid;
    EXCEPTION
      WHEN OTHERS THEN
```

```
            DBMS_OUTPUT.put_line('EXCEPTION caught '||sqlcode||
            ' '||sqlerrm);
END;
/
```

The important things to note are:

- Both the original and thumbnail objects to be populated must be selected from the database.

- Image processing is done on the original image with the thumbnail image object specified as a target.

- The thumbnail must be updated into the database.

Note that again we are incomplete without a commit. We will do this outside the procedures.

5.1.4 Obtaining the Thumbnail in a File—Exporting the Image

After the thumbnail is created, we may want to see the results. Or, we may be using the database as an image-processing engine. The following procedure exports the thumbnail into a file on the file system.

```
create or replace procedure download_thumbnail(prikey_id
number)
as
    th          Ordsys.OrdImage;
    thisrowid urowid;
    ctx         raw(64):=null;
BEGIN

    select t.thumb, rowid into th, thisrowid from photos t
        where id = prikey_id;
    th.export(ctx, 'file', 'IMAGEDIR',  prikey_id ||
    '_thumb.jpg');
    EXCEPTION
      WHEN OTHERS THEN
        DBMS_OUTPUT.put_line('EXCEPTION caught '||sqlcode||
         ' '||sqlerrm);
```

```
END;
/
```

The important things to note are:

- The image to be exported must be selected.
- The image is exported using an object method. The database directory object is specified as well as the file name, which in this procedure would be of the form <PRIMARY_KEY>_thumb.jpg.

5.1.5 Putting It All Together

The following PL/SQL code uses the above procedures to import an image, create a thumbnail of the image using database image processing, and export the thumbnail into the file system. Note that we commit the changes after the processing step to make the new row permanent.

```
BEGIN
upload_image('t.img', 1, 'A sample Picture',
    'Could be anywhere');
make_thumbnail(1);
commit;
download_thumbnail(1);

END;
/
```

5.2 *inter*Media Java Proxy Classes

This section shows how to develop a JDBC Java application that stores and uses images in an Oracle database table.

5.2.1 Overview of ORDSYS.ORDImage (Oracle Database) and OrdImage (Java) Objects

Java programmers are intimately familiar with Java objects but are often unaware that Oracle Database is an object-relational database, and as such, supports storage and retrieval of objects. Oracle *inter*Media provides the database type ORDImage, which is used to store images in a database table just like any other relational data. Some *inter*Media functionality (such as thumbnail generation) may also be used if images are stored in BLOB (binary large object) columns, but Oracle Corporation recommends storing images in ORDImage columns. An example of an ORDImage object in a database table is illustrated in Figure 5.1.

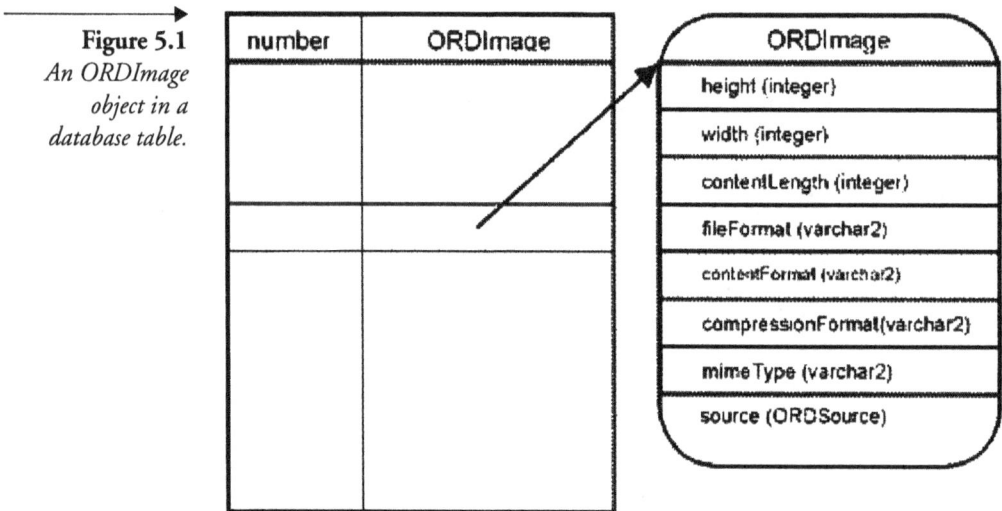

Figure 5.1
*An ORDImage
object in a
database table.*

number	ORDImage	ORDImage
		height (integer)
		width (integer)
		contentLength (integer)
		fileFormat (varchar2)
		contentFormat (varchar2)
		compressionFormat(varchar2)
		mimeType (varchar2)
		source (ORDSource)

Even though the JDBC specification does not support object-relational databases directly, Oracle *inter*Media database objects can be used in JDBC programs by means of the *inter*Media Java Client.

The *inter*Media Java Client contains high-performance proxy Java objects that allow for quick object property retrieval and convenient upload/download. The proxies forward any requests for computations back to the database server for the ORDImage object to execute. These client objects are in the oracle.ord.media.im package (found in the $ORACLE_HOME/ord/jlib/ordim.jar file).

A schematic diagram of how a database ORDSYS.ORDImage object is related to the Java ORDImage object is shown in Figure 5.2. It can't be stressed enough that ORDImage Java objects are merely proxies for database objects—they must be created from a database ORDImage object. These proxies are the same for the other media types such as OrdVideo, OrdAudio, and OrdDoc.

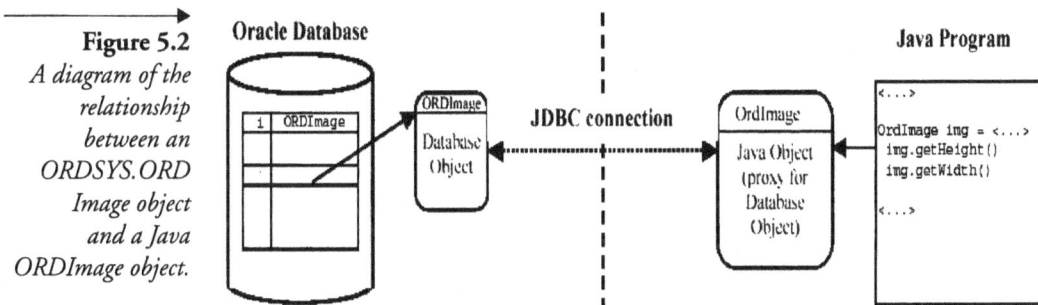

Figure 5.2
A diagram of the relationship between an ORDSYS.ORD Image object and a Java ORDImage object.

5.2.2   Setting Up the Required Java Environment— Imports and CLASSPATH

Imports

To use the OrdImage, OrdAudio, OrdVideo, and OrdDoc classes in your Java programs, the following import statement must be present.

```
import oracle.ord.im.OrdImage;
import oracle.ord.im.OrdAudio;
import oracle.ord.im.OrdVideo;
import oracle.ord.im.OrdDoc;
```

Note that the examples in this article also make use of several standard JDBC classes in the java.sql package and the Oracle JDBC extension classes OracleResultSet and OraclePreparedStatement that are included using the following import statements.

```
import java.sql.Connection;
import java.sql.SQLException;
import java.sql.DriverManager;
import java.sql.Statement;
import java.sql.PreparedStatement;
import java.sql.ResultSet;
import oracle.jdbc.OracleResultSet;
import oracle.jdbc.OraclePreparedStatement;
```

CLASSPATH

To connect to the database and use OrdImage objects, the following jar files must be in your CLASSPATH:

1.   The Oracle JDBC drivers

   ■ $ORACLE_HOME/jdbc/lib/ojdbc14.jar (preferred)

   ■ $ORACLE_HOME/jdbc/lib/classes12.jar (deprecated)

2.   The SQLJ runtime

   ■ $ORACLE_HOME/sqlj/lib/runtime12.jar

3.   The Oracle *inter*Media Java Client library

   ■ • $ORACLE_HOME/ord/jlib/ordim.jar

Setting the CLASSPATH on the command line

■ Windows (assumes %ORACLE_HOME% has been set):

```
setCLASSPATH=%ORACLE_HOME%\jdbc\lib\
ojdbc14.jar;%ORACLE_HOME%\ord\jlib\
ordim.jar;%ORACLE_HOME%\sqlj\lib\runtime12.jar;
```

■ UNIX (assumes that $ORACLE_HOME has been set):

```
setenv CLASSPATH ${ORACLE_HOME}/jdbc/lib/
ojdbc14.jar:$ORACLE_HOME/ord/jlib/
ordim.jar:$ORACLE_HOME/sqlj/lib/runtime12.jar:
```

Setting the CLASSPATH using JDeveloper 10g:

1.   Go to the project properties (right click on your project and choose properties).

2.   Navigate to the Profiles/Development/Libraries option and choose the three libraries shown below, and in Figure 5.3.

   ■ Oracle JDBC
   ■ Oracle *inter*Media
   ■ SQLJ Runtime

Documentation

The documentation (in Javadoc format) for the *inter*Media Java classes can be found from the main list of Oracle Documentation Books (under the

Figure 5.3
Selecting Libraries
for an interMedia
Project in
JDeveloper.

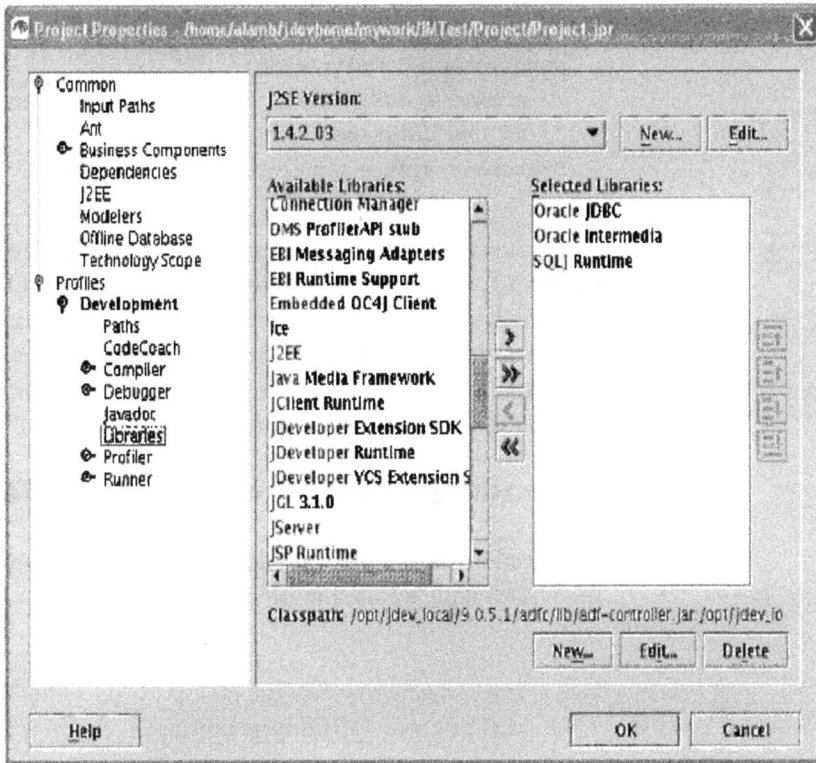

heading of "*inter*Media Java Classes Reference"). The Oracle documentation is included with the Database install, and it can be found on OTN at http://www.oracle.com/pls/db10g/db10g.homepage (click on the Books tab).

5.2.3   Creating the JDBC Connection

Oracle *inter*Media can be used with both Oracle JDBC drivers (thin or oci) and the Connection object is created in the normal way, except that the AutoCommit flag must be set to false. For example:

```
// register the oracle jdbc driver with the JDBC
// driver manager
DriverManager.registerDriver(new
oracle.jdbc.driver.OracleDriver());

Connection conn = DriverManager.getConnection(connectString,
username, password);
```

```
// Note: it is CRITICAL to set the autocommit to false so that
// two-phase select-commit of BLOBS can occur.
conn.setAutoCommit(false);
// create a JDBC Statement object to execute SQL
// in the database
Statement stmt = conn.createStatement();
```

As shown above, the Connection that is established must have the Auto-Commit flag set to false because *inter*Media uses BLOB columns internally to store data. Since BLOB updates in Oracle Database require a two-stage select-commit process, if the AutoCommit flag is set to true (the default) then BLOB operations will fail with the exception: java.sql.SQLException: ORA-01002: fetch out of sequence.

5.2.4 Uploading Images from Files into Tables

This section shows how to upload images that are stored in disk files into the photos table we used in previous chapters.

1. Insert a new row into the table with ID set to 1 and image initialized to a new ORDImage object.

```
// insert a row into photos
String rowInsertSQL = ("insert into photos (id, description,
location, image, thumb) values (1,'Dogs',
  'At Home',ordsys.ordimage.init(),ordsys.ordimage.init())");
stmt.execute(rowInsertSQL);
```

2. Get a proxy for the ORDImage database object in row 1 in the OrdImage Java proxy object imageProxy (note that since we will be uploading data into the ORDImage's underlying BLOB column, the row must be selected with the FOR UPDATE clause).

```
// select the new ORDImage into a java proxy OrdImage object
(imageProxy)
String rowSelectSQL = "select image from photos where id = 1
for update";
OracleResultSet rset =
(OracleResultSet)stmt.executeQuery(rowSelectSQL);
rset.next();
```

```
OrdImage imageProxy = (OrdImage)rset.getORAData("image",
OrdImage.getORADataFactory());
rset.close();
```

3. Load the image data from the dogs.gif file into the ORDImage object (and by extension into the database) by calling the loadDataFromFile method on the Java proxy object.

    ```
    imageProxy.loadDataFromFile("dogs.gif");
    ```

4. Automatically detect the image's height, width, file format, and so on by calling setProperties() on the proxy object. Calling setProperties() on the proxy object forwards the request to the database to execute ORDImage.setProperties() on the server.

    ```
    imageProxy.setProperties();
    ```

5. Update photos to reflect the changes we have made to the ORDImage object (uploaded data and filled in properties).

    ```
    String updateSQL = "update photos set image=? where id=1";
    OraclePreparedStatement opstmt =
    (OraclePreparedStatement)conn.prepareStatement(updateSQL);
    opstmt.setORAData(1, imageProxy);
    opstmt.execute();
    opstmt.close();
    ```

Note: If you call ORDimage.setProperties() on an image that is not one of *inter*Media's supported formats, a java.sql.SQLException that encapsulates an IMG-00705 error such as the following is thrown.

```
java.sql.SQLException: ORA-29400: data cartridge error
IMG-00705: unsupported or corrupted input format
```

5.2.5   Creating the JDBC Connection, Uploading Images from Files into Tables, and Retrieving Image Properties

Once images are in Oracle Database, you can access image metadata using either standard SQL queries or the Java proxy accessor methods. In the following examples, we demonstrate how to use the Java proxy accessor methods to access the properties of the goats.gif file that we uploaded in the previous section. Note that the properties that may be selected are height; width; fileFormat (JPEG, GIFF, and so on); contentFormat (monochrome and so on); contentLength (number of bytes of image data); and mimeType.

One may access an image's height and width by calling the accessors getHeight() and getWidth() on the *inter*Media Java proxy objects. To do this, first the image is selected into a proxy object (imageProxy), and then the getHeight() and getWidth() methods are called.

```
String rowSelectSQL = "select image from photos where id = 1";
OracleResultSet rset =
(OracleResultSet)stmt.executeQuery(rowSelectSQL);
rset.next();
OrdImage imageProxy = (OrdImage)rset.getORAData("image",
OrdImage.getORADataFactory());
rset.close();
int height = imageProxy.getHeight();
int width = imageProxy.getWidth();
```

The above code results in height = 375 and width = 500 when using the example dogs.gif file.

5.2.6   Creating Thumbnails and Changing Formats

We now illustrate how to create an ORDImage object that contains a thumbnail of an existing ORDImage object using the processCopy() method. To use the processCopy() method, the programmer describes the desired properties of the output image and provides the input image. For example, the following description generates a JPEG thumbnail image of size 75 × 100 pixels: `'fileformat=jfif fixedscale=75 100'`.

The following example shows how to insert a new ORDImage object into a second row of photos, and then shows how to generate a JPEG thumbnail of the goats.gif image in the new row with the `'maxscale=100   100 fileformat=jfif'` processCopy command.

```
// get the source and Destination ORDImage objects
String srcSelectSQL = "select image, thumb from photos where
    id=1";
OracleResultSet rset =
    (OracleResultSet)stmt.executeQuery(srcSelectSQL);
rset.next();
OrdImage srcImageProxy = (OrdImage)rset.getORAData("image",
OrdImage.getORADataFactory());
OrdImage dstImageProxy = (OrdImage)rset.getORAData("thumb",
OrdImage.getORADataFactory());
rset.close();

// call the processCopy method (processing occurs on the
SERVER)
srcImageProxy.processCopy("maxscale=100 100 fileformat=jfif",
    dstImageProxy);

// update the destination image in the second row
String dstUpdateSQL = "update photos set thumb=? where id=1";
OraclePreparedStatement opstmt =
(OraclePreparedStatement)conn.prepareStatement(dstUpdateSQL);
opstmt.setORAData(1, dstImageProxy);
opstmt.execute();
opstmt.close();
```

5.2.7   Downloading Image Data from Tables into Files

An ORDImage database object can be downloaded into a local disk file with the following steps.

1.   Select the ORDImage object from the database into an OrdImage Java proxy.

2.   Call the getDataInFile() method on the OrdImage Java proxy to download the image data into a file.

An example of these two steps to download the image in row 2 to "row2.jpg" is shown below.

```
// export the data in row 1
String exportSelectSQL = "select thumb from photos where id =
    1";

OracleResultSet rset =
(OracleResultSet)stmt.executeQuery(exportSelectSQL);

// get the proxy for the image in row 1
rset.next();
OrdImage imageProxy = (OrdImage)rset.getORAData("thumb",
    OrdImage.getORADataFactory());
rset.close();

// call the getDataInFile method to write the ORDImage in row
// 1 to disk
imageProxy.getDataInFile("thumb_1.jpg");
```

5.3   Oracle C++ Call Interface

Media data in Oracle can be inserted, accessed, and manipulated in any language that can perform PL/SQL operations. Oracle *inter*Media does supply convenience proxy classes for Java, but these are not necessary to access the full functionality of *inter*Media. In this section, the Oracle C++ Call Interface (OCCI) is used to perform the same processing as is performed by Java. The same *inter*Media processing can also be performed using Oracle Callable Interface (OCI).

5.3.1   Includes and C++ Namespaces

The following includes and namespaces are used with this example. The file occi.h is found in <ORACLE_HOME>/rdbms/public/occi.h.

```
#include <iostream>
#include <fstream>
#include <occi.h>
#include <unistd.h>
#include <string>
using namespace oracle::occi;
using namespace std;

#define BUFSIZE 16384
```

5.3.2   Creating the Connection

The connection is created, as you would in any OCCI program, with the following code.

```
Environment *env = Environment::createEnvironment
                            (Environment::DEFAULT);
Connection *conn = env->createConnection
                            (username, password, url);
```

5.3.3   Populating the Image Row from a File

For the population of the image row, OCCI must have AutoCommit set to false. Unlike JDBC, by default, OCCI sets AutoCommit off by default. Also, the AutoCommit settings are a member of the Statement class, not the Connection class.

The following OCCI method inserts an image into the database, populates the image raw data using the OCCI Blob and Stream classes, and then uses an anonymous PL/SQL block to set the properties of the image.

```
void insertImageRow (Connection *conn, unsigned int id,
         string descrip, string location, string fName)
  throw (SQLException)
{

  //
  // Open input file to populate blob
  //
  ifstream inFile;
  inFile.open(fName.data(), ios::in | ios::binary );
  if (!inFile)
  {
    cout << fName; cout << " file not found\n";
    return;
  }

  //
  // Insert row returning ID and blob to be populated
  //
```

1. Insert a new row into the table with ID set to 1 and image and thumb initialized to a new ORDImage object.

```
Statement *stmt = conn->createStatement
  ( "Insert into Photos t values \
      (:v1, :v2, :v3, \
      Ordimage.Init(), OrdImage.Init()) returning \
      ROWID, t.image.getContent() into :v4, :v5");
stmt->setInt(1, id);
stmt->setString(2, descrip);
stmt->setString(3, location);
stmt->registerOutParam(4, OCCISTRING, 50);
stmt->registerOutParam(5, OCCIBLOB);
```

2. Execute the statement and retrieve the unique row ID and BLOB from ORDImage object.

```
stmt->executeUpdate();
string rid = stmt->getString(4);
Blob blob = stmt->getBlob(5);

//
// Populate interMedia blob from file using Stream
// interface
//
unsigned int bufsize=BUFSIZE;
char *buffer = new char[bufsize];
```

3. Copy data from file into the BLOB stream. The method writeLastBuffer is required to end the BLOB stream writes.

```
Stream *strm = blob.getStream();
while(inFile)
{
  inFile.read((char *)buffer, bufsize);
  strm->writeBuffer(buffer,inFile.gcount());
}
strm->writeLastBuffer(buffer, 0);
blob.closeStream(strm);
inFile.close();
```

```
                        delete[] buffer;

                        //
                        // In the same transaction, Set the image properties
                        // and create a thumbnail
                        //
```

4.   Create a PL/SQL block of code to retrieve *inter*Media objects
        from the row that was just inserted, set a default MIME type, and
        attempt to populate metadata in the object from the image binary
        data using setProperties(). If we are successful in getting image
        metadata into the image object, a thumbnail of the image is cre-
        ated and copied into the thumb object.

```
        stmt->setSQL
          ("DECLARE \
              img ORDIMAGE; \
              thumbnail ORDIMAGE; \
            BEGIN \
              select image, thumb into img, thumbnail from \
                  Photos where rowid = :v1 for update; \
              img.setMimetype(:v2); \
              BEGIN \
                img.setProperties(); \
                img.processCopy( \
                  'fileFormat=JFIF maxScale=128 128', \
                  thumbnail); \
              EXCEPTION WHEN OTHERS THEN thumbnail := NULL; \
              END; \
              update Photos set image=img, \
                      thumb=thumbnail where rowid = :v1; \
            END;");
        stmt->setString(1, rid);
        // set default mime type based upon file Extension in
        // case of processing failure (image/<FILE_EXTENSION>)
        stmt->setString(2, "image/" +
                  fName.substr(fName.find_last_of(".") + 1));

        stmt->executeUpdate();
        conn->commit();
        conn->terminateStatement (stmt);
```

```
    cout <<
       "Populating and initializing the Image - Success"
       << endl;

    return;
}
```

5.3.4 Extracting the Thumbnail from the Database into a File

The extraction of an image from the database into the file is simply done with a select statement, obtaining the BLOB stream, and copying the stream data from the database into the file.

```
void writeThumbnailFile (Connection *conn, unsigned int id,
                         string fprefix)
  throw (SQLException)
{
  cout << "createStatement\n";
```

1. Select the binary data into and Mimetype of the image from the row with the passed ID.

```
Statement *stmt = conn->createStatement
  ("Select t.thumb.getContent(), t.thumb.getMimetype() \
     from Photos t where t.id= :v1");
stmt->setInt(1, id);
ResultSet *rset = stmt->executeQuery ();

if (rset->next ())
{
```

2. Get the binary data into an OCCI BLOB object and the MIME type into a string.

```
Blob blob = rset->getBlob (1);
string mimeType = rset->getString(2);

string fName = fprefix + "." +
    mimeType.substr(mimeType.find_last_of("/") + 1);
```

```
cout << "Output file name is " << fName << endl;

ofstream outFile;
outFile.open(fName.data() , ios::out | ios::binary);
if (!outFile)
{
  cout << fName; cout <<
    " file could not be created\n";
  conn->terminateStatement (stmt);
  return;
}

unsigned int bufsize=BUFSIZE;
char *buffer = new char[bufsize];
```

3.   After creating the output file, using part of the mimetype as the
     file extension (for example, image/jpeg would create a .jpeg file),
     copy the contents of the Blob into the

```
Stream *inStream = blob.getStream (1,0);
    while (1)
    {
      int bytesRead =
              inStream->readBuffer(buffer, bufsize);
      if (bytesRead < 0) break;
    outFile.write(buffer, bytesRead);
    }
    blob.closeStream(inStream);
    outFile.close();
    delete[] buffer;
  }
  conn->commit();
  conn->terminateStatement (stmt);

  return;
}
```

5.4   C# Using Oracle Data Provider for .NET (ODP.NET)

Media data stored with *inter*Media data can easily be accessed and handled in many Microsoft environments. These environments include C# and Visual Basic by using the Oracle Data Provider for .NET (ODP.NET). The example given in the previous sections of this chapter will be repeated in this section to illustrate the steps taken to use *inter*Media with .NET.

ODP.NET allows for access to the Oracle database. This runtime component provides the programming interface to execute database functionality.

A programmer using .NET will typically be using Microsoft's Visual Studio .Net. In this case, they would probably want to also install Oracle Developer Tools for Visual Studio .NET.

5.4.1   Prerequisites for Using Oracle with Visual Studio .NET

To access the Oracle database, it is necessary that ODP.NET is installed. To effectively use Visual Studio with Oracle databases, it is best to install Oracle Developer Tools for Visual Studio .NET. Both of these products are installed by default when the Oracle client is installed on the Windows system.

5.4.2   Preparing the Visual Studio Project to Use ODP.NET

To set up your Visual Studio C# project to make use of ODP.NET, the project should make a reference to Oracle.DataAccess. This reference will then be used by Visual Studio for object reference information.

5.4.3   Object References

The following namespaces are defined to be used in this program. The "using" directive allows us to reference types without having to fully qualify the namespace they are part of.

```
using System;
using System.Data;
using System.IO;
using Oracle.DataAccess.Types;
Using Oracle.DataAccess.Client;
```

5.4.4 Creating the Connection

The database connection is created with the following code.

```
//
// get connection to database
//
OracleConnection dbConn =
    new OracleConnection("User ID=scott;" +
                         "Password=tiger;" +
                         "Data Source=ORCL10g");
dbConn.Open();
```

5.4.5 Creating the Database Commands to Insert a Row

In this program, to increase the efficiency somewhat in the case of multiple inserts, the database commands are created once and then reused to create new rows in the database. The following code is used to create these commands.

```
private static OracleCommand insertCommand;
private static OracleParameter paramDesc;
private static OracleParameter paramID;
private static OracleParameter paramLoc;
private static OracleParameter paramBlob;
private static OracleParameter paramRowid;

private static OracleCommand processCommand;
private static OracleParameter paramRowidIn;
private static OracleParameter paramMime;

private static void setupCommands(OracleConnection conn)
{
    //
    // Initilze insert command for reuse as well as params
    //
```

1. Create the command that will insert a new row into the database returning the row ID and BLOB to be populated with the contents of the file.

```
insertCommand = new OracleCommand
   ("Insert into Photos t values" +
   "(:1, :2, :3, Ordimage.Init(), OrdImage.Init())" +

   " returning " +
   "t.image.getContent(), ROWID into:4, :5",
   conn);
paramID = new OracleParameter("id",
                      OracleDbType.Int32,
                      ParameterDirection.Input);
insertCommand.Parameters.Add(paramID);
paramDesc = new OracleParameter("desc",
                      OracleDbType.Varchar2,
                      ParameterDirection.Input);
insertCommand.Parameters.Add(paramDesc);
paramLoc = new OracleParameter("loc",
                      OracleDbType.Varchar2,
                      ParameterDirection.Input);
insertCommand.Parameters.Add(paramLoc);
paramBlob = new OracleParameter("imgblob",
                      OracleDbType.Blob,
                      ParameterDirection.Output);
insertCommand.Parameters.Add(paramBlob);
paramRowid = new OracleParameter("rowid",
                      OracleDbType.Varchar2,
                      ParameterDirection.Output);
paramRowid.Size = 50;
insertCommand.Parameters.Add(paramRowid);

//
// Initialize setproperties and thumbnail creation
// command and parameters
//
```

2. Create the command that will set a default MIME type and attempt to set the properties of the image. If successful, a thumbnail is created.

```
processCommand = new OracleCommand
      ("DECLARE " +
      "  img ORDIMAGE; "+
      "  thumbnailORDIMAGE; " +
```

```
            "BEGIN " +
            "  select image, thumb into" +
            "   img, thumbnail fromPhotos " +
            "   where rowid = :1 for update; " +
            "  img.setMimetype(:2); "+
            "  BEGIN " +
            "    img.setProperties(); " +
            "    img.processCopy('fileFormat=JFIF " +
            "        maxScale=128 128', thumbnail); " +
            "  EXCEPTION WHEN OTHERS THEN " +
            "    thumbnail := NULL;   " +
            "  END;" +
            "  update Photos set image=img, " +
            "    thumb=thumbnail where rowid= :1; " +
            "END;",  conn);
    paramRowidIn = new OracleParameter("id",
                       OracleDbType.Varchar2,
                       ParameterDirection.Input);
    processCommand.Parameters.Add(paramRowidIn);
    // set default mime type based upon file Extension in
    // case of setProperties failure(image/<FILE_EXTENSION>)
    paramMime = new OracleParameter("mime",
                       OracleDbType.Varchar2,
                       ParameterDirection.Input);

    processCommand.Parameters.Add(paramMime);
}
```

5.4.6 Populating the Image Row

For the population of the image row, ODP.NET must have AutoCommit
set to false, which it is by default.

The following C# method inserts an image into the database, populates
the image raw data using the BLOB class, and then sets the properties of
the image. This is accomplished with the commands created in the previous
section, only the parameter values for these commands need to be set.

```
//
//Insert image in row and create thumbnail
//
private static void insertImageRow (OracleConnection conn,
```

```
                              uint id,
                              string descrip,
                              string location,
                              string fName)
        {
        //
        // Open input file to populate blob
        //
        BinaryReader inStream =
            new BinaryReader(
                File.Open(fName,System.IO.FileMode.Open));

        //
        // Start transaction
        //
```

1.   Start a transaction for the two commands.

```
        OracleTransaction trans =
            conn.BeginTransaction(IsolationLevel.ReadCommitted);

        //
        // Insert row into DB returning ID and blob to be
        // populated
        //
```

2.   Insert the row into the database, setting the necessary input parameters.

```
        paramID.Value = System.Convert.ToUInt32(id);
        paramDesc.Value = descrip;
        paramLoc.Value = location;
        paramRowid.Size = 50;
        insertCommand.ExecuteNonQuery();

        //
        // Obtain the rowid and media blob for transaction use
        //  .
```

3.   Get the returned parameters, the row ID, and the BLOB to populate.

```
OracleBlob blob =
  (OracleBlob)insertCommand.Parameters["imgblob"].Value;
OracleString rid =
  (OracleString)insertCommand.Parameters["rowid"].Value;

//
// Populate interMedia blob from file using stream
// interface
//
```

4. Copy the file to the BLOB.

```
long written = 0;
int bufsiz = blob.OptimumChunkSize * 8;
while(written < inStream.BaseStream.Length)
{
    byte [] buf = inStream.ReadBytes(bufsiz);
    blob.Write(buf, 0, buf.Length);
    written += buf.Length;
}
blob.Close();

  //
  // In the same transaction, Set the image properties
  // and create a thumbnail
  //
```

5. Set the input parameters and process the BLOB in the database.

```
paramRowidIn.Value = paramRowid.Value;
// set default mime type based upon file Extension in
// case of setProperties failure(image/<FILE_EXTENSION>)
paramMime.Value = "image/" +
          fName.Substring(fName.LastIndexOf(".") + 1);


processCommand.ExecuteNonQuery();
```

6. Commit the transaction; after this command, the row is available in the database.

```
        trans.Commit();
        return;
}
```

5.4.7 Extracting the Thumbnail from the Database into a File

The extraction of an image from the database into the file is simply done with a select command, obtaining the BLOB stream, and copying the stream data from the database into the file. The MIME type is also obtained and used to provide a file extension.

```
//
// Get thumbnail from the Photos table and put it in a file
//
private static void writeThumbnailFile
            (OracleConnection conn, uint id, string fprefix)
{
    //
    // Create select command to get thumnail image using ID
    //
```

1. Prepare and execute the SQL command to obtain the MIME type and binary thumbnail image.

```
OracleCommand cmd = new OracleCommand
        ("Select t.thumb.getContent(), " +
         " t.thumb.getMimetype() from Photos t " +
      "where t.id= :v1", conn);
OracleParameter paramID = new OracleParameter("id",
            OracleDbType.Int32,
            System.Convert.ToUInt32(id),
            ParameterDirection.Input);
cmd.Parameters.Add(paramID);

    //
    // Execute the command as a reader commmand
    //
    OracleDataReader reader = cmd.ExecuteReader();
    if (!reader.Read())
    {
```

```
                    Console.WriteLine("No data found for {0}",
                                    cmd.CommandText);
                 return;
            }

            //
            // Obtain the binary data and mimetype from the SELECT
            //
```

2.   Get the query results into local data types.

```
            OracleBlob blob = reader.GetOracleBlob(0);
            string mimeType = reader.GetString(1);

            //
            // Use the mimetype to create a file extension
            //
            string fName = fprefix + "." +
        mimeType.Substring(mimeType.LastIndexOf("/")+ 1);

            //
            // Create output file
            //
            BinaryWriter outStream = new BinaryWriter
                 (File.Open(fName,System.IO.FileMode.CreateNew));

            //
            // Write binary contents from database into file
            //
```

3.   Copy from the thumbnail BLOB to the output file.

```
            byte [] buf = new byte[blob.OptimumChunkSize * 8];
            long bytesWritten = 0;
            while (bytesWritten < blob.Length)
            {
                int len = blob.Read(buf, 0, buf.Length);
                outStream.Write(buf, 0, len);
                bytesWritten += len;
            }
```

```
       // Clean up
       outStream.Close();
       cmd.Dispose();

     return;
   }
```

5.5   Java Advanced Imaging *inter*Media APIs

It can be the case that the processing capabilities of *inter*Media do not include what is needed for a particular application. Perhaps it is necessary to merge two images, sharpen edges, or do other image-processing functions not available in *inter*Media.

Being the case that users may need additional image-processing capabilities, *inter*Media provides convenience classes so that Java Advanced Imaging (JAI) can interact with data stored in *inter*Media.

Some of the details are not covered here since they are covered in the previous chapters (e.g., creating the database connection).

The *inter*Media JAI I/O classes used in this demo are:

- oracle.ord.media.jai.io.BlobInputStream
- oracle.ord.media.jai.io.BlobOutputStream

There are other *inter*Media JAI I/O classes as well that are not directly used in this example, which are:

- oracle.ord.media.jai.io.BfileInputStream
- oracle.ord.media.jai.io.ByteArraySeekableOutputStream
- oracle.ord.media.jai.io.FileSeekableOutputStream
- oracle.ord.media.jai.io.MemoryCacheSeekableOutputStream
- oracle.ord.media.jai.io.SeekableOutputStream

All of the JAI-related *inter*Media classes are included in the Oracle *inter*Media jar file ordim.jar.

The example in the following section will do the following steps:

- Load the image into JAI from the file system.

- Create a row in the database for the image and thumbnail.

- Use JAI to encode the image as JPEG and store it into the database.

- Use JAI to create a JAI PlanarImage from the database for processing.

- Use JAI to scale the image to a half-size thumbnail image.

- Use JAI to encode and store this image into the database as a PNG image.

- Commit the row update.

- Reread the thumbnail image from the database into a JAI PlanarImage.

- Use Java image processing to paint a logo into the thumbnail in the lower right corner of the image.

- Use JAI to write the thumbnail with the logo into the file system.

5.5.1 JAI Includes

To prepare for processing, the following JAI classes are included. These classes include the classes provided by Oracle *inter*Media that allow JAI clients to access media stored in the database.

```
import javax.media.jai.*;
import javax.media.jai.operator.*;
import com.sun.media.jai.widget.DisplayJAI;
import com.sun.media.jai.codec.*;

import oracle.ord.media.jai.io.BlobInputStream;
import oracle.ord.media.jai.io.BlobOutputStream;
```

5.5.2 Creating the Database Row

The database row is created, as in the previous Java example, on a JDBC connection with AutoCommit turned off.

```
/**
 * Play with the image using Oracle and JAI
 */
```

```
void insertImageRow(int id, String desc,
                    String loc, String fileName,
                    Connection conn ) throws Exception
{
   //
   // Create JAI PlanarImage from file. We will
   // Stream this image, using JAI, into the
   // database using a java OutputStream.
   //
   //
   PlanarImage src = JAI.create("fileload", fileName);

   //
   // Create new row with image
   //
```

1. Create a statement to insert the row returning the ROWID and image objects.

```
CallableStatement cstmt =
  conn.prepareCall (
  "begin " +
  "insert into photos t (id, description, " +

   "                   location, image, thumb) " +
   " values (?, ?, ?, ORDImage.init(), " +
   "         ORDImage.init())" +
   " returning rowid, t.image, t.thumb into " +
   "              ?, ?, ? ; " +
  "end;");

// Register input parameters
cstmt.setInt(1, id);
cstmt.setString(2, desc);
cstmt.setString(3, loc);
// Register Output Parameters
// RowID, Image and Thumbnail image
cstmt.registerOutParameter(4, Types.VARCHAR);
cstmt.registerOutParameter(5, Types.STRUCT,
                           "ORDIMAGE");
cstmt.registerOutParameter(6, Types.STRUCT,
                           "ORDIMAGE");
```

2. Execute the statement and obtain the ROWID and image objects.

```
int rowsUpdated  = cstmt.executeUpdate();
String rowid = cstmt.getString(4);
OrdImage imgObj = (OrdImage)
  ((OracleCallableStatement)cstmt).getORAData(5,
                    OrdImage.getORADataFactory());
OrdImage thumbObj = (OrdImage)
  ((OracleCallableStatement)cstmt).getORAData(6,
                    OrdImage.getORADataFactory());
cstmt.close();

//
// Populate image BLOB with JAI image using JAI
// to convert the image to jpg
// And using the interMedia BlobOutputStream for JAI
//
```

3. Use *inter*Media to create JAI-usable output stream and JAI to encode images as JPEGs and place them into database BLOB.

```
BlobOutputStream bos =
  new BlobOutputStream((java.sql.Blob)
                    imgObj.getContent());
JAI.create("Encode", src, bos, "JPEG" , null);
bos.close();

//
// Set the image properties
//
```

4. Tell the database to set the image properties.

```
imgObj.setProperties();

//
// re-Create JAI image from database Blob based
// stream using the interMedia BlobInputStream class
//
```

5. As an exercise, use the newly created image in the database as input to JAI.

```
BlobInputStream bis =
    new BlobInputStream((java.sql.Blob)
                            imgObj.getContent());
src = JAI.create("Stream", bis);

//
// Use JAI to make thumbnail here
//
ParameterBlock pb = new ParameterBlock();
pb.addSource(src);          // The source image
pb.add(0.5F);               // The xScale
pb.add(0.5F);               // The yScale
pb.add(0.0F);               // The x translation
pb.add(0.0F);               // The y translation
pb.add(new InterpolationNearest());//Scale algorithm


// scale the image using JAI
```

6. Use JAI to scale the image from the database.

```
PlanarImage thumb = JAI.create("Scale", pb, null);

//
// Save thumbnail image into database as PNG format
//
```

7. As we have done with the image, use JAI and *inter*Media JAI classes to store the scaled image as a PNG image. Use *inter*Media to set the properties of the image.

```
bos = new BlobOutputStream((java.sql.Blob)
                            thumbObj.getContent());
JAI.create("Encode", thumb, bos, "PNG" , null);
bos.close();
thumbObj.setProperties();
```

```
//
// Update database row with JAI created thumbnail
//
```

8. Update the row with the image and thumbnail and commit the transaction.

```
OraclePreparedStatement updateImages =
    (OraclePreparedStatement)conn.prepareStatement(
        "Update photos set image= ?, thumb = ? " +
        "    where rowid = ?" );
updateImages.setORAData(1, imgObj);
updateImages.setORAData(2, thumbObj);
updateImages.setString(3, rowid);
updateImages.execute();
updateImages.close();

//
// Commit the transaction
//
conn.commit();

//
// Display original and thumbnail image
//
add(new DisplayJAI(src), BorderLayout.NORTH);

add(new DisplayJAI(thumb), BorderLayout.WEST);
}
```

5.5.3 Get the Thumbnail Image, Put a Logo on the Image, and Put the Image into a File

Now that the image is in the database, we can query the database to obtain the thumbnail. Unlike what we have done in the past, a logo will be painted into the thumbnail. This additional functionality is here to demonstrate the ease of processing images from the database. In a real application, we would probably put the logo on the thumbnail when the row was inserted into the database.

```
    void writeThumbnailFile(int id, Connection conn)
                                        throws Exception
  {
      //
      // Select the thumbnail
      //
```

1. Obtain the thumbnail image from the database.

```
      OraclePreparedStatement selectThumb =
          (OraclePreparedStatement)conn.prepareStatement(
            "select thumb from photos where id = ?" );
      selectThumb.setInt(1, id);
      OracleResultSet rset =
          (OracleResultSet)selectThumb.executeQuery();
      rset.next();
      OrdImage thumbObj =
          (OrdImage)rset.getORAData(1,
                          OrdImage.getORADataFactory());
      selectThumb.close();

      //
      // Get the thumbnail into a JAI image
      //
```

2. Use JAI and *inter*Media JAI classes to load an image into JAI PlanarImage

```
      BlobInputStream bis =
        new BlobInputStream((java.sql.Blob)
                              thumbObj.getContent());
      PlanarImage thumbnail = JAI.create("Stream", bis);
      //
      // Get the logo to place into lower right
      //
```

3. Load a logo image from a prepopulated logos table. Use the first logo in the table.

```
OraclePreparedStatement selectLogo =
    (OraclePreparedStatement)conn.prepareStatement(
        "select logo from logos where id = 1" );
rset = (OracleResultSet)selectLogo.executeQuery();
rset.next();
OrdImage logoObj =
    (OrdImage)rset.getORAData(1,
                        OrdImage.getORADataFactory());
selectLogo.close();
bis = new BlobInputStream
            ((java.sql.Blob)logoObj.getContent());
PlanarImage logo = JAI.create("Stream", bis);

//
// Now that we have the thumbnail and logo,
// draw logo into lower right corner.
//
BufferedImage thumbBi =
                thumbnail.getAsBufferedImage();
```

4.   Paint the logo into the lower right corner of the thumbnail.

```
Graphics2D g2d = thumbBi.createGraphics();
g2d.drawImage(logo.getAsBufferedImage(),
        null,
        thumbnail.getWidth()-logo.getWidth(),
        thumbnail.getHeight()-logo.getHeight());

//
// Save the thumbnail with logo into a file
//
```

5.   Create a file in PNG format with the thumbnail with the logo file.

```
JAI.create("filestore", thumbBi,
        "thumbLogo" + id + ".png", "PNG", null);

//
// Display the image with logo
```

```
            //
            add(new DisplayJAI(thumbBi), BorderLayout.EAST);

            addWindowListener(new WindowAdapter() {
                    public void windowClosing(WindowEvent e)
                        { System.exit(0); }
            });
            pack();
            show();
        }
```

5.5.4 Running the Sample

To run the sample, the methods in the previous two sections are included into a class with the following signature.

```
    public class jaiIm extends Frame {

        public static void main(String[] args) throws Exception {
            if (args.length != 4) {
                System.out.println("usage: java jaiIm " +
                "connectionString username password inputFile");
                System.out.println("e.g.   java laiIm " +
                "jdbc:oracle:oci:@inst1 scott tiger " +

                    "myImage.jpg");
                System.exit(-1);
            }

            // register the oracle jdbc driver with the JDBC
            //driver manager
```

1. Connect to the database, and make sure to set AutoCommit to false.

```
            DriverManager.registerDriver
                    (new oracle.jdbc.driver.OracleDriver());
            Connection conn =
                DriverManager.getConnection(args[0], args[1],
                                        args[2]);
```

```
// Note: it is CRITICAL to set the autocommit to
// false so that two-phase select-commit of BLOBS
// can occur.
conn.setAutoCommit(false);

jaiIm jaiim = new jaiIm();
```

2. Perform the processing in the previous two sections.

```
jaiim.insertImageRow(17, "jai Description",
                         "jai location",
                         args[3], conn);
jaiim.writeThumbnailFile(17, conn);
}
```

The execution of the example given above will result in the display shown in Figure 5.4, as well as a new database row and thumbnail with logo file. The top image is the original image, the lower left image is the thumbnail image, and the lower right is the thumbnail with logo image. Note that the logo has some transparent pixels so the image appears to wrap the text.

Figure 5.4
*Original Image,
Scaled Image,
Scaled Image
with Overlay*

5.6   Summary

The examples in this section are just quick examples of how to use *inter*Media from some APIs. More complete and intensive data storage and manipulation are possible.

To use *inter*Media from an Oracle database requires an API that can perform SQL operations, operate on binary database BLOBS, and make use of PL/SQL procedures. Since these are the only requirements, the examples given in this section are only a subset of the APIs that can make use of *inter*Media. The processing using these other APIs will be similar to those examples that do not have *inter*Media convenience classes.

In addition to these requirements, *inter*Media provides convenience APIs for some interfaces. These include the Java and JAI environments.

6

Loading Media

A very important consideration in a database-backed media application is how the data is loaded into the database. Depending on where the data comes from, and who is responsible for loading it, very different methods will be optimal. For example, an online photo album application will have very different loading requirements than a bank check image electronic storage and transmission application.

In the photo album example, it is clearly necessary to have users upload their pictures from their browsers or a custom desktop application that can batch an upload of a large number of pictures. Most photo album applications provide both.

In the batch processing environment of digitally scanning bank checks and storing them, the volume of data is critical and must be addressed. Loading the media will likely involve multiple streams of data that may need to load tens of thousands of checks per hour. Once in the database, these checks can then be transmitted for digital clearance or displayed to users from their online banking application.

In this chapter, we will look at various ways of loading *inter*Media data into the database.

6.1 PL/SQL

We have seen previous examples of loading data using PL/SQL from the file system in introductory sections. In this section we will look in more detail about using *inter*Media to load data using PL/SQL. We will not be describing nondatabase storage, except in the context of preparation to load the media into the database. Some of the features of loading using *inter*Media PL/SQL methods include:

- Supports and has many media-specific methods available to create or modify media objects.

- Uses methods, for example, setProperties(), setMimeType(), and so forth, to set attributes.

- Provides an interface that may already be familiar to SQL users.

- Provides immediate error feedback when procedures are compiled interactively from SQL.

- Requires target media stored in file systems to be on a device that is local to the database server.

- Sets image attributes in the import() method with an automatic call to the setProperties() method (for supported formats).

- Sets audio, video, and supported media data attributes, but not automatically as part of the import() method. The script must call the import() method and call the setProperties() method.

*inter*Media object methods can be used to load multimedia data from the following data sources:

- A media file from the file system
- Media from the Internet using HTTP
- Media using a custom data source plug-in

6.1.1   Loading from Local Files

Most users will be concerned with loading media from files. Please note that the files must be local to the database computer file system, not to where a user is running PL/SQL.

For an HTTP source, the images are pulled from websites using HTTP requests, not being pushed into the database from forms submitted by users. This could be useful in creating an archive of images from the database.

If the user has specialized requirements, like pulling and/or pushing image data from a proprietary image archive only accessible from an API, a custom data source plug-in may be written by the user.

Here is an example of loading an image, audio, and video onto the database into the same row from files local to the database server.

```
DECLARE
  img ORDImage;
  aud ORDAudio;
  vid ORDVideo;
  ctx RAW(64) := NULL;
  row_id urowid;
BEGIN
  -- Insert a new row into the pm.online_media table
  DELETE FROM pm.online_media WHERE product_id = 3003;
  INSERT INTO pm.online_media
          (product_id,
           product_photo,
           product_audio,
           product_video)
  VALUES (3003,
          ORDImage.init('FILE', 'MEDIA_DIR', 'laptop.jpg'),
          ORDAudio.init('FILE', 'MEDIA_DIR', 'laptop.mpa'),
          ORDVideo.init('FILE', 'MEDIA_DIR', 'laptop.rm'))
    RETURNING product_photo, product_audio, product_video,
rowid
    INTO img, aud, vid, row_id;

  -- Bring the media into the database and populate
  -- the attributes
  img.import(ctx);
  -- ORDImage.import also calls ORDImage.setProperties;

  aud.import(ctx);
  aud.setProperties(ctx);

  vid.import(ctx);
  vid.setProperties(ctx);

  -- update the table with the properties we have extracted
  UPDATE pm.online_media
  SET    product_photo = img,
         product_audio = aud,
         product_video = vid
  WHERE  rowid = row_id;

  COMMIT;
END;
/
```

Note that the image does not require a setProperties() method call since this is done implicitly.

6.1.2 Loading from an HTTP Source

For an HTTP source, the images are pulled from websites using HTTP requests, not being pushed into the database from forms submitted by users. This could be useful in creating an archive of images from the database.

Loading from an HTTP source is very similar to loading from a file source. The only difference is that the location of the data is specified differently. However, you may need to set some additional parameters using the utl_http package. In the following example the proxy server is set to www-proxy.acme.com on port 80 except for computers in the *.acme.com domain.

```
DECLARE
   img ORDImage;
   thumbnail ORDImage;
   ctx RAW(64) := NULL;
   row_id urowid;
BEGIN

   utl_http.set_proxy('www-
   proxy.us.acme.com:80','*.us.acme.com');

   INSERT INTO photos
          (id,
           description,
           location,
           image,
           thumb)
   VALUES (202,
           'Goats',
           'Fields in Maine',
           ORDImage.init(),
           ORDImage.init())
   RETURNING image, thumb, rowid INTO img, thumb, row_id;

   -- Bring the media into the database and populate
   -- the attributes
   img.importFrom(ctx, 'HTTP',
```

```
                          'www.oracle.com/admin/images','oralogo.gif');

          -- ORDImage.import also calls ORDImage.setProperties;

          img.processCopy('fileFormat=JFIF maxScale=128 128',
          thumbnail);

          -- Update and commit the row
          update photos set image=img, thumb=thumbnail where rowid =
          row_id;
          commit;

       END;
       /
```

You can see that the difference is mostly how the image source is specified. For an HTTP source we specify the type as `'HTTP'`, the Web server (without the http://), and Web server path as `'www.oracle.com/admin/images'`, and the endpoint as the file `'oralogo.gif'`.

6.1.3 Loading from a User Written Source

If the user has specialized requirements, like pulling and/or pushing image data from a proprietary image archive only accessible from an API, a custom data source plug-in may be written by the user.

6.1.4 Unrecognized Formats

Because of the rich plethora of media formats that exist, both proprietary and public domain, old and new, it may be the case that when loading media data into the database, the format of the media is not recognized by *inter*Media. In this case, the user may have to set metadata about the media manually. The most important information to gather is the MIME type of the media. This can typically be determined by either file extension, or for HTTP data, the MIME type passed as part of the HTTP response in the Content-Type header field.

You may also want to avoid the processing of the media data that determines the metadata for performance reasons. You may already know what type of data is being inserted, and either know other metadata or simply be uninterested in fully specifying the full metadata. For example, if you are batch loading check images that are always the same height, width, and

MIME type, and that is all the metadata you are interested in, you can set this metadata manually and avoid the extra overhead of the setProperties method. Time-based media types may require scanning the entire data stream to collect metadata.

The image import method is slightly different from the import methods used by audio, video, and document objects. If used without extra parameters, or without metadata, it will perform a setProperties implicitly.

The following example shows an image object being loaded into the database, setting the type of the media manually.

```
create or replace procedure upload_image_noset
    (file_name varchar2,
     prikey_id number,
     descr varchar2,
     loc varchar2)
as
    imgobj          ORDSYS.ORDImage;
    ctx          raw(64):=null;
    thisrowid urowid;

BEGIN
    insert into photos t (id, description, location,
        image, thumb)
          values (prikey_id, descr, loc,
                    ORDSYS.ORDImage.init(),
                    ORDSYS.ORDImage.init())
          returning rowid, t.image into thisrowid, imgobj;

    -- Make Sure import does not call setProperties
    imgobj.fileFormat := 'OTHER';

    imgobj.importFrom(ctx, 'FILE', 'IMAGEDIR', file_name);

    -- Set the properties manually
    imgobj.mimeType := 'image/vnd.fujixerox.edmics-rlc';
    imgobj.height := 321;
    imgobj.width := 123;

    update photos t set t.image=imgobj where rowid =
      thisrowid;
END;
/
```

It may also be that only a portion of the images you are loading cannot be recognized. In this case, you may want to catch the exception and set MIME type metadata information explicitly as in the following example.

```
create or replace procedure upload_image_setmime
    (file_name varchar2,
     prikey_id number,
     descr varchar2,
     loc varchar2)
as
    imgobj          ORDSYS.ORDImage;
    ctx             raw(64):=null;
    thisrowid       urowid;
    ext             varchar2(10);
BEGIN
    insert into photos t (id, description, location, image,
thumb)
            values (prikey_id, descr, loc,
                        ORDSYS.ORDImage.init(),
ORDSYS.ORDImage.init())
          returning rowid, t.image into thisrowid, imgobj;


    BEGIN
      imgobj.importFrom(ctx, 'FILE', 'IMAGEDIR', file_name);


    EXCEPTION
      WHEN OTHERS THEN
        -- Is this an unsupported format error?
        if (INSTR(sqlerrm, 'IMG-00705') != 0) then
          -- Metadata cannot be automatically set. Try and
          -- set mimetype by file extension
          ext := SUBSTR(file_name, INSTR(file_name,'.'));
          if (UPPER(ext) = '.RLC') then
            imgobj.fileformat := 'OTHER';
            imgobj.import(ctx);
            imgobj.setMimeType
                ('image/vnd.fujixerox.edmics-rlc');
          elsif (UPPER(ext) = '.DWG') then
            imgobj.fileformat := 'OTHER';
```

```
                imgobj.import(ctx);
                imgobj.setMimeType('image/vnd.dwg');
            else
                raise; -- Could not determine mimetype
            end if;
        else
            raise;
        end if;
    END;

    update photos t set t.image=imgobj where rowid =
        thisrowid;

END;
```

Something like the above could also be done on HTTP data passing the Content-Type from the Request or Response header to set the MIME type.

For audio and video, loading unrecognized data using PL/SQL is much more straightforward. If you know that format is not recognized, you can simply skip the setProperties() step and set what you do know about the media in the object. Setting metadata for audio and video can be an expensive operation that may include scanning the entire file for some formats. So, depending on your loading needs, you may want to set the metadata manually. Here is a similar example of loading an audio and setting the MIME type of the data if we can figure out what it is. A video load would be very similar.

```
create or replace procedure upload_audio_setmime
    (file_name varchar2,
     prikey_id number,
     descr varchar2,
     loc varchar2)
as
    audobj        ORDSYS.ORDAudio;
    ctx           raw(64):=null;
    thisrowid     urowid;
    ext           varchar2(10);
BEGIN
    insert into sounds t (id, description, location, sound)
        values (prikey_id, descr, loc,
```

```
                    ORDSYS.ORDAudio.init())
            returning rowid, t.sound into thisrowid, audobj;


         audobj.importFrom(ctx, 'FILE', 'AUDIODIR', file_name);

    BEGIN

      audobj.setproperties(ctx);

    EXCEPTION
      WHEN OTHERS THEN
          -- Metadata cannot be automatically set. Try and set
          -- mimetype by file extension
          ext := SUBSTR(file_name, INSTR(file_name,'.'));
          if (UPPER(ext) = '.QCP') then
              audobj.setMimeType('audio/EVRC-QCP');
          elsif (UPPER(ext) = '.AMR') then
              audobj.setMimeType('audio/AMR');
          else
              raise; -- Could not determine minmetype
          end if;
    END;

    update sounds t set t.sound=audobj where rowid =
        thisrowid;

  END;
  /
```

With audio and video, since setProperties() is never called explicitly, we don't need to identify the exception type.

Another way to handle unrecognized media formats is to use your own media parser. For example, if metadata extraction fails, you may want to set the metadata in the media object using your own parser.

```
DECLARE
  img ORDImage;
  row_id urowid;
BEGIN
```

```
Select image, rowid into img, row_id from photos where ID
    = 10 for update;
begin
    img.setProperties();
    EXCEPTION
      WHEN OTHERS THEN
        -- Is this an unsupported format error?
        if (INSTR(sqlerrm, 'IMG-00705') != 0) then
            myMediaPackage.mySetProperties(img);
        else
            raise;
        end if;
end;

    update photos set image=img where rowid=row_id;
    commit;
END;
```

In myMediaPackage.mySetProperties(img) you would use the BLOB, and a stored procedure, a stored JAVA procedure, or an external procedure to parse the data and set the appropriate attributes in the image object.

6.1.5   PL/SQL Loading Methods Performance Considerations

When loading media into the database using *inter*Media PL/SQL methods, the following items should be considered for best performance:

- Disable logging on LOB columns. Re-execute the procedure to recover a failed data load transaction. This avoids the large amount of binary data being copied into the REDO log file for rolling forward. It is important to realize that this means that you will be responsible for saving the media data, before the next database backup, in the case of database failure (if there is not an alternate database failure recovery mechanism).

- Load the media data in smaller groups if you run out of resources.

- Do not use the Oracle cache option for LOB columns. You can turn on caching after the load operation is complete by using the SQL ALTER TABLE MODIFY LOB CACHE statement.

- Use the INSERT RETURNING clause to obtain empty *inter*Media objects that were just inserted into the database for data loading later in the procedure.

- Use ROWIDs to reference rows that are being worked on. The ROWID is obtained in either a SELECT ROWID ... INTO statement or an INSERT RETURNING ROWID ... INTO clause.

- If you can set the object metadata manually, rather than having the metadata populated with media-processing functions (using the setProperties() method either explicitly or implicitly) you can increase performance.

6.2   SQL*Loader

Another option for loading *inter*Media data into the database is SQL*Loader. The main advantage over PL/SQL and external table loading (covered in the next section) is that using SQL*Loader allows you to load the media over the network. The main disadvantage to SQL*Loader is that object-relational methods, like setProperties(), cannot be invoked with it. These methods can be invoked after the images are loaded if necessary in another procedure.

However, the lack of ability to call methods may not be an issue if it is decided to skip automatic metadata extraction and set the metadata manually. You can use this technique to populate as much known metadata in the media object as you like.

Here is an example of an SQL*Loader control file that loads the raw images into a table, and also sets minimal metadtata, the MIME type, in the image object.

```
LOAD DATA
INFILE *
INTO TABLE photos
APPEND
FIELDS TERMINATED BY ','
(id,
 description,
 location,
 image column object
     (
         mimetype,
```

```
                          source column object
                          (
                            localData_fname FILLER CHAR(12),
                            localData LOBFILE(image.source.localData_fname) raw
                            terminated by EOF
                          )
                        )
                      )
```

```
BEGINDATA
3,Goats,Hampshire,image/gif,goats.gif,
4,Flowers,Vermont,image/jpg,flowers.jpg,
```

To Invoke SQL*Loader, the following command line is used:

```
sqlldr control=loadimage.ctl log=loadimage.log userid=scott/
tiger@remotedb
```

As you can see, the ID, the MIME type, and the raw image binary data is loaded in the table. If it is necessary to set further properties of the images, a PL/SQL procedure can be written to scan through the rows and set the image properties, as in the following example.

```
CREATE OR REPLACE Procedure SetPropsAfterSQLLoader
IS
    total_val number(6);
    cursor c is
      select image, rowid from photos for update;

BEGIN

    total_val := 0;

    FOR row_rec in c
    LOOP
        -- Try not to set properties on images already done
        if (row_rec.image.getWidth() is null) then
          row_rec.image.setProperties();
          update photos t set t.image = row_rec.image
                              where rowid = row_rec.rowid;
        end if;
```

```
        END LOOP;
      commit;
  END;
  /
  show errors;
```

6.3   External Tables

Somewhere between PL/SQL and SQL*Loader, is the functionality of database external tables. These tables have the ability to define database tables from flat files stored on the file system. This features uses similar technology to PL/SQL and SQL*Loader.

Note that it is possible to load data using parallel processing that can be tuned with external tables. To load media from external tables, five things are necessary to set up:

1.   A file that holds the table data.

2.   A directory specification.

3.   An external table data file.

4.   A table defined on the data file.

5.   A procedure to copy the data to media objects.

The file that holds the table could contain the following data that looks much like an SQL*Loader table:

```
10,Goats,Somewhere over the rainbow,goats.gif
11,Flowers,Field in NH,flowers.jpg
:
:
:
```

As we have seen before, a directory specification must be defined from a user who has the create directory privilege, and use of that directory must be assigned to the user.

```
SQL> CREATE DIRECTORY LOADMEDIADIR AS 'C:\LOADMEDIADIR';
SQL> GRANT READ ON DIRECTORY LOADMEDIADIR TO SCOTT;
```

Now that the directory definition and data file have been created, a table definition can be defined that will allow the database to see this file as a read-only SQL table:

```
create table EXTERNAL_MEDIA_TABLE
   (id VARCHAR2(10), Descr VARCHAR2(40), loc VARCHAR2(40),
blobdata BLOB)
      ORGANIZATION EXTERNAL
       (TYPE ORACLE_LOADER DEFAULT DIRECTORY LOADMEDIADIR
       ACCESS PARAMETERS
         (RECORDS DELIMITED BY NEWLINE
           FIELDS terminated by ',' (id CHAR(2),
                         descr CHAR(40),
                         loc CHAR(40), b char(50))
            COLUMN TRANSFORMS (blobdata from LOBFILE(b))
          )
         LOCATION ('tst_ext.dat'))
       PARALLEL;
```

The table we define does not define a *inter*Media type because the definition of an object-relational type is not supported with external tables. Of importance here is the COLUMN TRANSFORMS clause. This clause takes the file name specified in the data file and transforms it into a BLOB. At this point we can do some standard SQL operation on the table we have just defined, for example:

```
SQL> SELECT ID, DESCR, LOC FROM EXTERNAL_MEDIA_TABLE;
```

At this point, we are ready to move the data to a fully-qualified database media table. This is done with a PL/SQL procedure. This procedure will copy the BLOB data from the external table into an internal table, get the properties of the image, and populate the thumbnail with a scaled down version of the image.

```
Declare
    cursor c is
       select id, descr, loc, blobdata from
EXTERNAL_MEDIA_TABLE;
      img ORDSYS.ORDIMAGE;
      thmb ORDSYS.ORDIMAGE;
```

```
            thisrowid urowid;
begin

    for rec in c
    LOOP
        insert into photos t (id, description, location, image,
                                thumb)
            values (rec.id, rec.descr, rec.loc,
                    ORDSYS.ORDImage.init(),
                    ORDSYS.ORDImage.init())
            returning rowid, t.image, t.thumb into thisrowid, img,
                    thmb;

        img.source.localdata := rec.blobdata;

        img.setproperties();

        img.processCopy('fileFormat=JFIF maxScale=128 128',
                    thmb);

        update photos t set t.image=img, t.thumb=thmb where
                rowid = thisrowid;

        commit;

    END LOOP;
end;
/

drop table EXTERNAL_MEDIA_TABLE;
```

We use a cursor to select all the records from EXTERNAL_MEDIA_
TABLE. This information is inserted into the database table as well as some
initialized media data types. The BLOB data is then copied to the image
object, and a setProperties() method extracts metadata from the image. We
could catch any exceptions here and handle them by rejecting the image, or
perhaps set MIME type based on file extension, but in this case, we are sat-
isfied that the input data is a standard that is understood. The thumbnail is
then created and the row updated.

After the data is loaded, the external table can be dropped.

Oracle Data Pump

Data Pump can be used to export media data into a binary file, load this file into another database, or move media data from one database to another over the network. By itself, it cannot do an initial load of multimedia data into the database, but it is worth mentioning here because it is a powerful tool for moving media data from place to place.

Data Pump may be used in various situations where you need to move media data. One such example would be to synchronize media data from a central website to sites around the world so that local customers or users have faster access. Another example may be to distribute the media-processing load. An application that has to load hundreds of thousands of images per hour that require processing, like metadata extraction, format conversion, and scaling, may choose to distribute the load by performing image processing into satellite systems before using Data Pump to move the data to a centralized site.

One way to export media data using Data Pump is to use the expdp utility. This can easily create a Data Pump binary file. For example:

```
C:\>expdp scott/tiger TABLES=photos DUMPFILE=DPDIR:photos.dmp
LOGFILE=DPDIR:photos.log
```

After the Data Pump file is created, it can be used to import data into another database.

To import the data into another database the impdp command can be used as follows:

```
C:\>impdp scott/tiger TABLES=photos DIRECTORY=DPIMPDIR
DUMPFILE=photos.dmp
```

You can also use Data Pump to directly transfer information from one database to another. To copy directly from one database to another using Data Pump, a network link must be created in the target database:

```
SQL> create Database Link remote connect to scott identified
by tiger using 'remotedb';
```

You can then use impdp on this system to import a table directly from a remote database into a local target database:

```
C:\>impdp scott/tiger TABLES=photos DIRECTORY=dpdir
NETWORK_LINK=remote
```

Note that the DIRECTORY clause is still necessary if you want a log of the import operation. The log will be created in the directory specified.

If you only want to add rows from a remote database to the local target database into an existing table, the CONTEXT=DATA_ONLY clause is used:

```
C:\>impdp scott/tiger TABLES=photos DIRECTORY=dpdir
NETWORK_LINK=remote  CONTENT=DATA_ONLY
```

6.4 Transportable Tablespaces

Database tablespaces are files that are a part of the database. These tablespace files contain the data that are stored in tables, in the case we are interested in, where the media table data is stored.

One feature of the Oracle Database Enterprise Edition is transportable tablespaces. A transportable tablespace allows a system administrator to move a subset of a database from one database and plug it into another database. This can be a table partition, a table, or a set of tables. This can be useful for a number of media applications including:

- Incremental backups of media database.
- Copying media data to other media databases.
- Archival of historical media.

Moving data using transportable tablespaces is quicker than import/export or Data Pump operations. This is because the tablespace file is simply copied from one system to another. The transportable tablespace metadata is imported into the target database to make it available.

To be transportable, a set of tablespaces to be transported must be self-contained. That is to say that references within the tablespace cannot reference data outside the tablespace set, for example, an index in the tablespace referencing a table outside the tablespace set.

To make use of transportable tables, it is typically necessary to partition the media tables into a number of tablespaces. You may also want to place the binary media data into a tablespace separate from the other table data. You can then transport these tablespaces as a tablespace set.

To create a table that will be used for historical archiving, it can be partitioned so that only a certain date range is placed into the tablespace. When the data is ready to be archived, it can be removed from the database and placed in archive.

Let us assume that we do want to archive pictures after every month. First, we will need a tablespace for each month. Using a SYSDBA account, we create the following tablespaces:

```
CREATE TABLESPACE augustPhotos DATAFILE 'augustPhotos.dbf'
SIZE 20M;
CREATE TABLESPACE septemberPhotos DATAFILE
'septemberPhotos.dbf' SIZE 20M;
```

From a user account, we can now create the photos table with the addition of a date to segment the photographs by date.

```
CREATE TABLE photos
                  (id           NUMBER PRIMARY KEY,
                  description   VARCHAR2(40) NOT NULL,
                  location      VARCHAR2(40),
                  created       DATE,
                  image         ORDSYS.ORDIMAGE,
                  thumb         ORDSYS.ORDIMAGE)
        PARTITION BY RANGE (created)
        (partition august VALUES LESS THAN
            (TO_DATE('01-SEP-2005'))
            tablespace augustphotos,
        partition september VALUES LESS THAN
            (TO_DATE('1-OCT-2005'))
            tablespace septemberPhotos);
```

We can add partitions as needed, for example:

```
CREATE TABLESPACE octoberPhotos DATAFILE 'octoberPhotos.dbf'
SIZE 20M LOGGING;
ALTER TABLE photos ADD PARTITION october VALUES LESS THAN
(TO_DATE('01-NOV-2005')) tablespace octoberPhotos;
```

To move the August partition from the photos table, and make the tablespace transportable and self-contained, all outside references must be removed. To do this, we have to exchange the table data into another table and remove the partition from the photos table.

```
CREATE TABLE photos_august
                (id          NUMBER PRIMARY KEY,
                 description VARCHAR2(40) NOT NULL,
                 location    VARCHAR2(40),
                 created     DATE,
                 image       ORDSYS.ORDIMAGE,
                 thumb       ORDSYS.ORDIMAGE)
            tablespace augustphotos;
```

```
ALTER TABLE photos
    EXCHANGE PARTITION august WITH TABLE photos_august
    WITHOUT VALIDATION;
```

```
ALTER TABLE PHOTOS DROP PARTITION august;
```

From an SYSDBA account, to move this tablespace to another database, we make the tablespace read-only:

```
ALTER TABLESPACE augustPhotos READ ONLY;
```

We then use Data Pump to gather the metadata necessary to transport the tablespace from one system to the next.

```
C:\>EXPDP system/welcome1 DUMPFILE=augustPhotos.dmp
DIRECTORY=dpdir    TRANSPORT_TABLESPACES='augustPhotos';
```

At this point, the Data Pump metadata file, augustPhotos.dmp, and tablespace file, augustPhotos.dbf, are copied to the target system using your favorite utility.

On the target system,

```
C:\>IMPDP system/manager1 DUMPFILE=AUGUSTPHOTOS.dmp
DIRECTORY=dpimpdir TRANSPORT_DATAFILES=c:\plsql\
AUGUSTPHOTOS.DBF
```

If we want to make the tablespace writeable, we can do this using the alter command on the target and original database from an SYSDBA account:

```
SQL> ALTER TABLESPACE READ WRITE;
```

At this time we may want to add this partition to an existing partitioned table in the target database. Let us assume this table is named photos_archive with the same definition as the photos_table. The first thing we need to do is to add a partition to the target table:

```
SQL> ALTER TABLE photos_archive ADD PARTITION august VALUES
LESS THAN (to_date('01-SEP-2006'));
```

At this point, we exchange this partition with the table we just added to the database:

```
SQL> alter table photos_archive exchange partition august
with table photos_august WITHOUT VALIDATION;
```

Now, we have added the archived photos to the photos_archive table.

6.5   HTTP Form Load

In many applications, loading of the data through Web forms is desirable. Media applications are no exception. There are many techniques to create server Web applications to load media data. These are covered in other chapters.

The one thing that is common to all loading of HTTP data is the HTML code necessary to download. For media applications, you must download a file that is local to the client system. A Web form to upload media will require the following code:

- The enclosing form has the attribute `method="post"`.

- The enclosing form has the attribute `enctype="multipart/form-data"`.

- The form has an input form element with the `type="file"` attribute.

Following is a simple example of a Web form that uploads a file to a Web server.

```
<form action="http://www.oracle.com/upload_media"
      enctype="multipart/form-data" method="post">
<p>
Input file name:<br>
<input type="file" name="mediafile" size="40">
</p>
<p>
<input type="submit" value="Upload">
</p>
</form>
```

You can have as many file input fields as you like to upload more than one media file at a time.

The most important advantage of using a Web form as an interface is the fact that Web browsers are ubiquitous. There is no need to ship an application out to clients.

6.6   Thick Client Loading

Another way to load media data into the database is to use a thick client. If you have ever dealt with having to upload digital images to a site to order prints, you will have noticed that many allow upload of images from either a Web browser or their custom written application that you can download from their site. They created the thick client to make their service more usable and friendly.

A thick client can have many advantages including:

- A more user-friendly interface that includes drag, drop, cut, and paste so that you can easily select a number of files to be uploaded in a batch.

- Since you have control of the upload data stream, it is possible to create an application that will restart failed batch uploads at the point of failure.

- Better feedback to the user on upload status, how much time is left, percent done, etc.

Examples of loading data with a thick client have been given in the introduction to *inter*Media's API section.

6.7   Summary

There are numerous ways to load media data and to move media data from one database to another. This chapter has outlined a number of these techniques.

Which method that is chosen will depend highly on the type of data, the volume of data, and where the data is coming from. For example, if the data is coming from users, it is probably best to use a Web form so that they can insert the media directly into the database and analyze the media. If the data is coming from a high-speed scanner, it may be best to load the data from the scanner result files and skip the somewhat expensive step of extracting metadata from the media by analyzing the media since most of this metadata is known beforehand.

7

Planning inter*Media Applications*

7.1   Introduction

This chapter is about planning a rich-media application from the point of gathering the requirements to testing the implemented system. The application may be a straight forward rich-media application rather like the Family Picture Book (see Chapter 3) with a simple Web user interface connecting to the database. Or as increasingly is the case the rich-media application will be part of a more complex information system where interoperability of the component parts might be a significant requirement.

In this chapter we will introduce various techniques to collect the requirements, plan the stages of the implementation, prototype, and test the system. This is a good point to reflect on what is special about rich-media applications so that we can recognize where there would be problems in development.

- The applications are often novel so there may be few or no existing systems that we can learn from.

- The collection of rich-media data and its related metadata is a much more significant problem than in text-only applications and will need to be planned.

- The data itself may be the product or service being provided to the customer.

- Identifying what the users actually want and what will be useful to them is more difficult, particularly where content-based retrieval (see Chapter 13) is a requirement.

- Uncertainty about user and technology requirements may increase the risk in terms of time and resources required to develop the system.

- The presentation of the rich media could be through a number of different channels—desktop, Web interface, mobile phone, PDA, iPOD, etc.

Information systems (IS) have been getting more complex. There are many reasons for this. Early systems were based on batch processing where data entry and report generation were in the hands of the IT departments themselves. Now end users are responsible for their own IS, and the complexity of the IS tasks has changed to cover not just operational issues but decision making. An organization may have acquired systems from many different vendors that need to be integrated, so that metadata and interoperability are important. The advent of the Internet has meant the public may interact with an organization's systems remotely using many different channels—interactive TV and mobile and handheld digital devices. Complex and highly interactive organizational systems must be capable of supporting external users such as the public, whose interaction with a system may be remote, infrequent, and nonroutine, as well as internal employees with different and specific training needs. Forecasters suggest this would mean "useable information and services anywhere and anytime" through multichannel access (Dunckley, L. (2006) Practice in Public Sector IT:Usability and Accessibility Performance. Seibel White Paper.). The way the technology is deployed is vital for its success. As Joaquim Roigé, a director at Healthcare Project Management at Indra in Spain, warns, "This is a new challenge to developers—scarce resources ... means we need to be selective when we consider the alternative technologies customers may use to access our systems. We need to match the interface channel to the task. There is a matrix of channels to services deployed that is something I feel is not currently sufficiently analyzed."

This raises a number of significant questions for IS providers, such as

1.   How can we improve our understanding, analysis, and design of rich media applications to meet future human needs in a resource-effective way?

2.   How do we support the communities of the future in an era of ambient, pervasive, ubiquitous, and mobile computing? Which technology will be useful and acceptable?

3.   How can we achieve quantifiable return on investment by selecting the right tools and effective methodologies, integrating systems, and deploying standards?

There are many excellent books about requirements gathering, IS project management, and software engineering, some of which are included in the references to this chapter. So here we will focus on those techniques that can be particularly useful for rich-media application development. We will also encourage you to explore the employment of some of the newer tools and techniques that can be used for novel application development with uncertain requirements.

In this chapter we also will look at some illustrative cases as well as tools and techniques that are available to address the problems mentioned above.

7.2   Gathering Requirements

Hardly a day goes by without some report in the press that a computer system has failed or been shockingly over budget. In 1994, for example, *Scientific American* reported that three quarters of all large systems were "operating failures" that either did not function as intended, or are not used at all. In this context success can be described as *being used effectively for the uses and users for which it was commissioned*. Even worse, it also appears that computer systems are now so pervasive in everyday life that they can kill. Unfortunately, it is well known that problems in medical systems can harm patients seriously if not detected and solved in time. Recently, Koppel et al. (2005) conducted a field study of a hospital's order-entry system where doctors used the software to specify medications for patients. The study reported 22 ways in which the order-entry system caused patients to get the wrong medicine. Most of these issues were identified as usability problems.

One reason that ICT systems appear to fail is because of a lack of effective user engagement. This can be overcome by incorporating user-centered design (UCD) within development. Thomas Landauer (1995) reviewed the value of UCD based on a wide variety of reported studies where "some kind of UCD was intentionally applied." While the average gains were impressive (50%) individual studies reported gains in performance from 0% (NASA) to 720% (IBM). Landauer claims, based on studies, that without UCD a user interface has typically 40 flaws.

Requirements are often referred to as user needs. We need to know who the users of the information system are and how they carry out their work.

Shifting our focus from the input to the design process, how should information systems meet *all* the needs of *different* users? Often system developers may merely equate user needs with utility. Landauer (1995, p. 218) has outlined how designers tend to take a system-centered point of view, and programmers, who are involved day and night with a program, cannot put themselves in the place of a new user. Developers who are working on their own do not have sufficient domain knowledge, either to be sure of recognizing all usability problems and consequently the design factors to solve these problems, or to be confident of accurately prioritizing these problems with reference to actual user concerns.

Clearly users require systems to perform functions for which they were devised, but their needs are much wider. Smith (1997) has classified three distinct types of user needs: functional, aspirational, and physical.

- *Functional needs,* which are the requirement of the information system to perform the specific tasks that the users require it to do in the operational situation: media upload, download, searching, indexing, and media-specific operations.

- *Aspirational needs* represent the requirement to support the medium- to long-term personal goals of the user. How does the rich-media functionality fit the user's work context, ranging from the clear need for job security to the less-tangible desires for interpersonal affiliation in the work place? Does the functional design fit the organizational and national culture? Are we introducing functions that require the user to learn new skills and concepts and perhaps unlearn previous ways of doing things? Database professionals may need to become familiar with image-processing concepts to exploit all the functionality supplied by *inter*Media.

- *Physical needs* are the needs of the information system to perform its tasks in a manner well suited to the physical characteristics of the user, including workstation ergonomics and interface requirements. Have we considered accessibility to the rich media—how is it presented?

These different classes of user needs lead us to recognize that there are actually a number of different kinds of requirements that we need to identify at the start of the application development.

7.2.1 Functional Requirements

Functional requirements capture what the product should do. For a rich-media application this will include collection of media, storage, compression, update, formatting, retrieval, classification, and display. However, we also have to decide how the functionality will be distributed between the database and the APIs. At what point do we compress the data and when do we generate thumbnails and carry out feature extraction?

7.2.2 Data Requirements

Data requirements capture issues in terms of:

- Volatility—how often is the data changed? In a rich-media application the data will probably be more stable than is something like a transactional database.

- Persistence—how long must the data remain accessible? This is likely to be a longer timespan than for transactional data as the rich media usually has a higher value.

- Accuracy—how accurate must the data be? Compression (lossy and lossless) and resolution.

- Aggregation—what is the need to summarize and filter the information?

- Value—can it be easily replaced?

- Metadata—standards, ownership.

- Amounts of data—rich media will have significant storage requirements.

7.2.3 Environmental Requirements—Context of Use

Environmental requirements capture the circumstances in which the product will be used. This could be the physical or working environment. At one extreme, what would the system need to be operated at a Mt. Everest base camp at 30,000 feet? Will users be wearing protective clothing? Is the working environment noisy and dusty, such as a textile factory?

The social environment is also important particularly for rich-media applications. Is it public or private? Is it shared or single user? Is it synchronous or asynchronous?

What about the organizational and cultural environment? When we introduce a new computer system we may change work patterns and disrupt working practices. When a European ERP system was implemented in Malaysia there were problems because of the disclosure of pricing information to lowly paid staff. This had not been recognized as a problem by the European developers—the concept of privacy and confidentiality is different in Malaysia than in Western societies.

7.2.4 User Requirements

User requirements capture the characteristics of the user group, their abilities, and skills. Computer users are not all the same, so how do we differ?

- Age, gender, expertise?
- Culture—psychological differences?
- Adaptability? Learning ability?
- Discretion—can the users choose to use the system or is it essential for their work?

7.2.5 Usability Requirements

Usability requirements capture the usability goals and measures for the product. In terms of standards this refers to efficiency, effectiveness, and user satisfaction. In addition, recent legislation has added accessibility requirements. The Web Content Accessibility Guidelines 1.0 were developed by the Web Content Accessibility Guidelines Working Group (WCAG WG) and became a W3C Recommendation in 1999.

The following case study demonstrates how requirements can be complex to identify and document.

The U.K. Identity System Case Study

This is interesting because the U.K. identity system has been described as the largest computer system in the world. ID cards will provide legal U.K. residents, including foreign nationals, with an easy and secure way of proving who they are.

The system's sponsors claim that ID cards will be linked to their owners by unique biometric identifiers (e.g., fingerprints), which means there will be a much stronger way of protecting people's identities. Background checks will ensure that claimed identities are real and not stolen, and will prevent criminals from using multiple identities.

The exact format of an ID card is not yet decided but it is likely that it will be a credit card–size plastic card featuring the holder's photograph and a chip storing basic personal information. The ID scheme is more than just issuing a piece of plastic to every adult in the United Kingdom. It is about recording on a central database personal information that will be linked to biometric data. The card should be convenient for the citizens and provide a simple means to check a person against the record in the database. Security in protecting a person's identity from theft and preventing criminals from creating multiple identities is another key requirement of the database. Public acceptance of the technology for data capture and information retrieval is important.

The U.K. Identity Cards Bill is presently going through Parliament and includes the following proposals:

- National identification register
- National identity registration number
- Collection of biometrics
- U.K. citizens must disclose personal data

The identity system will collect the following data for every citizen:

- Name
- Birth coordinates
- Current and previous addresses
- Residential status
- Biometric details

In addition, it is planned that the database will hold records of all dealings with individuals and an audit trail of access to the records for security and integrity reasons.

Since the act is currently under consideration, the system has not yet been fully specified but the following could happen:

- Everybody may have to register.
- You must notify the system every time you change your address.

- You may have to keep an appointment to provide biometric data such as
    - Fingerprints
    - Facial image
    - Iris scan
    - Signature

A national registration register would be created to cover:

- Every U.K. citizen from 16 years and 3 months and older.
- Every U.K. citizen would be assigned an NIRN (national identity registration number).
- Every U.K. citizen would be issued an actual ID card with some of this data.

There are a number of rich media issues such as image formats for capture and storage, upload, indexing, and content-based image retrieval (CBIR) requirements that are currently not specified.

The following sections deal with tools and techniques for gathering requirements, the use of scenarios, and user stories.

7.2.6 **Tools and Techniques**

Participation and cooperation between users and developers needs to be carefully planned. If we skip on the requirements stage we run the risk of developing a system that the users do not want and will not use. If we use too many resources on the requirements stage we will run out of resources or go over budget. This section looks at the different ways in which requirements can be gathered and documented in order.

- To understand what techniques are available for gathering requirements.

- To appreciate their strengths and weaknesses.

- To understand which techniques to choose for specific applications.

The first question we have to answer is, who are the users? In the ID case study there are a number of different stakeholders. The U.K. government has stated it wants to use the system to deal with identity theft, illegal immigration and working, misuse of public services, organized crime, and terrorism. But how can we find out what the users of the system, the public, and the people who will work with the system actually want?

The problem is not that there is a lack of methods; there is a wide range but there is little guidance to choose methods for a particular application and to plan a well-grounded requirements acquisition program. Table 7.1 gives a list of the classical requirements methods, together with their advantages and disadvantages particularly in terms of rich-media applications.

However, the requirement-gathering techniques listed in Table 7.1 vary in terms of:

- Objectives—an investigation to open up the design space, or a confirmation of a design or building consensus.

- Cost involved—time and difficulty of analysis.

- Richness of the information—ethnography can provide rich information but it will involve sifting through lots of low-value observations to find the gold nugget.

- Density of the information—"signal to noise" ratio—can we distinguish the key relevant information easily from the background information?

- Reliability of the information collected—if the technique were repeated would the data be the same?

- Objectivity/subjectivity of the process—how much interpretation does the developer or evaluator have to make?

- Possibility of bias—are we seeing the true picture or has it been slanted in some way that could mislead us in the next stages of design?

Several of the methods in Table 7.1 mention *situatedness*. This has been described as the context that provides the multiple perspectives needed for the understanding that permits all voices to be heard in good faith. In our terms it usually means seeing the real-world working situation, and has given rise to context-based design methods.

Every requirement-gathering method has disadvantages and errors can occur. Even with a well-established method, if the method is poorly

Table 7.1 *Requirement-gathering Techniques for Rich-media Applications*

Technique	Good For	Data Collected	Advantages	Disadvantages
Question-naires and surveys	Specific questions	Quantitative Qualitative	Low cost Many people can be surveyed	Lacks situated-ness Relies on recollection and honesty
Interviews, structured and unstructured	Exploring issues	Mostly qualitative	Designer can meet and understand users	Designer must select representative users carefully Lacks situated-ness Relies on recollection and honesty
Focus groups	Multiple viewpoints	Mostly qualitative	Highlights issues of consensus and conflict	Group must be homogeneous Group must not be dominated by users with specific issues
Ethnography field methods	Situatedness	Qualitative	Designer can see actual context of use Can use video and audio to support technique	High cost, low information content
Remote viewing or evaluation	Some Situatedness	Quantitative Qualitative	Designer can see remote context and take measurements	Designer cannot meet users and may not understand what is going on

Table 7.1   *Requirement-gathering Techniques for Rich-media Applications (continued)*

Technique	Good For	Data Collected	Advantages	Disadvantages
Virtual ethnography	Some situatedness	Quantitative Qualitative	Facilitated by some groupware and ERP systems More efficient than traditional ethnography	Designer cannot meet users

planned and the sources of error are not recognized and managed, then errors can result. Methods can be biased in different ways.

The "principle of triangulation" is a good idea. Basically, this means that more than one method should be applied to be able to look at the system from different perspectives. This is a way of checking which requirements are stable and valid across user groups and should give more reliable results.

Many of these techniques assume there is some kind of existing system that we can study or ask users about. Nokia is a company that has developed many novel rich-media communication products successfully so it is worth noting its development approach, which is summarized as follows:

- User-centered design
- Contextual approach
- Ethnographic approach
- Data gathering includes market research
- Scenarios and task models
- Iterative prototyping: design–build–evaluate

When we are faced with developing completely new systems or concepts, scenarios can be useful.

What Are Scenarios?

Scenarios are informal narratives, usually collaboratively constructed by a team in order to describe human work processes. The scenarios should include more than a simple description of the workflow. The term *scenario-based design* is used to cover a range of tools and techniques that all have a number of common objectives.

Scenarios are useful both for detailed design and also for the design of new concepts and products. In particular they are useful as a basis for overall design to

- Identify human goals and motivations.

- Identify design alternatives.

- Extend and deepen understanding of the problem.

In terms of software development, these contribute to

- technical implementation

- cooperation within design teams

- communication in a multidisciplinary team

- evaluation of prototypes at a later stage in development.

Extreme programming (XP) is a popular agile development method that employs user stories to document requirements and engage users in development. User stories are also an important part of the planning process and serve the same purpose as use cases but are not the same. They are used to create time estimates for the release planning meeting. They are also used instead of a large requirements document. User stories are written by the customers as things that the system needs to do for them. They are similar to usage scenarios, except that they are not limited to describing a user interface. They are in the format of about three sentences of text written by the customer in the customer's terminology without "techno-syntax."

In Chapter 3 we introduced the Family and Friends Picture Book with some outline user stories:

Matt is interested in astronomy, and his set of photos is mainly focused on the solar system. He captures images from his telescope as well as gets them from various sources, including the Internet. He needs to identify images from the night sky at different locations and times of the year.

User stories also drive the creation of the acceptance tests. In XP one or more automated acceptance tests must be created to verify that the user story has been correctly implemented.

One of the biggest misunderstandings with user stories is how they differ from traditional requirements specifications. The biggest difference is in the level of detail. User stories should only provide enough detail to make a reasonably low-risk estimate of how long the story will take to implement. When the time comes to implement the story, developers will go to the customer and receive a detailed description of the requirements face to face.

As an essential part of the plan, developers estimate how long the stories might take to implement. Each story will be assigned an "ideal development time" as an estimate of completion time in weeks, such as 1, 2, or a maximum of 3 weeks. This ideal development time is how long it would take to implement the story in code if there were no distractions, no other assignments, and the developers knew exactly what to do. An estimate that is longer than 3 weeks means the story needs to be broken down further. Less than 1 week indicates the story is at too detailed a level, therefore, some stories may need to be combined. About 80 user stories (plus or minus 20) are regarded as a perfect number to create a release plan during the planning stage.

Another difference between stories and a requirements document is a focus on user needs. At this stage the developers should try to avoid details of specific technology, database, layout, and algorithms. The developers should try to keep stories focused on user needs and benefits as opposed to specifying GUI layouts.

*inter*Media *Application Development*

Much of what we have said would apply to all information systems, but for a rich-media development we will need to plan

- Loading large volumes of rich media into the database.
- Associating the correct metadata.
- Indexing the media content for future search and retrieval.
- Delivering the rich-media content efficiently.

There are several possibilities for loading rich-media data into the database, which we covered in detail in Chapter 6:

- API: an application programming interface.

- Database table replication: copying from one Oracle database into another keeps databases, such as those used for production and deployment, synchronized.

- SQL*Loader: a high-volume, bulk loader that deals with large quantities of multimedia content very efficiently, using direct path access.

- PL/SQL procedures: often used as an alternative to SQL*Loader.

- WebDAV: a standard extension to HTTP.

These are covered in detail in the relevant chapters, especially Chapters 4 and 5.

An important issue is the storage of the media as there are several possibilities, including:

- Binary large objects, or BLOBS, stored within the database.

- File-based large objects, or BFILES, stored in local operating system-specific file systems.

- URLs containing image, audio, and video data stored on any HTTP server, such as the Oracle Application Server.

- Specialized media storage servers.

The option of storing multimedia content outside the database can be useful for managing large or new multimedia repositories that already reside as flat files on erasable or read-only devices. This data can be conveniently imported and exported between BLOBS and the external BFILE source at any time. However, as these alternative designs involve a tradeoff between security, manageability, and ease of delivery, this is an area where prototyping (section 7.5) can be of benefit.

*inter*Media facilitates associating metadata with the relevant rich-media objects. This is explained in Chapter 8 where we see how by using the media object types, the metadata is extracted from the media using the appropriate encapsulated methods and loaded into attributes of the object type. Specific application metadata, such as the name of the artist who created the media, can be extracted when required and returned to the application as an XML string. The way metadata issues are supported by *inter*Media is covered in Chapter 10.

7.3　Define Architecture

When we have a reasonable concept of the requirements, the next stage is to consider the architecture of the proposed system. It is often not appreciated that the choice of technical architecture has significance for other issues such as interoperability, connectivity, and usability. This is because you cannot add on usability late in the development of complex customer-centric systems. The choice of architecture will enable or restrict the way the system is implemented. When we define the architecture we must consider

- Integration necessary between different private and public bodies in order to provide customer centricity seamlessly and cost-effectively.

- Significant technological investment in legacy systems.

- Many standards that affect IS are set at a national, not international, level but for rich media there are a number of important international standards as well.

- Current projects and implementations often do not mandate standards but only suggest them for consideration.

This is a good point to consider enterprise architecture (EA) and whether the proposed rich-media system is intended to fit seamlessly into an existing EA. In the last decade the ability to combine disparate streams of information to improve decision making, develop business innovations, and streamline operations was perceived as giving a company a competitive advantage over others that might be overwhelmed by information overload. The development of the concept of the information architecture also changed the emphasis of software development from using a single development methodology and supplier to supporting diversity within an overarching framework. Now the interconnectivity of the Web is creating the need for organizations' separate EAs to achieve a level of compatibility and interoperability. The development of EA encountered technical problems, such as interfacing products from different hardware and software vendors, but the primary impediment was the web of organizational factors such as management commitment, data responsibility, data centralization, system design, and staffing. User participation and management commitment are the most significant factors in the success of enterprisewide modeling. End-user managers and their staff must actively engage in defining data elements and relationships among data because they are in the best position to determine the relative importance of data elements to the business. This means negotiating to replace or adapt existing data models.

Table 7.2 presents Zachman's enterprise architecture. This is a useful way of providing a framework for the planning of application and information systems. The original ISA framework had three columns that represented the data, function, and network representing the *what, how,* and *where* of an IS. They relate to columns A, B, and C of the full framework. A later version of the ISA framework (Sowa and Zachman, 1992) consisted of a table of 30 cells, organized in 6 columns of 5 rows, since they recognized the need to add further perspectives relating to people *who*, motivation *why*, and events *when*. As a level-based approach the ISA moves from generalized business objectives progressively to more detailed planning levels from the general to the specific and from the nontechnical to the technical issues. Zachman's original model was ahead of its time in that it recognized the need for the "planner" row to set the business context of an IS. The planning row provides a predominantly business viewpoint while the lower rows give a technological viewpoint. The framework as it applies to enterprises is simply a logical structure for classifying and organizing the descriptive representations of an enterprise that are significant to the management of the enterprise as well as to the development of the enterprise's systems. Thus, the data column would require the development of one consistent logical data model for the whole organization.

Applications

Note: For the ID system, we can start to specify the cells as follows:

- DATA, *What*—Things important to the business: protecting personal identity, preventing criminals from creating multiple IDs, strengthening homeland security, preventing illegal immigration, controlling access to public services.

- FUNCTION, *How*—Background checks on identities, collect biometrics, issue ID cards, register adult residents, audit use.

- NETWORK, *Where*—Locations: all U.K. regions.

- PEOPLE, *Who*—Important organizations: Interol, NSA, CIA, U.K. Passport Office, U.K. service providers.

Table 7.2 *Zachman's Enterprise Architecture*

	DATA *What*	FUNCTION *How*	NETWORK *Where*	PEOPLE *Who*	TIME *When*	MOTIVATION *Why*
SCOPE CONTEXTUAL Planner	List of things important to the business	List of processes the business performs	List of locations where business operates	List of organizations important to the business	List of events/ cycles important to the business	List of business goals/ strategies Ends/means
BUSINESS MODEL Owner	e.g., Semantic model	Business process model	Business logistics system	Work-flow model	Master schedule	Business plan Ends = Business objective Means = Business strategy
SYSTEM MODEL Designer	e.g., Logical data model	Application architecture I/O user views	Distributed systems architecture	Human interface architecture People = Role Work = Deliverable	Processing structure	Business rules model Ends = Structural assertion Means = Action assertion
TECHNOLOGY MODEL Builder	e.g., Physical data model	System design	Technology architecture	Presentation architecture People = User Deliverable= Screen format	Control structure	Rule design End = Condition Means = Action
DETAILED REPRESENTATION Subcontractor	e.g., Data definition	Program language statements I/O control block	Network architecture Node = Address Link = Protocol	Security architecture People = Identity Work = Job	Timing definition Time = Interrupt Cycle = Machine cycle	Rule specification End = Subcondition Means = Step

Table 7.2 *Zachman's Enterprise Architecture (continued)*

	DATA *What*	FUNCTION *How*	NETWORK *Where*	PEOPLE *Who*	TIME *When*	MOTIVATION *Why*
FUNC-TIONING ENTER-PRISE	e.g., DATA	e.g., FUNC-TION	e.g., NET-WORK	e.g., ORGA-NIZATION	e.g., SCHED-ULE	e.g., STRATEGY

7.3.1 Technical Architecture

The technical architecture selected will depend on requirements for interoperability, connectivity, and usability. Probably the most well-known current architecture is the client-server system but the Oracle *inter*Media architecture is most easily represented as a three-tier architecture—the data server tier, the application server tier, and the client tier (Figure 7.1). Oracle Application Server and Oracle Database install Oracle HTTP Server powered by the Apache HTTP Server. Oracle HTTP Server serves mainly the static HTML files, images, and so forth that a Web application uses, and is usually located in the file system where Oracle HTTP Server is installed.

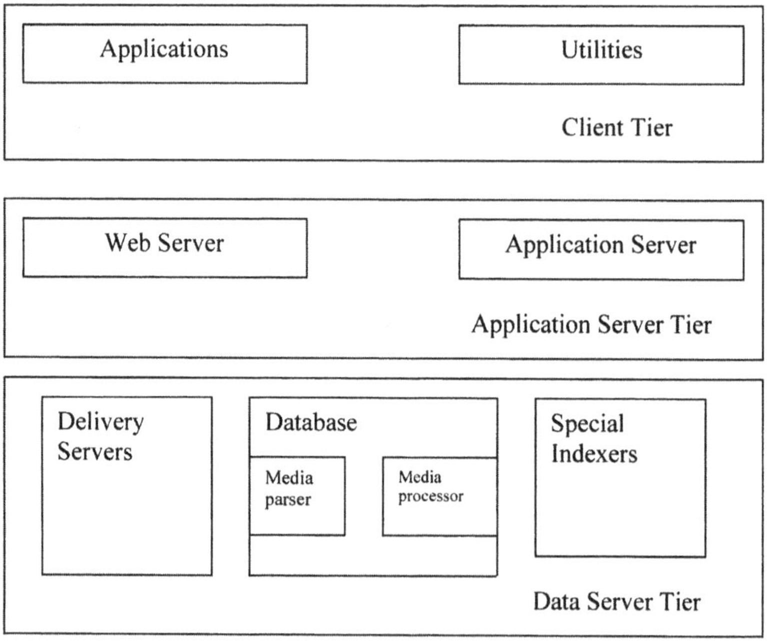

Figure 7.1 *Three Tier Architecture*

7.3.2 Client-server Architecture

The lowest tier, the data server, contains the database. Within this are two important components: the media parser, which takes the rich-media content and parses out the media format, and metadata. The media processor supports the processing of images within the database (see Chapter 8). Both of these run on the Oracle Java Virtual Machine. The delivery servers are special servers connected to plug-ins that get the rich-media content out of the database and deliver this to thin clients. RealNetworks Helix and Microsoft Windows Media are streaming servers that are examples of these. The special indexers are third-party indexers that can perform functions, such as speech recognition and building speech-to-text time base indexers for specialized applications. Also within the data server tier is the XML schema used for loading media content into the XML DB, which makes it easy to manage the media content as part of an XML document.

The application server tier includes the Web server and the *inter*Media class libraries, such as the JSP tag library for JSP application development. Also in the middle tier is Webdav—a Web distributed authoring and versioning protocol. Webdav is a standard extension to HTTP that makes upload and download of media to remote clients easy. Another middle-tier component is for multimedia delivery over wireless connections. This component provides for media adaptation to suit delivery channel characteristics and output devices.

In this way downloading or delivery of all multimedia content is supported either in batch or as streaming for certain audio and video formats. The data types can always be delivered from the database to the client in batch, synchronous mode. For some data types, more specialized delivery services are available (see Figure 7.2). For certain audio and video formats, the media object types can be delivered in an isochronous or stream fashion, making it possible to play it as it arrives using the RTSP protocol. Oracle *inter*Media support for these special protocols is through peer-level servers from third-party partners such as RealNetworks and Microsoft.

Using the Java database connectivity (JDBC) interface, you can quickly develop applications for use on any tier (client, application server, or database) to manipulate and modify audio, image, and video data, or heterogeneous media data stored in a database. Oracle *inter*Media Java Classes makes it possible for JDBC result sets to include both traditional relational data and *inter*Media columns of object-type media data, to easily select and operate on the result set, to access object attributes, and to invoke object methods. Through Java class libraries, Java clients can retrieve multimedia objects in JDBC result sets and send them to a browser. These same clients can use the Java Advanced Imaging (JAI) package used by Oracle *inter*Media to perform sophisticated, client-side image processing. Thick clients can also use a Java Media Framework (JMF) player to play, upload, and download audio or video clips from Oracle *inter*Media. This is described in Chapter 9 on Java application development.

7.3.3 Alternative Architectures

We can also develop *inter*Media application through PL/SQL. The Oracle HTTP Server contains other modules or plug-ins that extend its functions. One of these modules is the mod_plsql module, also known as the PL/SQL Gateway (Figure 7.2), which serves data dynamically from the database to Web browsers by calling PL/SQL stored procedures. The PL/SQL Gateway receives requests from a Web browser in the form of PL/SQL servlets or PL/SQL server pages that are mapped to PL/SQL stored procedure calls. PL/SQL stored procedures retrieve data from the database and generate an HTTP response containing the data and code from the PL/SQL Web Toolkit to display the generated Web page in a Web browser. The PL/SQL Web

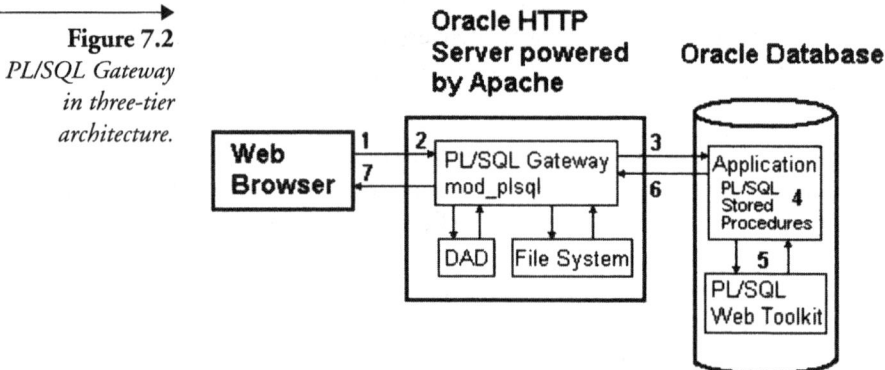

Figure 7.2
*PL/SQL Gateway
in three-tier
architecture.*

Toolkit contains a set of packages that can be used in the stored procedures to get the information required, construct HTML tags, and return header information to the client Web browser.

Oracle HTTP Server contains the PL/SQL Gateway or mod_plsql module, the database access description (DAD) that contains the database connection information, and the file system where static HTML files and images are stored for use by Web applications. From the PL/SQL Gateway, the response is returned to the HTTP Server for hosting as a formatted

Web page for the client Web browser. Usually, the returned formatted Web page has one or more additional links, and each link, when selected, sends another request to the database through the PL/SQL Gateway to execute one or more stored procedures. The generated response displays data on the client Web page usually with additional links, which, when selected, execute more stored procedures that return the generated response for display as yet another formatted Web page, and so forth. This is how the PL/SQL application in the PL/SQL development environment is designed to work.

Web application developers who use the PL/SQL development environment create a PL/SQL package specification and body that describe procedures and functions that comprise the application. The package specification defines the procedures and functions used by the application, and the package body is the implementation of each procedure and function. All packages are compiled and stored in the database to perform specific operations for accessing data in the database and formatting HTML output for Web page presentation. To invoke these stored PL/SQL procedures, Web application developers use the request/response PL/SQL servlets and PL/SQL server pages (PSP) to allow Web browser clients to send requests and get back responses using HTTP.

Oracle HTTP Server maps a URL entered in a browser to a specific PL/SQL procedure stored in the database. It does this by storing specific configuration information by means of a DAD for each stored procedure. Thus, each DAD contains the database connection information that is needed by the Web server to translate the URL entered into a database connection in order to call the stored procedure.

A key determinant of successful IS implementation is the technical architecture (shown in Table 7.2). However, currently client-server systems provide limited support for distributed architectures required for complex systems involving rich media. Several alternative technologies have been put forward as solutions:

- Grid technology has the potential to allow both competition and interoperability not only among applications and toolkits, but also among implementations of key services. Interoperability could be achieved by both standards in communication and data security, storage, and processing, and by policy initiatives, including organizational protocols, financing procedures, and legal frameworks.

- Web services are loosely coupled reusable software components that semantically encapsulate discrete functionality. They provide a distributed computing technology for publishing, discovering, and consuming business services on the Internet or within an intranet using standard XML protocols and formats. Web services standards are giving service definition a structure but challenges remain. If a service could not define its security, availability, integrity, and environment, an acceptable definition of service would not be achieved.

■ Open grid services architecture (OGSA) is one approach that is suggested as an architecture unifying grid and Web services technology to address flexibility and reliability and to improve the interoperability of grid systems.

■ Hub-based approaches achieve interoperability by employing a connectivity hub for data exchange that is composed of a common object model and a set of process flows that run across a variety of systems independently of the communication technology and the underlying data models and applications.

If barriers, in terms of legacy systems, silo processes, and heterogeneous connectivity are to be overcome, an innovative approach has to be developed. The hub-based approach provides a technical solution that is compatible with the separation of data, function, and network columns of the EA (see Table 7.2). There are also concerns that service-oriented architectures will not solve interoperability problems alone because of shortcomings especially in the aspects of scalability and interoperability. Peer-based SOA (PSOA) will lead to point-to-point solutions (1:1 interfaces) that are not the best solutions, since they are not scalable or cost-effective—the cost and effort of developing and maintaining such interfaces grows exponentially when new systems are added. Every new system may need as many interfaces as the already existing systems and theoretically, if every system is to be connected with each other, the number of interfaces is $N*(N-1)/2$, N being the total number of systems. Therefore, the idea of a connectivity hub for data exchange clearly appears to be the solution to the problem of N:N interfaces. In order to integrate consistently different data models, different data definitions and data formats, different semantics and different meanings, a hub would reduce the complexity to a 1:N basis by means of a common object model as a composite of application data models. Discussions and white papers concerning these alternative architectures can be found on the Oracle Technology Network website.

7.4   Data Modeling

In Table 7.2, for historic reasons, there are two separate columns devoted to *data* and *function* although in object-oriented development these are not separated. In the next sections we will look in more detail at the specifications of parts of these columns.

7.4.1   Define Schema

In most organizations, analysis, development, and database teams have tended to work for different managers, business units, and other business organizations. These separate teams are working toward a common goal and need to work together. One of the great potential advantages of adopting UML would be that different IT professionals, who tend to be involved in different stages of the lifecycle, should be able to use a consistent set of modeling techniques and communicate effectively with one another. In the past database designers have tended to use entity models for logical database design while application programmers used a variety of programming design techniques.

This is even more important in incremental development where different parts of the same system may be being changed constantly. As the developers build the applications they uncovers new requirements and the database team also uncover new requirements building the database.

In Figure 7.3 we can see a representation of development from analysis to implementation. At the analysis stage a UML class diagram is used to design the conceptual schema instead of the extended ER model often used in relational database development. UML has the advantage that it permits the design of the entire system, facilitating different system views. The design phase would include a logical design that was independent of any product and a specific design based on Oracle without considering tuning or optimizing at this stage. The logical design (see Table 7.2 SYSTEM MODEL) has an object-relational design that can be used by all the product implementations, forms, Java, etc. and can make migration between products easier. It is useful in the design phase to develop an SQL:1999 schema for interoperability purposes and use an extended UML graphical representation to support documentation and understandability. It also makes the development of the database schema easier as it shows the correct order in which we will need to compile each new object type (or UDT). The implementation phase (see Table 7.2, builder layer) will include some

Figure 7.3

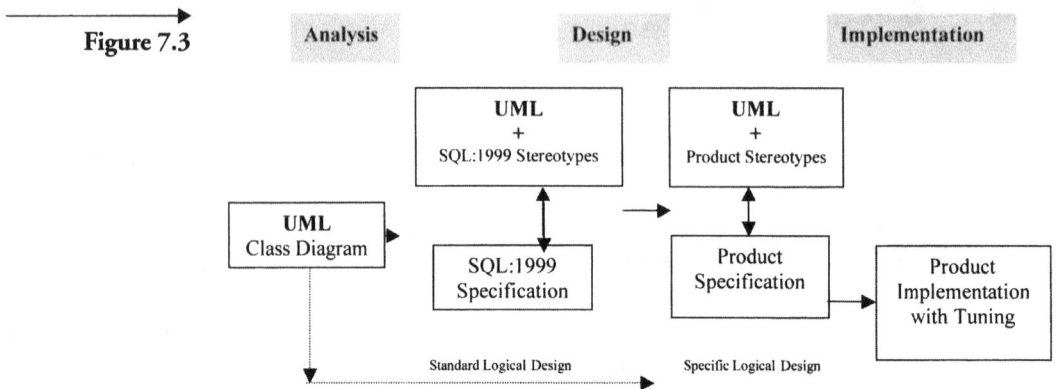

physical design tasks to fine-tune the schema to improve response time and storage space.

Table 7.3

UML	SQL:1999	Oracle Object-Relational Types
Class	Structured type	Object type
Class extension	Typed table	Table of object type
Attribute	Attribute	Attribute
Multivalued	ARRAY	VARRAY/Nested table
Composed	ROW/Structured type in column	Object type in column
Calculated	Trigger/Method	Trigger/Method
Association	Table Constraints	Generalisation row
One-to-One	REF/[REF]	REF/[REF]
One-to-Many	[REP]/[ARRAY]	[REF]/[Nested table/VARRAY]
Many-to-Many	ARRAY/ARRAY	Nested table/Nested table VARRAY/VARRAY
Aggregation	ARRAY	Nested table/VARRAY of references
Composition	ARRAY	Nested table/VARRAY of objects
Generalization	Types/Typed tables	FINAL/INSTATIABLE types

The process will require transformations between UML, SQL:1999, and Oracle. Table 7.3 provides some guidelines for transforming a conceptual UML-based schema into SQL:1999 schema and into Oracle object-relational types.

In UML only persistent classes (marked by the stereotype *<<persistent>>*) have to be transformed into a class in the database schema. This may mean defining the object type as well as its extension as an object table. Each UML class method is specified in the definition of the object type as the signature of the method so that the method belongs to that type. The body of the method can then be defined separately.

Each attribute of the UML class is transformed into an attribute of the type. Multivalued attributes are represented as collection types. Oracle supports VARRAY and NESTED TABLE collection types. Using a VARRAY is recommended if the maximum number of elements is known and small and the entire collection is to be retrieved. If the number of elements is unknown it is better to use a NESTED TABLE, which can also be queried easily. Composed attributes can be defined as an object type without extension (not defining the object table). Derived attributes should be implemented by means of a trigger or a method.

In the U.K. ID card system, each citizen's details could be held together with their current and previous addresses. Figure 7.4 represents the transformation using graphical notations. Note the collection type has no methods of its own.

Figure 7.4

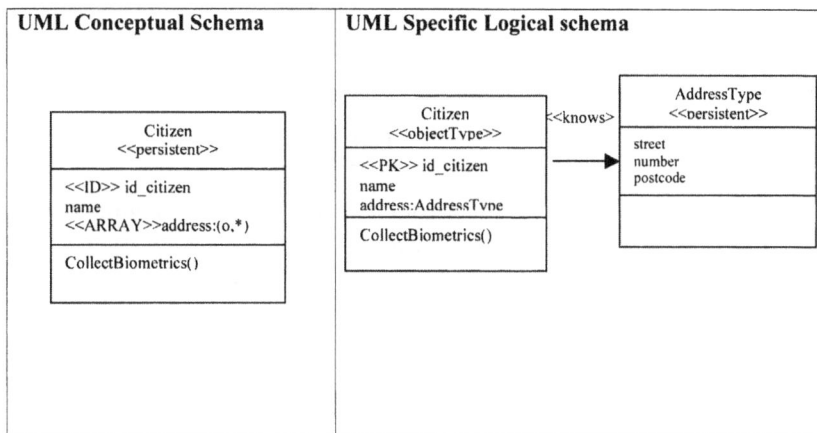

This extension of UML (Table 7.4) defines a set of stereotypes, tagged values, and constraints that enable applications to be modeled in object-

Table 7.4   *Stereotypes for Database Design*

	Database Element	UML Element	Stereotype	Icon
Architectural	Database	Component	«Database»	
	Schema	Package	«Schema»	
Conceptual	Persistent class	Class	«Persistent»	
	Multivalued attribute	Attribute	«MA»	
	Calculated attribute	Attribute	«DA»	
	Composed attribute	Attribute	«CA»	
	Identifier	Attribute	«ID»	
Logical	Table	Class	«Table»	
	View	Class	«View»	
	Column	Attributes	«Column»	
	Primary key	Attributes	«PK»	
	Foreign key	Attributes	«FK»	
	NOT NULL constraint	Attributes	«NOTNULL»	
	Unique constraint	Attributes	«Unique»	
	Trigger	Constraint	«Trigger»	
	CHECK constraint	Constraint	«Check»	
	Stored procedure	Class	«Stored Procedure»	
Physical	Tablespace	Component	«Tablespace»	
	Index	Class	<<Index>>	

relational databases and follows the recommendations of Marcos et al. (2005).

In Table 7.5 we show how the SQL:1999 stereotypes can be implemented.

Table 7.5 *SQL:1999 Stereotypes*

Structured Type Metamodel class: Class. Description: A *«UDT»* allows the representation of new user-defined data types. Icon: None. Constraints: Can only be used to define value types. Tagged values: None.	**Typed Table** Metamodel class: Class. Description: It is defined as *«Object Type»*. It represents a class of the database schema that should be defined as a table of a structured data type. Icon: `<<table>>` Constraints: A typed table implies the definition of a structured type, which is the type of the table. Tagged values: None.
Knows Description: A *«Knows»* association is a special relationship that joins a class with a user-defined data type *«UDT»* that is used with the class. It is a unidirectional relationship. The direction of the association is represented by an arrow at the end of the user defined type used by the class. Icon: None. Constraints: Can only be used to join an *«Object Type»* class with a *«UDT»* class. Tagged values: None.	**REF Type** Description: A *«REF»* represents a link to some *«Object Type»* class. Icon: ●→ Constraints: A *«REF»* attribute can only refer to an *«Object Type»* class. Tagged values: The *«Object Type»* class to which it refers.
ARRAY Metamodel class: Attribute. Description: An *«Array»* represents an indexed and bounded collection type. Icon: ☐☐☐ Constraints: The elements of an *«Array»* can be of any data type except the *«Array»* type. Tagged values: The basic types of the array. The number of elements.	**ROW Type** Metamodel class: Attribute. Description: A *«row»* type represents a composed attribute with a fixed number of elements, each of them can be of different data type. Icon: ☰ Constraints: Has no methods. Tagged values: The name for each element and its data type.

Table 7.5   *SQL:1999 Stereotypes (continued)*

	Deferred Method
Redefined Method	Metamodel class: Method.
Metamodel class: Method.	Description: A *«def»* method is a method that defers its implementation to its child classes.
Description: A *«redef»* method is an inherited method that is implemented again by the child class.	Icon: None.
Icon: None.	Constraints: It has to be defined in a class with children
Constraints: None.	
Tagged values: The list of parameters of the method with their data types. The data type returned by the method.	Tagged values: The list of parameters of the method with their data types. The data type returned by the method.

7.5   Prototyping

7.5.1   Why Prototype?

The aim of ITC development is *usefulness*, but it is difficult to define, whereas the concept of usability is well established and enshrined in an ISO standard (ISO 9241-11.3). The consequences of poor usability design are evident as

- User dissatisfaction and even rejection.
- Wasted resources and time as users resort to "working around" the system.
- Dangers of incomplete data entry.
- Error propagation.
- Adverse economic impact.

Investing in usability means planning this into the system development from the earliest stages in the lifecycle, rather than delaying the user input until the final stages of testing. This is because problems of usability can be difficult to solve. When a problem is identified too late in the development there is an inevitable tendency to "quick fix" the problem even if it were clear there could be something fundamentally wrong with the product. We need an early focus on the users to help developers understand how users think about the whole system not just the interface. Introducing a user focus and maintaining it throughout the development makes good economic sense.

As the design process has become more complex, technology has given us some support. This means that we can now create interactive prototypes fairly easily and explore different design options early in the development. We can use online questionnaires to provide users with opportunities to give feedback through our websites so that we can continuously monitor usage and collect information about errors. We can capture information about user behavior and interactions remotely. Although this can generate large amounts of data, it can be difficult to interpret without the use of HCI specialists. This means we should consider the use of multidisciplinary teams with developers, managers, users, and HCI specialists working together. These ideas are built into a number of agile development methods such as dynamic systems design method (DSDM) and extreme programming (XP).

However, some developers are still reluctant to engage directly with users. Too often "user testing" is just letting another developer or someone trusted by the development team use the system. Some organizations also worry about the commercial implications of showing early design concepts to users. But the payoff in terms of the system's quality and the professional development of software engineers can be considerable. There are also guidelines and heuristics to help designers, although these are less well known than one might expect. Talking informally with a group of U.K. developers recently, we were surprised how few were aware of simple heuristics, such as that displaying text in uppercase makes it less readable and would be inefficient for users. Another problem is that some developers are still not aware of the requirements of accessibility in terms of font, color, animation, and effectively labeling images through metadata. This may partly be the way usability is presented in the literature. HCI books are notoriously wordy and some heuristics are quite vague and deal with slippery concepts such as "naturalness."

For example, recent changes in legislation in the United States and European Union (EU) place an obligation to make ITC systems accessible for disabled people (WAI initiative). Therefore, we need to design systems with flexibility in mind. Following accessibility guidelines should ensure that all kinds of websites, including multimedia, work well for all users. When we improve usability for disabled users we will automatically improve the system for everybody. Since the Web has a strong visual bias, we need to ensure access for people with vision impairments.

Another problem technological advances pose is that we can no longer design systems with the same degree of predictability. The risk in system development is much higher. It is very easy to cite numerous expensive IT failures. Since both the investment and risk is high, prototyping and piloting these systems is essential. While prototyping is now popular, piloting is less widely used but can be essential when untried technology is being considered, such as the U.K. ID card system. Another key issue is evaluating the prototype user interfaces in a timely and efficient manner.

7.5.2 What Is Prototyping?

There are many variations of prototyping but all methods involve the creation of some kind of prototype, even though the prototype itself can range from just a rough sketch to a working prototype the user can interact with. The objective is, however, the same: to anticipate the future use of a product by trialing the prototype with users because the product is not yet available. We can distinguish two basic types of prototyping strategies:

1.   The throwaway approach where the prototype is redeveloped or translated.

2.   The evolutionary approach where the prototypes themselves become delivered systems.

Many different terms are used to describe the product of these processes. Prototypes have been described as external or internal from the viewpoint of the users and can also be said to have *horizontal* or *vertical* functionality. This is outlined in Figure 7.5. In *horizontal prototyping* the whole, albeit limited, version of the required system is prototyped and at each iteration of the evolutionary process more and more detail of the system is added. This is in contrast to *vertical prototyping* where a full version of one part of the system is developed. Typically horizontal prototypes are mock-ups, however, their influence on the software development is not profound because they do not allow the user to evaluate their requirements fully. Vertical prototypes are of much greater interest because they can exhibit more functionality and would normally be expected to have

- A user interface

- Supporting data structures and storage

- Algorithms or data manipulations

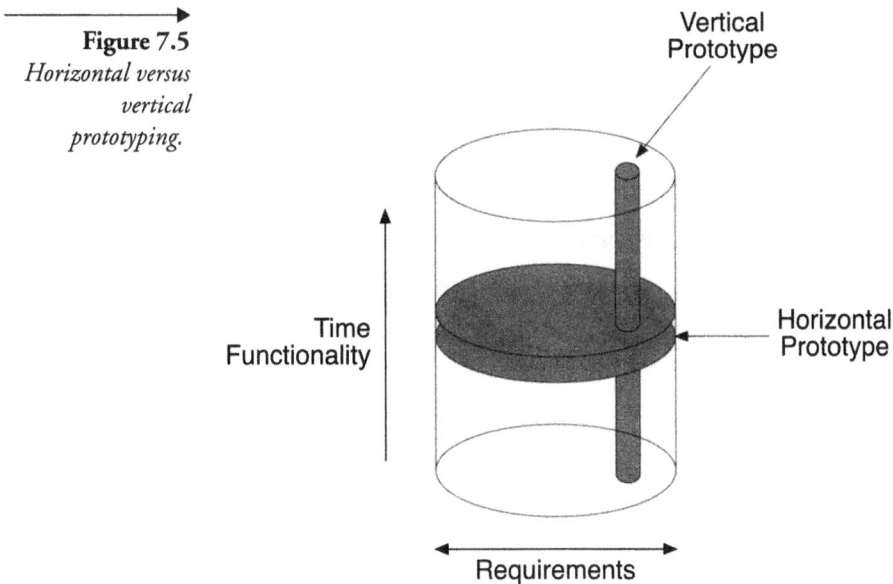

Figure 7.5
Horizontal versus vertical prototyping.

Currently the terms low fidelity and high fidelity are also being used to distinguish two kinds of prototypes that are particularly important for user requirements.

7.5.3 Low-fidelity Prototypes

These are used early in the lifecycle and are called low fidelity because they may not resemble the end product very strongly and are created very quickly from low-cost materials. This is usually a rough-cut external user interface that can be paper, whiteboard, flip charts, or a mock-up produced in a software package, such as Microsoft Word or PowerPoint, that has no interactivity. It is useful to provide the "look and feel" of an interface but it lacks the ability to demonstrate effectively how the user interacts with the system because it will have strictly limited functionality. A so-called first-cut prototype should include menus, layout outline, and dialogue to represent how the user would navigate around the system, but this would not be detailed.

A simple technique for developing low-fidelity prototypes that involve users in design sessions is called PICTIVE (plastic interface for collaborative technology initiatives through video exploration). This technique was developed by a team of designers led by Muller working for Sun Microsystems and first published in 1992. Variants of the method are now quite widely used. The method uses low-cost familiar office materials (e.g., colored pens, Post-it® notes, highlighters, colored paper, and tape).

- Large sheets of paper represent screens or windows.

- Smaller papers or large Post-it notes represent dialog boxes or menus.

- Icons are drawn onto the paper or may be produced prior to the sessions.

- Colored acetate represents highlighting fields or windows.

- Paper widget sets can also be used when a particular target environment is known.

The participants then create a low-fidelity design by building up the structure from a series of Post-it notes layered on a paper screen by users and developers working together. This is particularly useful for rich-media applications where the users may not be able to articulate in words what they want and may suggest requirements that would be technically difficult to realize. The design session can be participative and negotiable. Several alternative designs can be easily explored in detail very quickly. For example, in the case of a Web interface, the design based on a "frame" look and feel can be contrasted with one based on tabs or pull-down menus. The position and size of image and video windows can be explored as well as the way the media would be queried and navigated. One of the advantages of this approach is that participants can explain both the static design of the screen and its dynamic behavior. Several screens will typically be developed and the users and developers can check how to navigate between screens and menus very easily. Obviously, I do not know of its successful use for audio.

It is important that PICTIVE materials can be changeable and extensible by the participants. Once the group has produced a mock-up interface using PICTIVE materials, users can then walk through the mock-up narrating and explaining their work scenarios. Participants can

- Annotate the materials by writing and drawing on the design.

- Rearrange or replace the materials to explain how work can be done differently.

- Reduce social distance between users and designers.

Figure 7.6

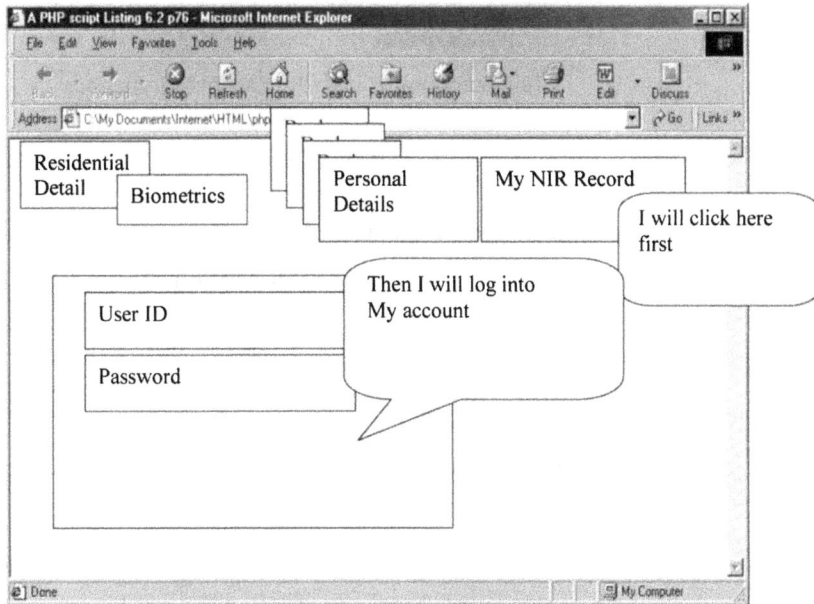

The strongest use for PICTIVE has been in design of visual interfaces based on user-enacted scenarios. In the original method the PICTIVE sessions were videoed. The video records form a way of documenting the design decisions so that developers can check the group discussions that lead to the PICTIVE design. As well as the video the developers have a set of notes from the session and the PICTIVE prototype itself. One of the strongest reasons for using PICTIVE is that it is a low-cost way of carrying out parallel prototyping. This opens out the design space by producing alternatives. One way of doing this is to deliberately plan PICTIVE sessions with different user groups.

7.5.4 High-fidelity Prototypes

This kind of prototype will be much more refined and interactive, capturing essential features of the proposed design in some detail. The key characteristic is that these prototypes are interactive and the user can appear to complete a task and so a much more extensive evaluation is possible. This kind of prototype takes more time and resources to develop and consequently there is a temptation to allow this kind of prototype to develop into the actual product. In evolutionary prototyping these prototypes are not considered to be "throw-away," although low-fidelity and high-fidelity prototypes could be developed at various stages in both horizontal and vertical prototyping.

Characteristics of high-fidelity prototypes are:

- Complete functionality
- Extensive interaction
- Include navigation and information flow
- Prototype responds to user in a way that represents final product

The advantages are:

- Usability testing can be conducted early in design–build–evaluate cycles.
- Realistic comparisons with competitive products can be made.
- Provides a "living" specification for developers.
- Can be effective marketing tools.

The disadvantages are:

- Expensive and time-consuming
- Requires significant programming effort
- Difficult to investigate design alternatives because of expense and duplication
- Many important design decisions may be made too rapidly to be validated

Oracle provides a suitable application development framework in JDeveloper. Within this system you can set up a number of projects within an application. An application is the highest level of the control structure and serves as a collector for the subparts. This means it is possible to create a high-fidelity prototype for one part of the application that has been identified as suitable while traditional application development continues for other parts of the application. Within JDeveloper we can access the database directly through the SQL worksheet so that DBA functions can be carried out here and the media loaded.

Figure 7.7

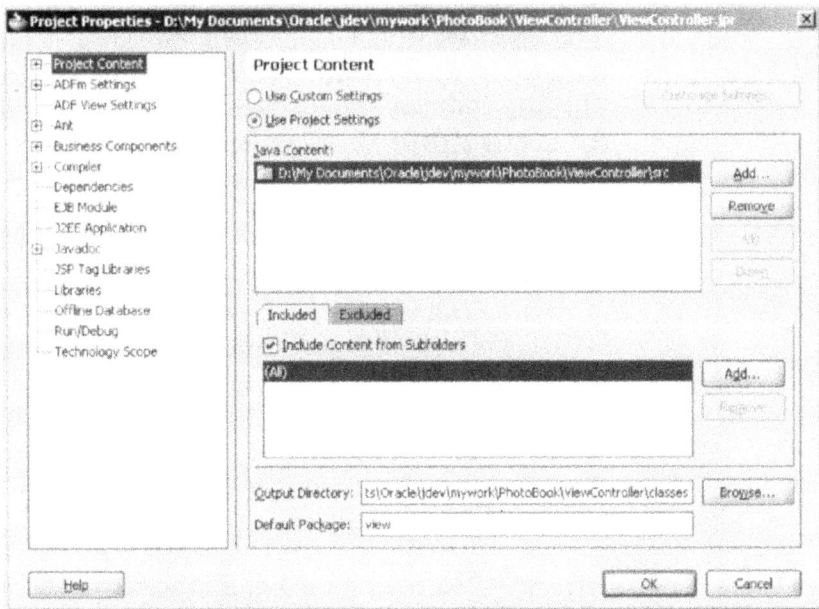

Figure 7.8

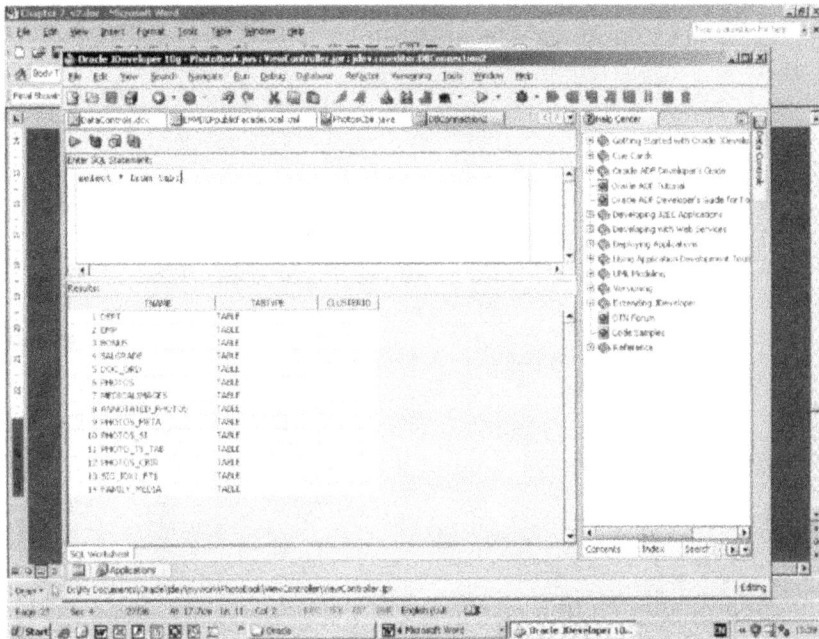

Since JDeveloper supports every stage of the development lifecycle through a single IDE it overcomes many of the disadvantages of prototyping such as version control and refactoring. In this way modeling, coding, debugging, testing, and tuning can be carried out in the same environment. JDeveloper includes UML modelers that can be integrated with creating EJB and simple Java classes. This includes support for the main UML models, such as a Class Modeler, Use Case Modeler, Activity Modeler, and a Sequence Diagram Modeler.

It includes a TopLink Mapper that enables developers to visually map Java objects to databases and other data sources.

At the user interface level JDeveloper provides a visual layout editor for HTML, JSP, and JSF in such a way that it can support interfaces for multichannel applications. A component called the Property Inspector allows the developer to simply specify attributes of visual components. For Web applications Oracle ADF also includes ADF faces. These are a set of JSF components that can be used to define advanced HTML with functionality provided by JSF architecture.

Figure 7.9

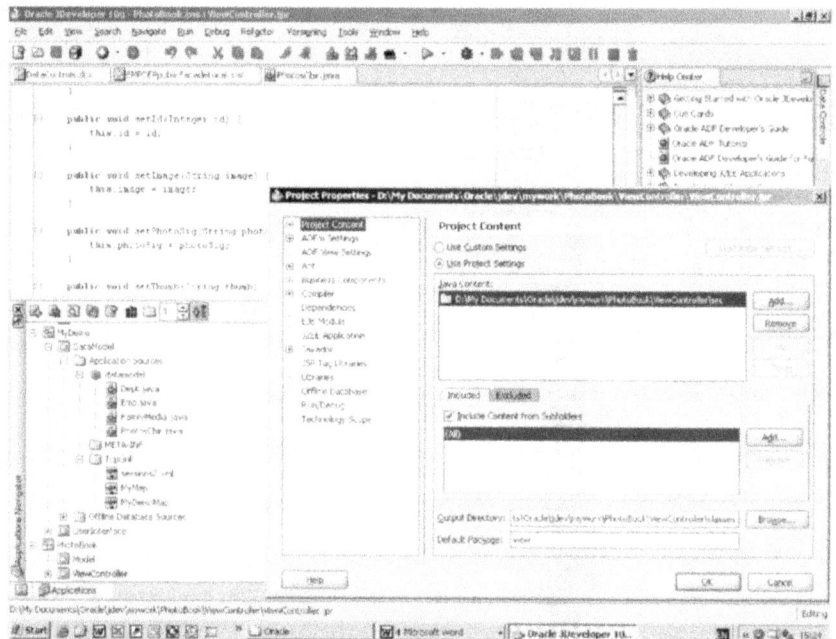

It is often assumed that prototyping ensures the design will be user-centered. This was not part of the original concept and it is still not universal. The characteristics of the users who will interact with the system—their experience, frequency of use, location, equipment, and authority level—are all significant. Experienced users can overlook the obvious and make assumptions that inexperienced users would not. This affects many stages of user-centered design from identification of requirements to evaluation. Users carry out tasks in response to events that occur within their sphere of responsibility. Special attention must be taken of all the objects the user employs so that these can be integrated into the way systems work even if they (objects) are not part of the system.

However, in practice there are several problems with prototyping, particularly

- Learning curve
  - There can be high expectations of high productivity that do not take into account the need for tools and training.
- Tool efficiency
  - Prototyping tools are generally less efficient than conventional programming languages (slow, large memory requirements, larger code).
- New roles for people—users must be involved
- Prototype itself (what is it—product, representation?)
- Ending prototyping—it can be difficult to stop—at each iteration users keep suggesting improvements and so do the developers
- Accuracy—this is important in user testing
- Acceptance

At the center of a prototyping development is a build-and-test cycle. It is important to evaluate the prototype and identify redesign issues. There are broadly two categories of interface evaluation methods that have been used:

1. Inspection methods conducted by usability experts that are cheaper and can be deployed in the early stages of the development process. However, the actual context of use is usually missing, hence these methods are often criticized for not addressing a "true picture" and are less reliable with new technological systems;

2. Field methods (sometimes called ethnography), involving real users in their real context who are able to contextualize the evalu-

ation. This tends to be time-consuming and expensive. Also, it requires the system, or a good robust prototype of it, to be developed and deployed.

On the positive side, newer usability methods are being developed that emphasize the context of use, can be deployed by interdisciplinary teams, and require less training. A realistic factor is that employing social scientists is cheaper than employing software developers so that the payoff from a small ethnographic pilot can be considerable provided the social scientists understand the design objectives and issues, and speak the same language as the developers.

During the build and test stage of prototyping a range of products are generated, some of these are in the form of documentation, for example:

- Task specification
- System functionality specification
- Interface functionality specification
- Screen layout and behavior
- Design rationale
- User feedback
- Performance criteria
- Reusable code

Given these reservations, prototyping can still be a powerful development tool. In one interview, a developer reflected on a career in which prototyping had played an important part before the introduction of modern tools or RAD and emphasized the prospective nature of user ownership and belief:

If you've been out there in the hard world, I'm sure you'll know there have been some beautifully written systems which have been a total failure, because essentially the customer didn't believe in them, or the users didn't believe in them. And there have been some absolute monstrosities, especially Mickey Mouse systems written on PCs by the users themselves, that fell down at every instance, that had no integrity and all of the dreadful sins, but they loved it because it was theirs. And a key difference in prototyping is that you sit down with the user with a PC, or a screen painter, or whatever it is, but you sit there and you go through it with him. And by the time that you finished this exercise whether it's just taken a day, a week, a month…. It didn't matter how good, bad, or indifferent it was, they would make it work. In fact it was usually pretty good as well. But the winning of their hearts and minds was a major breakthrough in my opinion because they invested the time and they took ownership.

—Quoted from Tudhope et al.

This developer emphasizes that crucial factors in whether the system will eventually "work" are the future activities and motivation of the user and that these are influenced strongly by previous prototyping experience, via either direct involvement or as "ambassador" users. However, just chatting with users about a screen can be inefficient and too open so that requirements drift occurs. It can be more efficient to plan a succession of developer–user interactive sessions, which we call DUCE sessions.

A DUCE session could take place in a usability lab but it is intended that the session should be held in the user's workplace in a realistic context. This method is intended to be used by developers actively involved in design decisions rather than HCI specialists.

The objective of the DUCE session is to make the users explain their normal working practice in relation to the prototype and while they are interacting with it. In order to assist the users to verbalize their experience, the developer is required to ask them a number of open questions as they work through the scenarios. The developer should also make a video and audio recording of the evaluation session for later analysis and takes notes of issues expressed. The question framework is shown in Figure 7.10.

The questioning style we are aiming for is more exploratory and less inquisitorial. For example, questions in the style of "Why did you do that?" are excluded because this would make the designer too dominant in the conversation. A checklist is provided in Figure 7.11 showing the theoretical cognitive stage (Norman, 1986) on the left and corresponding questions to ensure that each stage of cognition involved in completing the task is discussed by the user and developer.

Figure 7.10
*Eliciting user
comments in a
DUCE session.*

For each task/goal:
　　Ask the user to explain what he/she is attempting
　　For each subtask:
　　　　Ask the user to explain what he/she is attempting
　　　　For each stage in Norman's model of interaction:
　　　　　　Consider asking a question from the checklist
　　　　Next stage
　　　Next subtask
　　Next task

Table 7.6　*Checklist of questions*

User's Cognitive Stage	Potential Question
1. Form a goal	a) How does the screen help you select a way of achieving your task?
2. Form an intention	b) How does the screen suggest that what you are about to do is simple or difficult?
3. Specify the action sequence 4. Execute the action	c) How does the system let you know how you are making progress?
5. Perceive the resultant system state 6. Interpret the resultant state	d) What is the most important part of the information visible now? e) How has the screen changed in order to show what you have achieved?
7. Evaluate the outcome	f) How do you know that what you have done was correct? g) How would you recognize any mistakes?

7.6　Refine Requirements

The next problem is how to refine the requirements in light of information from data-gathering activities and prototyping. An important issue is prioritizing these. MoSCoW rules (from Dai Clegge of Oracle) is a technique that can help:

MUST HAVE for fundamental requirements (minimum usable subset).

SHOULD HAVE for important requirements but not fundamental.

COULD HAVE for those that could be left out.

WANT TO HAVE BUT WILL NOT HAVE THIS TIME AROUND.

The MoSCoW rules are very important as they form the basis of the decisions the developers will make over the whole project and during the time boxes. *Time boxing* is a technique for making sure prototyping development does not get out of control.

Improving design following user testing is often challenging because attempting to remove one fault can introduce other problems. Therefore, it is important that the designers are presented with actual user comments rather than a reinterpretation of them. This is based on observations that actual comments appear to have more impact motivating designers to change their design than evidence from experts that could be dismissed as merely opinion.

We recommend a meeting to thrash this out, which we call a team evidence analysis (TEA) session. This is because it involves problem solving where a team of developers needs to collaborate. In these days of outsourcing, the team may be distributed geographically and in different time zones, so the session may need technology such as groupware to facilitate it. In general, the way that designers convert data from usability evaluations into design decisions is not clear. One approach is based first on the user importance (the number of users encountering the problem and its importance to the user); secondly on the difficulty to repair the problem; and thirdly in relation to cost-benefit analysis (the relationship between user importance and cost of repair).

What kind of teams are most effective? We have found through experimental study of teams of developers that teams who work together are more effective at resolving design issues than developers working alone, and that having actual users' comments were more useful than the participation of an HCI specialist.

7.7 Test Infrastructure

The ISO standard (ISO/IEC 9126 [1991]) defines six quality characteristics and describes a software product evaluation process model. This standard describes

1.   Internal quality

2.   External quality

3.   Quality of use

The external quality manifested by software is the result of internal software attributes. The quality characteristics provide a framework for specifying quality requirements for software and making trade-offs between software product quality characteristics (see Figure 7.11). The objective is to achieve the necessary and sufficient quality to meet the real needs of users. These can be stated and implied needs. User requirements can be specified by quality-in-use metrics, which in turn can be used when a product is evaluated. Achieving a product that satisfies a user's need normally requires an iterative approach to software development with continual feedback from the user's perspective.

Figure 7.11

Principle Quality Factors

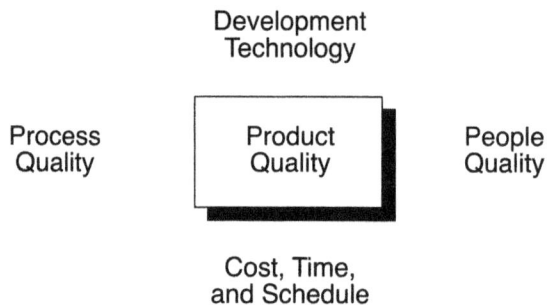

Development
Technology

Process
Quality

Product
Quality

People
Quality

Cost, Time,
and Schedule

Quality in use is the user's view of quality of the software product when it is used in a specific environment and a specific content of use. It measures the extent to which users can achieve their goals in a particular environment. It does not measure the properties of the software itself. The effective testing of the modules requires planning the test, including test data. Use cases form the basis of test cases and scenarios. See Figure 7.12.

Oracle JDeveloper demonstrated the advances in RAD tools. Without tool support testing and debugging user interface code can be challenging as user interface events can be difficult to disentangle. The UI debugger provides an easy way to monitor user interface execution with UI snapshots, event tracking, and graphical object display. We can also integrate with open source testing frameworks.

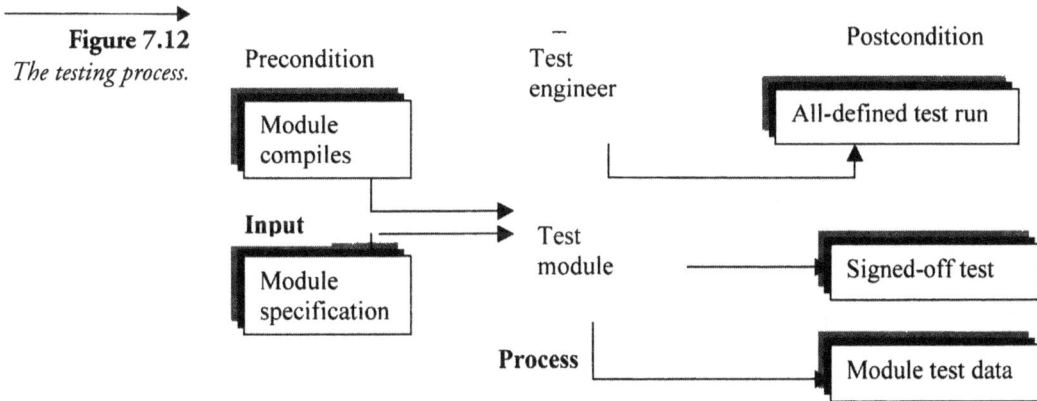

Figure 7.12
The testing process.

The ISO standard defines usability as the extent to which the software product can be understood, learned, used, and attractive to the user when used in specified conditions.

Understandability	The capability to enable the user to understand whether the software is suitable and how it can be used for particular tasks and conditions for use.
Learnability	The capability to enable the user to learn to use its application.
Operability	The capability to enable the user to operate and control its application (controllability, error tolerance, and conformity to user expectations).

Usability metrics should be objective, empirical, use a valid scale, and be reproducible. To be classed as empirical, data must be obtained from observation or a psychometrically-valid questionnaire.

The context of use includes the users, tasks, the physical, system, and social environment in which the software product is used. Usability metrics can be obtained by simulating a realistic working environment in a usability laboratory.

Quality in use metrics include:

- Efficiency metrics—can the user achieve specified goals with completeness and accuracy?
- Productivity metrics—resources used (e.g., time to complete task, user's effort, materials, or financial costs).

- Safety metrics—level of risk of harm.

- Satisfaction metrics—users' attitudes.

Table 7.7   *Metrics for the Usability of Multimedia Applications (ISO/IEC TR 9126-2)*

Metrics	Definition
Task completion	What proportion of the tasks are completed, x = A/B
Task effectiveness	What proportion of the tasks are completed correctly, x = A/B
Error frequency	Number of errors made by users, x = A
Help frequency	Number of accesses to help, x = A
Task productivity	M2 = M1/T, where M1 is task effectiveness, T is task time
Satisfaction scale	x = A, where A is questionnaire responses
Operational frequency of use	Does the user use the software frequently Actual use/Opportunity of use, x = A/B
Media device utilization balancing	Degree of synchronization between different media over set period of time – X = ST/T, where ST sync time is time devoted to continuous resource, T = time period for dissimilar media to finish tasks with synchronization

Effort type is the productive time associated with a specific project task, while individual effort is the productive time needed by the individual to complete a specified task. The task effort is the accumulated value for each individual over the whole project.

Understandability metrics are significant guides for rich-media applications. These include:

- Functional understandability: the number of user interface functions where purposes are easily understood by the user, compared with the number of functions, x = A/B.

- Location understandability: the number of user interface functions where purposes are easily understood by the user, compared with the number of functions, x = A/B (can the user locate functions by exploring the interface?).

- Operability metrics:
    - Number of input items that check for valid data, x = A/B
    - Number of functions that can be cancelled, x = A/B
    - Number of functions that can be customized for access by users who have accessibility problems, x = A/B

- Physical accessibility: number of functions successfully accessed by users with physical handicaps

There are two time behavior metrics that are important for rich media:

- Response time—estimated time to complete task

- Throughput time—number of tasks that can be performed over unit of time

How many users do we need to test our systems? Landauer and Nielsen seem to suggest that with five users we would uncover 80% of the problems, however, ISO/IEC TR 9126-2 suggests that for reliable results a sample of at least eight users is necessary, although useful information can be obtained from smaller groups. Users should carry out the tests without any hints or external assistance.

7.8   References

Beck, K. *Extreme Programming Explained: Embrace Change.* Boston: Addison-Wesley, 1999.

Dunckley, L. (2006) Practice in Public Sector IT:Usability and Accessibility Performance. Seibel White Paper.

Goguen, J. "Requirements Engineering as the Reconciliation of Social and Technical Issues," in *Requirements Engineering: Social and Technical Issues*, M. Jirotka and J. Goguen, eds. London: Academic Press, 1994, pp. 165–200.

Koppel R, Metlay J.P., Cohen A, Abaluck B, Russell Localio A, Kimmel, S.E, and Strom,B.L. (2005) *Role of Computerized Physician Order Entry Systems in Facilitating Medication Errors.* JAMA. 2005;293:1197-1203.

Landauer, T. K. *The Trouble with Computers.* Boston: MIT Press, 1995.

Lindsay, P. H., and Norman, D. A. (1972). *Human information processing: An introduction to psychology.* New York: Academic Press.

Marcos,E., Vela,B. and Cavero,J.M. (2003) A Methodological Approach for Object-Relational Database Design using UML .Journal Software and Systems Modeling Volume 2, Number 1 / March,Pages 59-72.

Naiburg, E. J., and R. A. Maksimchuk.*UML for Database Design*. Boston: Addison-Wesley, 2001.

Norman, D. A. (1986), Cognitive Engineering, in Norman, D. A. and Draper, S. W. (eds.) User Centered Systems Design.

Pinheiro, F.A.C., and J. A. Goguen. "An Object-oriented Tool for Tracing Requirements," *IEEE Software*, 13, no. 2 (March 1996):52–64.

Smith, A. (1997) Human-Computer Factors: A Study of Users and Information Systems. McGraw-Hill Higher Education.

Smith, A. and L. Dunckley. "Early Prototype Evaluation and Redesign: Structuring the Design Space Through Contextual Techniques." *Interacting with Computers*, 14, no. 6 (Dec. 2002): 821–843.

Sommerville, I.P. *Software Engineering Seventh Edition*. Boston: Addison-Wesley, Wokingham, 2000.

Stapleton, J. *DSDM—Dynamic Systems Development Method*. Boston: Addison-Wesley, 1997.

Suchman, L. "Representations of Work." *Communications of the ACM*, 38, no. 9 (1995):33–68.

Tudhope, D., Beynon-Davies,P. and Mackay, H. (2000) Prototyping Praxis: Constructing Computer Systems and Building Belief. Human-Computer Interaction 2000, Vol. 15, No. 4, Pages 353-383.

8

Media in Object Types

This chapter looks in greater detail at the nature and characteristics of the different kinds of media objects and the specific needs for text, audio, image, and video applications. Through a study of this chapter the reader will develop a broad overview of the role of media objects within database development and should then be able to understand

- The general features of a variety of media object types and their deployment in relational and object tables.
- The role played by SQL objects to develop more complex objects.

8.1   Media Objects

In Chapter 3 we learned that object types have the general structure shown in Figure 8.1.

Figure 8.1
Classes and object types.

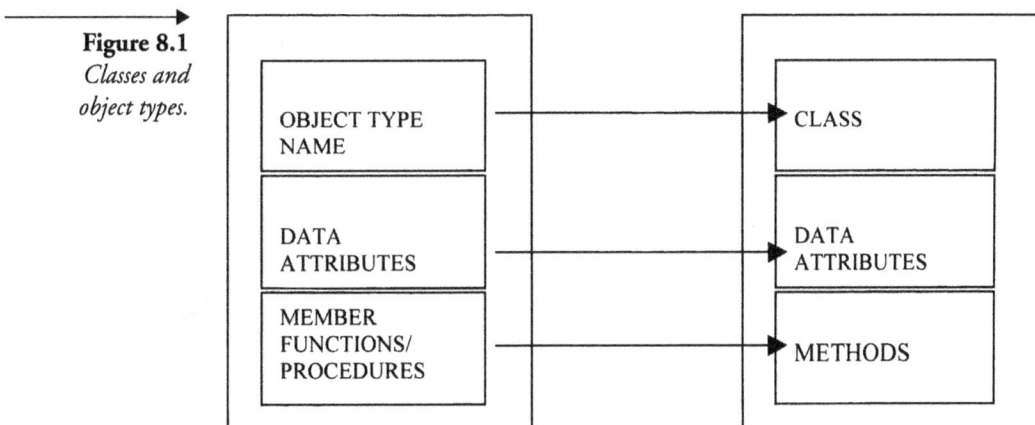

A key concept in SQL:1999 is that user-defined data types would make it easier for applications developers to work with complex and unstructured data. A user-defined data type is a theoretical construct that is implemented in Oracle as an object type. In an Oracle implementation, an object type is equivalent in the concept of a class in UML, with three kinds of components. It must have a *name* that uniquely identifies it within the database schema, it can have *attributes* that are either *built-in* types or other object types, and *methods* that describe the operations that can be applied to the object type known as member functions or procedures. In an object type there may be several attributes. These attributes will normally have *built-in* data types drawn from the traditional system-defined data types, such as INTEGER, CHARACTER, etc., or may be object types, such as a set of color values. As we found in Chapter 3 an object type is one created by or for the database developer. This concept of TYPE has an advantage that only certain operations can be allowed, that is, are valid for a given type. For example, arithmetic operations will only be valid for a numeric data type; finding the time intervals between two dates can only apply to datetime data types. When object types are created, the developer can also specify the operations (methods) that can be applied to them.

Even in the original relational model there was no restriction on the kinds of things that could be defined as types, but this theoretical ability has only been available in practice recently. So now we can have types made up from maps, images, and videos by using object types that we studied in Chapter 3, such as SI_StillImage type. The values of a type may only be manipulated by the operators defined on that domain. For example, SI_StillImage type has an operator called SI_Thumbnail(height,width) that would derive a new thumbnail image from the specified SI_StillImage object using the height and width provided as parameters.

In Chapter 3 we listed the attributes of the *inter*Media object types, for example, the ORDImage object type. Every object type has methods associated with it that deal with

- The construction of instances of the type.
- Setting and getting individual attribute values.
- The specific nature of the media type, such as image processing operations.

Although Oracle *inter*Media provides a set of image, audio, and video object types sufficient for most common application requirements, including popular Web formats, these types can be extended to support many application-specific requirements, for example:

- New or specialized formats

- New compression and decompression schemes (codecs)

- Specialized indexes

- Customized query optimization and methods

- New data sources

- Specialized data-processing algorithms

Applications can easily add multiple image, audio, and video columns, or mixed columns containing any of these types as objects to existing and new relational tables.

Before we look at the different media types individually we need to get an understanding of ORDSource. This is a special object type from which all the media types derive properties and methods. The ORDSource type has a set of methods that are basic to all the *inter*Media types. In addition, the other types (image, audio, and video) have their own specialized methods that we cover separately later in this chapter.

In UML the class is not a collection of objects, it is a definition of the object's data and operations. In the same way, *inter*Media ORDAudio, ORDDoc, ORDImage, and ORDVideo object types provide wrapper methods from ORDSource to do the following:

- Set the source of the data as local or external (ORDSource.setLocal) depending on whether the data is within the database or in the external file system.

- Modify the time an object was last updated (ORDSource.setUpdateTime).

- Set information about the external source type, location, and name of the data (ORDSource.setSourceInformation) that we need when we load the data.

- Transfer data into or out of the database (ORDSource.importFrom).

■ Obtain information about the local data content, such as its length, location, or its handle to the BLOB, put the content into a temporary BLOB, or delete it, for example, using the ORDSource.getContentInTempLob() method.

■ Access source data by opening it, reading it, writing to it, trimming it, and closing it, for example, using the ORDSOURCE.trim method.

We can see how this system works by taking ORDImage as an example. The ORDSource object type is incorporated in all the specific media types and examples of its attributes are shown in Table 8.1 for image media. We do not call its methods directly, instead users are advised to use those methods provided for the specific types. There are a number of methods available to manipulate the image instances.

This means that when ORDSYS.ORDImage is used as a data type for a column in a table that column will include all attributes of the ORD-Source type and the ORDImage type. These are shown below with sample data for the Picture Book case study. Table 8.1 (a) displays specific image attributes. The MIME type is used to specify the nature of the data in the

Table 8.1   *(a) ORDImage Attributes with Sample Data*

Source	MIME Type	Height	Width	Content Length	File Format	Content Format	Compression Format
cats	image/jpeg	132	147	301,000	JFIF	24BITRGB	JEPG
chardonnay	image/jpeg	223	157	80,000	JFIF	24BITRGB	JEPG
europa	image/gif	150	150	9,820	GIFF	24BITRGB	GIFLZW
frank	image/tiff	221	224	15,700	TIFF	24BITRGB	None
goldfinch	image/bmp	200	200	117,000	BMPF	24BITRGB	None
isaac	image/tiff	334	266	99,100	TIFF	8BITBW	None
kiran	image/jpeg	480	640	80,000	JFIF	24BITRGB	JEPG

body of a MIME entity, by giving media type and subtype identifiers. The MIME header field is simply a set of parameters, specified in an attribute/ value notation (see Chapter 2). In general, the top-level media type is used to declare the general type of data, while the subtype specifies a specific format for that type of data. Table 8.1 (b) shows the corresponding values for the attributes of the source attribute of the ORDImage type (which is of type ORDSource). This tells us that all the media data is local and stored in BLOBS.

Table 8.1   *(b) ORDSource Attributes with Sample Data*

Object	localData	srcType	srcLocation	srcName	updateTime	Local
cats	BLOB	FILE	C:\image	Cats.jpg	02/11/02:12:26	1
chardonnay	BLOB	FILE	C:\image	Chardonnay.jpg	02/11/02:12:26	1
europa	BLOB	FILE	C:\image	Europa1.gif	22/11/01:21:46	1
frank	BLOB	FILE	C:\image	Frank300.tif	2/11/02:12:26	1
goldfinch	BLOB	FILE	C:\image	Goldfinc.bmp	02/11/02:12:26	1
isaac	BLOB	FILE	C:\image	Isaac.tif	9/19/02:07:08	1
kiran	BLOB	FILE	C:\image	Kiran.jpg	19/09/02:17:58	1

Note: The metadata values (height, width, etc.) can be captured from the media during the insertion of the instances by extraction from the media metadata rather than being entered by the user (see Section 8.3.3). The three ORDSource attributes (src-Type, srcLocation, srcName) are only required for external media sources but are important information for loading the image media into the database.

8.2   Methods Available for ORDImage Object Type

*inter*Media supports image processing, such as image format transcoding, image cutting, image scaling, and generating thumbnail images. In addition, specifically when the destination image file format is RAW Pixel (RPIX) format or Microsoft Windows Bitmap (BMPF) image format, *inter*Media supports a variety of operators for changing the format characteristics.

We will start by creating a new table to illustrate the ORDImage methods:

```
CREATE TABLE photos
    (ID               NUMBER NOT NULL,
     IMAGE            ORDSYS.ORDIMAGE)
    LOB (IMAGE.SOURCE.LOCALDATA) STORE AS (CHUNK 32K)
```

We can now use the methods of ORDImage, which can be invoked in two ways:

```
object_typename.method()
```

Or we can use it with an expression such as a PL/SQL variable:

```
object_expression.method()
```

Now we can add an image using the INIT() method, described in Chapter 3, to initialize the image column as an empty BLOB, followed by the importFrom method, which will accept an external image file and import this into the database. This is illustrated by the next PL/SQL procedure:

```
CREATE or replace PROCEDURE img_import
AS
    img      ORDSYS.ORDIMAGE;
    ctx      raw(64) :=null;
BEGIN
    INSERT INTO photos(id, image)
    VALUES (4310,ORDSYS.ORDIMAGE.INIT());
        img.importFrom(ctx,'file','PHOTO_DIR','graduation.jpg')
            returning image into img;
    UPDATE  photos SET image=img WHERE id=4310;
END;
```

In this procedure we use the declaration

```
ctx      raw(64) :=null;
```

This is for the source plug-in context information and should be allocated and initialized to NULL. We will use this kind of variable for all the different media types.

The statement

```
INSERT INTO photos(id, image)
    VALUES (4310,ORDSYS.ORDIMAGE.INIT());
```

effects the creation of an empty image in the row identified by 4310. The importFrom method stores image data in the database from the directory named as 'PHOTO_DIR' and implicitly calls the setProperties() method to set the height, width, fileFormat, and other object fields appropriately extracted from the image metadata.

This is the full specification of the method:

```
img.importFrom(ctx,'file','PHOTO_DIR','graduation.jpg');
```

The object types include a number of data manipulation methods, for example, specifically for image media using ORDImage:

- Format and compression conversion
- Scaling
- Cropping
- Copying

The first set of methods we will study are concerned with the status of images before or after processing. For example, processCopy() and process() are member functions of ORDSYS.ORDIMAGE that can access and manipulate the following attributes:

- Source
- Content length
- Width
- Height
- MIME type
- File format
- Content format
- Compression format

Note there are operators of the same name that process BFILES and BLOBS through the relational interface. We can use these operators in the statement such as object_name.setProperties(). In the following procedure an image is selected from the database and copied into a variable **obj** that is used with the setProperties() method to extract the values of some image attributes that can then be displayed.

```
CREATE OR REPLACE PROCEDURE get_image_props
AS
 obj ORDSYS.ORDimage;
BEGIN
 SELECT p.image INTO obj FROM photos p
  WHERE p.id = 4310 FOR UPDATE;
 obj.setProperties();
 DBMS_OUTPUT.PUT_LINE('Image file format: ' ||
obj.getFileformat);
 DBMS_OUTPUT.PUT_LINE('Image Compression: ' ||
obj.getCompressionFormat);
 DBMS_OUTPUT.PUT_LINE('Image Content format: ' ||
obj.getContentformat);
 DBMS_OUTPUT.PUT_LINE('Image Mime Type: ' ||
obj.getMimeType);
 DBMS_OUTPUT.PUT_LINE('Image size: ' ||
obj.getContentLength);
 DBMS_OUTPUT.PUT_LINE('Image Height: ' || obj.getHeight);
 DBMS_OUTPUT.PUT_LINE('Image Width: ' || obj.getWidth);
 UPDATE  photos p set p.image = obj
   WHERE  p.id = 4310;
 COMMIT;
END;
```

When we execute this procedure we find the following.

```
SQL> execute get_image_props
Image file format: JFIF
Image Compression: JPEG
Image Content format: 24BITRGB
Image Mime Type: image/jpeg
Image size: 73874
Image Height: 360
Image Width: 564
```

Properties extracted from the *inter*Media object types can be stored in an XML-formatted CLOB or in individual relational columns as we showed in Table 8.1.

Both process methods process() and processCopy() carry out three types of operations:

1. Image formatting—change the layout of the data within the image storage but do not change the semantic content or visual appearance of the image (e.g., converting a 24-bit image to 8 bits; color to greyscale; compression).

2. Image processing—change the way the image looks (e.g., contrast; cut, flip, gamma, which corrects the brightness of the image; mirror; rotate; scale; quantize, which will change a number of properties including dither). (See Chapter 2.)

3. Format—specific—only for raw pixel or BMPF (e.g., changes channel order, R,G,B).

The main difference between the process() and processCopy() methods is that the latter method accepts separate source and destination ORDImage instances so the original image and the changed image are both retained. In the case of process() method, the source and destination ORDImage instances are the same so the original image becomes the destination image and is written into the same storage space as the source image replacing it so that it is permanently altered. For example:

```
Object_name.processCopy(VERB, new_object_name)
```

```
Object_name.process(VERB)
```

In general when we use these process methods, any number of operators can be combined as long as the command statement makes sense. In Figure 8.2 we can see some of the effects of using process verbs on the same source image: (a) is the original image, (b) is the result of using the cut verb, and (c) is the result of using two verbs, gamma and rotate. Some operators only work with certain image formats, for example, JPEG, while others require data in raw pixel format.

When we use these methods the IN parameter relates to a number of operators—process verbs—included in a single method. The process verbs include:

- Flip
- Gamma
- Contrast

- Quantize
- Tiled
- FileFormat
- MaxScale

The full list of verbs is displayed in Table 8.2. FileFormat is the single most important detail when specifying the output for process() method. Its value determines the range of content and compression formats allowed and whether or not compression quality will be useful.

Table 8.2 *Image Processing Verbs*

Process Verb	Effect	Usage Example
Rotate	Changes orientation	'rotate=45 '
Gamma	Changes RGB values to make image lighter or darker	'gamma="0.3"'
Contrast	Changes pixels range	Contrast 150 210
Cut	Crops image to rectangle from upper left value to lower right	Cut 00 200 200
Scale	Changing scale (e.g., to produce a thumbnail)	scale=2
		scale="0.51"
		scale="0.15"
compressionQuality	Expressed as integer(=>0 and <=100)	compressionQuality=50
	MAXCOMPRATIO (smallest image, lowest quality)	compressionQuality= MAXCOMPRATIO
	HIGHCOMP	compressionQuality= HIGHCOMP
	MEDCOMP default	compressionQuality= MEDCOMP
	LOWCOMP	compressionQuality= LOWCOMP

Table 8.2   *Image Processing Verbs (continued)*

Process Verb	Effect	Usage Example
	MAXINTEGRITY (largest image, best quality)	compressionQuality= MAXINTEGRITY
	An integer value between 0 and 100	compressionQuality=50
compressionFormat	Specifies the compression algorithm to encode the image data, such as HUFFMAN3, FAX3, and FAX4—common in TIFF images	compressionFormat=JPEG
contentFormat	Concerned with 8-bit … monochrome, etc.	
	Use 256 colors with lookup table	contentFormat=8bitlut
	Use 24-bit true color	contentFormat=24bitrgb
fileFormat	Changes output to specified file format	fileFormat=TIFF
fixedScale	Scales to fixed size in pixels (width, height)	fixedScale=32 32
maxScale	Scales to maximum size preserving aspect ratio	maxScale=50 50
flip	Swap scan lines from top to bottom	flip
mirror	Swap columns of an image from left to right	mirror
tiled	Forces output to be tiled. for TIFF only.	tiled
xScale	Scale on x-axis by given factor.	xScale="0.1"
yScale	Scale on y-axis by given factor.	yScale="0.1"
Page	Used with "multipage" images produced by some scanners. For TIFF only.	Page=0

Table 8.2   *Image Processing Verbs (continued)*

Process Verb	Effect	Usage Example
Quantize	ERRORDIFFUSION ORDEREDDITHER THRESHOLD MEDIANCUT	quantize=ordereddither

Note: Quotes are required around floating point values to correctly interpret values according to the user's NLS_TERRITORY setting.

Following this approach we can change an image into a thumbnail using processCopy(), combined with the scale verbs:

```
BEGIN
  SELECT image, thumb INTO obj_1, obj_2
   FROM photos
   WHERE id = img_id FOR UPDATE;
   obj_1.processCopy('maxScale=32 32', obj_2);
  UPDATE photos SET thumb = obj_2
   WHERE id=img_id;
  COMMIT;
End;
```

In this example we have used processCopy() because we want to keep the original image and the thumbnail. This example takes the stored image into the variable obj_1 and uses the processCopy() method to generate and store the thumbnail in obj_2. The statement

```
obj_1.processCopy('maxScale=32 32', obj_2);
```

follows the same pattern for all the process verbs (i.e., input image + process verb = output image). See Table 8.3 and Figure 8.2.

Table 8.3   *Verbs used with methods Process() and ProcessCopy()*

Input Image	Process Verb	Output Image
GIF file	'fileformat=jfif'	JPEG file

Table 8.3 *Verbs used with methods Process() and ProcessCopy()*

JPEG	'maxscale=200 200'	JPEG file
JPEG file	'fileformat=tiff scale="0.4"	Outputs TIFF file
TIFF file	'fileFormat=giff rotate=90'	Gives GIF file

Figure 8.2
Image processing within the database.

| (a) The original image | (b) Cut = 00 100 100 | (c) Uses mirror with gamma |

The gamma processing verb changes the R,G,B band values of the image. The values gamma1, gamma2, and gamma3 are the denominators of the gamma exponent applied to the input image. If only one value is specified, then that value is applied to *all* color components (either gray, or red, green, and blue) of the input image as shown in Figure 8.2(c). If three values are specified then gamma1 is applied to the red component of the image, gamma2 to the green component, and gamma3 to the blue component.

To brighten an image, specify gamma values greater than 1.0; typical values are in the range 1.0 to 2.5. To darken an image, specify gamma values smaller than 1.0 (but larger than 0).

The *mirror* operator places an image's scanlines in inverse order such that the pixel columns are swapped from left to right. This operator accepts no values.

The rotate and gamma operators are illustrated in the following procedures.

```
CREATE OR REPLACE PROCEDURE image_process1
AS
 obj ORDSYS.ORDimage;
BEGIN
```

```
SELECT p.image INTO obj FROM photos p
  WHERE p.id = 4310 FOR UPDATE;
obj.process('rotate=45 gamma="0.3"');--rotate and darken
 obj.process('quantize=ordereddither');
 DBMS_OUTPUT.PUT_LINE('Image file format: ' ||
obj.getFileformat);
 DBMS_OUTPUT.PUT_LINE('Image Compression: ' ||
obj.getCompressionFormat);
 DBMS_OUTPUT.PUT_LINE('Image Content format: ' ||
obj.getContentformat);
 DBMS_OUTPUT.PUT_LINE('Image Mime Type: ' ||
obj.getMimeType);
 DBMS_OUTPUT.PUT_LINE('Image size: ' ||
obj.getContentLength);
DBMS_OUTPUT.PUT_LINE('Image Height: ' || obj.getHeight);
DBMS_OUTPUT.PUT_LINE('Image Width: ' || obj.getWidth);
 UPDATE  photos p set p.image = obj
   WHERE  p.id = 4310;
 COMMIT;
END;
```

The procedure above illustrates how we can perform image processing by selecting an image from the database and using the process method to produce the changes in orientation and color. The cut verb will select a rectangular area from upper left (x,y) with dimensions width, height. In the next example the cut verb is specified.

Figure 8.3
Examples of effects of processing verbs.

| (a) Quantize | (b) Crop, quantize using dither | (c) Resize x,y scales |

```
CREATE OR REPLACE PROCEDURE image_process2
  AS
   obj ORDSYS.ORDimage;
  BEGIN
   SELECT p.image INTO obj FROM photos p
```

```
     WHERE p.id = 4310 FOR UPDATE;
   obj.process('cut=0 0 200 200');
   obj.process('contrast=150 210');
   obj.process('flip');
   obj.process('mirror');
   DBMS_OUTPUT.PUT_LINE('Image file format: ' ||
obj.getFileformat);
   DBMS_OUTPUT.PUT_LINE('Image Compression: ' ||
obj.getCompressionFormat);
   DBMS_OUTPUT.PUT_LINE('Image Content format: ' ||
obj.getContentformat);
   DBMS_OUTPUT.PUT_LINE('Image Mime Type: ' ||
obj.getMimeType);
   DBMS_OUTPUT.PUT_LINE('Image size: ' ||
obj.getContentLength);
 DBMS_OUTPUT.PUT_LINE('Image Height: ' || obj.getHeight);
 DBMS_OUTPUT.PUT_LINE('Image Width: ' || obj.getWidth);
   UPDATE  photos p set p.image = obj
     WHERE  p.id = 4310;
   COMMIT;
 END;
```

We can see the difference in the images in Figures 8.2 and 8.3 but in addition we can see the results of the properties:

<SQL> execute image_process2

Image file format: JFIF

Image compression: JPEG

Image content format: 24BITRGB

Image MIME type: image/jpeg

Image size: 3012

Image height: 200

Image width: 200

The quantize verb (see Figure 8.3 for its affect) is used to improve the quality of a poor image by using a specific quantize method such as

- ERRORDIFFUSION
- ORDEREDDITHER
- THRESHOLD
- MEDIANCUT

The Quantize verb is used in the procedure image_process1 in a statement such as

```
quantize=ordereddither
```

There are two forms of the contrast operator. We can use

```
Contrast =<p>
```

where <p> maps a percentage of the pixel values, p, to the entire output range. Or,

```
Contrast=<lower> <upper>
```

This linearly maps the input image's pixels in the range between upper and lower to the entire output range. It is also possible to map the color bands (R,G,B) to different ranges (e.g., Contrast 150 210).

8.2.1 Dealing with Image Metadata

There are specialized methods available for dealing with image metadata that are described in Chapter 2. ORDImage has methods to get and write the metadata into special XML documents.

The photos table stores two instances of an image: the full-size photograph and a thumbnail image. This table can also store up to four different image metadata documents. These documents are stored in the columns named `metaORDImage`, `metaEXIF`, `metaIPTC`, and `metaXMP`, and represent image metadata from the ORDImage, EXIF, IPTC, and XMP metadata formats, respectively. The metadata columns are of type `XMLType`, and they are bound to the corresponding metadata XML schemas that *inter*Media provides. We can modify the photos table to create a table that holds the metadata as well.

```
CREATE TABLE photos_meta
                    ( id            NUMBER PRIMARY KEY,
                      description   VARCHAR2(40),
                      metaORDImage XMLTYPE,
                      metaEXIF      XMLTYPE,
                      metaIPTC      XMLTYPE,
                      metaXMP       XMLTYPE,
                      image         ORDSYS.ORDIMAGE,
                      thumb         ORDSYS.ORDIMAGE )
LOB(image.source.localdata)  -- storage images with 32K chunk
  STORE AS (chunk 32k)
LOB(thumb.source.localdata)  -- but the thumbnails with only
16k
  STORE AS (chunk 16k)
-- and bind the XMLType columns to the interMedia metadata
schemas
XMLType COLUMN metaORDImage
  XMLSCHEMA "http://xmlns.oracle.com/ord/meta/ordimage"
  ELEMENT "ordImageAttributes"
XMLType COLUMN metaEXIF
  XMLSCHEMA "http://xmlns.oracle.com/ord/meta/exif"
  ELEMENT "exifMetadata"
XMLType COLUMN metaIPTC
  XMLSCHEMA "http://xmlns.oracle.com/ord/meta/iptc"
  ELEMENT "iptcMetadata"
XMLType COLUMN metaXMP
  XMLSCHEMA "http://xmlns.oracle.com/ord/meta/xmp"
  ELEMENT "xmpMetadata";
```

The following PL/SQL procedure extracts metadata from an image and stores it in the specified metadata columns in the photos_meta table. This procedure demonstrates the getMetadata() method, which returns an array of XML documents. The root element of each document is examined to determine the metadata type. The UPDATE statement stores the documents in the corresponding columns in the photos_meta table.

The getMetadata() Method

The ORDImage getMetadata method is a member function that accepts the metadata type as a string parameter that specifies the types of embedded metadata to extract and return an XMLSequenceType, for example, getMetadata(metadata type). It extracts the specified types of metadata from the image and returns an array of schema-valid XML documents. If no matching metadata is found, an empty array is returned.

The input parameter can be the metadata type specified as follows: ALL, ORDIMAGE, XMP, EXIF, and IPTC-IIM. The default value is ALL. When the value of the input parameter metadata type is ALL, and more than one type of supported metadata is present in the image, this method returns several XML documents, one for each type of metadata found. For other values of the input parameter, the method returns zero, if the metadata of that type were absent or a single XML document conforms to one of the metadata standards XMP, EXIF, and IPTC-IIM. Each document returned is stored as an instance of XMLType, and is based on one of the metadata schemas. The method XMLType.getNamespace() can be used to determine the type of metadata represented in that document.

```
CREATE OR REPLACE PROCEDURE extractMetadata(inID IN INTEGER)
IS
    img             ORDSYS.ORDIMAGE;
    metav           XMLSequenceType;
    meta_root       VARCHAR2(40);
    xmlORD          XMLType;
    xmlXMP          XMLType;
    xmlEXIF         XMLType;
    xmlIPTC         XMLType;

BEGIN
 -- select the image
SELECT image INTO img
FROM photos_meta WHERE id = inID;
-- extract all the metadata
metav := img.getMetadata( 'ALL' );

-- process the result array to discover what types of metadata
were returned

FOR i IN 1..metav.count() LOOP
  meta_root := metav(i).getRootElement();
  CASE meta_root
    WHEN        'ordImageAttributes' THEN xmlORD := metav(i);
    WHEN        'xmpMetadata' THEN xmlXMP := metav(i);
    WHEN        'iptcMetadata' THEN xmlIPTC := metav(i);
    WHEN        'exifMetadata' THEN xmlEXIF := metav(i);
```

```
      ELSE NULL;
    END CASE;
  END LOOP;


  -- Update metadata columns
  --
  UPDATE photos_meta
  SET metaORDImage = xmlORD,
      metaEXIF = xmlEXIF,
      metaIPTC = xmlIPTC,
      METAXMP = xmlXMP
  WHERE id = inID;


  END;
```

The putMetadata() Method

This method accepts XML data in the form of a valid XML document and a string that specifies its metadata type. The XMLType should contain a schema valid XML document for the indicated metadata type. If the value of the metadata type parameter is XMP, the root element should contain a well-formed RDF document. This is the default type. For example:

```
putMetadata(xml Data IN NOCOPY XMLType, metadata type IN
VARCHAR2 DEFAULT 'XMP' encoding IN VARCHAR2 DEFAULT 'UTF-8');
```

This specifies the character encoding to be used in the image file. Valid values are UTF-8, UTF-16, UTF-16BE, and UTF-16LE. The default is UTF-8. Why is this necessary?

Different image file formats support different encodings, and may restrict the binary metadata packet size. The putMetadata() method creates a binary packet suitable for embedding in the target image file. The packet is encoded according to the value of the encoding parameter. If the value of the metadata type parameter is XMP, a new XMP packet is written to the image, replacing any existing XMP packets. A binary metadata packet generated from the same XML document input may have different sizes for different encodings. The following are the restrictions of the supported image formats:

- GIF89a supports UTF-8 encoding only.

- JPEG requires a binary packet size of less than 65,502 bytes.

- TIFF requires a binary packet size of less than 4 gigabytes.

The following PL/SQL procedure demonstrates the putMetadata() method. This procedure accepts six arguments. The entry_id argument identifies the image in the photos_meta table to be updated. The remaining arguments (title, creator, date, description, and copyright) are strings that will be formatted into an XMP packet and embedded within the target image.

This example creates an XML document instance based on the *inter*Media XML schema for XMP metadata. The schema for XMP metadata defines a single, global element <xmpMetadata>. The <xmpMetadata> element contains a single, well-formed RDF document. The RDF document contains a single <RDF> element that is derived from the RDF namespace. This RDF document is constructed using elements defined by the Dublin Core Schema (see Chapter 2).

The call to the putMetadata() method embeds the metadata document into the image file. The UPDATE statement stores the new image and the new metadata back in the photos_meta table.

```
CREATE OR REPLACE PROCEDURE write_metadata
( entry_id IN VARCHAR2,
                        title IN VARCHAR2,
                        creator IN VARCHAR2,
                        date IN VARCHAR2,
                        description IN VARCHAR2,
                        copyright IN VARCHAR2 )
     IS
        img              ORDSYS.ORDImage;
        xmp              XMLType;
        buf              VARCHAR2(5000);
     BEGIN
     -- select the image
     SELECT image INTO img
     FROM photos_meta WHERE id = entry_id FOR UPDATE;

     -- Create the XMP packet it must be schema valid
     -- to "http://xmlns.oracle.com/ord/meta/xmp"
     -- and contain an <RDF> element. This example uses
```

```
-- the Dublin Core schema.

buf := '<xmpMetadata xmlns="http://xmlns.oracle.com/ord/meta/
xmp"
         xsi:schemaLocation="http://xmlns.oracle.com/ord/meta/
xmp
            http://xmlns.oracle.com/ord/meta/xmp"
         xmlns:xsi="http://www.w3.org/2001/XMLSchema-instance"
>
   <rdf:RDF xmlns:rdf="http://www.w3.org/1999/02/22-rdf-
syntax-ns#">
   <rdf:Description about="" xmlns:dc="http://purl.org/dc/
elements/1.1/">';

IF title IS NOT NULL THEN
   buf := buf || '<dc:title>' || htf.escape_sc(title) || '</
dc:title>';
END IF;

IF creator IS NOT NULL THEN
   buf := buf || '<dc:creator>' || htf.escape_sc(creator)
             || '</dc:creator>';
END IF;
IF date IS NOT NULL THEN
   buf := buf || '<dc:date>' || htf.escape_sc(date)
             || '</dc:date>';
END IF;
IF description IS NOT NULL THEN
   buf := buf || '<dc:description>' ||
htf.escape_sc(description)
             || '</dc:description>';
END IF;
IF copyright IS NOT NULL THEN
   buf := buf || '<dc:copyright>' || htf.escape_sc(copyright)
             || '</dc:copyright>';
END IF;

buf := buf || '
   </rdf:Description>
   </rdf:RDF>
   </xmpMetadata>';
```

```
-- create the XML document
xmp := XMLType.createXML(buf, 'http://xmlns.oracle.com/ord/
meta/xmp');

-- write the metadata
img.putMetadata( xmp, 'XMP' );

-- update the image
UPDATE photos_meta SET image = img,
    metaXMP = xmp
WHERE id = entry_id;

END;
```

*inter*Media can work with DICOM images in basically the same way as GIF or TIFF images but we would need to create a table to hold the metadata that refers to the appropriate XML schema. This is illustrated by creating another version of the photos_meta table called medicalImages.

```
CREATE TABLE medicalImages
                        (id number primary key,
                         description VARCHAR2(40),
                         metadata XMLType,
                         image ORDSYS.ORDIMAGE,
                         thumb ORDSYS.ORDIMAGE)
LOB (image.source.localdata) -- store images with 32K chunk
  STORE AS (chunk 32K)
LOB (thumb.source.localdata) -- but the thumbnails with only
16K
  STORE AS (chunk 16K)
-- and bind the XMLType columns to the interMedia metadata
columns
XMLType column metadata
  XMLSCHEMA "http://xmlns.oracle.com/ord/meta/dicomImage"
  ELEMENT "DICOM_IMAGE";
```

We also provide a specialized method getDicomMetadata() to extract the metadata.

```
CREATE OR REPLACE PROCEDURE extractDicomMetadata(inID
INTEGER)
```

```
            IS
                local_image        ORDSYS.ORDIMAGE;
                local_id           INTEGER;
                dicom_metadata     XMLType := NULL;
            BEGIN
                SELECT image INTO local_image FROM medicalImages WHERE id =
            inID;
                -- extract DICOM metadata
                dicom_metadata :=
            local_image.getDicomMetadata('imageGeneral');
                IF (dicom_metadata IS NULL) THEN
                    DBMS_OUTPUT.PUT_LINE('metadata is NULL');
                ELSE
                    UPDATE medicalImages SET metadata = dicom_metadata where
            id = inID;
                END IF;
                -- let us print the namespace of the XML document
            containing the
                -- dicom metadata that we just extracted
                DBMS_OUTPUT.PUT_LINE('namespace: ' ||
            dicom_metadata.getNamespace());

            END;
```

The method is very similar to the getMetadata() method but the string parameter that specifies the type of DICOM metadata to extract has only one valid value, `imageGeneral`. All other values are ignored.

The DICOM standard includes a complete set of *encoding rules* for medical images. These encoding rules are also called *transfer syntax*. Oracle *inter*Media provides DICOM encoding rules that support metadata extraction and image content processing. Metadata extraction is supported by the getDicomMetadata() and setProperties() methods. Image content support is provided through the processCopy() and setProperties() methods.

8.3 Methods Available for ORDAudio Object Type

The ORDAudio object type has the following attributes:

- Description
- Source

- Format

- MIME type

- Comments

- Encoding

- Sample size and rate

- Number of channels

- Compression and duration

We can create a table to hold our family music such as:

```
CREATE TABLE AUDIO_ord
        (ID              NUMBER NOT NULL,
         DESCRIPTION     VARCHAR2(40) NOT NULL,
         AUDIO           ORDSYS.ORDAUDIO)
```

We will need to initialize the *inter*Media column, using the ORDAudio.INIT() method just as we did for images, before we can insert the audio data from a file in the directory. In this example we would have created the directory object AUDIO_DIR and granted access to users.

```
CREATE or replace PROCEDURE AUDIO_SAMPLE_import
AS
   my_aud      ORDSYS.ORDAUDIO;
   ctx      raw(64) :=null;
BEGIN
   INSERT INTO  AUDIO_ORD(id,description,audio)
      VALUES (1743,'Nocturne in C-sharpe Minor Chopin',
      ORDSYS.ORDaudio.INIT())
   RETURNING audio INTO my_aud;

my_aud.importFrom(ctx,'file','AUDIO_DIR','pianist_01.mp3');
   UPDATE  AUDIO_ORD SET audio=my_aud WHERE id=1743;
END;
```

This procedure uses the ORDAudio.INIT() method to initialize the BLOB within the ORDAudio object type. The ctx variable is used to hold the context information for the source. The importFrom() method transfers audio data from the specified external audio data source, in this case AUDIO_DIR directory, which must exist before we can use this method. The audio data is inserted into the source.localData attribute (of the embedded ORDSource object type) within the database.

The next procedure illustrates how audio data can be retrieved from the database, then its properties captured by the setProperties() method and stored in the appropriate attributes of the audio object type within the database.

```
CREATE OR REPLACE PROCEDURE audio_process1
AS
 obj ORDSYS.ORDAudio;
 ctx RAW(64) :=NULL;
BEGIN
 SELECT p.audio INTO obj FROM audio_ord p
  WHERE p.id = 1743 FOR UPDATE;
  obj.setProperties(ctx,FALSE);
 DBMS_OUTPUT.PUT_LINE('Audio file format: ' ||
obj.getFormat);
 DBMS_OUTPUT.PUT_LINE('Audio Compression: ' ||
obj.getCompressionType);
 DBMS_OUTPUT.PUT_LINE('Audio encoding: ' || obj.getEncoding);
 DBMS_OUTPUT.PUT_LINE('Audio Sampling Rate: ' ||
obj.getSamplingRate);
 DBMS_OUTPUT.PUT_LINE('Audio Duration: ' ||
obj.getAudioDuration);
 DBMS_OUTPUT.PUT_LINE('Audio size: ' || obj.getSampleSize);
 UPDATE audio_ord p
    SET p.audio = obj
    WHERE p.id = 1743;
COMMIT;
 EXCEPTION
  WHEN ORDSYS.ORDAudioExceptions.METHOD_NOT_SUPPORTED THEN
    DBMS_OUTPUT.PUT_LINE('METHOD_NOT_SUPPORTED caught');
    WHEN OTHERS THEN
    DBMS_OUTPUT.PUT_LINE('EXCEPTION CAUGHT');
 END;
```

When we execute the procedure we can check the properties.

```
SQL> EXECUTE audio_process1
Audio file format: MPGA
Audio Compression: LAYER3
Audio encoding: LAYER3
Audio Sampling Rate: 44100
Audio Duration: 250
Audio size:
```

The setProperties() method reads the audio metadata to capture the values of the object attributes and then stores them in the object attributes in the database. In this way the attributes of the audio data for which values are available are captured: compression type, duration, encoding type, format, MIME type, number of channels, sampling rate, and sample size. In this case the statement

```
obj.setProperties(ctx,FALSE);
```

shows the setComments parameter is FALSE. It would populate the comments field of the object with a rich set of format and application properties in XML form if the value of the setComments parameter is TRUE. The default value is FALSE. If the property cannot be extracted from the media source, then the respective attribute is set to NULL as in the above example where there is no value for the audio size.

We can process the audio data using the special method called *processAudioCommand*, which allows us to send a command and related arguments to the format plug-in for processing. We use this method to send any audio commands and their respective arguments to the format plug-in. Commands are not interpreted; they are taken and passed through to a format plug-in to be processed. We can extend support to a new format that is not understood by the ORDAudio object by preparing a package such as ORDPLUGINS.ORDX_<format>_AUDIO that supports that format.

8.4   Methods Available for ORDVideo Object Type

We'll start with a suitable table for the family to store its video data:

```
CREATE TABLE VIDEO_ord
    (ID              NUMBER NOT NULL,
```

```
DESCRIPTION     VARCHAR2(40) NOT NULL,
VIDEO           ORDSYS.ORDVIDEO)
```

ORDVideo has the following attributes:

- Description
- Source
- Height/width
- Format
- MIME type
- Comments
- Bit rate
- Sample size and rate
- Number of frames, rate, resolution
- Number of colors
- Compression and duration

There are separate methods to manipulate these attributes but one of the most useful is setProperties() again since it reads the video data to get the values of the video object's attributes and then stores them in the ORDVideo object. This method sets the properties for each of the attributes of the video data for which values are available: format, height, width, frame resolution, frame rate, video duration, number of frames, compression type, number of colors, and bit rate.

The method also populates the comments field of the object with a rich set of format and application properties in XML form if the value of the setComments parameter is TRUE.

We should begin using the init() method as soon as possible to allow you to more easily initialize the ORDVideo object type, especially if the ORDVideo type evolves and attributes are added in a future release. INSERT statements left unchanged using the default constructor (which initializes each object attribute) will fail under these circumstances. This can be achieved by the following statement.

```
BEGIN
 INSERT INTO video_ord (id, description, video)
 VALUES (1234,'Pond life video', ORDSYS.ORDVideo.init());
 COMMIT;
END;
```

We can then move video data from the specified external data source into the local source, using the importFrom() method:

```
CREATE OR REPLACE PROCEDURE VIDEO_imp
 AS
  obj ORDSYS.ORDVideo;
  ctx RAW(64) :=NULL;
BEGIN
  SELECT P.VIDEO INTO obj FROM video_ORD p
     WHERE p.id = 1234 FOR UPDATE;
  DBMS_OUTPUT.PUT_LINE('setting and getting source');
  DBMS_OUTPUT.PUT_LINE('--------------------------');
  -- Import data:

obj.importFrom(ctx,'file','VIDEO_DIR','CYCLIDIUM_GLAUCOMA.MOV
');
  -- Check size:
  DBMS_OUTPUT.PUT_LINE('Length is '
    ||TO_CHAR(obj.getContentLength(ctx)));
  UPDATE VIDEO_ORD p SET P.video = obj WHERE id = 1234;
  COMMIT;
  EXCEPTION
        WHEN ORDSYS.ORDSourceExceptions.METHOD_NOT_SUPPORTED
THEN
          DBMS_OUTPUT.put_line('Source METHOD_NOT_SUPPORTED
caught');
        WHEN
ORDSYS.ORDSourceExceptions.SOURCE_PLUGIN_EXCEPTION THEN
          DBMS_OUTPUT.put_line('SOURCE PLUGIN EXCEPTION
caught');
        WHEN ORDSYS.ORDVideoExceptions.METHOD_NOT_SUPPORTED
THEN
          DBMS_OUTPUT.put_line('VIDEO METHOD_NOT_SUPPORTED
EXCEPTION caught');
        WHEN ORDSYS.ORDVideoExceptions.VIDEO_PLUGIN_EXCEPTION
THEN
```

```
                          DBMS_OUTPUT.put_line('VIDEO PLUGIN EXCEPTION
        caught');
                  WHEN OTHERS THEN
                      DBMS_OUTPUT.PUT_LINE('EXCEPTION Caught');
        END;
```

In this procedure we have used a number of exceptions to trap problems with the source and the video plugin. For example note that the ORDSourceExceptions.METHOD_NOT_SUPPORTED is raised when the importFrom( ) method is called but the method is not supported by the source plug-in being used. Similarly, the VIDEO_PLUGIN_EXCEPTION is raised when the video plug-in raises an exception. Here is an example of the use of setProperties():

```
CREATE OR REPLACE PROCEDURE video_props
  AS
    obj ORDSYS.ORDVideo;
    ctx RAW(64) :=NULL;
  BEGIN
    SELECT p.video INTO obj FROM VIDEO_ORD p
      WHERE p.id  = 1234 FOR UPDATE;
    obj.setProperties(ctx,FALSE);
    UPDATE VIDEO_ORD p SET p.video = obj
      WHERE p.id = 1234;
    COMMIT;
    EXCEPTION
    WHEN ORDSYS.ORDVideoExceptions.VIDEO_PLUGIN_EXCEPTION THEN
      DBMS_OUTPUT.PUT_LINE('ORDVideoExceptions.VIDEO_PLUGIN_EXCEPTION
caught');
    WHEN OTHERS THEN
      DBMS_OUTPUT.PUT_LINE('exception raised');
  END;
```

The statement obj.setProperties(ctx,FALSE) operates on the video stored into the obj variable. The subsequent UPDATE statement stores the properties captured back into the database with the actual video data. In this case the setComments() parameter is set to FALSE.

Object type

We can use get methods to retrieve individual attribute values or we can use the getAllAttributes method to generate a string that contains the main settings.

```
CREATE OR REPLACE PROCEDURE get_video_props
AS
 obj ORDSYS.ORDVideo;
 tempLob    CLOB;
 ctx RAW(64) :=NULL;
BEGIN
 SELECT p.video INTO obj FROM video_ord p
  WHERE p.id = 1234;
 DBMS_OUTPUT.PUT_LINE('getting comma separated list of all
attributes');
 DBMS_OUTPUT.PUT_LINE('-------------------------------------
-------');
 DBMS_LOB.CREATETEMPORARY(tempLob, FALSE, DBMS_LOB.CALL);
 obj.getAllAttributes(ctx,tempLob);

DBMS_OUTPUT.PUT_LINE(DBMS_LOB.substr(tempLob,DBMS_LOB.getLeng
th(tempLob),1));
 COMMIT;
 EXCEPTION
  WHEN ORDSYS.ORDVideoExceptions.METHOD_NOT_SUPPORTED THEN
   DBMS_OUTPUT.PUT_LINE('VIDEO METHOD_NOT_SUPPORTED EXCEPTION
caught');
  WHEN OTHERS THEN
   DBMS_OUTPUT.PUT_LINE('EXCEPTION CAUGHT');
END;
```

Looking at the output of this procedure we can see that the obj.getAllAttributes(ctx,tempLob) statement produces a string that includes a list of video data attributes separated by comma (,) (i.e., format, MIME type, width, height, format, frameResolution, frameRate, videoDuration, numberOfFrames, compressionType, numberOfColors, and bitRate).

```
SQL> EXECUTE get_video_props
getting comma separated list of all attributes
------------------------------------------------
```

```
                   format=MOOV,mimeType=video/
                   quicktime,width=160,height=120,frameResolution=NULL,frameRate
                   =24,videoDuration=17,numberOfFrames=408,compressionType=RPZA,
                   numberOfColors=16,bitRate=NULL
```

These video data attributes are available from the header of the formatted video data and can be extracted from the video data itself. The statement

```
                   DBMS_OUTPUT.PUT_LINE(DBMS_LOB.substr(tempLob,DBMS_LOB.getLeng
                   th(tempLob),1));
```

is used to store the extracted data in a temporary CLOB, which is manipulated by the DBMS_LOB package to produce the formatted string.

The next procedure shows how to set up an alternative approach, selecting the attribute values one by one.

```
CREATE OR REPLACE PROCEDURE get_video_ATTRIBUTES
 AS
  obj ORDSYS.ORDVideo;
  ctx RAW(64) :=NULL;
  res INTEGER;
  width INTEGER;
  height INTEGER;
 BEGIN
  SELECT p.video INTO obj FROM video_ord p
   WHERE p.id  = 1234;
  DBMS_OUTPUT.PUT_LINE('getting attributes');
  DBMS_OUTPUT.PUT_LINE('-----------------------------------------------');
obj.getFrameSize(width, height);
  DBMS_OUTPUT.PUT_LINE('width :' || width);
  DBMS_OUTPUT.PUT_LINE('height :' || height);
 res := obj.getFrameResolution();
  DBMS_OUTPUT.PUT_LINE('resolution : ' ||res);
 res:= obj.getNumberOfColors();
DBMS_OUTPUT.PUT_LINE('number of colors : ' ||res);
 res:= obj.getNumberOfFrames();
DBMS_OUTPUT.PUT_LINE('number of frames : ' ||res);
  COMMIT;
  EXCEPTION
   WHEN ORDSYS.ORDVideoExceptions.METHOD_NOT_SUPPORTED THEN
    DBMS_OUTPUT.PUT_LINE('VIDEO METHOD_NOT_SUPPORTED EXCEPTION caught');
```

```
WHEN OTHERS THEN
  DBMS_OUTPUT.PUT_LINE('EXCEPTION CAUGHT');
END;
```

Sample output:

```
getting attributes
-----------------------------------------------
width : 160
height : 120
resolution :
number of colors : 16
number of frames : 408
```

As in the case of ORDAudio, setProperties() will extract the available object attributes but when the property cannot be extracted, the attribute is set to null, as in the cas of reolution.

8.5   Methods Available for ORDDoc Object Type

The purpose of the ORDDoc object type is to integrate the storage, retrieval, and management of heterogeneous media data within the database. The ORDDoc type can store any heterogeneous media data including audio, image, and video data in a database column. Instead of having separate columns for audio, image, text, and video objects, we can use one column of ORDDoc objects to represent all types of multimedia. ORDDoc can automatically extract metadata from data of a variety of popular audio, image, and video data formats.

ORDDoc has the following attributes:

- Source
- File format
- MIME type
- Content length
- Comments

ORDDoc methods can also be used to extract application attributes and store them in the comments attribute of the object in XML form. The comments attribute is a CLOB so that can hold a large amount of text.

The family may want to store heterogeneous data in a table that uses the ORDSY.ORDDoc object types to store media instances, such as favorite recipes with images of the product. First we would create a suitable table.

```
CREATE TABLE doc_ord
   (ID                NUMBER NOT NULL,
    DESCRIPTION       VARCHAR2(40),
    my_doc            ORDSYS.ORDDOC)
```

As before we need to initialize the ORDDoc object instance that sets the embedded BLOB data type to EMPTY_BLOB, using the special INIT() method.

```
BEGIN
INSERT INTO doc_ord (id,description,my_doc)
   VALUES (1242, 'A recipe for Hungarian
Goulash',ORDSYS.ORDDoc.init('file', 'FILE_DIR',
'recipe.doc'));
END;
```

In the following procedure the importFrom() method is used to transfer data from the external source into the local database.

```
CREATE OR REPLACE PROCEDURE DOC_imp
AS
   obj ORDSYS.ORDDoc;
   ctx RAW(64) :=NULL;
BEGIN
   SELECT my_doc INTO obj FROM doc_ord
      WHERE id=1242 FOR UPDATE;
   DBMS_OUTPUT.PUT_LINE('setting and getting source');
   DBMS_OUTPUT.PUT_LINE('--------------------------');
   -- set source to a file
   -- import data
   obj.importFrom(ctx,'file','FILE_DIR','recipe.doc',FALSE);
   -- check size
   DBMS_OUTPUT.PUT_LINE('Length:'||
```

```
         TO_CHAR(DBMS_LOB.GETLENGTH(obj.getContent)));
    DBMS_OUTPUT.PUT_LINE(obj.getSource());
    UPDATE doc_ord SET my_doc=obj WHERE id=1242;
    COMMIT;
    EXCEPTION
      WHEN ORDSYS.ORDSourceExceptions.METHOD_NOT_SUPPORTED THEN
        DBMS_OUTPUT.PUT_LINE
           ('ORDSourceExceptions.METHOD_NOT_SUPPORTED caught');
      WHEN ORDSYS.ORDDocExceptions.DOC_PLUGIN_EXCEPTION THEN
        DBMS_OUTPUT.put_line('DOC PLUGIN EXCEPTION caught');
END;
```

This gives the following results:

```
SQL> execute doc_imp
setting and getting source
--------------------------
Length: 43520
file://FILE_DIR/recipe.doc
```

This object type has a slightly different importFrom() method that has a parameter set_prop with IN and data type BOOLEAN. This is a value that determines whether the setProperties() method is called. If the value of this parameter is TRUE, then the setProperties() method is called to read the media data to get the values of the object attributes and store them in the object attributes; otherwise, if the value is FALSE, the set Properties() method is not called. The default value is FALSE as in this case.

In the above examples we have used the *inter*Media object types as composite data types for columns in relational tables. Alternatively, we can create our own object types based on *inter*Media object types and methods. Here is an example of an image type that can be used for text-based retrieval through anotation stored in the *description* attribute:

```
CREATE TYPE AnnotatedImage AS OBJECT
    ( image ORDSYS.ORDImage,
      description CLOB,
      MEMBER PROCEDURE SetProperties(
SELF IN OUT AnnotatedImage),
      MEMBER PROCEDURE Copy(
dest IN OUT AnnotatedImage),
```

```
      MEMBER PROCEDURE ProcessCopy(
command IN VARCHAR2,
    dest IN OUT AnnotatedImage)
  );
```

In this case we have specified three methods as part of the type. Using stored procedures as methods gives a number of advantages. Since stored procedures only require the calling parameters, the transmission of whole results sets or intermediate tables required for SQL statements is avoided and network traffic can be reduced. Stored procedures are executed in compiled format that greatly reduces code execution times. Stored procedures are also a way of controlling development and are an essential part of the object-relational development.

Two different kinds of methods can be created:

1.   Function or procedure member methods are used to process information and can accept arguments. Methods that are functions always return a value.

2.   Comparison methods that have a distinct purpose to deal with the comparison of object types that are much more complex than the traditional data types.

The member procedures are specified in the type body as follows.

```
CREATE TYPE BODY AnnotatedImage AS
  MEMBER PROCEDURE SetProperties(SELF IN OUT AnnotatedImage)
IS
  BEGIN
    SELF.image.setProperties();
    SELF.description :=
        'This is an example of using Image object as a
subtype';
  END SetProperties;
  MEMBER PROCEDURE Copy(dest IN OUT AnnotatedImage) IS
  BEGIN
    SELF.image.copy(dest.image);
    dest.description := SELF.description;
  END Copy;
  MEMBER PROCEDURE ProcessCopy(command IN VARCHAR2,
```

```
                                  dest IN OUT AnnotatedImage) IS
  BEGIN
    SELF.Image.processCopy(command,dest.image);
    dest.description := SELF.description;
  END ProcessCopy;
END;
```

In the statement

```
SELF.image.setProperties();
```

the setProperties() method is called with an empty parameter list because its
arguments are the attributes of the object of which it is a member, the
image attribute of the type AnnotatedImage. This is called a *selfish style* of
invocation. In general, object methods are invoked by using the style
Type_name.method() or object_expression.method().

After creating the new type, you can use it as you would any other type,
for example, as a data type in a relational table.

```
CREATE TABLE annotated_photos
(id         NUMBER,
 an_image   AnnotatedImage)
```

When we insert this into the table we will invoke the INIT() method of
the *inter*Media image data type ORDImage. For example, to use an image
as an external BFILE source we would state, as follows.

```
INSERT INTO annotated_photos
 VALUES
 (1001,
    AnnotatedImage(ORDSYS.ORDImage.init('file',
        'PHOTO_DIR','raven.bmp'),'')
 )
```

We can use the following procedure with this table:

```
CREATE OR REPLACE PROCEDURE proc_annotate
AS
    myimage AnnotatedImage;
BEGIN
```

```
SELECT an_image
INTO myimage
FROM ANNOTATED_PHOTOS
WHERE id = '1002';
myimage.SetProperties;
DBMS_OUTPUT.PUT_LINE
    ('This image has a description of a raven ');
DBMS_OUTPUT.PUT_LINE(myimage.description);
UPDATE   ANNOTATED_PHOTOS
SET an_image = myimage;
END;
```

If we execute the procedure we get the following output:

```
SQL> EXECUTE proc_annotate;
This image has a description of a raven
This is an example of using Image object as a subtype
```

Note that one of the messages has come from the table column and one from the type method.

Using object types gives a much wider choice to the developer but one question is what kind of type to select. *inter*Media provides the ability to extract content and format metadata from media sources (image, audio, and video files), and collects and organizes this metadata as an XML formatted CLOB. Once metadata has been extracted and stored, you can index the metadata for powerful full text and thematic media searches using Oracle Text. Thus, the database can be queried to locate the media data based on the metadata extracted from the media. The development of methods and member functions are discussed in later chapters dealing with PL/SQL and Java.

We can use object-relational concepts to develop object types based on *inter*Media object types as shown

```
CREATE TYPE photo_type AS OBJECT
(    id                NUMBER,               ◄
     description       photo_detail_t,    ◄────── Object type
     image             SI_StillImage,◄
     thumb             ORDSYS.ORDIMAGE◄────── Object type
     MEMBER FUNCTION
     Get_description   RETURN NUMBER);◄────────── Function
```

We can see that this definition of the photo_type includes several *object types* and a *function*. Some of the attributes are themselves complex. The *description* attribute has a photo_detail_t data type and the *image* attribute is specified with SI_StillImage data type. We do not have to list the methods available with this object type as they are encapsulated and available to photo_type. We can also specify methods associated with the photo_type object that reflect real-world user requirements. Therefore, for the photo_type we could have a method that extracted details of the description of the photo. We could also store the photo_type in object tables where each row of the object table corresponds to a single photo_type object and the columns of the table are the attributes of the photo_type.

8.6   SI_StillImage Object Type

This is a special object type that provides compatibility with the SQL/MM part of the SQL:1999 standard (see Chapter 3). This object type has an extended list of attributes, shown in Table 8.4. As with the other *inter*Media types, the SI_StillImage media data will be held in a BLOB in an encapsulated ORDSource object that is the data type of the content_SI attribute. The structure of this object type is complex in that it embeds ORDSource, includes attributes specified in SQL:1999, and includes some attributes that have proved useful for the ORDImage object type but are not yet part of the standard (e.g., MIME type and compression format). As this is a highly composite object type it has many methods available. Another difference is that this object type will need to use the DBMS_LOB package to manipulate the BLOB data type embedded in this object type.

Table 8.4   *Attributes of SI_StillImage Object Type*

Attribute	Type	Comment
content_SI	ORDSYS.ORDSOURCE	SQL Standard—an ORDSource object that contains the binary image or BLOB
contentLength_SI	INTEGER	Length of the image in bytes
format_SI	VARCHAR2(4000)	Image format
height_SI	INTEGER	The number of lines of the image

Table 8.4 *Attributes of SI_StillImage Object Type (continued)*

Attribute	Type	Comment
width_SI	INTEGER	The number of columns of the image
Oracle attribute extensions:		
mimeType_ora	VARCHAR2(4000)	The MIME type information—not in SQL standard
contentFormat_ora	VARCHAR2(4000)	Type of image (monochrome, etc.)
compressionFormat_ora	VARCHAR2(4000)	Compression algorithm
retainFeatures_SI	INTEGER	Flag that indicates whether or not image features will be extracted and cached
Oracle extension attributes to cache image features:		
averageColorSpec_ora	SI_Color	Cached SI_Color object
colorsList_ora	colorsList	Cached array of colors
frequenciesList_ora	colorFrequenciesList	Cached array of color frequencies
colorPositions_ora	colorPositions	Cached array of color positions
textureEncoding_ora	textureEncoding	The cached array of textures

8.6.1 SI_StillImage Methods

We will focus on this object type's methods but the SQL/MM standard requires that for each StillImage constructor or method, there is an equivalent SQL function or procedure. Each function or procedure is presented with its equivalent constructor or method. Although the description, parameters, usage notes, and exceptions, subsections frequently refer to the method, these subsections are also applicable to the equivalent SQL function or procedure. To quote from the Oracle *Inter*Media Reference Manual, "All SQL functions and procedures are created as standalone functions in the ORDSYS schema with invoker rights. A public synonym with the corresponding function or procedure name is created for all SQL functions and procedures." Therefore, we do not need to specify the schema name when a function or procedure is called. For example, use ORDSYS.SI_MkAvgClr(averageColor) to make the call without the synonym, and use SI_MkAvgClr(averageColor) to make the call based on the method with the synonym. All database users can call these functions and procedures.

The object type can be used as the data type of columns in a table, for example:

```
CREATE TABLE photos_SI
(id              NUMBER PRIMARY KEY,
                 description VARCHAR2(40) NOT NULL,
                 location    VARCHAR2(40),
                 image       SI_StillImage,
                 thumb       SI_StillImage)
```

There are three groups of SI_StillImage methods:

1.   Constructor methods

2.   Basic image-processing methods

3.   Advanced image feature extraction methods (covered in Chapter 11)

There are three different types of constructor methods (summarized in Table 8.5) for the SI_StillImage object type, and it is strongly suggested that these are used in preference to the default constructor.

Table 8.5   *Constructor Methods for SI_StillImage*

Constructor Method Name	Function	Comment
SI_StillImage(content)	Initalizes the image and extracts parameters from image file	Accepts BLOB parameter used with DBMS_BLOB package
SI_StillImage(content, explicitFormat)	Constructs an SI_StillImage object from a specified image and a format	Useful for unsupported image formats
SI_StillImage(content, explicitFormat, height, width)	Constructs an SI_StillImage value from a specified image	Useful for unsupported image formats

Table 8.5   *Constructor Methods for SI_StillImage*

Constructor Method Name	Function	Comment
SI_MkStillImage1()	Makes a new SI_StillImage object	Initializes the SI_StillImage attributes with values extracted from the image

Using SI_StillImage(content)

This is used to construct the type by initializing the SI_StillImage attributes as follows:

- content_SI.localData is initialized with the specified image.

- contentLength_SI is initialized with the length of the image extracted from the specified image.

- format_SI is initialized with the format of image extracted from the specified image.

- height_SI is initialized with the height of image extracted from the specified image.

- width_SI is initialized with the width of image extracted from the specified image.

Using the DBMS_LOB Package

We can use a special package DBMS_LOB provided for manipulating LOBS. The DBMS_LOB package also processes BFILES. DBMS_LOB is a package that is based on working with LOB locators. It consists of a number of routines for manipulating LOBS. Most of these are listed in Table 8.6, together with a brief note on their purpose and an example of their use. Before users can access the package, the SYS user must either execute both dbmslob.sql and prvtlob.plb scripts or execute the catproc.sql script. Then users can be granted privileges to use the package.

Table 8.6   *Routines Provided by DBMS_LOB Package*

DBMS_LOB Routines	Purpose	Example of Use
DBMS_LOB.OPEN	Open the BFILE	DBMS_LOB.OPEN(Lob_loc, DBMS_LOB.LOB_READONLY);

Table 8.6   *Routines Provided by DBMS_LOB Package (continued)*

DBMS_LOB Routines	Purpose	Example of Use
DBMS_LOB.READ	Read data from a LOB starting at a specified offset	DBMS_LOB.READ(Lob_loc, Amount, Position, Buffer);
DBMS_LOB.WRITE	Write data to a LOB from a specified offset	DBMS_LOB.WRITE (locator, amount, offset, text)
DBMS_LOB.WRITEAPPEND	Write data to the end of a LOB	DBMS_LOB.WRITEAP-PEND(lob_loc, amount, text)
DBMS_LOB.SUBSTR	Return part of a LOB value starting at a specified offset	SELECT DBMS_LOB.SUBSTR(note,5,12)
DBMS_LOB.INSTR	Return the numerical position of part of a LOB value	SELECT DBMS_LOB.INSTR(note,' Rian')
DBMS_LOB.GETLENGTH	Gets the length of a LOB	SELECT DBMS_LOB.GETLENGTH(note)
DBMS_LOB.TRIM	Trims a LOB value to the specified shorter length	DBMS_LOB.TRIM(lob_loc, no_bytes)
DBMS_LOB.CREATETEMPO-RARY	Creates a temporary LOB that exists for a session and is useful if a LOB is being changed and then stored again	
DBMS_LOB.COPY	Copies part or the whole of a LOB to another LOB	DBMS_LOB.COPY(to_lob, from_lob, no_bytes, from_offset, to_offset)
DBMS_LOB.APPEND	Appends the content of a LOB to another LOB	DBMS_LOB.APPEND(to_lob, from_lob)
DBMS_LOB.COMPARE	Compares to similar LOB types	DBMS_LOB.COMPARE(lob_1, lob_2, no_bytes, offset1,offset2)
DBMS_LOB.ERASE	Erases part or the whole of a LOB, starting at a specified offset	DBMS_LOB.ERASE (lob_loc, no_bytes, offset)
DBMS_LOB.LOADFROMFILE	Loads BFILE data into an internal LOB	DBMS_LOB.LOADFROMFILE(from_lob, to_lob, no_bytes, from_offset, to_offset)
DBMS_LOB.CLOSE	Close the BFILE	DBMS_LOB.CLOSE(Lob_loc);

The following example demonstrates how to insert an image into a StillImage object column using the PL/SQL routine DBMS_LOB.LOADFROMFILE.

```
CREATE OR REPLACE PROCEDURE SI_Image_imp
AS
    lobd   blob;
    fils   BFILE := BFILENAME('PHOTO_DIR','raven.bmp');
BEGIN
    DBMS_LOB.CREATETEMPORARY(lobd, TRUE);
    DBMS_LOB.fileopen(fils, DBMS_LOB.file_readonly);
    DBMS_LOB.LOADFROMFILE(lobd, fils,
DBMS_LOB.GETLENGTH(fils));
    DBMS_LOB.FILECLOSE(fils);
    INSERT INTO  photos_si (id, description, image)
        VALUES(1235, 'Raven averages 24 inches',
new ORDSYS.SI_StillImage(lobd));
    DBMS_LOB.FREETEMPORARY(lobd);
    COMMIT;
END;
```

In this procedure we specify the location of the image file and BFILENAME function adds the data into the variable *fils*, which is a BFILE. Then we create a temporary BLOB by using the DBMS_LOB package, open the BFILE, and load the file into it. The BFILE is closed and then the temporary LOB used as the IN parameter for the SI_StillImage() method is used to insert the data into the object.

Using SI_StillImage(content, explicitFormat)

We can also use a constructor that lets us specify the image format, height, and width when the specified image is an unsupported image format by using the following statement:

```
newimage := NEW SI_StillImage(lobd, 'psp', 570, 1168);
```

This constructor has the advantage that we can specify the image format when the specified image is in an unsupported image format and initializes the SI_StillImage attributes as follows:

- content_SI.localData is initialized with the specified image.
- contentLength_SI is initialized with the length of the image extracted from the specified image.
- format_SI is initialized with the specified image format.
- height_SI is initialized with the height of the image extracted from the specified image.
- width_SI is initialized with the width of the image extracted from the specified image.

If the constructor function is not able to extract the height and width values from the specified image, then we can assign value to them as follows:

```
myImage.height_SI := height
myImage.width_SI := width
```

The following procedure illustrates this, where a Paint Shop Pro image is stored into a temporary BLOB, and since this is a proprietory format, the height and width cannot be extracted, so these are assigned:

```
CREATE OR REPLACE PROCEDURE SI_Image_imp_format
AS   lobd BLOB;
     fils BFILE := BFILENAME('PHOTO_DIR','cats.psp');
     newimage SI_StillImage;
     height NUMBER;
     width NUMBER;
     myimage SI_StillImage;

BEGIN
     -- Put the blob in a temporary LOB:
     DBMS_LOB.CREATETEMPORARY(lobd, TRUE);
     DBMS_LOB.FILEOPEN(fils, DBMS_LOB.FILE_READONLY);
     DBMS_LOB.LOADFROMFILE(lobd, fils,
DBMS_LOB.GETLENGTH(fils));
     DBMS_LOB.FILECLOSE(fils);
     -- Create a new SI_StillImage object for this image (which
has an
     -- unsupported format):
     newimage := NEW SI_StillImage(lobd, 'psp');
```

```
    -- If the stored height and width values are NULL, the
following will set
    -- them appropriately. Alternatively, you could use the
    -- SI_StillImage(content, explicitFormat, height,width)
constructor:
    height := 570;
    width := 1168;
    IF (newimage.SI_Height is NULL) THEN
        newimage.height_SI := height;
    END IF;
    IF (newimage.SI_Width is NULL) THEN
        newimage.width_SI := width;
    END IF;
    -- Insert the image into the si_media table, then free the
temp LOB
    INSERT INTO  photos_si (id, description, image)
        VALUES (33, 'two siamese cats',newimage);
    DBMS_LOB.FREETEMPORARY(lobd);
    -- Make sure that the height and width were stored as
expected:
    SELECT image INTO myimage FROM PHOTOS_SI WHERE id=33;
    height := myimage.SI_height;
    width := myimage.SI_width;
    DBMS_OUTPUT.PUT_LINE('Height is ' || height || ' pixels.');
    DBMS_OUTPUT.PUT_LINE('Width is ' || width ||  ' pixels.');
    COMMIT;
END;
```

The explicitFormat parameter must be the same as the format extracted from the image otherwise an error will be returned. An error will also be generated if the explicitFormat parameter value indicates an unsupported format but the format extracted is not NULL.

Note: query the SI_IMAGE_FORMATS view in SI_INFORMTN_ SCHEMA for a list of the supported image formats.

Using SI_StillImage(content, explicitFormat, height, width)

This constructor lets you specify the image format, height, and width when the specified image is an unsupported image format. It is very similar to the previous constructor method except that it allows you to specify values for the height and width of images with unsupported formats. It is not intended to be used to change an image into a thumbnail.

```
CREATE OR REPLACE PROCEDURE SI_Image_exp_format
AS
    lobd BLOB;
    fils BFILE := BFILENAME('FILE_DIR','cats.psp');
    newimage SI_StillImage;
    height NUMBER;
    width NUMBER;
    myimage SI_StillImage;
BEGIN
    -- Put the blob in a temporary LOB:
    DBMS_LOB.CREATETEMPORARY(lobd, TRUE);
    DBMS_LOB.FILEOPEN(fils, DBMS_LOB.FILE_READONLY);
    DBMS_LOB.LOADFROMFILE(lobd, fils,
DBMS_LOB.GETLENGTH(fils));
    DBMS_LOB.FILECLOSE(fils);
    -- Create a new SI_StillImage object for this image (which
has an
    -- unsupported format)
    newimage := SI_StillImage(lobd, 'psp', 570, 1168);
    -- Insert the image into the si_media table, then free the
temp BLOB
    INSERT INTO  photos_si (id, description, image)
        VALUES (33, 'two siamese cats',newimage);
    DBMS_LOB.FREETEMPORARY(lobd);
    -- Make sure that the height and width were stored as
expected
        SELECT image INTO myimage
        FROM photos_si WHERE id=33;
    height := myimage.SI_height;
    width := myimage.SI_width;
    DBMS_OUTPUT.PUT_LINE('Height is ' || height || ' pixels.');
    DBMS_OUTPUT.PUT_LINE('Width is ' || width ||  ' pixels.');
    COMMIT;
END;
```

Using SI_MkStillImage1()

An alternative approach will create a new SI_StillImage object using the
SI_MkStillImage1() function and the PL/SQL package
DBMS_LOB.LOADFROM FILE:

```
CREATE OR REPLACE PROCEDURE SI_Image_imp2
    AS
```

```
    lobd blob;
    fils BFILE := BFILENAME('PHOTO_DIR','robin.bmp');
BEGIN
    DBMS_LOB.CREATETEMPORARY(lobd, TRUE);
    DBMS_LOB.FILEOPEN(fils, dbms_lob.file_readonly);
    DBMS_LOB.LOADFROMFILE(lobd, fils,
dbms_lob.getlength(fils));
    DBMS_LOB.FILECLOSE(fils);
    INSERT INTO photos_si (id,description, image)
      VALUES (1236, 'small bird red breast',
SI_MkStillImage1(lobd));
    DBMS_LOB.FREETEMPORARY(lobd);
    COMMIT;
END;
```

8.6.2 Methods for Image Processing

The SI_StillImage object type has a number of important methods, listed in Table 8.7.

Table 8.7 *SI_StillImage Object Type Methods*

Image Processing Method	Function	Comment
SI_ClearFeatures	Disables image feature caching and sets feature attributes to NULL	Used to remove the processing overhead associated with feature synchronization
SI_InitFeatures()	Extracts the image features and caches them in the SI_StillImage object	This method is recommended for users needing image matching
SI_Thumbnail()	Derives a thumbnail image, size is 80 × 80 pixels from the specified SI_StillImage object	Preserves the image aspect ratio so the resulting thumbnail size will be as close to 80 × 80 pixels as possible
SI_Thumbnail(height, width)	Derives a thumbnail image of specified size	Does not preserve the image aspect ratio

SI_InitFeatures() extracts the image features and caches them in the SI_StillImage object. This method needs to be called once, after which SI_StillImage will manage the image features such that every time the image is processed, new image features will automatically be extracted. This method is recommended for users who will be image matching.

This method is not in the first edition of the SQL/MM Still Image standard, but has been accepted for inclusion in the next version. The following procedure will extract the image features and cache them in an SI_StillImage object.

```
CREATE OR REPLACE PROCEDURE SI_FEATURES_IMP
  AS
  myimage SI_StillImage;
BEGIN
  SELECT IMAGE INTO myimage FROM photos_SI
    WHERE id = 1239 FOR UPDATE;
  myimage.SI_InitFeatures;
  UPDATE photos_SI
   SET IMAGE = myimage where id=1239;
  DBMS_OUTPUT.PUT_LINE('Image feature caching enabled');
  COMMIT;
END;
SQL> execute si_features_imp
Image feature caching enabled

PL/SQL procedure successfully completed.
```

In contrast, SI_ClearFeatures() disables image feature caching and sets the value of all internal image feature attributes to NULL. We would call this method to remove the processing overhead associated with feature synchronization if we were not interested in image matching. This method does nothing for unsupported image formats. This method is not in the first edition of the SQL/MM StillImage standard, but it has been accepted for inclusion in the next version.

```
CREATE OR REPLACE PROCEDURE SI_CLEAR_FEATURES
  AS
   myimage SI_StillImage;
BEGIN
  SELECT IMAGE INTO myimage FROM photos_SI
    WHERE id = 1239 FOR UPDATE;
```

```
    UPDATE photos_SI
      SET IMAGE = myimage where id=1239;

    myimage.SI_ClearFeatures;
    DBMS_OUTPUT.PUT_LINE('Image feature caching disabled');
    COMMIT;
  END;
```

There are two methods for producing a thumbnail image from a SI_Image instance. SI_Thumbnail() derives a thumbnail image from the specified SI_StillImage object. The default thumbnail size is 80 × 80 pixels. Because this method preserves the image aspect ratio, the resulting thumbnail size will be as close to 80 × 80 pixels as possible.

```
CREATE OR REPLACE PROCEDURE SI_Image_thumb
  AS
    myimage SI_StillImage;
     myThumbnail SI_StillImage;
     height number;
     width number;
  BEGIN
    SELECT image INTO myimage FROM  photos_SI WHERE id = 1239;
    width := myimage.SI_width;
    height := myimage.SI_height;
    DBMS_OUTPUT.PUT_LINE('Height is ' || height || ' pixels.');
    DBMS_OUTPUT.PUT_LINE('Width is ' || width ||  ' pixels.');
    myThumbnail := myimage.SI_Thumbnail;
    width := myThumbnail.SI_width;
    height := myThumbnail.SI_height;
    DBMS_OUTPUT.PUT_LINE('Height is ' || height || ' pixels.');
    DBMS_OUTPUT.PUT_LINE('Width is ' || width ||  ' pixels.');
  UPDATE photos_SI
  SET thumb = myThumbnail
  WHERE id =1239;
  END;
SQL> execute SI_Image_thumb
Height is 1320 pixels.
Width is 1407 pixels.
Height is 75 pixels.
Width is 80 pixels.

PL/SQL procedure successfully completed.
```

Alternatively, we can generate a new thumbnail image from the specified SI_StillImage object using the height and width specified. This method does not preserve the aspect ratio. Create a new thumbnail image from an SI_StillImage object with the specified height and width using the SI_Thumbnail(height, width) method:

```
CREATE OR REPLACE PROCEDURE SI_Image_thumb_size
AS
    myimage SI_StillImage;
    myThumbnail SI_StillImage;
    height number;
    width number;
BEGIN
  SELECT image INTO myimage FROM Photos_si WHERE id = 1235;
  width := myimage.SI_width;
  height := myimage.SI_height;
  DBMS_OUTPUT.PUT_LINE('Height is ' || height || ' pixels.');
  DBMS_OUTPUT.PUT_LINE('Width is ' || width || ' pixels.');
  myThumbnail := myimage.SI_Thumbnail(129,121);
  width := myThumbnail.SI_width;
  height := myThumbnail.SI_height;
  DBMS_OUTPUT.PUT_LINE('Height is ' || height || ' pixels.');
  DBMS_OUTPUT.PUT_LINE('Width is ' || width || ' pixels.');
UPDATE photos_SI
SET thumb = myThumbnail
WHERE id = 1235;
END;
Procedure created.

SQL> execute SI_Image_thumb_size
Height is 200 pixels.
Width is 200 pixels.
Height is 129 pixels.
Width is 121 pixels.

PL/SQL procedure successfully completed.
```

There are a number of attributes associated with the requirements for image matching. These are covered in Chapter 13 on advanced query processing.

8.7 Object Tables

We can use user-defined types in two ways: to specify an attribute in a relational table or to generate an object table from the type. There are good design reasons why we should only create one object table for each user-defined type in order to maintain consistency throughout the database; otherwise, as explained later, we may end up with dangling REFs.

An object table is a special kind of table that holds objects and provides a relational view of the attributes of those objects. In Chapter 3 we created an object table from a photo_ord type based on the *inter*Media ORDImage type.

```
CREATE TYPE photo_ty AS OBJECT
  ( id           NUMBER,
          description VARCHAR2(40),
          location    VARCHAR2(40),
          image       ORDSYS.ORDIMAGE,
          thumb       ORDSYS.ORDIMAGE);
```

Then we created the object table:

```
CREATE TABLE photo_ty_tab OF photo_ty
(CONSTRAINT PK_photo_ty_tab PRIMARY KEY(id))
```

Note: In Oracle, object tables will not be listed in the system table called tab and cannot be shown by the query SELECT * FROM TAB, but we can use DESCRIBE to look at the structure of objects and object tables.

When an object table is formed, each object forms a complete row of the object table:

- Objects that appear in object tables are called *row objects*.
- Every row object in an object table has an associated object identifier (OID).
- The OID uniquely identifies the object in an object table.
- The OID can be used to construct object references to row objects that are an alternative to foreign keys.

- The OID allows object types and relational tables to refer to the row objects in the object table.

Oracle automatically assigns a unique system-generated identifier called the OID for each row object. Object references are used to fetch and navigate objects. We can regard the use of the OID as a compromise as it could be said to conflict with relational theory and it is not very meaningful in an object-relational database. Oracle manages object access by creating and maintaining an index of the OID column of the object table.

We specified a primary key for the photo_table, using the ID attribute. Oracle recommends the use of primary-key based identifiers for more efficient loading of the object table because system-generated object identifiers need to be remapped by the DBMS using user-specified keys.

8.8   Summary

In this chapter we have covered the basic methods of the ORDSYS object types focusing on the constructor and image-processing methods. These methods allow rich media to be stored in the specialized object types in the ORDSource object type either internally in the database or externally. We have illustrated how routine image-processing operations can be carried out with the ORDImage object type without removing the images from the database or using specialized image-processing software. Some image processing can also be carried out with the SI_StillImage object type that is included for interoperability purposes.

9

J2EE/ADF Application Development

9.1 Introduction

This chapter will introduce the development of applications using J2EE technologies, such as Java, Java Server Pages (JSP), and Java Server Faces (JSF), as well as Oracle's Application Development Framework (ADF).

Oracle's Application Development Framework (ADF) is a collection of technologies that can be used to automate the complexities of developing an application using J2EE's model-view-controller (MVC) design paradigm. This allows the developer to concentrate on the business logic. ADF is based on proven J2EE technologies, such as Java Server Faces (JSF), and business components from previous versions of Oracle JDeveloper.

Development of a rich-media application using Java and J2EE technologies is much quicker and easier with the use of an integrated development environment (IDE) such as JDeveloper. This is especially true when the IDE includes wizards to access media data. However, some may choose, for various reasons, not to use an IDE for development. For this reason, this chapter will show how an IDE can be used for *inter*Media data as well as plain code samples. The reason for this is that the concepts presented here can be used for multiple J2EE IDEs as well as for those developing J2EE applications without the use of an IDE.

Some may choose to use plain Java applications to access media, while others will integrate this media access into JSP pages. The choice of using plain Java or JSP technology is typically one made outside of the question of where the media is going to be managed. The concepts in this chapter are how to use these J2EE technologies to use media professionally managed in the database using these technologies.

9.2   Application Development Framework

To make J2EE development simpler and more accessible, Oracle JDeveloper introduces the Oracle Application Development Framework (Oracle ADF), a J2EE development framework based on the model-view-controller (MVC) architecture that implements design patterns and eliminates infrastructure coding. Oracle ADF has four layers:

1. **The business services layer**—provides access to data from various sources and handles business logic.

2. **The model layer**—provides an abstraction layer on top of the business services layer, enabling the view and controller layers to work with different implementations of business services in a consistent way.

3. **The controller layer**—provides a mechanism to control the flow of the Web application.

4. **The view layer**—provides the user interface to the application.

Oracle ADF integrates seamlessly with *inter*Media at all layers, thus providing great flexibility and simplicity in the way in which developers can create media-rich Java applications.

On the business services layer, developers can drag and drop tables from the database browser onto the UML diagram to generate business services that provide Java interfaces to these tables. *inter*Media object types are automatically recognized by Oracle ADF and corresponding domain classes are created on this layer. The same mechanism also makes the *inter*Media object transparent in the drag-and-drop operations on the model layer and the controller layer.

On the view layer, developers can create a media-rich JSP/UIX application as any other JSP/UIX application by the drag-and-drop business services component from JDeveloper Data Control Palette. Render value tag and input render tag will automatically bind user interface components with *inter*Media domain objects so that users are able to view, insert, update, and delete multimedia content just like handling other textual data in the JSP/UIX application. The developers can debug or run the JSP/UIX application from inside the JDeveloper. When the development work is done, the developers can deploy the JSP/UIX application to an application server in the form of WAR file or EAR file from the JDeveloper.

Finally, developers can choose to program directly against the underlying *inter*Media ADF Integration Package. The *inter*Media ADF Integration Package includes the *inter*Media ADF domain classes and a set of utility classes. The `OrdImageDomain`, `OrdAudioDomain`, `OrdVideoDomain`, and `OrdDocDomain` *inter*Media ADF domain classes are available since Release 9i of JDeveloper. These domain classes are wrappers of the *inter*Media Java Client classes described earlier and inherit all the underlying multimedia retrieval, upload, and manipulation methods.

The *inter*Media business components domain classes support the `DomainOwnerInterface`, `LobInterface`, `AttributeList`, and `XMLDomainInterface` of the Oracle ADF, and so provide built-in, integrated multimedia capabilities. The utility classes support the retrieval, rendering, and uploading of multimedia content. For example, any application can use the *inter*Media ADF domain classes to facilitate uploading multimedia into the database. Servlet and JSP applications can use the `OrdURL-Builder` and `OrdPlayMedia` classes to build URLs and retrieve multimedia content from the database. `OrdURLBuilder` constructs URLs that locate *inter*Media objects using the ADF run-time framework, while `OrdPlayMedia` interprets the URLs to fetch the *inter*Media content from the database and deliver it to the browser.

To illustrate this point, we will take the steps necessary to create a very simple media application using JDeveloper ADF.

9.2.1 Creating the Model Component

To create a model component to interface to the database and retrieve and upload media from the photos table that was created in previous samples, business components are used.

To create the model, we must first create an application and database connection. This is accomplished using simple wizards. The Database Connection connects to a database where the photos table was created.

After creating a JDeveloper application and database connection, we create a project to hold the model and use a JDeveloper wizard to create the model. In the General category, Projects or ADF Business Components is selected. We choose Business Components to create a component that can retrieve/insert data from/to a database table. See Figure 9.1.

After naming the model project "MediaProject" we accept the defaults in the next screen that specifies the paths. After the second step in creating the project, the following screen shown in Figure 9.2 is displayed to guide

Figure 9.1

*Creating the
Database
Connection*

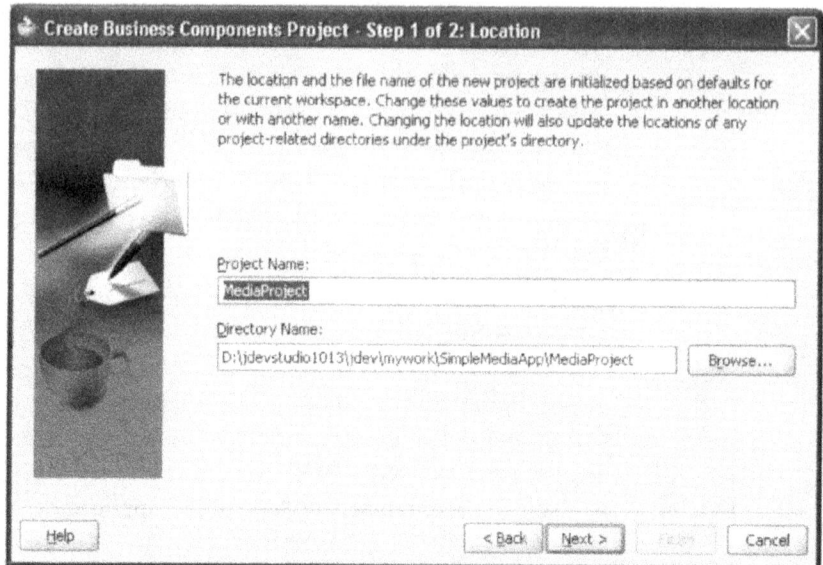

us through creating the business object from database tables. In this screen we choose the database connection we had defined previously.

After defining the connection to use, it is time to select the table to build the business component to use. JDeveloper displays a list of database tables when the Tables object type checkbox is selected. The photos table is selected by identifying the object type as a table and selecting the Photos table, as shown in Figure 9.3

The next step is to create an Updatable View Object (Figure 9.4). This updatable view business object allows for a view that can be updated by the application. The following step would be to create read-only view objects that we will skip.

After skipping the read-only object view selection, we take the defaults on the next screen that define the package and application module name. On the last screen of this wizard, we can optionally create a business components diagram of this module. This can be useful to understand the configuration of the business object. We choose to create a diagram.

At this point, we have created a business object that can be used by a model component.

Figure 9.2
*Business
Component
Initialization*

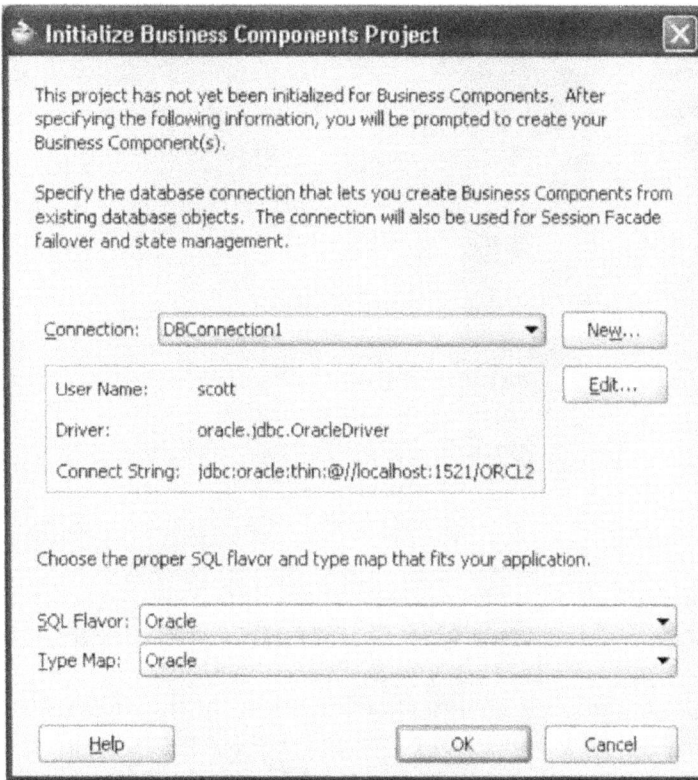

Initialize Business Components Project

This project has not yet been initialized for Business Components. After specifying the following information, you will be prompted to create your Business Component(s).

Specify the database connection that lets you create Business Components from existing database objects. The connection will also be used for Session Facade failover and state management.

Connection: DBConnection1   New...

User Name:	scott
Driver:	oracle.jdbc.OracleDriver
Connect String:	jdbc:oracle:thin:@//localhost:1521/ORCL2

Edit...

Choose the proper SQL flavor and type map that fits your application.

SQL Flavor: Oracle
Type Map: Oracle

Help   OK   Cancel

Figure 9.3
*Create Business
Component Step 1*

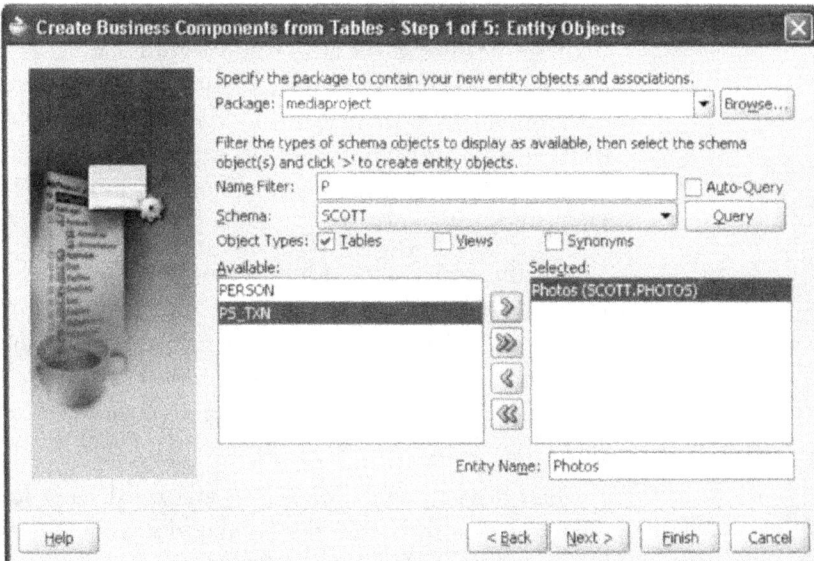

Create Business Components from Tables - Step 1 of 5: Entity Objects

Specify the package to contain your new entity objects and associations.
Package: mediaproject   Browse...

Filter the types of schema objects to display as available, then select the schema object(s) and click '>' to create entity objects.
Name Filter: P   ☐ Auto-Query
Schema: SCOTT   Query
Object Types: ☑ Tables   ☐ Views   ☐ Synonyms

Available: Selected:
PERSON   Photos (SCOTT.PHOTOS)
PS_TXN

Entity Name: Photos

Help   < Back   Next >   Finish   Cancel

Figure 9.4
*Creating Business
Component Step 2*

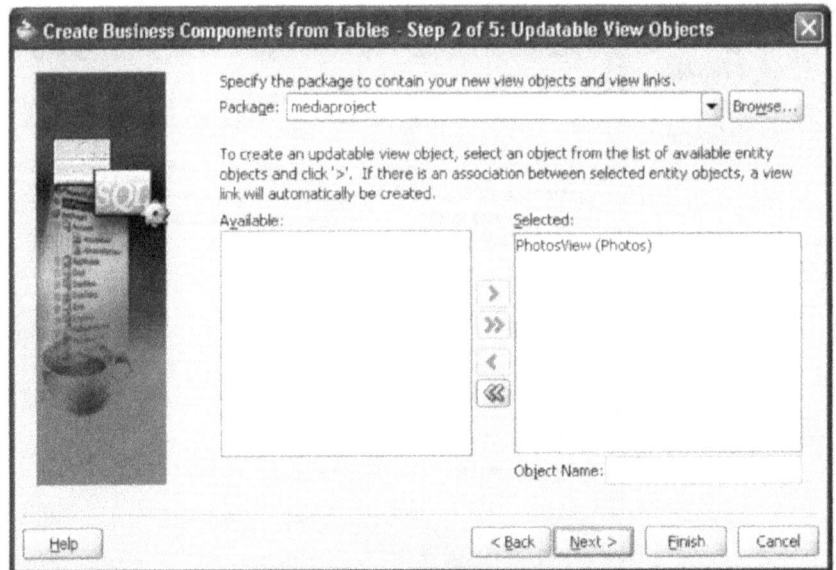

Figure 9.4
*Creating Business
Component Step 2*

9.2.2   Creating the Controller and View Components

To create a JSF application, we use the JDeveloper. First an empty project is created and then we create a new JSF page control and configuration (faces configuration) into the project. This controller will handle the control component of the JSF application. After these steps, JDeveloper has the appearance shown in Figure 9.5.

After creation of the faces configuration file, named faces-config.xml by default, JDeveloper immediately brings the faces configuration file to the foreground and displays it in a Design GUI. To see the actual XML source code, you can press the source tab at the lower portion of the center screen. At this point, there is no actual content in the JSF application, so the Design GUI is empty.

On the upper right side there is a Palette that contains components. Using the mouse, drag a JSF page component from the Palette onto the Design screen. At this point the Design screen contains a page that will be invoked by the JSF controller. We double click on the page to bring up the Create JSF JSP wizard. On the second screen of the wizard the newly created JSP is named browse.jsp, as shown in Figure 9.6.

After this page of the wizard, we take the defaults for the next screen and then continue to choose the tag libraries we will use. We choose the tag libraries illustrated in Figure 9.7.

Figure 9.5
Initial Component Diagram

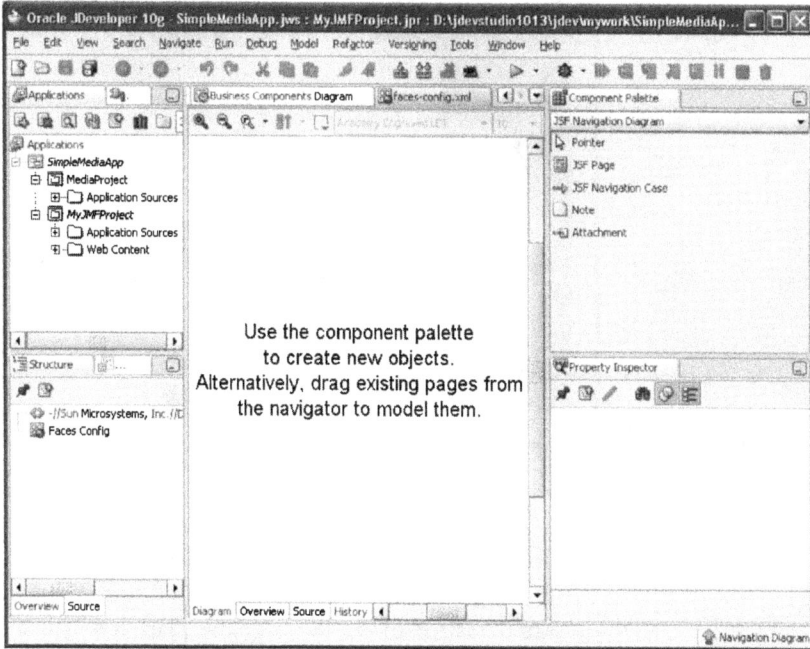

Figure 9.6
Create JSF JSP Step 1

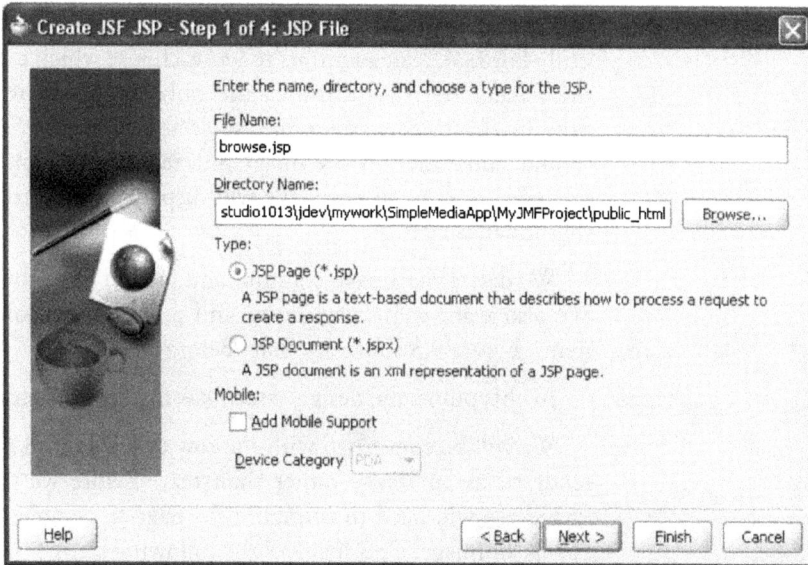

Then, click Finish to take the rest of the defaults for this new JSP page. In a real application, we would at least review and verify the default choices, and perhaps change them to what the development environment requires.

Figure 9.7
Create JSF JSP
Step 2

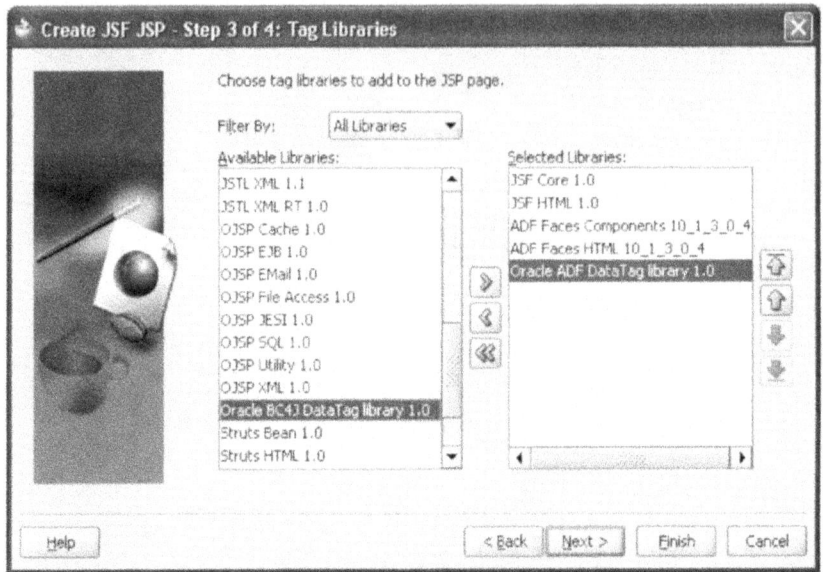

After creation of the JSF page, we place it within a JSP Editor. From our Palette, we choose data controls, expand AppModuleDataControl, and locate the PhotosView1 component. This component is dragged onto the JSP screen. A dialog appears, and we choose Create->Table->ADF Read-Only Form. A dialog appears to let us choose which columns will appear on the screen. For this example, the only image we want to display is the thumbnail image in the table, since it will display a list. We could, and should, show the full size image in a real application by creating a link on this page to a detail page. We will display all the text fields, as well as the thumbnail image.

We delete the Image column, and are left with the rest of the columns. We also want some navigation and a submit button, so we check these items. Figure 9.8 shows the state before we continue.

At this point, the design screen has the appearance shown in Figure 9.9.

We will be concerned with the row called Thumb. This row needs to be rendered as an image rather than text. Before we can render this as an image, we will need to configure the page to be able to render the thumbnail as an image. This involves the following steps:

- Changing the binding of Thumb to use the OrdValueHandler in the page definition file.

Figure 9.8
*JSF JSP
Form Fields*

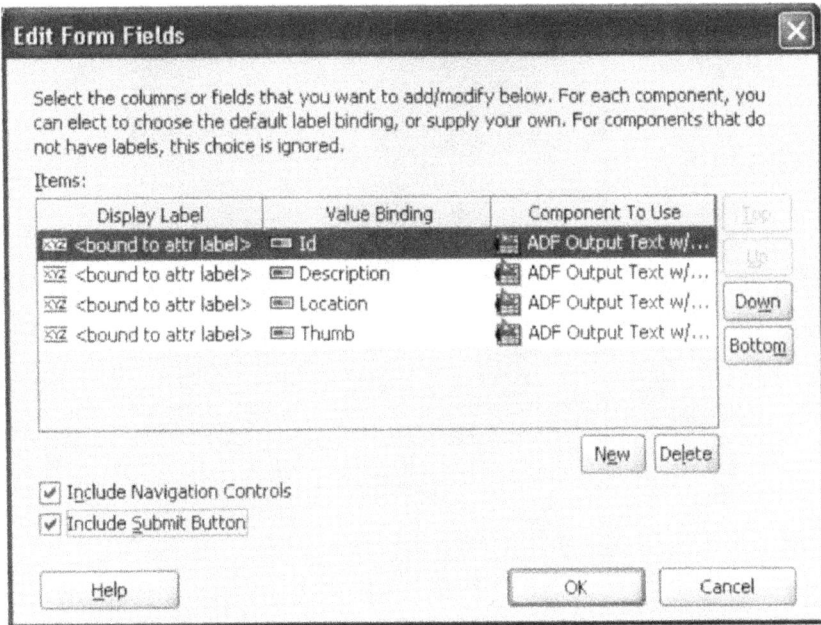

Figure 9.8
*JSF JSP
Form Fields*

- Creating a servlet endpoint for the handler to use to get or put media in *inter*Media objects.

- Changing the JSP page to use OrdValueHandler.

For the first set, we use the navigator on the left side to expand the application sources in MyJMFProject. In the list is a package called myjmf-project.pageDefs. This project includes definitions for each of the JSF pages in the project. After expanding the myjmfproject.pageDefs project and opening browsePageDef.xml, we can see the definitions for each of the fields. The definition that will be modified is highlighted. See Figure 9.10.

The highlighted definition for Thumb will be a custom input handler set to OrdDomainValueHandler. After this change, the XML segment describing Thumb will be the following:

```
<attributeValues id="Thumb" IterBinding="PhotosView1Iterator"
    CustomInputHandler="OrdDomainValueHandler">
  <AttrNames>
    <Item Value="Thumb"/>
  </AttrNames>
</attributeValues>
```

Figure 9.9

JSP Form Design

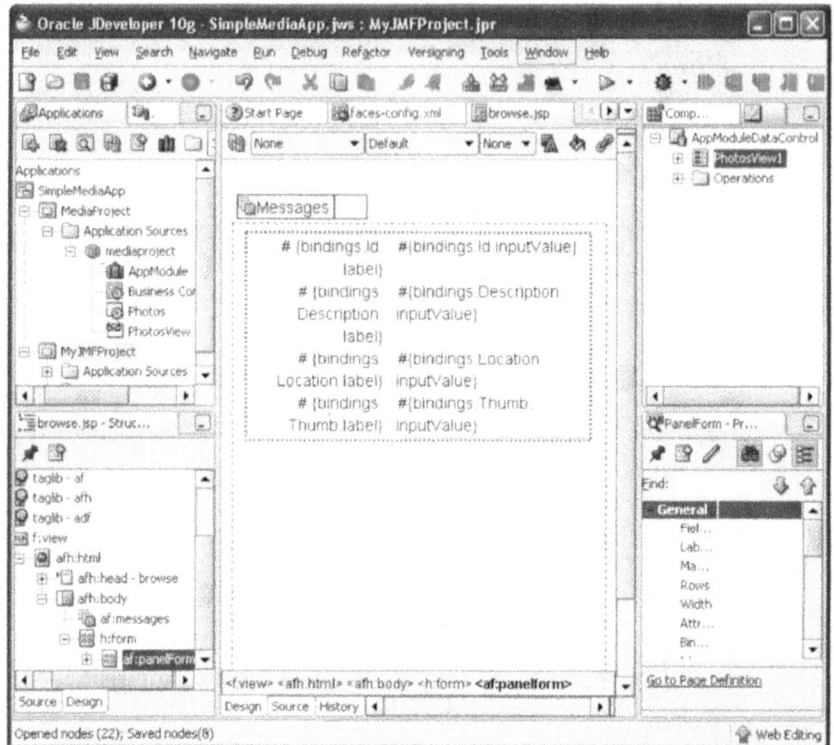

At this point, we need to create a servlet endpoint for media requests. The OrdDomainHandler uses the OrdDeliverMedia servlet. Creation of this endpoint is done by modifying web.xml. To open web.xml, use the navigator to expand Web Content and then WEB-INF. Open web.xml. The Following XML segment is added to the XML file to define the servlet that will be used for getting (or putting) media from (or to) the database. This XML segment is placed within the upper-level <web-app> tag. This change needs to only be done once in the project, not like the change of the InputHandler that needs to be done for every page that will want to display media from the database or insert media into the database.

```
<filter-mapping>
    <filter-name>adfBindings</filter-name>
    <servlet-name>ordDeliverMedia</servlet-name>
</filter-mapping>

<servlet>
```

Figure 9.10

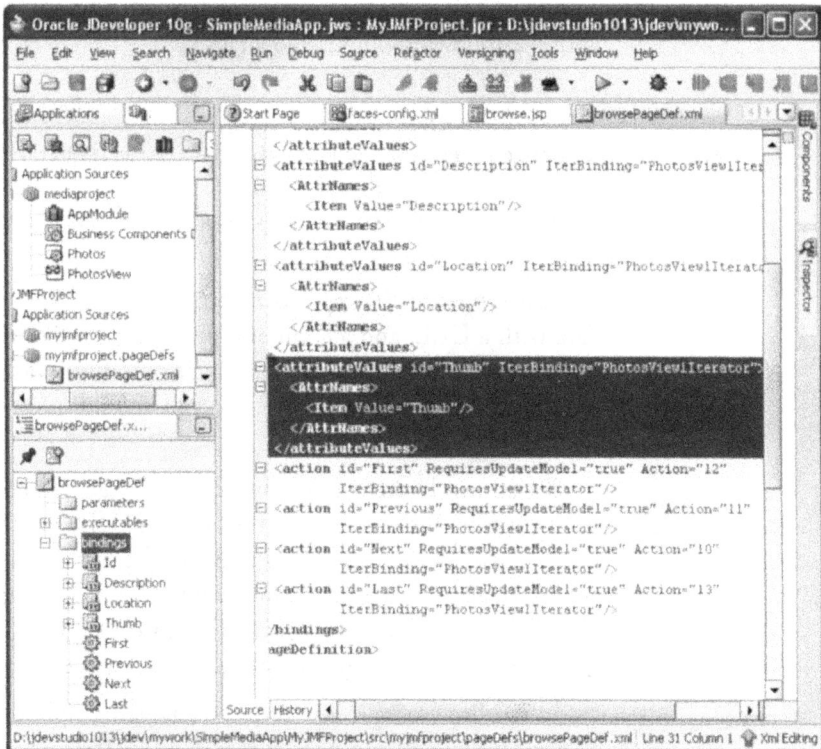

Figure 9.10

```
<servlet-name>ordDeliverMedia</servlet-name>
<servlet-class>oracle.ord.html.OrdPlayMediaServlet</
servlet-class>
    <init-param>
        <param-name>releaseMode</param-name>
        <param-value>Stateful</param-value>
    </init-param>
</servlet>

<servlet-mapping>
    <servlet-name>ordDeliverMedia</servlet-name>
    <url-pattern>ordDeliverMedia</url-pattern>
</servlet-mapping>
```

At this point, we have to go into the source code of the JSP. Select the tab for browse.jsp. Choose the Source tab at the lower part of the main screen. Find the following code in browse.jsp:

```
<af:outputText value="#{bindings.Thumb.inputValue}"/>
```

Change this text to output media with the MIME type of the media with the following objectMedia tag:

```
<af:objectMedia
source="#{bindings.Thumb.inputValue.source}"

contentType="#{bindings.Thumb.inputValue.media.mimeType}"/>
```

The ObjectMedia tag has a source, which indicates the source of the data with a URL, and a contentType, that is the MIME type of the media. If the media is an image, an image tag is produced, otherwise an anchor tag is produced (for nonimage media, you should add something within the ObjectMedia tag to click on).

We are nearly there! Now, only one thing is left to be done before we can see the image. We need to add the jar file BC4JHTML.jar to the project. To do this, highlight the MyJMFProject in the navigator, right click on it, and choose Project Properties. Now highlight Libraries and click on the Add Library button. Select BC4JHTML and click OK. Click OK to leave the project properties dialog. We are ready to test the JSP page.

To test browse.jsp, select it in the navigator, right click, and select run. If all went well, you should see something like the screen in Figure 9.11.

To create a form to edit or create media in the database is quite similar. The differences are:

- The form must be changed to be of type multipart/form data. This can be done in many ways, like double clicking on the <h:form> element on the lower left. The <h:form> element should end up looking like:

```
<h:form enctype=îmultipart/form-data
```

- The form field to edit/create the media field must be changed to accept a file. The wizard will put in code that looks like the following:

```
<af:inputText value="#{bindings.Image.inputValue}"
 label="#{bindings.Image.label}"
 required="#{bindings.Image.mandatory}"
 columns="#{bindings.Image.displayWidth}">
```

Figure 9.11

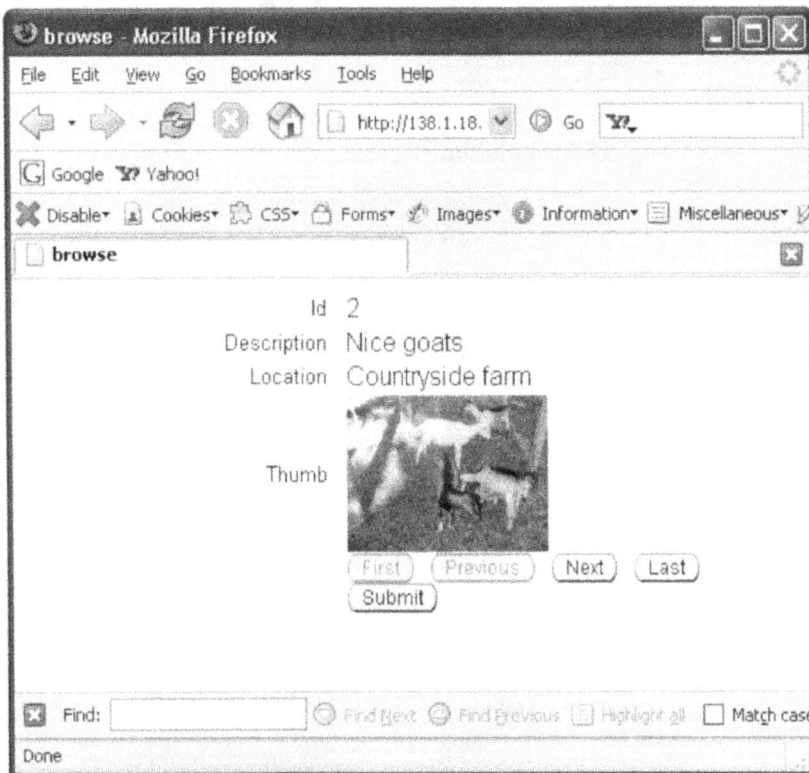

```
<af:validator binding="#{bindings.Image.validator}"/>
</af:inputText>
```

- This should be changed to something like the following that will create a field to accept a filename for update/insert and also display the media when updating an existing record:

```
<af:panelLabelAndMessage>
 <af:inputFile value="#{bindings.Image.inputValue}"
simple="true">
 <af:validator binding="#{bindings.Image.validator}"/>
 </af:inputFile>
 <af:objectMedia source="#{bindings.Image.inputValue.source}"
 contentType="#{bindings.Image.inputValue.media.mimeType}"/>
</af:panelLabelAndMessage>
>
```

9.3   *inter*Media Java Server Pages Tag Library

Oracle *inter*Media provides a custom Java Server Pages (JSP) tag library that lets users easily generate multimedia HTML tags in Java Server Pages, and upload multimedia data into *inter*Media objects in the database.

The *inter*Media JSP tag library is used with Oracle JDeveloper, however, the application can be deployed on the J2EE platform of your choice.

9.3.1   Retrieving Multimedia Data Using the *inter*Media JSP Tag Library

Oracle *inter*Media Java Classes for servlets and JSP uses the OrdHttpResponseHandler class to retrieve media data from an Oracle database and deliver it to a browser or other HTTP client from a Java servlet or JSP page.

Multimedia Tag Library provides media retrieval tags, which JSP developers can use to generate complete HTML multimedia tags or create multimedia retrieval URLs for inclusion in the customized use of an HTML multimedia tag. The media retrieval tags are embedAudio, embedImage, embedVideo, and mediaURL.

Example of Retrieving Multimedia Data Using the interMedia JSP Tag Library

The `PhotoAlbum.jsp` file is one component of a sample JSP application that uses tags from the Multimedia Tag Library to retrieve media data from the database and deliver it to a browser, which displays the media in a simple photograph album application. Example 2-1 shows the tags mediaUrl and embedImage.

The `PhotoAlbum.jsp` file generates the HTML code that displays the contents of the database table named Photos, including the contents of the description, location, and thumb columns. The contents of the thumb column in the photos table are displayed as thumbnail images that link to the full-size images that are stored in the image column in the Photos Table. From the browser, users can click a thumbnail image to view the full-size image.

```
[1] <%@ page language="java" %>
[2] <%@ taglib prefix="ord" uri="/Web-inf/intermedia-
    taglib.tld" %>
```

```
<%@ taglib prefix="sql" uri="/web-inf/sqltaglib.tld" %>

<%
[3] public static final String escapeHtmlString(String input)
    {
        StringBuffer sb = new StringBuffer();

        for (int i = 0; i < input.length(); i++)
        {
            char ch = input.charAt(i);
            switch (ch)
            {
                case '<':
                    sb.append("&lt;");
                    break;

                case '>':
                    sb.append("&gt;");
                    break;
                case '&':
                    sb.append("&amp;");
                    break;
                case '"':
                    sb.append("&quot;");
                    break;
                case ' ':
                    sb.append(" ");
                    break;

                default:
                    sb.append(ch);
            }

        }

        return sb.toString();
    }
%>

<%-- HTML header --%>
<HTML LANG="EN">
```

```
<HEAD>
<TITLE>interMedia JavaServer Pages Photo Album Demo</TITLE>
</HEAD>

<BODY>

   <%-- Page heading --%>
[4] <TABLE BORDER="0" WIDTH="100%">
   <TR>

    <TD COLSPAN="2" BGCOLOR="#F7F7E7" ALIGN="CENTER">
    <FONT SIZE="+2">
      <I>inter</I>Media JavaServer Pages Photo Album Demo
      </FONT>
    </TD>
   </TR>
   </TABLE>

   <P>
   <TABLE BORDER="1" CELLPADDING="3" CELLSPACING="0"
   WIDTH="100%"
    SUMMARY="Table of thumb nail images">
   <TR BGCOLOR="#336699">
     <TH id="description"><FONT
     COLOR="#FFFFFF">Description</FONT></TH>
     <TH id="location"><FONT COLOR="#FFFFFF">Location
     </FONT></TH>
     <TH id="image"><FONT COLOR="#FFFFFF">Image</FONT></TH>
   </TR>

   <% int rowCount = 0; %>
[5] <sql:dbOpen connId = "myConn" dataSource="jdbc/OracleDS"
    />
    <sql:dbQuery connId = "myConn" queryId="myQuery"
    output="jdbc">

    SELECT id, description, location from photos order by
    description
    </sql:dbQuery>
    <sql:dbNextRow queryId="myQuery">
    <%
```

```
[6]    String id = myQuery.getString(1);
       String description = myQuery.getString(2);
       String location = myQuery.getString(3);
    %>
[7]     <TR>
        <TD HEADERS="description">
          <%= escapeHtmlString(description) %>
        </TD>
        <%
          if ( location != null )
            out.print( "<TD HEADERS=\"location\">" +
              escapeHtmlString(location) + "</TD>" );
          else
            out.print( "<TD HEADERS=\"location\"> </TD>"
                       );
        %>

        <TD HEADERS="image">
[8]      <ord:mediaUrl dataSourcename="jdbc/OracleDS"
                        table = "photos"
                        column = "image"
                        key = "<%=id%>"
                        keyColumn = "id"
                        id = "urlId">
[9]        <A HREF="<%= urlId.getUrl()%>">
[10]         <ord:embedImage dataSourceName="jdbc/OracleDS"
                        table = "photos"
                        column = "thumb"
                        key = "<%= id %>"
                        keyColumn = "id"
                        alt =
             "<%=escapeHtmlString(description)%>"
                        border="1" />

          </A>
         </ord:mediaUrl>
       </TD></TR>

[11] <% rowCount ++; %>
     </sql:dbNextRow>
     <sql:dbCloseQuery queryId="myQuery"/>
```

```
<sql:dbClose connId="myConn"/>

<TR>
<TD SCOPE="col" COLSPAN="3" ALIGN="CENTER">
<FONT COLOR="#336699"><B><I>
<%
    if (rowCount == 0)
    {
      out.println(" The photo album is empty");
    }
    else
    {
      out.println
  (" Select the thumb-nail to view the full-size image");
    }
%>
    </I></B></FONT></TD>
  </TR>
<%-- Finish the table --%>
</TABLE>

</P>

 <P>
<TABLE WIDTH="100%">
  <TR BGCOLOR="#F7F7E7">
    <TD COLSPAN="3" ALIGN="CENTER">
      <A HREF="PhotoAlbumUploadForm.jsp">Upload new photo</A>
    </TD>
  </TR>
</TABLE>
</P>

</BODY>
</HTML>
```

The Java, SQL, and HTML statements in the `PhotoAlbum.jsp` file perform the following operations:

1. Declare Java as the script language used in the JSP page. (This line of code is a JSP directive.)

2. Provide the prefix and uri attributes. The value of the uri attribute indicates the location of the tag library descriptor (TLD) file for the tag library. The prefix attribute (ord) specifies the XML namespace identifier, which should be inserted before each occurrence of the library's tags in the JSP page. (These two lines of code are Multimedia Tag Library directives.)

3. Declare a method that provides escape sequences to interpret some commonly used special characters in HTML. (This is called a method declaration statement.)

4. Use an HTML table to display the entries of the photos table in the database. (This is an HTML program.)

5. Open the database connection, perform a query on the photos table, and then loop over the retrieved result set.

6. Retrieve data from the result set.

7. Begin to display the entries in the table.

8. Create a script variable named urlId that points to the image column of the photos table in the database. (This line of code shows the Multimedia JSP tag mediaUrl.)

9. Provide a link that points to the URL stored in the script variable.

10. Generate the HTML <IMG> tag that displays the thumb column of the photos table (see embedImage for information about the HTML output). The HTML <A HREF> tag uses the JSP tag embedImage as the link anchor. (This line of code shows the Multimedia JSP tag embedImage.)

11. End the loop then close the query and the database connection.

9.3.2 Uploading Multimedia Data Using the *inter*Media JSP Tag Library

Oracle *inter*Media Java Classes for servlets and JSP uses the OrdHttpUploadFile class to facilitate the handling of uploaded media files. This class provides a simple application programming interface (API) that applications call to load media data into the database.

File uploading using HTML forms encodes form data and uploaded files in POST requests using the multipart/form-data format. The

OrdHttpUploadFormData class facilitates the processing of such requests by parsing the POST data and making the contents of regular form fields and the contents of uploaded files readily accessible to a Java servlet or JSP page.

Multimedia Tag Library provides media upload tags, which facilitate the development of multimedia applications that upload media data into the database. The media upload tags are storeMedia, uploadFile, and upload-FormData.

The `PhotoAlbumInsertPhoto.jsp` file is one component of a sample JSP application that uses tags from Multimedia Tag Library to upload media files into a database. The following example shows the tags uploadFormData, uploadFile, and storeMedia.

```
[1] <%@ page language="java" %>
<%@ taglib prefix="ord" uri="/Web-inf/intermedia-taglib.tld"
%>
<%@ taglib prefix="sql" uri="/web-inf/sqltaglib.tld" %>


[2] <ord:uploadFormData formDataId = "fd">

[3]  <ord:uploadFile
          parameter = "photo"
          fullFileName = "ffName"
          shortFileName = "sfName"

          length = "fLength" >

     <%
[4]   if (ffName == null || ffName.length() == 0)
      {
    %>
      <jsp:forward
      page="PhotoAlbumUploadForm.jsp?error=
      Please+supply+a+file+name."/>
    <%
        return;
      }

      if (fLength.intValue() == 0)
```

```
        {
    %>
        <jsp:forward
        page="PhotoAlbumUploadForm.jsp?error=
        Please+supply+a+valid+image+file."/>
        <%
        return;
        }

        String description = fd.getParameter("description");
        String location = fd.getParameter("location");
[5]     if ( description == null || description.length() == 0 )
        {
            description = "Image from file: " + sfName + ".";
            if(description.length() > 40)

            {
                description = description.substring(0, 40);
            }
        }

        java.util.Vector otherValuesVector =
        new java.util.Vector();
        otherValuesVector.add(description);
        otherValuesVector.add(location);
    %>

    <%String id = "original"; %>
[6] <sql:dbOpen connId = "myConn" dataSource="jdbc/OracleDS"
                 commitOnClose="true"/>

    <sql:dbQuery connId = "myConn" queryId=
    "myQuery" output="jdbc">
        SELECT photos_sequence.nextval from dual
    </sql:dbQuery>

    <sql:dbNextRow queryId="myQuery">
        <% id = myQuery.getString(1); %>
    </sql:dbNextRow>

    <sql:dbCloseQuery queryId="myQuery"/>
```

```
[7] <ord:storeMedia
        conn = "<%=
(oracle.jdbc.driver.OracleConnection)myConn.getConnection()
%>"
        table = "photos"

        key = "<%=id%>"
        keyColumn = "id"
        mediaColumns = "image"
        mediaParameters = "photo"
        otherColumns = "description, location"
        otherValues = "<%=otherValuesVector%>"
    />


[8] <sql:dbSetParam name = "myid" value = "<%=id%>"/>
    <sql:dbExecute connId = "myConn" bindParams="myid">
      {call generateThumbNail(?)}
    </sql:dbExecute>

  <sql:dbClose connId = "myConn" />

  </ord:uploadFile>

</ord:uploadFormData>


<%-- HTML header --%>
<HTML LANG="EN">
<HEAD>
<TITLE>interMedia JavaServer Pages Photo Album Demo</TITLE>
</HEAD>

[9] <META HTTP-EQUIV="REFRESH"
CONTENT="2;URL=PhotoAlbum.jsp">


<BODY>

 <%-- Page heading --%>
  <TABLE BORDER="0" WIDTH="100%">
   <TR>
     <TD COLSPAN="2" BGCOLOR="#F7F7E7" ALIGN="CENTER">
```

```
        <FONT SIZE="+2">
         <I>inter</I>Media JavaServer Pages Photo Album Demo
         </FONT>
       </TD>
      </TR>
    </TABLE>


    <%-- Display header and instructions --%>
    <P>
    <FONT SIZE=3 COLOR="#336699">
    <B>Photo successfully uploaded into photo album</B>
    </FONT>
    <HR SIZE=1>
    </P>
    <P>
Please click the link below or wait for the browser to refresh
the page.
    </P>


    <%-- Output link to return to the main page --%>
    <P>
    <TABLE WIDTH="100%">
      <TR BGCOLOR="#F7F7E7">
        <TD COLSPAN="3" ALIGN="CENTER">
        <A HREF="PhotoAlbum.jsp">Return to photo album</A>
        </TD>

      </TR>
    </TABLE>
    </P>


    <%-- Finish the page --%>
    </BODY>
    </HTML>
```

The Java, SQL, and HTML statements in the `PhotoAlbumInsert-Photo.jsp` file perform the following operations:

1. Declare Java as the script language used in the JSP page (JSP directive). Provide the location of the TLD file and the required ord and sql prefix attributes. (These are Tag Library directives.)

2. Create a script variable named fd, which is an instance of the oracle.ord.im.OrdHttpUploadFormData object. (This line of code shows the multimedia JSP tag uploadFormData.)

3. Create the script variables ffName, sfName, and fLength, which contain the full file name, short file name, and file length of the uploaded media, respectively. (This line of code shows the multimedia JSP tag uploadFile.)

4. Provide error checking.

5. Generate a default description if no description is provided.

6. Open the database connection and get the next unique ID for the photos table in the database.

7. Upload the media data into the image column of the photos table, and the description and location information into the description and location columns of the photos table. (This line of code shows the multimedia JSP tag storeMedia.)

8. Call a PL/SQL procedure to populate the thumb column of the photos table from the uploaded image column.

9. Display a message of success and then direct the JSP page back to the main page (`PhotoAlbum.jsp`).

9.4 *inter*Media Java Proxy Classes

The image proxy classes were introduced in chapter 2. Aside from the OrdImage class, the other classes are OrdAudio, OrdVideo, and OrdDoc. These classes make the functionality of the *inter*Media classes available to Java programs outside the database. They also include utility classes to make programming common functions more convenient.

The database table used for proxy classes can be created from the Java program or previously using standard SQL. In this chapter, it is assumed that the table is created outside the Java program. Most client programs should not be performing database definition language (DDL) statements that, in most cases, are left to the DBA.

9.4.1   A Note on the Context Parameter

You will note that many of the methods have a context parameter. You may wonder why it is there and why you should care. In most cases you should not, however, it is not used by most *inter*Media users.

Where it is used is if you have a user-written source plug-in. This may be something like a legacy laser disk picture server that can only be accessed using an API. If you do have a system like this, you may need to store a context when the system is opened. Perhaps device handles, current position, etc.

So, if you write a user-written source plug-in, you do care about the context parameter and you will store your context there. If you are using the Database BLOB source, the HTTP source, or file source, you should not worry about the context parameter, except to know you need to pass it in many of the APIs.

9.4.2   Preparing to Use the Proxy Classes

The proxy classes must be associated with a media object in the database. They are used to represent the database media objects in the Java program. The creation of the media object can be done from Java with a simple insert statement, after the object is created, and it can be associated with a proxy class and its contents manipulated. To create the association between the proxy class and the database media object, JDBC is used. To use the proxy classes, the following actions may be taken:

- Create a JDBC connection, with AutoCommit set to off unless no SQL update operations are to occur, then the programmer can choose either AutoCommit on or off.
- A new media row may be created.
- Obtain the media object into a CallableStatement or ResultSet from a procedure or a select statement.
- Use the proxy classes.
- Update the proxy classes.

Creating the JDBC Connection

The creation of a JDBC connection is the same as you would do for using an SQL connection on any database, except it is typically important to set

AutoCommit to off for operations that will update the database. Note that AutoCommit is set on by default in JDBC connections. For example:

```
// register the oracle jdbc driver with the JDBC driver
manager
DriverManager.registerDriver(new
oracle.jdbc.driver.OracleDriver());


Connection conn = DriverManager.getConnection(connectString,
username, password);


// Note: for update operations, it is CRITICAL to set the
autocommit to false so that
// two-phase select-commit of BLOBS can occur.
conn.setAutoCommit(false);
```

Creating a New Media Row with the Media Objects and Create the Proxy Objects

To create a new media row, a simple insert statement is executed with the media column inserted. Typically, when you insert a new media object, you are going to put media data into it in subsequent operations, so to avoid round trips, you may want to return the initialized media object. To be a bit more efficient, we will insert and return the image object in one step using a JDBC CallableStatement block.

```
// After prepare, this can be used over and over again.
      CallableStatement cstmt =
        conn.prepareCall (
        "begin " +
        "insert into photos t (id, description, location,"
        + image, thumb) " +
        " values (?," +
        "'Desc that should be an input param''," +
        "'A place that should be an input param too', " +
        "ORDImage.init(), ORDImage.init())" +
   " returning rowid, t.image, t.thumb into ?, ?, ? ; " +
        "end;");

      // Register input parameters
      cstmt.setInt(1, 17);
      // Register Output Parameters
```

```
        cstmt.registerOutParameter(2, Types.VARCHAR);  // rowid
        ((OracleCallableStatement)cstmt).registerOutParameter
                    (3, Types.STRUCT, "ORDIMAGE");
        // image
        ((OracleCallableStatement)cstmt).registerOutParameter
                    (4, Types.STRUCT, "ORDIMAGE");
        // thumb

            int rowsUpdated  = cstmt.executeUpdate();

            String rowid = cstmt.getString(2);
            // Obtain the proxy objects
            OrdImage imgObj =

(OrdImage)((OracleCallableStatement)cstmt).getORAData
                    (3,
  OrdImage.getORADataFactory());
            OrdImage thumbObj =

(OrdImage)((OracleCallableStatement)cstmt).getORAData
                    (4,
  OrdImage.getORADataFactory());
```

Execute an SQL Select Statement to Return a Media Column for Existing Rows and Obtain the Proxy Objects

To return the media rows from an existing or just inserted row, we could also use a standard select statement.

```
// select the new ORDImage into a java proxy OrdImage object
(imageProxy)

String rowSelectSQL = "select image from photos where id = 1
for update";
OracleResultSet rset =
(OracleResultSet)stmt.executeQuery(rowSelectSQL);
rset.next();
OrdImage imageProxy = (OrdImage)rset.getORAData("image",
OrdImage.getORADataFactory());
rset.close();
```

Note that the `for update` clause should only be used if there is a potential of the media, or row, being updated. The media is typically updated through the proxy object.

Use the Proxy Classes

Once obtained, the proxy classes can be used. They can be used to retrieve media or attributes, or they can be used to modify the media and attributes. They are like any other Java object except that the modifications can be made permanent in the database.

One example of using a proxy class would be to create an image using Image IO. This image then can be used in other display objects, like an ImageIcon that can be put into various controls, like a JLabel that can be displayed in a frame.

```
InputStream is =
    imgObj.getContent().getBinaryStream();
ImageInputStream iis =
    ImageIO.createImageInputStream(is);
    Image image = ImageIO.read(iis);
    ImageIcon imgIcon = new ImageIcon(image);
    JLabel label = new Jlabel(imgIcon);
```

Another example is to use the methods provided to perform image processing and modify images in the database. For example:

```
imgObj.loadDataFromFile("goats.gif");
imgObj.setProperties();
imgObj.processCopy("fileFormat=JFIF maxScale=128 128",
    thumbObj);
```

Update the Media Objects in the Databases

If you change the Java proxy object during processing, these changes do not become permanent until the row is updated and the current transaction committed. Here is an example of updating and committing the update after proxy object changes.

```
OraclePreparedStatement insertImg =
    (OraclePreparedStatement)conn.prepareStatement(
    "Update photos Set image = ?, thumb = ? " +
```

```
                                " where rowid = ?" );

                        insertImg.setORAData(1, imgObj);
                        insertImg.setORAData(2, thumbObj);
                        insertImg.setString(3, rowid);
                        insertImg.execute();
                        insertImg.close();
                        conn.commit();
```

9.4.3   **OrdAudio, OrdImage, OrdAudio, and OrdDoc**

Common methods for OrdAudio, OrdImage, OrdVideo, and OrdDoc

Table 9.1 contains a signature and brief description of the common methods. For full information, see the *interMedia Java Classes Reference Manual.*

Table 9.1   *Common Methods*

Method Signature	Description
void clearLocal()	Clears the local attribute to indicate that the media data is stored externally.
int closeSource(byte[ ] [ ] ctx)	Closes a plug-in data source.
void deleteContent()	Deletes media stored locally in the source BLOB.
void export (byte[ ] [ ] ctx, String srcType, String srcLocation, String srcName)	Exports data from the source BLOB into a file.
Oracle.sql.BFILE getBFILE()	Returns a BFILE locator from the database when the media is stored in a file outside the database.
Oracle.sql.BLOB getContent()	Returns the BLOB locator from the local-Data attribute.
getContentLength()	Returns the length of the media data.
byte[ ] getDataInByteArray()	Returns a byte array containing the media data from the localData BLOB attribute.
boolean getDataInFile(String filename)	Writes the data from the database specified by the localData BLOB attribute to a local file.

Table 9.1 *Common Methods (continued)*

Method Signature	Description
`InputStream getDataInStream()`	Returns an InputStream object from which the data in the database BLOB specified by the localData attribute.
`static oracle.sql.ORADataFactory getORADataFactory()`	Returns the OrdAudio ORADataFactory interface for use by the getORAData() method.
`String getFormat()`	This method returns the value of the format attribute as a string.
`String getMimeType()`	This method returns the value of the mimeType attribute as a string.
`String getSource()`	Returns the source information in the form srcType://srcLocation/srcName.
`String getSourceLocation()`	Returns the value of the srcLocation attribute.
`String getSourceName()`	This method returns the value of the srcName attribute.
`String getSourceType()`	This method returns the value of the srcType attribute.
`java.sql.Timestamp getUpdateTime()`	This method returns the value of the updateTime attribute.
`boolean isLocal()`	This method returns true if the data is stored in the database in a BLOB; false otherwise.
`boolean loadDataFromByteArray(byte[ ] byteArr)`	Loads data from a byte array into the database BLOB specified by localData; it replaces any existing content and updates the Update Time.
`boolean loadDataFromFile(String filename)`	Loads data from a file local to the Java program into the database BLOB specified by localData; it replaces any existing content and updates the Update Time.
`boolean loadDataFromInputStream(Input Stream inpStream)`	Loads data from an InputStream into the database BLOB specified by localData; it replaces any existing content and updates the Update Time.

Table 9.1 *Common Methods (continued)*

Method Signature	Description
`void setFormat(String format)`	Sets the value of the format attribute.
`void setLocal()`	Sets the value of the local attribute to indicate that the media data is stored locally in the database in a BLOB specified by the localData attribute.
`void setMimeType(String mimeType)`	Sets the value of the mimeType attribute.
`setSource(String srcType, String srcLocation, String srcName)`	Sets the values of the srcType, srcLocation, and srcName attributes.
`void setUpdateTime(java.sql.Timestamp currentTime)`	Sets the value of the updateTime attribute.

OrdImage Noncommon Methods

Table 9.2 shows the OrdImage noncommon methods.

Table 9.2 *OrdImage Noncommon Methods*

Method Signature	Description
`boolean checkProperties()`	Checks if the properties of the image data are consistent with the attributes of the OrdImage Java object.
`void copy(OrdImage dest)`	Copies all the attributes of the current OrdImage. If the media is stored locally in a BLOB, the BLOB is also copied.
`String getCompressionFormat()`	Returns the value of the compressionFormat attribute.
`String getContentFormat()`	Returns the value of the contentFormat attribute.
`int getHeight()`	This method returns the value of the height attribute.
`int getWidth()`	This method returns the value of the width attribute.

Table 9.2   *OrdImage Noncommon Methods (continued)*

Method Signature	Description
`void importData(byte[ ] [ ] ctx)`	Imports data from an external source into the database BLOB specified by the local-Data attribute. Calls setProperties() after obtaining the data unless the setFormat() method sets the format attribute.
`importFrom(byte[ ] [ ] ctx, String srcType, String srcLocation, String srcName)`	Imports data from an external source, specified by the method parameters, into the database BLOB specified by the local-Data attribute. Calls setProperties() after obtaining the data unless the setFormat() method sets the format attribute.
`void process(String cmd)`	Performs one or more image-processing operations on the image data in the database BLOB specified by the localData attribute.
`void processCopy(String cmd, OrdImage dest)`	Copies the image data to the destination object and performs one or more image-processing operations on the image data.
`void setCompressionFormat(String compressionFormat)`	Sets the value of the compressionFormat attribute.
`void setContentFormat(String contentFormat)`	Sets the value of the contentFormat attribute.
`setContentLength(int contentLength)`	Sets the value of the contentLength attribute, but does not affect the media itself.
`void setHeight(int height)`	Sets the value of the height attribute.
`void setProperties()`	Parses the image data properties and sets the values of the attributes in the OrdImage Java object.
`void setProperties(String description)`	Writes the characteristics of a foreign image into the appropriate attribute fields. See the *inter*Media Reference Guide for the format of this string.
`void setWidth(int width)`	Sets the value of the width attribute.

OrdAudio Noncommon Methods

Table 9.3 shows the OrdAudio noncommon methods.

Table 9.3   *OrdAudio Noncommon Methods*

Method Signature	Description
`boolean checkProperties(byte[ ] [ ] ctx)`	Checks if the properties of the audio data are consistent with the attributes of the OrdAudio object.
`CLOB getAllAttributes(byte[ ] [ ] ctx)`	Returns the values of the audio properties in a temporary CLOB in a form defined by the format plug-in.
`String getContentFormat()`	Returns the value of the contentFormat attribute.
`String getAttribute(byte[ ] [ ] ctx, String name)`	Returns the value of the requested audio property defined by user-defined format plug-ins.
`int getAudioDuration()`	This method returns the value of the audioDuration attribute.
`Oracle.sql.CLOB getComments()`	Returns the CLOB locator from the comments attribute.
`String getCompressionType()`	Returns the value of the compressionType attribute.
`oracle.sql.BLOB getContentInLob(byte[ ] [ ] ctx, String mimetype[ ], String format[ ])`	Returns the data from the BLOB specified by the localData attribute in a temporary BLOB in the database.
`int getContentLength()`	Returns the length of the audio data.
`int getContentLength(byte[ ] [ ] ctx)`	Returns the length of the audio data using source plug-in context information. Not supported for all source types.
`String getDescription()`	Returns the value of the description attribute.
`String getEncoding()`	This method returns the value of the encoding attribute.
`int getNumberOfChannels()`	Returns the value of the numberOfChannels attribute.

Table 9.3   *OrdAudio Noncommon Methods (continued)*

Method Signature	Description
`int getSamplingRate()`	Returns the value of the samplingRate attribute.
`void importData(byte[ ] [ ] ctx)`	Imports data from an external source into the database BLOB specified by the local-Data attribute.
`importFrom(byte[ ] [ ] ctx, String srcType, String srcLocation, String srcName)`	Imports data from an external source, specified by the method parameters, into the database BLOB, specified by the local-Data attribute. Calls setProperties() after obtaining the data unless the setFormat() method sets the format attribute.
`int openSource(byte[ ] userarg, byte[ ] [ ] ctx)`	Opens a data source for a plug-in if necessary.
`byte[ ] processAudioCommand(byte[ ] [ ] ctx, String cmd, String args, byte[ ] [ ] result)`	Calls the format plug-in in the database to execute a command implemented by a user-written plug-in.
`byte[ ] processSourceCommand(byte[ ] [ ] ctx, String cmd, String args, byte[ ] [ ] result)`	Calls the user-written source plug-in in the database to execute a command.
`int readFromSource(byte[ ] [ ] ctx, int startpos, int numbytes, byte[ ] [ ] buffer)`	Reads data from the data source.
`void setAudioDuration(int audioDuration)`	Sets the value of the audioDuration attribute.
`void setComments(oracle.sql.CLOB comments)`	Sets the value of the comments attribute.
`void setCompressionType(String compressionType)`	Sets the value of the compressionType attribute. Set automatically for some formats with setProperties(Byte[][]).
`void setDescription(String description)`	Sets the value of the description attribute.
`void setEncoding(String encoding)`	Sets the value of the encoding attribute. May be set with setProperties(Byte[][]).

Table 9.3   *OrdAudio Noncommon Methods (continued)*

Method Signature	Description
`void setKnownAttributes(String format, String encoding, int numberOfChannels, int samplingRate, int sampleSize, String compressionType, int audioDuration)`	Sets the values of the known attributes of the OrdAudio Java object. SetProperties(Byte[][]) may set these as well.
`void setNumberOfChannels(int numberOfChannels)`	Sets the value of the numberOfChannels attribute.
`void setProperties(byte[ ] [ ] ctx)`	Parses the audio data properties and sets the values of the attributes in the OrdAudio Java object.
`void setProperties(byte[ ] [ ] ctx, boolean setComments)`	Parses the audio data properties, sets the values of the attributes in the OrdAudio Java object, and optionally populates the CLOB specified by the comments attribute.
`void setSampleSize(int sampleSize)`	Sets the value of the sampleSize attribute.
`void setSamplingRate(int samplingRate)`	Sets the value of the samplingRate attribute.
`int trimSource(byte[ ] [ ] ctx, int newLen)`	Trims the data to the specified length by source plug-ins that support the operation.
`int writeToSource(byte[ ] [ ] ctx, int startpos, int numbytes, byte[ ] buffer)`	Writes data to the data source for source plug-ins that support it.

OrdVideo Noncommon

Table 9.4 shows the OrdVideo noncommon methods.

OrdDoc Noncommon

Table 9.5 shows the OrdDoc noncommon methods.

Table 9.4   *OrdVideo Noncommon Methods*

Method Signature	Description
`boolean checkProperties(byte[ ] [ ] ctx)`	Checks if the properties of the audio data are consistent with the attributes of the OrdAudio object.
`CLOB getAllAttributes(byte[ ] [ ] ctx)`	Returns the values of the audio properties in a temporary CLOB in a form defined by the format plug-in.
`String getContentFormat()`	Returns the value of the contentFormat attribute.
`String getAttribute(byte[ ] [ ] ctx, String name)`	Returns the value of the requested audio property defined by user-defined format plug-ins.
`int getBitRate()`	Returns the value of the bitRate attribute.
`Oracle.sql.CLOB getComments()`	Returns the CLOB locator from the comments attribute.
`String getCompressionType()`	Returns the value of the compressionType attribute.
`oracle.sql.BLOB getContentInLob(byte[ ] [ ] ctx, String mimetype[ ], String format[ ])`	Returns the data from the BLOB specified by the localData attribute in a temporary BLOB in the database.
`int getContentLength()`	Returns the length of the audio data.
`int getContentLength(byte[ ] [ ] ctx)`	Returns the length of the audio data using source plug-in context information. Not supported for all source types.
`String getDescription()`	Returns the value of the description attribute.
`String getEncoding()`	This method returns the value of the encoding attribute.
`int getFrameRate()`	Returns the value of the frameRate attribute.
`int getFrameResolution()`	Returns the value of the frameResolution attribute.
`int getHeight()`	Returns the value of the height attribute.

Table 9.4 *OrdVideo Noncommon Methods (continued)*

Method Signature	Description
`int getNumberOfColors()`	Returns the value of the numberOfColors attribute.
`int getNumberOfFrames()`	Returns the value of the numberOfFrames attribute.
`int getVideoDuration()`	Returns the value of the videoDuration attribute.
`int getWidth()`	Returns the value of the width attribute.
`void importData(byte[ ] [ ] ctx)`	Imports data from an external source into the database BLOB specified by the local-Data attribute.
`importFrom(byte[ ] [ ] ctx, String srcType, String srcLocation, String srcName)`	Imports data from an external source, specified by the method parameters, into the database BLOB, specified by the local-Data attribute. Calls setProperties() after obtaining the data unless the setFormat() method sets the format attribute.
`int openSource(byte[ ] userarg, byte[ ] [ ] ctx)`	Opens a data source for a plug-in if necessary.
`byte[ ] processSourceCommand(byte[ ] [ ] ctx, String cmd, String args, byte[ ] [ ] result)`	Calls the user-written source plug-in in the database to execute a command.
`byte[ ] processVideoCommand(byte[ ] [ ] ctx, String cmd, String args, byte[ ] [ ] result)`	Calls the format plug-in in the database to execute a command implemented by a user-written plug-in.
`int readFromSource(byte[ ] [ ] ctx, int startpos, int numbytes, byte[ ] [ ] buffer)`	Reads data from the data source.
`void setBitRate(int bitRate)`	Sets the value of the bitRate attribute.
`void setComments(oracle.sql.CLOB comments)`	Sets the value of the comments attribute.
`void setCompressionType(String compressionType)`	Sets the value of the compressionType attribute. Set automatically for some formats with setProperties(Byte[][]).

Table 9.4   *OrdVideo Noncommon Methods (continued)*

Method Signature	Description
void setDescription(String description)	Sets the value of the description attribute.
void setEncoding(String encoding)	Sets the value of the encoding attribute. May be set with setProperties(Byte[][]).
void setFrameRate(int frameRate)	Sets the value of the frameRate attribute.
void setFrameResolution(int frameResolution)	Sets the value of the frameResolution attribute.
void setHeight(int height)	Sets the value of the height attribute.
void setNumberOfColors(int numberOfColors)	Sets the value of the numberOfColors attribute.
public void setNumberOfFrames(int numberOfFrames)	Sets the value of the numberOfFrames attribute.
void setProperties(byte[ ] [ ] ctx)	Parses the audio data properties and sets the values of the attributes in the OrdAudio Java object.
void setProperties(byte[ ] [ ] ctx, boolean setComments)	Parses the audio data properties, sets the values of the attributes in the OrdAudio Java object, and optionally populates the CLOB specified by the comments attribute.
void setVideoDuration(int videoDuration)	Sets the value of the videoDuration attribute.
void setWidth(int width)	Sets the value of the width attribute.
int trimSource(byte[ ] [ ] ctx, int newLen)	Trims the data to the specified length by source plug-ins that support the operation.
int writeToSource(byte[ ] [ ] ctx, int startpos, int numbytes, byte[ ] buffer)	Writes data to the data source for source plug-ins that support it.

Table 9.5   *OrdDoc Noncommon Methods*

Method Signature	Description
`Oracle.sql.CLOB getComments()`	Returns the CLOB locator from the comments attribute.
`oracle.sql.BLOB getContentInLob(byte[ ] [ ] ctx, String mimetype[ ], String format[ ])`	Returns the data from the BLOB specified by the localData attribute in a temporary BLOB in the database.
`int getContentLength()`	Returns the length of the audio data.
`void importData(byte[ ] [ ] ctx)`	Imports data from an external source into the database BLOB specified by the local-Data attribute.
`importFrom(byte[ ] [ ] ctx, String srcType, String srcLocation, String srcName)`	Imports data from an external source, specified by the method parameters, into the database BLOB, specified by the local-Data attribute. Calls setProperties() after obtaining the data unless the setFormat() method sets the format attribute.
`int openSource(byte[ ] userarg, byte[ ] [ ] ctx)`	Opens a data source for a plug-in if necessary.
`byte[ ] processSourceCommand(byte[ ] [ ] ctx, String cmd, String args, byte[ ] [ ] result)`	Calls the user-written source plug-in in the database to execute a command.
`int readFromSource(byte[ ] [ ] ctx, int startpos, int numbytes, byte[ ] [ ] buffer)`	Reads data from the data source.
`void setComments(oracle.sql.CLOB comments)`	Sets the value of the comments attribute.
`void setProperties(byte[ ] [ ] ctx)`	Parses the audio data properties and sets the values of the attributes in the OrdAudio Java object.
`void setProperties(byte[ ] [ ] ctx, boolean setComments)`	Parses the audio data properties, sets the values of the attributes in the OrdAudio Java object, and optionally populates the CLOB specified by the comments attribute.

Table 9.5   *OrdDoc Noncommon Methods (continued)*

Method Signature	Description
`int trimSource(byte[ ] [ ]` `ctx, int newLen)`	Trims the data to the specified length by source plug-ins that support the operation.
int writeToSource(byte[ ] [ ] ctx, int startpos, int numbytes, byte[ ] buffer)	Writes data to the data source for source plug-ins that support it.

9.4.4   OrdImageSignature Methods

OrdImageSignature is used as a proxy to the database OrdImageSignature database type. This signature describes the contents of the image in terms of color, shape, and texture. The image signature is used for image-matching applications. This is a quick list of the methods available.

To use these methods, the OrdImageSignature object must be populated and associated with a signature object in the back end. See Table 9.6 and the following code, for example.

```
/ select the ORDImageSignature into a java proxy
OrdImageSignature object (imageSigProxy)
String rowSelectSQL = "select imageSig from photos";
OracleResultSet rset =
(OracleResultSet)stmt.executeQuery(rowSelectSQL);
rset.next();
OrdImageSignature imageSigProxy =
            (OrdImageSignature)rset.getORAData("image",
OrdImage.getORADataFactory());
```

Table 9.6   *OrdImageSignature Methods*

Method Signature	Description

`static float`
`evaluateScore(OrdImage`
`Signature signature1,`
`OrdImageSignature signature2,`
`String attrWeights)`
	Compares two image signatures, returning a score that indicates the degree of difference between the image signatures.

Table 9.6 *OrdImageSignature Methods (continued)*

Method Signature	Description
void generateSignature(OrdImage img)	Reads data from the data source. Generates an image signature for the specified image. The signature is stored in the OrdImageSignature object. Must be updated and committed into the database to be stored.
static oracle.sql.ORADataFactory getORADataFactory()	Returns the OrdImageSignature ORADataFactory interface for use by the getORAData() method.
static int isSimilar(OrdImageSignature signature1, OrdImageSignature signature2, String attrWeights, float threshold)	Compares two image signatures, returning a status that indicates if the degree of difference between the image signatures is within a specified threshold.

9.5 *inter*Media Java Classes for Servlets

The *inter*Media Java Classes for servlets are utility classes used to help with the delivery and upload on media to and from the Web using the HTTP protocol. These classes make it easy to write a servlet to deliver or upload media from and to the database. These classes depend on a JDBC connection and the proxy classes that were discussed earlier in this chapter to manipulate the database media.

For delivery of media from the database, these classes can take the *inter*Media proxy objects and the contents, with the correct HTTP headers populated from the media objects, as a response to an HTTP request.

For upload of media, these classes help parse the multipart/form-data request returning both text and file parts of the form. This is quite a convenience to the programmer.

The classes that are used for media retrieval are:

- OrdHttpResponseHandler—used in a Java servlet to deliver media to an HTTP client, like a browser.

- OrdHttpJspResponseHandler—used in a JSP to deliver media to an HTTP client. Note that JSP engines are not required to be capable of delivering binary data.

The classes used to upload media data into the database are:

- OrdHttpUploadFormData—this class parses the upload request so that the programmer does not have to do this. Returns parts of the request to the programmer as demanded.

- OrdHttpUploadFile—a representation of a file that is part of the upload request.

- OrdMultipartFilter—the class that implements the javax.servlet.Filter interface in servlet 2.3. A filter preprocesses the request before the servlet is called. It must be defined in the servlet parameter file for the servlet pattern being used and wraps the multipart HttpServletRequest in OrdMultipartWrapper.

- OrdMultipartWrapper—the wrapper around multipart/form-data request when OrdMultipartFilter is used. This wrapper wraps the servlet's HttpServletRequest object so that multipart fields can be easily accessed without parsing (which is done in the filter).

For uploading media into the database, it should be noted that you should either use the first two classes above or the last two. You should not mix the two to avoid unnecessary reprocessing of the request.

One thing that should definitely be implemented for both methods in a real application is JDBC connection pooling. To connect to the database on every request would make access to any database data very expensive.

9.5.1   Media Delivery

Media Delivery Using JSPs

Note that not all JSP engines are capable of delivering nontext data. If this is the case with your servlet engine, you will be required to use a servlet. To deliver media using a JSP using OrdHttpJspResponseHandler, you need the following:

- A JSP that will deliver the media.

- Java code to return the media.

The JSP is just an endpoint of a URL. It can inspect the request and reject it. The JSP can then call a method to obtain the media. Typically this uses information in the request for finding the media, for example, an ID.

The JSP can then call one of the OrdHttpJspResponseHandler methods to send the media data. This data can be in the form of one of the media proxy objects, or a BFILE, BLOB or InputStream. If you want to send media using a BFILE, BLOB, or InputStream, you will also need to supply a MIME type and a time stamp indicating the last update time. This information is already in the media objects, so it is not necessary when sending media from *inter*Media proxy classes.

In the following example, we have defined a data source in OC4J data-sources.xml. Your data source may be defined differently. The definition used for the examples is as follows:

```
<data-source

class="oracle.jdbc.pool.OracleConnectionPoolDataSource"
        name="jdbc/pool/OracleMediaPoolDS"
        location="jdbc/pool/OracleMediaPoolDS"
        url="jdbc:oracle:thin:@localhost:1521:orcl10g"
        username="scott"
        password="tiger"
    />
```

An example of a JSP that delivers *inter*Media images follows:

```
<%@ page import="oracle.ord.im.OrdHttpJspResponseHandler" %>
<%@ page import="oracle.ord.im.OrdImage" %>
<%@ page import="oracle.ord.im.OrdMediaUtil" %>
<%@ page
import="oracle.jdbc.pool.OracleConnectionPoolDataSource" %>
<%@ page import="oracle.jdbc.pool.OraclePooledConnection" %>
<%@ page import="oracle.jdbc.driver.OracleConnection" %>
<%@ page import="oracle.jdbc.OraclePreparedStatement" %>
<%@ page import="oracle.jdbc.OracleResultSet" %>

<jsp:useBean id="handler" scope="page"
```

```
                    class="oracle.ord.im.OrdHttpJspResponseHandler"/>

        <%
            //
            // Get ID of image to fetch. We could get other parameters
            // as well
            //
            boolean imageSent = false;
            String id = request.getParameter( "id" );
            if ( id != null && !"".equals(id) )
            {
                //
                // Use a try block to ensure the JDBC connection is
                // released
                //
                OracleConnection conn = null;
                try
                {
                    //
                    // Get a connection from the pool. The SQL would
                    // be better
                    // done from a factory....
                    //
                    javax.naming.InitialContext ic =
                            new javax.naming.InitialContext();
                    OracleConnectionPoolDataSource ds =
                        (OracleConnectionPoolDataSource)
                            ic.lookup("jdbc/pool/OracleMediaPoolDS");
                    OraclePooledConnection pc =
                                (OraclePooledConnection)
                                ds.getPooledConnection();
                    conn = (OracleConnection)pc.getConnection();

                    //
                    // Here, we go to the database and select an image
                    // from the database, Returns null if image not
                    // found or
                    // image column is null (not populated).
                    //
                    String imgSelectSQL ="select image from photos
                    where id = "+id;
```

```
                    OraclePreparedStatement stmt =
                        (OraclePreparedStatement)
                        conn.prepareStatement(imgSelectSQL);
                    OracleResultSet rset =
                        (OracleResultSet)stmt.executeQuery();
                    rset.next();
                    OrdImage imageProxy = (OrdImage)
                        rset.getORAData("image",
                        OrdImage.getORADataFactory());
                    rset.close();

                    if ( imageProxy == null)
                    {
                        response.setStatus( response.SC_NOT_FOUND );
                        return;
                    }

                    //
                    // Send this image.
                    //
                    handler.setPageContext( pageContext );
                    handler.sendImage( imageProxy );
                    imageSent = true;
                }
                finally
                {
                    //
                    // Ensure the JDBC connection is released
                    //
                    if (conn != null) conn.close();
                }
                // Go to not found error
                if (imageSent) return;
            }
        %>


        <%-- The request does not include a key to the row --%>
        <html lang="EN"><head><title>ExampleMediaDelivery.jsp -
        malformed URL</title></head>
        <body><h1>ExampleMediaDelivery.jsp - malformed URL</h1>
        </body></html>
```

Media Delivery Using Servlets

Media delivery using servlets and the *inter*Media classes for JSP and servlets require that the data is obtained and then sent using the method necessary for the data type being sent.

The class that is used to deliver *inter*Media data from a servlet is OrdHttpResponseHandler. This class implements the send methods to send the contents of a proxy object or other types of objects, including BLOBS, to the HTTP client.

The following servlet example presents a form to the user, and when a row is found in the table, displays the thumbnail and full-size image. Please note that this servlet could have better performance by caching the more recent results of queries. Three requests are made to retrieve the data: one to populate the HTML, one to obtain the thumbnail image, and one to obtain the full-size image. Remember that each image, or multimedia, request will be a new request to the server. In this example, we use metadata from the image on the first request to populate the width and height of the image. The following is an example JSP that delivers data.

```
import java.io.IOException;
import java.io.PrintWriter;
import java.sql.Connection;
import java.sql.SQLException;
import java.sql.Types;
import java.sql.PreparedStatement;
import javax.servlet.ServletException;
import javax.servlet.ServletConfig;
import javax.servlet.http.HttpServlet;
import javax.servlet.http.HttpServletRequest;
import javax.servlet.http.HttpServletResponse;
import javax.naming.NamingException;
import oracle.jdbc.OracleResultSet;
import oracle.jdbc.pool.OracleConnectionPoolDataSource;
import oracle.jdbc.pool.OraclePooledConnection;
import oracle.jdbc.driver.OracleConnection;
import oracle.ord.im.OrdImage;
import oracle.ord.im.OrdHttpResponseHandler;
import oracle.ord.im.OrdMultipartWrapper;

public class deliveryServlet extends HttpServlet
{
```

```java
OracleConnection conn = null;
String servletURL = null;

/**
 * Servlet initialization method.
 */
public void init( ServletConfig config ) throws
    ServletException
{
  super.init(config);
}

/*
 * Get a pooled database connection
 */
private void getPooledConnection() throws SQLException,
    NamingException
{
  javax.naming.InitialContext ic = new
      javax.naming.InitialContext();
  OracleConnectionPoolDataSource ds=
      (OracleConnectionPoolDataSource)
      ic.lookup("jdbc/pool/OracleMediaPoolDS");
  OraclePooledConnection pc = (OraclePooledConnection)
                              ds.getPooledConnection();
  conn = (OracleConnection)pc.getConnection();
  // conn.setAutoCommit(false); // just query. No need for
  // this
}

/*
 * Process an HTTP GET request used to deliver an image
   column
 */
public void doGet( HttpServletRequest request,
                   HttpServletResponse response )
    throws ServletException, IOException
{
  String id = request.getParameter( "id" );
  String what = request.getParameter( "what" );
  if (!"image".equalsIgnoreCase(what)) what = "form";
```

```
        // set a default

    if ("form".equalsIgnoreCase(what))
    {
    String servletURL = request.getRequestURL().toString();
      try
    {
      if (conn == null) getPooledConnection();
       PrintWriter out = response.getWriter();
       response.setContentType( "text/html" );
       out.println( "<HTML><BODY>" +
                      "<H1>Display Images</H1>" +
                       "<FORM action=\"" + servletURL + "\">" +
               " Enter Row ID:<INPUT type=\"text\" name=\"id\
  " /><BR/>");
          if (id != null)
          {
            PreparedStatement stmt =
              conn.prepareStatement("select description,"+
             "location, " +
                                         "thumb, image "+
                            " from photos where id = ?" );
          stmt.setString( 1, id );
          OracleResultSet rset =
          (OracleResultSet)stmt.executeQuery();
          //
          // Fetch the row from the result set.
          //
          if ( rset.next() )
          {
            //
            // Get columns from query
            //
           String location = rset.getString(1);
           String description = rset.getString(2);
            OrdImage thumb =
               (OrdImage)rset.getORAData(3,
               OrdImage.getORADataFactory());
            OrdImage img =
               (OrdImage)rset.getORAData(4,
           OrdImage.getORADataFactory());
            out.println("<B>Description: </B>" +
```

```
                    description+ "<BR/>");
                    out.println("<B>Location: </B>" + location+
                    "<BR/>");
                    if (thumb != null &&
                        thumb.getMimeType().startsWith("image/"))
                    if (thumb != null &&
                        thumb.getMimeType().startsWith("image/"))
                    {

                      String thmbWidthStr =  thumb.getWidth() == 0 ?
                      "" :
                        "WIDTH=\"" + thumb.getWidth()  + "\" ";

                      String thmbHeightStr =  thumb.getHeight() == 0
                        ? "" :
                          "HEIGHT=\"" + thumb.getHeight()  + "\" ";
                      out.println("<B>Thumbnail: </B>" +
                          "<IMG SRC=\"" + servletURL + "?id=" + id +
                                  "&what=image&col=thumb\" " +
                                        thmbWidthStr +
                                        thmbHeightStr +
                              "/>" );
                    }
                    if (img != null &&
                    img.getMimeType().startsWith("image/"))
                    {
                      String imgWidthStr =  img.getWidth() == 0 ? ""
                          :
                          "WIDTH=\"" + img.getWidth()  + "\" ";
                      String imgHeightStr =  img.getHeight() == 0 ?
                              "" :
                          "HEIGHT=\"" + img.getHeight()  + "\" ";

                      out.println("<B>Image: </B>" +
                          "<IMG SRC=\"" + servletURL + "?id=" + id +
                                  "&what=image&col=image\" " +
                                        imgWidthStr +
                                        imgHeightStr +
                              "/>" );
                    }
                  }
```

```
           else
           {
             //
             // Print not found
             //
             out.println("<H2>Row with ID\"" + id +
                         "\" Not Found</H2><BR/>");
           }
         }
         out.println("</FORM></BODY></HTML>");
       }
       catch (Exception e)
       {
        conn  = null; // Get another connection next time.
         throw new ServletException(e);
       }
     }
     else
     {
       try
       {
      if (conn == null) getPooledConnection();
         String col = request.getParameter("col");
         if (col == null) col = "thumb";
         //default to the thumbnail column
         PreparedStatement stmt =
           conn.prepareStatement( "select " + col +
                " from photos where id = ? " );
         stmt.setString( 1, id );
         OracleResultSet rset =
                 (OracleResultSet)stmt.executeQuery();

         //
         // Fetch the row from the result set.
         //
         if ( rset.next() )
         {
           //
           // Get the OrdImage object from the result set.
           //
           OrdImage img =
```

```
                        (OrdImage)rset.getORAData(1,
                OrdImage.getORADataFactory());

            //
            // Create an OrdHttpResponseHandler object, then
            // use it to get
            // the image from the database and deliver it to
            // the browser.
            //
            OrdHttpResponseHandler handler =
              new OrdHttpResponseHandler( request, response );
            handler.sendImage( img );
          }
          else
          {
            //
            // Row not found, return a suitable error.
            //
            response.setStatus( response.SC_NOT_FOUND );
          }

          //
          // Close the result-set and the statement.
          //
          rset.close();
          stmt.close();
        }
        catch (Exception e)
        {
         conn  = null; // Get another connection next time.
          throw new ServletException(e);
        }
      }
    }
  }
```

9.5.2 Media Upload Classes for Servlets

The media upload classes are convenience classes to help parse a request
with media in a servlet environment. It can be quite a bit of code to parse a
multipart/form-data POST request. These classes perform this parsing for

you. If you want total control over the parsing of the form, you are not required to use these classes to upload media data. You can parse the request yourself.

Uploading *inter*Media media over HTTP using Java is done through a servlet. To upload data to the database you need:

- A Web page form that

  - Sends the form data in multipart/form-data format in an HTTP POST request.
  - Has at least one input field of type file.

- A servlet that will accept the form from the client.

  - This servlet will have a connection to the database.
  - This servlet will either create a new row in the database for the media or populate an existing row.

There are two techniques that you can use with the convenience classes to upload media. The first is to have all the code in the servlet to parse the multipart/form-data POST request. The second is to make use of the servlet filter provided by *inter*Media. This will parse the request before the servlet code is called and wrap the request in an OrdMultipartWrapper object that has all the functionality of an HttpServletRequest object plus much of the functionality that OrdHttpUploadFormData has. The first technique is called the *request parsing technique*, the second is called the *filter technique*.

One important note when uploading media data from the Web is to know the maximum size of the data. If this data is very large, perhaps a 10-gigabyte movie, it is certainly best for the servlet to cache this movie in a file rather that Java's virtual memory. You can set the limit of the Java virtual memory use with either technique. In the filter technique, you would call the OrdHttpUploadFormData setMaxMemory method to set the maximum size of virtual memory use and the directory to use for temporary files. For the filter technique, these settings are set as part of the filter configuration. These parameters should always be set to prevent exhausting Java memory event if you don't think the data will ever be that large. A mistake, or mischief, could cause problems for your Web server.

One nice feature of using these classes to upload files into *inter*Media database objects is that they populate the MIME type of the object from the HTTP request before attempting to get properties from the binary data.

In the case that the binary data is not recognized by *inter*Media media parsing the MIME type will still be set to an appropriate value. A browser typically sets the MIME type of data it is uploading based on the file extension.

The result of using either the parsing technique or filtering technique is the standard parameters from a form request in string objects and the file parts of the form in OrdHttpUploadFile objects. The OrdHttpUploadFile objects are used to provide information about the file, such as MIME type, file name, and length, and populate the database with file data from the request in *inter*Media proxy objects or a standard database BLOB.

To upload media from a browser requires an appropriate HTML form. A very simple example of an HTML form that uploads an image follows.

```
<HTML>
<BODY>
<FORM action="http://localhost:8888/servlet/uploadServlet"
name="uploadForm"
      method="post" enctype="multipart/form-data">
<P>
 Location?    <INPUT type="text" name="location"/><BR/>
 Description? <INPUT type="text" name="description"/><BR/>
 Image File?  <INPUT type="file" name="photo"/><BR/>
 <INPUT type="submit" value="Submit" />
</P>
</FORM>
</BODY>
</HTML>
```

In the following example a database sequence object is created to assign an ID number to added media. It is preferable to use sequences rather than the maximum ID plus one because two users may be trying to insert media at the same time. With a sequence, we can guarantee that simultaneous update requests do not try to use the same ID. This sequence is created with the following SQL statement.

```
SQL> create sequence photos_sequence;
```

This example is a servlet that handles the upload request from the preceding form. This servlet works with either the filter technique or parsing using OrdHttpUploadFormData. To use the filter method, the filter must be put into the servlet filter chain. Each technique will be described in more detail in subsequent sections, but a simple example servlet follows.

```java
import java.io.IOException;
import java.io.PrintWriter;
import java.sql.Connection;
import java.sql.SQLException;
import java.sql.Types;
import javax.servlet.ServletException;
import javax.servlet.ServletConfig;
import javax.servlet.http.HttpServlet;
import javax.servlet.http.HttpServletRequest;
import javax.servlet.http.HttpServletResponse;
import javax.naming.NamingException;
import oracle.jdbc.OracleCallableStatement;
import oracle.jdbc.OraclePreparedStatement;
import oracle.jdbc.OracleResultSet;
import oracle.jdbc.pool.OracleConnectionPoolDataSource;
import oracle.jdbc.pool.OraclePooledConnection;
import oracle.jdbc.driver.OracleConnection;
import oracle.ord.im.OrdImage;
import oracle.ord.im.OrdHttpUploadFile;
import oracle.ord.im.OrdHttpUploadFormData;
import oracle.ord.im.OrdHttpResponseHandler;
import oracle.ord.im.OrdMultipartWrapper;

public class uploadServlet extends HttpServlet
{
    OracleConnection conn = null;
    OrdHttpUploadFormData formData = null;

    /**
     * Servlet initialization method.
     */
    public void init( ServletConfig config ) throws
    ServletException
    {
        super.init(config);
    }

    /*
```

```
 * Get a pooled database connection
 */
private void getPooledConnection() throws SQLException,
NamingException
{
  javax.naming.InitialContext ic = new
  javax.naming.InitialContext();
  OracleConnectionPoolDataSource ds =
  (OracleConnectionPoolDataSource)
          ic.lookup("jdbc/pool/OracleMediaPoolDS");
  OraclePooledConnection pc = (OraclePooledConnection)
          ds.getPooledConnection();
  conn = (OracleConnection)pc.getConnection();
  conn.setAutoCommit(false);
  // Update or put Media, need this
}


/*
 * Process an HTTP Post request used to upload a new photo
 * into the album
 */
public void doPost( HttpServletRequest request,
                    HttpServletResponse response )
    throws ServletException, IOException
{
    String description = null;
    String location = null;
    OrdHttpUploadFile photo = null;

    if (request instanceof OrdMultipartWrapper)
    {
        //
        // This request was parsed by OrdMultipartFilter,
        // use it.
        //
        OrdMultipartWrapper ordMultiPartWrapper =
                (OrdMultipartWrapper)request;

        //
        // Get the description, location and photo from the
```

```
            // wrapper
            //
            description =
                    ordMultiPartWrapper.getParameter(
                    "description" );
            location = ordMultiPartWrapper.getParameter(
                    "location" );
            photo = ordMultiPartWrapper.getFileParameter(
                    "photo" );
        }
        else
        {
            // Parse the data using OrdHttpUploadFormData
            //
            // Create an OrdHttpUploadFormData object.
            //
            formData = new OrdHttpUploadFormData( request );
            if ( !formData.isUploadRequest() )
            {
              return;
            }

            //
            // Parse the multipart/form-data message.
            // (10 meg max before using file), use system
            // temp directory
            formData.setMaxMemory(10 (1024*1024), null);
            formData.parseFormData();

            //
            // Get the description, location and photo.
            //
            description = formData.getParameter( "description"
                );
            location = formData.getParameter( "location" );
            photo = formData.getFileParameter( "photo" );
        }
        //
        // Make sure a valid image file was provided.
        //
        if ( photo == null ||
```

```
                    photo.getOriginalFileName() == null ||
                    photo.getOriginalFileName().length() == 0 ||
                    photo.getContentLength() == 0
                 )
          {
             return;
          }

        try
    {
        if (conn == null)
            getPooledConnection(); //Get connection if needed
        //
        // Get a value for the ID column of the new row
        //
        OraclePreparedStatement stmt =
              (OraclePreparedStatement)conn.prepareStatement(
                    "select photos_sequence.nextval from dual"
                     );
        OracleResultSet rset =
              (OracleResultSet)stmt.executeQuery();
        if ( !rset.next() )
            throw new ServletException( "new ID not found" );
        String id = rset.getString( 1 );
        rset.close();
        stmt.close();

        //
        // Prepare and execute a SQL statement to insert the
        // new row.
        //
        OracleCallableStatement cstmt =
              (OracleCallableStatement)
              conn.prepareCall (
                 "begin " +
                 "insert into photos t " +
                    "    (id, description, location, image," +
                       "thumb) " +
                    "values (?, ?, ?, ORDImage.init()," +
                       "ORDImage.init())" +
                    " returning rowid, t.image, t.thumb into " +
```

```
                    "?, ?, ? ; " +
                    "end;");
         cstmt.setString( 1, id );
         cstmt.setString( 2, description );
         cstmt.setString( 3, location );
         cstmt.registerOutParameter(4, Types.VARCHAR);
         // rowid
    cstmt.registerOutParameter(5, Types.STRUCT,
             "ORDIMAGE"); // image
    cstmt.registerOutParameter(6, Types.STRUCT,
             "ORDIMAGE"); // thumb
         cstmt.executeUpdate();
         cstmt.close();

         String rowid = cstmt.getString(4);
         // Obtain the proxy objects
         OrdImage image = (OrdImage)
                     cstmt.getORAData(5,
                     OrdImage.getORADataFactory());
         OrdImage thumb = (OrdImage)
                     cstmt.getORAData(6,
                     OrdImage.getORADataFactory());
         cstmt.close();

         //
         // Load the photo into the database and set
         // the properties.
         //
         photo.loadImage( image );
         if (formData != null) formData.release();
         // Release any resources

         //
         // Try to copy the full-size image and process it to
         // create the thumb-nail. This may not be
         // possible if the image format is
         // not recognized.
         //
         try
         {
             image.processCopy( "maxScale=50,50", thumb );
```

```
        }
        catch ( SQLException e )
        {
            thumb.deleteContent();
            thumb.setContentLength( 0 );
        }

        //
        // Prepare and execute a SQL statement to update the
        // full-size and
        // thumb-nail images in the database.
        //
        stmt =
            (OraclePreparedStatement)conn.prepareStatement(
            "update photos set image = ?, thumb = ? where" +
            "rowid = ?" );
        //
        stmt.setORAData( 1, image );
        stmt.setORAData( 2, thumb );
        stmt.setString( 3, rowid );
        stmt.execute();
        stmt.close();

        //
        // Commit the changes.
        //
        conn.commit();
    }
    catch (Exception se)
    {
        conn = null; // We may need a new connection
        if (formData != null)
            formData.release();//Release any resources
        throw new ServletException(se);
    }
    // Print a response page (or we could redirect here
        PrintWriter out = response.getWriter();
    response.setContentType( "text/html" );
    out.println( "<html><body>" +
                "<h1>Upload Sucessful</h1>" +
                "<input type=\"button\" onclick=
```

```
                          \"history.go(-1)\" "+
                              "value=\"back\"/>" +
                      "</body></html>");

          }

      }
```

Media Upload Using OrdHttpUploadFormData

The following example servlet shows how the multipart/form-data request is parsed.

```
         // Parse the data using OrdHttpUploadFormData
         //
         // Create an OrdHttpUploadFormData object.
         //
[1]      OrdHttpUploadFormData formData =
                         new OrdHttpUploadFormData( request );
[2]      if ( !formData.isUploadRequest() )
         {
            return;
         }

         //
         // Parse the multipart/form-data message.
         //
[3]      formData.parseFormData();

         //
         // Get the description, location and photo.
         //
[4]      description = formData.getParameter( "description" );
         location = formData.getParameter( "location" );
[5]      photo = formData.getFileParameter( "photo" );
```

To receive media and other form data from an HTTP request, the following steps are taken:

1. Create the OrdHttpUploadFormData object using the servlet request, HttpServletRequest.

2. Test the object to make sure it is a multipart/form-data request.

3. Parse the request.

4.   Get text parameters from the request.

5.   Get a file from the request in OrdHttpUploadFile format.

Media Upload Using OrdMultipartFilter

To use a filter in J2EE, the filter parameters must be set in web.xml for the Web application the servlet is running from. You need to specify the filter and filter parameters, and then specify which servlet will use the filter. The *inter*Media HTTP filter only filters requests. An example snippet from web.xml is shown below that will cause the filter to be invoked, parsing the multipart/form-data, before our servlet is invoked.

```
<filter>
    <filter-name>ordMultipartFilter</filter-name>
    <filter-class>oracle.ord.im.OrdMultipartFilter
        </filter-class>
    <init-param>
        <param-name>tempDir</param-name>
        <param-value>d:\temp</param-value>
    </init-param>
    <init-param>
        <param-name>maxMemory</param-name>
        <param-value>10000000000</param-value>
    </init-param>
</filter>

<filter-mapping>
    <filter-name>ordMultipartFilter</filter-name>
    <url-pattern>/servlet/tstPhotoAlbumServlet
        </url-pattern>
</filter-mapping>
```

When the above code is set correctly, the section of the example servlet that uses the filter method will be used. This section is:

```
[1]  if (request instanceof OrdMultipartWrapper)
     {
         //
         // This request was parsed by OrdMultipartFilter, use it.
         //
[2]     OrdMultipartWrapper ordMultiPartWrapper =
```

```
                              (OrdMultipartWrapper)request;

        //
        // Get the description, location and photo from the wrapper
        //
[3]     description = ordMultiPartWrapper.getParameter( "description" );
        location = ordMultiPartWrapper.getParameter( "location" );
[4]     photo = ordMultiPartWrapper.getFileParameter( "photo" );
    }
```

When using OrdMultipartWrapper to receive media data and other form data from an HTTP request, the following stepts are taken:

1. Test if the HttpServletRequest has been wrapped in OrdMultipartWrapper by OrdMultipartFilter.

2. Cast the request to OrdMultipartWrapper for convenience.

3. Obtain the text parts of the request as string objects.

4. Obtain the file part of the request as an OrdHttpUploadFile object.

9.6   Summary

Oracle *inter*Media provides a rich set of features for the J2EE environment. It has support for servlets, JSPs and representing database *inter*Media objects as Java objects. *inter*Media can also be used effectively with Oracle JDeveloper, as this application development tool can recognize *inter*Media objects.

10

Image Metadata Support

10.1   Introduction

Metadata, to put it simply, is data about data. The metadata for an image is data about the image. This metadata may be used to store information such as:

- Camera settings
- Who created the image
- When the image was taken
- Where the image was taken
- Copyright information
- Contact information
- Legal use information
- Relevant keywords for the image
- User-defined metadata (workflow data, etc.)

Additionally, there is metadata associated with DICOM medical images. This information may include:

- Patient information
- Study information
- Equipment information
- Series information

This metadata is stored within the image file itself, typically at the beginning of the file. Most imaging tools such as Adobe Photoshop® include the functionality to view and modify this information.

The metadata within the image file is either in binary format (IPTC, EXIF) or XML (XMP). When extracted by *inter*Media, all metadata formats are returned as XML. If the format is a binary format, it is converted to XML. This XML format is easier to use with database features such as XML DB and to search with Oracle Text. The kinds of metadata that can be extracted are

- EXIF—exchangeable image file format
- IPTC-IIM—International Press Telecommunications Council, information interchange model
- XMP—extensible metadata platform
- *inter*Media metadata

The EXIF standard focuses on camera setting information, such as camera settings, what kind of camera, and the time the picture was taken, and is inserted by most digital cameras when the photograph is taken.

The IPTC-IIM standard is used mostly to add "file information" useful in press applications. This information includes data like caption, news category, author, legal use, keywords, copyright, or dateline. IPTC-IIM is a frozen legacy standard that has been superseded by XMP.

XMP is the newest standard that is flexible. It can contain any kind of information and encompasses both EXIF and IPTC-IIM standards. It is also used in job processing and workflow applications. It is seen as data that may be updated by applications along a workflow.

The *inter*Media image metadata can be obtained from all *inter*Media supported image formats. It includes format metadata, such as height, width, and file format. For other embedded metadata, the image metadata that can be extracted from or inserted into images using *inter*Media is shown in Table 10.1.

Insertion of metadata is supported using *inter*Media, however, *inter*Media can only put XMP, the newest and most flexible format, into images. This fits in nicely with the view of XMP that it is updated by the applications that use it. When XMP metadata is put into an image by *inter*Media, the non-XMP metadata already in the image is preserved.

Table 10.1 *interMedia Metadata Insert Extraction Capabilities*

File Type	EXIF Metadata	IPTC-IIM Metadata	XMP Metadata
JPEG	Extract	Extract	Extract/insert
JPEG2000			Extract/insert
GIF			Extract/insert
TIFF	Extract	Extract	Extract/insert

Bear in mind that if an image is processed, with either the process or processCopy ORDImage methods, the resulting image will not have metadata attached. Since the format or size may change, the original metadata may not be correct, so it is intentionally not preserved.

This metadata in images is of great importance in finding images or having your images found. It is used in image searches, including Web and desktop image search engines. Typically, most image Web search engines use the HTTP <IMG> tag ALT attribute. This attribute indicates the text to display if the image is not displayed because of an error or the browser cannot display it (as in a text-based browser), or is set not to display images. Image search is also done using HTTP text near the image. An image website would be well advised to make image metadata available so their images can be found by potential customers. Keywords from the metadata stored in the images can be extracted and placed into the ALT attribute to make sure Web search engines can find the image on keyword searches.

Because of the increased use of embedded image metadata by applications, it is an area that most image applications need to consider for use in finding images in the database or on the Web.

10.2 Metadata Schemas

The XML schemas, in DTD format, for all of the XML metadata types are registered with XML DB by *inter*Media. This registration allows for schema validation, which is important when setting the metadata, and binding XMLTYPE columns to a particular XML representation. Validation for registered schemas is quicker since the schema is already parsed.

These XML schemas are registered with XML DB using the following schema namespace names for use with *inter*Media:

- http://xmlns.oracle.com/ord/meta/exif
- http://xmlns.oracle.com/ord/meta/iptc
- http://xmlns.oracle.com/ord/meta/xmp
- http://xmlns.oracle.com/ord/meta/ordimage
- http://xmlns.oracle.com/ord/meta/dicom

The following database table is defined by binding each XMLTYPE in the table to one of these schemas:

```
create table ImagesWithMetadata (item_id number primary key,
                                 exifMeta XMLTYPE,
                                 iptcMeta XMLTYPE,
                                 xmpMeta XMLTYPE,
                                 image ordsys.ordimage)
XMLTYPE COLUMN EXIFMETA
  XMLSCHEMA "http://xmlns.oracle.com/ord/meta/exif"
  ELEMENT "exifMetadata"
XMLTYPE COLUMN IPTCMETA
  XMLSCHEMA "http://xmlns.oracle.com/ord/meta/iptc"
  ELEMENT "iptcMetadata"
XMLTYPE COLUMN XMPMETA
  XMLSCHEMA "http://xmlns.oracle.com/ord/meta/xmp"
  ELEMENT "xmpMetadata"
;
```

The schemas define the structure of the XML data, and also implicitly, the structure of the storage in the database. This structure is in the form of an object-relational type. By default, the XML data is stored in structured storage.

To see what XML types were created by the table above we can describe them as follows.

```
SQL> describe ImagesWithMetadata;
 Name                                     Null?    Type
 ---------------------------------------- -------- ---------------------------

 ITEM_ID                                  NOT NULL NUMBER
 EXIFMETA                                          SYS.XMLTYPE(XMLSchema "http:
```

	//xmlns.oracle.com/ord/meta/
	exif" Element "exifMetadata"
	) STORAGE Object-relational TYPE "exifMetadata192_T"
IPTCMETA	SYS.XMLTYPE(XMLSchema "http:
	//xmlns.oracle.com/ord/meta/
	iptc" Element "iptcMetadata"
	) STORAGE Object-relational TYPE "iptcMetadataType94_T"
XMPMETA	SYS.XMLTYPE(XMLSchema "http:
	//xmlns.oracle.com/ord/meta/
	xmp" Element "xmpMetadata") STORAGE Object-relational TY
IMAGE	PE "xmpMetadataType100_T" ORDSYS.ORDIMAGE

If you want to go further, you can then describe the types that XML DB has created for the *inter*Media schema definition.

```
SQL> describe ORDSYS."iptcMetadataType94_T";
ORDSYS."iptcMetadataType94_T" is NOT FINAL
Name                                     Null?    Type
---------------------------------------- -------- ----------------------------

SYS_XDBPD$                                        XDB.XDB$RAW_LIST_T
recordVersion                                     NUMBER(38)
objectName                                        VARCHAR2(4000 CHAR)
editStatus                                        VARCHAR2(4000 CHAR)
urgency                                           NUMBER(38)
category                                          VARCHAR2(4000 CHAR)
supplementalCategory                              ORDSYS.supplementalCategory9
                                                  5_COLL
fixtureIdentifier                                 VARCHAR2(4000 CHAR)
```

keyword	ORDSYS.supplementalCategory9 5_COLL
contentLocation	ORDSYS.contentLocation97_COL L
instructions	VARCHAR2(4000 CHAR)
dateCreated	DATE
timeCreated	VARCHAR2(4000 CHAR)
digitalCreationDate	DATE
digitalCreationTime	VARCHAR2(4000 CHAR)
byline	ORDSYS.byline99_COLL
city	VARCHAR2(4000 CHAR)
subLocation	VARCHAR2(4000 CHAR)
provinceState	VARCHAR2(4000 CHAR)
country	VARCHAR2(4000 CHAR)
location	VARCHAR2(4000 CHAR)
transmissionReference	VARCHAR2(4000 CHAR)
headline	VARCHAR2(4000 CHAR)
credit	VARCHAR2(4000 CHAR)
source	VARCHAR2(4000 CHAR)
copyright	VARCHAR2(4000 CHAR)
contact	ORDSYS.supplementalCategory9 5_COLL
caption	VARCHAR2(4000 CHAR)
captionWriter	ORDSYS.supplementalCategory9 5_COLL
languageId	VARCHAR2(4000 CHAR)

You can go as far as you like down the tree, which resembles an XML tree, as some of the elements are expressed as types, collections, or collections of collections. For example, if we look at the keyword element, we see it is of type "ORDSYS.supplementalCategory95_COLL." We can describe this type:

```
SQL> describe ORDSYS."supplementalCategory95_COLL"
 ORDSYS."supplementalCategory95_COLL" VARRAY(2147483647) OF
 VARCHAR2(4000 CHAR)
```

This is a VARRAY type. Using XML schema definition XML DB annotations allows specification of the storage parameters for any of the types above. For example, if the captions in your images are greater than 4,000 bytes, you could specify storage of the caption in a CLOB instead of VARCHAR2(4000 CHAR).

To access information, you could use XML syntax as specified in a following section, or (not recommended) object-relational DOT notation used in types. It is best to refer to the XML elements in XML XPath format so that the XML schema storage can be changed without forcing the application to change. For example, the following SELECT statement is preferred.

```
SQL> select extract(iptcMeta,'/iptcMetadata/city/text()',
  2 'xmlns=http://xmlns.oracle.com/ord/meta/iptc')
  3 from ImagesWithMetadata;
Malibalipuram
```

The following is the nonpreferred DOT notation way to select the information (using the pseudo-type XMLDATA as the root element of the document). For example, if the storage of the XML document was changed to CLOB, this example SELECT would not work.

```
SQL> select t.iptcMeta."XMLDATA"."city" from
     ImagesWithMetadata t;
Malibalipuram
```

If you would like to override the storage of the XML data type, this can be done by modifying the schema provided by *inter*Media and registering this XML DB schema as a local schema in your own database schema. This schema would have to be compatible with the XML document returned from getMetadata(). The idea here would be to change the XML DB parameters to better suit your application, not to change the XML document structure itself. For example, to replace the schema definition with the contents of myOrdImage.xsd that will be used for future table creations that use the "http://xmlns.oracle.com/ord/meta/ordimage" schema, the following may be used:

```
BEGIN
  DBMS_XMLSCHEMA.registerSchema(
    SCHEMAURL => 'http://xmlns.oracle.com/ord/meta/ordimage',
    SCHEMADOC => bfilename('IMAGEDIR','myOrdImage.xsd'),
    LOCAL => TRUE,
    GENTYPES => TRUE,
```

```
        GENTABLES => FALSE,
        CSID => nls_charset_id('AL32UTF8'));
    END;
    /
```

The "STORE AS CLOB" clause can also be used to bypass the default-structured storage. This will cause the XML document to be stored in a simple CLOB. For example, if we wanted the IPTC data stored in a CLOB we would use the following syntax:

```
XMLTYPE COLUMN IPTCMETA STORE AS CLOB
    XMLSCHEMA "http://xmlns.oracle.com/ord/meta/iptc"
    ELEMENT "iptcMetadata"
```

The general idea of XML DB structured storage is to store part, or all, of the XML document in object-relational fields rather than embedded into a CLOB as raw XML data. By doing this, XML data can be changed, or used as an index, without repeatedly parsing the entire XML document, an expensive operation. The data can be retrieved at any time as an XML document by incorporating these fields into the output when the XML document is requested.

There are many differences and advantages and disadvantages to storing XML data as either structured or unstructured, too many to cover here. Please refer to the XML DB Developers Guide for more information.

The biggest advantages of using structured data are to be able to extract information, update the type and index more efficiently, as well as being able to index using a B*Tree or Bitmap index. Unstructured storage provides the most raw throughput of input and output of the entire document and is most flexible in what kind of document can be stored.

10.3 Extracting Image Metadata

All *inter*Media metadata is extracted in the form of XML database objects. All of the metadata present in the image is returned as a database XMLSequence type. This sequence is like an array of XMLType. Each XMLType in the sequence contains the XML for one of the metadata sources. To identify what the XMLType contains, use the XMLType getRootElement() method.

Image metadata is extracted with the *inter*Media getMetadata() method. This method returns an XMLSequenceType with the following possible metadata:

- *inter*Media metadata (always returned, metadata from the *inter*Media object)
- EXIF metadata
- IPTC-IIM metadata
- XMP metadata

If you want to use the non-*inter*Media object metadata for searching purposes, it must be placed in the database row. For *inter*Media metadata, you can either use the XML representation from getMetadata(), or create an index on the *inter*Media object attributes. The following example shows metadata being extracted from an image while the image is being loaded. The metadata is then placed into the row that is being created.

```
create or replace procedure load_img_and_metadata(id number,
                                                   dir varchar2,
                                                   file_name
varchar2)
as
    imgobj     ORDImage;
    ctx        raw(64):=null;
    thisrowid  urowid;
    meta       xmlType := null;
    xmeta      xmlType := null;
    imeta      xmlType := null;
    emeta      xmlType := null;
    metas      xmlSequenceType;
BEGIN
    insert into ImagesWithMetadata (item_id, image) values
        (id, ORDSYS.ORDImage.init())
        returning rowid, image into thisrowid, imgobj;

    imgobj.setsource('FILE', dir, file_name);

    imgobj.import(ctx);
```

```
    --
    -- Get the metadata, skipping interMedia metadata
    --
    metas := imgobj.getMetadata('exif');
    if metas.count > 0 then emeta := metas(1); end if;
    metas := imgobj.getMetadata('iptc-iim');
    if metas.count > 0 then imeta := metas(1); end if;
    metas := imgobj.getMetadata('xmp');
    if metas.count > 0 then xmeta := metas(1); end if;


    --
    -- Put the metadata and the image into the row
    --
    update ImagesWithMetadata t set t.image=imgobj,
       t.exifMeta=emeta, t.iptcMeta=imeta, t.xmpMeta=xmeta
    where rowid = thisrowid;
    commit;

END;
/
```

Keywords and other information in the metadata can be selected from the metadata. Here are examples of selecting metadata information from XML data types.

1. This example selects all the keywords for each row in the database. The keywords are returned as a concatenated string for each row:

```
select t.xmpMeta.extract(
  '/xmpMetadata/rdf:RDF/rdf:Description/dc:subject/rdf:Bag/rdf:li/text()',
  'xmlns="http://xmlns.oracle.com/ord/meta/xmp"
        xmlns:rdf="http://www.w3.org/1999/02/22-rdf-syntax-ns#"
        xmlns:dc="http://purl.org/dc/elements/1.1/" ').getStringVal()
    "Keywords" from
  ImagesWithMetadata t;
```

2. This example selects all the keywords in the database row as individual rows in the result set for the image with the ID 1:

```
select value(li).extract('rdf:li/text()',
  'xmlns:rdf="http://www.w3.org/1999/02/22-rdf-syntax-ns#"'
  ).getStringVal() "keywords" from ImagesWithMetadata t,
  TABLE(xmlsequence(extract(t.xmpMeta,
  '/xmpMetadata/rdf:RDF/rdf:Description/dc:subject/rdf:Bag/rdf:li',
  'xmlns="http://xmlns.oracle.com/ord/meta/xmp"
  xmlns:rdf="http://www.w3.org/1999/02/22-rdf-syntax-ns#"
  xmlns:dc="http://purl.org/dc/elements/1.1/" '))) li where t.id=1;
```

3. This anonymous procedure extracts each keyword and prints it to the console:

```
declare
    doc xmltype;
    cnt number;
    keyword varchar2(100);
begin

    select xmpmeta into doc from ImagesWithMetadata where id = 1;


    select count(*) into cnt from TABLE(xmlsequence(extract(doc,
      '/xmpMetadata/rdf:RDF/rdf:Description/dc:subject/rdf:Bag/rdf:li',
      'xmlns="http://xmlns.oracle.com/ord/meta/xmp"
     xmlns:rdf="http://www.w3.org/1999/02/22-rdf-syntax-ns#"
     xmlns:dc="http://purl.org/dc/elements/1.1/" ')));

    for i in  1..cnt loop
      keyword := doc.extract(
      '/xmpMetadata/rdf:RDF/rdf:Description/dc:subject/rdf:Bag/rdf:li['
     || i || ']/text()',
           'xmlns="http://xmlns.oracle.com/ord/meta/xmp"
           xmlns:rdf="http://www.w3.org/1999/02/22-rdf-syntax-ns#"
           xmlns:dc="http://purl.org/dc/elements/1.1/"
           ').getStringVal();
    dbms_output.put_line('keyword [' || i || '] = ' || keyword);
    end loop;
end;
/
show errors;
```

10.4 Inserting Image Metadata

As well as extracting metadata, *inter*Media can insert metadata or modified metadata into the image. Only XMP metadata, the most flexible and extensible metadata standard, can be placed within the image binary using *inter*Media. After the image metadata is modified, the new values will be seen by users that access the image.

It is quite easy to insert XML metadata into an image, and in most cases there is existing metadata that is to be modified, so we will not have an example of inserting metadata into an image that has none.

The following example takes image XMP metadata from an original image and if it exists, places it in the thumbnail as well. This preserves the metadata.

```
DECLARE
    Img ORDSYS.ORDImage;
    Thumbnail ORDSYS.ORDImage;
    xmeta xmltype := NULL;
    metas xmlsequencetype;
BEGIN
  load_image1('t.img');
  SELECT pict, thumb INTO Img, Thumbnail
      FROM imagemeta WHERE item_id = 1 for update;

  metas := img.getMetadata('xmp');
  if metas.count > 0 then xmeta := metas(1); end if;

  Img.ProcessCopy('fileFormat=JFIF maxScale=800 800',
      Thumbnail);

  if not xmeta is null then
    Thumbnail.putMetadata(xmeta);
  end if;

  commit;

END;
/
```

A procedure can be written to add keywords to the XMP metadata. The following routine does this. It is a bit complicated, as it creates the XML fragment necessary for the keyword insertion. That is, it would be much simpler if we knew all the parent XML elements existed or at least one keyword was already present.

```
create or replace procedure add_keyword(id number, keyword varchar2)
as
    imgobj     ORDImage;
    thisrowid urowid;
    xmeta      xmlType := null;
    element    xmlType := null;
    prefix     varchar2(500) := '';
    suffix     varchar2(500) := '';
    elementXpath varchar2(500);
    tag        varchar2(20);

    dbg varchar2(2000);

    xmpNameSpaces varchar2(200) :=
        'xmlns="http://xmlns.oracle.com/ord/meta/xmp" ' ||
        'xmlns:rdf="http://www.w3.org/1999/02/22-rdf-syntax-ns#" ' ||
        'xmlns:dc="http://purl.org/dc/elements/1.1/"';

    ns_declarations varchar2(200) :=
            ' xmlns:dc="http://purl.org/dc/elements/1.1/" ' ||
            'xmlns:rdf="http://www.w3.org/1999/02/22-rdf-syntax-ns#" ';
BEGIN



    select image,  xmpMeta, rowid      into
            imgobj, xmeta,    thisrowid
    from ImagesWithMetadata where item_id=1 for update;



    elementXpath :=
                '/xmpMetadata/rdf:RDF/rdf:Description';

    -- Does the "rdf:Description node" exist?
    if  xmeta.existsNode(
        '/xmpMetadata/rdf:RDF/rdf:Description' ||
```

```
          '[namespace::* = "http://purl.org/dc/elements/1.1/"]'
        , xmpNamespaces) = 0
then -- No, Start XML fragment starting at rdf:Description
      prefix := prefix || '<rdf:Description ' ||
                  ns_declarations || '>';
      suffix :=  '</rdf:Description>' || suffix;
      ns_declarations := ''; -- Namespaces have now been declared.
      if tag is null then tag := 'rdf:Description'; end if;
else -- Yes rdf:Description exists, add to insert xpath
      elementXPath := elementXpath ||
          '[namespace::*="http://purl.org/dc/elements/1.1/"]';
end if;


if  xmeta.existsNode(
      '/xmpMetadata/rdf:RDF/rdf:Description' ||
      '[namespace::* = "http://purl.org/dc/elements/1.1/"]' ||
      '/dc:subject'
    , xmpNamespaces) = 0
then -- No, Add XML dc:subject XML fragment
      prefix := prefix || '<dc:subject ' || ns_declarations || '>';
      suffix :=  '</dc:subject>' || suffix;
      ns_declarations := ''; -- Namespaces have now been declared.
      if tag is null then tag := 'dc:subject'; end if;
else -- Yes, add to insert xpath
      elementXpath := elementXPath || '/dc:subject';
end if;


if  xmeta.existsNode(
      '/xmpMetadata/rdf:RDF/rdf:Description' ||
      '[namespace::* = "http://purl.org/dc/elements/1.1/"]' ||
      '/dc:subject/rdf:Bag'
    , xmpNamespaces) = 0
then -- No, Add XML rdf:Bag XML fragment
      prefix := prefix || '<rdf:Bag ' || ns_declarations || '>';
      suffix :=  '</rdf:Bag>' || suffix;
      ns_declarations := ''; -- Namespaces have now been declared.
      if tag is null then tag := 'rdf:Bag'; end if;
else -- Yes, add to insert xpath
      elementXpath := elementXPath || '/rdf:Bag';
end if;
```

```
--
-- Finally put in keyword (but only if it does not already exist)
--
if xmeta.existsNode(
        '//dc:subject/rdf:Bag[rdf:li="' || keyword || '"]',
        xmpNamespaces) = 0
then
    -- assemble XML fragment that needs to be inserted
    element := xmltype(prefix || '<rdf:li ' ||
        ns_declarations || ' >' ||
        keyword || '</rdf:li>' || suffix);
    if tag is null then tag := 'rdf:li'; end if;
    -- insert XML fragment
    select insertChildXML(xmeta,
            elementXpath,
            tag,
            element,
            xmpNamespaces)
    into xmeta from dual;
end if;


-- dbms_output.put_line(xmeta.getClobVal());
imgobj.putMetadata(xmeta);

update ImagesWithMetadata t set t.xmpMeta=xmeta,
        t.image=imgobj
where rowid = thisrowid;
commit;

END;
/
show errors;
```

10.5   Indexing Image Metadata

One of the advantages of using a database to store images is to be able to search for images in many ways, as well as having a centralized, manageable repository.

Indexing the XMLType may depend on how the XML table type is stored. The XMLType may be structured, that is shredded into components, or unstructured, that is any kind of XML data that can be described with an XML schema. Unstructured XMLType data is stored in a CLOB.

For structured XMLType data, indexes can be B*Tree, Bitmap, function-based, or text-based indexes. Text-based indexes can be either a more limited XML DB context index or a full-text index. For unstructured XML-Type data, the indexes that can be used are function-based or text-based indexes (context and full-text indexes).

The IPTC-IIM and EXIF *inter*Media schemas are well structured, and have well-defined XML schemas, provided by *inter*Media, associated with them. They would be good candidates for XML DB-structured storage and indexing of structured fields.

The XMP standard allows for almost anything to be placed into the XML. The *inter*Media XMP schema definition allows all the endless possibilities to be stored in this schema. Because of this, the *inter*Media schema definition defines the XML data to be stored in a CLOB. To use the standard database indexes on XMP would require a user-based local schema definition to define structured storage for the fields to be indexed.

One side effect of storing XML in a CLOB, rather than structured fields, is that the XML will have to be parsed and the index value obtained from the XML data on a row insert/update. If the XML field is in structured storage, the value is simply obtained from the database field, and although the indexing syntax looks as if were function based, it is in actuality field based.

A query done without an index will result in a full table scan. Of course, this is very inefficient. For example:

```
SQL> explain plan for select item_id from ImagesWithMetadata where
  2             extractValue(IPTCMeta, '/iptcMetadata/location/text()',
  3                'xmlns="http://xmlns.oracle.com/ord/meta/iptc"') = 'India';
SQL>
SQL> select plan_table_output from
table(dbms_xplan.display('plan_table',null,'serial'));
Plan hash value: 474266177
```

```
-------------------------------------------------------------------------------
| Id  | Operation         | Name              | Rows | Bytes | Cost (%CPU)| Time     |
-------------------------------------------------------------------------------
|   0 | SELECT STATEMENT  |                   |    1 |     9 |     3   (0)| 00:00:01 |
|*  1 |  TABLE ACCESS FULL| IMAGESWITHMETADATA |    1 |     9 |     3   (0)| 00:00:01 |
-------------------------------------------------------------------------------
```

```
Predicate Information (identified by operation id):
---------------------------------------------------

  1 - filter("IMAGESWITHMETADATA"."SYS_NC00738$"='India')
```

This plan indicates that an operation of "TABLE ACCESS FULL" will occur, this indicates the entire table will be scanned to find a row where the location is "India."

The following example creates an index on XML data for the location of the picture, which makes finding a picture from a specific location much more efficient.

```
CREATE INDEX iptc_location_idx
  ON ImagesWithMetadata(extractValue(IPTCMETA,
    '/iptcMetadata/location/text()',
    ' xmlns="http://xmlns.oracle.com/ord/meta/iptc" ' ));
```

Using "explain plan," we can see that this index will be a normal, more efficient database index search.

```
SQL> explain plan for select item_id from ImagesWithMetadata where
  2           existsNode(IPTCMeta, '/iptcMetadata/location/text()',
  3           'xmlns="http://xmlns.oracle.com/ord/meta/iptc"') = 'India';
SQL> select plan_table_output from
table(dbms_xplan.display('plan_table',null,'serial'));
```

Id	Operation	Name	Rows	Bytes	Cost(%CPU)	Time
0	SELECT STATEMENT		1	9	2 (0)	00:00:01
1	TABLE ACCESS BY INDEX ROWID	IMAGESWITHMETADATA	1	9	2 (0)	00:00:01
* 2	INDEX RANGE SCAN	IPTC_LOCATION_IDX	1		1 (0)	00:00:01

```
Predicate Information (identified by operation id):
---------------------------------------------------

  2 - access("IMAGESWITHMETADATA"."SYS_NC00738$"='India')
```

One of the issues in indexing XML data is if the data to be indexed is one value or multiple values. Many index types do not allow for multiple values for a single database row. For example, the IPTC-IIM XML for an image may contain multiple keyword fields as in the following example.

```
<iptcMetadata xmlns="http://xmlns.oracle.com/ord/meta/iptc"
```

```
xsi:schemaLocation="http://xmlns.oracle.com/ord/meta/iptc
http://xmlns.oracle.com/ord/meta/iptc"
 xmlns:xsi="http://www.w3.org/2001/XMLSchema-instance">
 <recordVersion>2</recordVersion>
 <objectName>ar21319</objectName>
 <keyword>land</keyword>
 <keyword>monument</keyword>
 <keyword>nature</keyword>
 <keyword>scenery</keyword>
 <keyword>architectural</keyword>
 <keyword>architecture</keyword>
 <keyword>building</keyword>
 <keyword>place of worship</keyword>
 <keyword>religious building</keyword>
 <keyword>structures</keyword>
 <keyword>temple</keyword>
 <keyword>sacred place</keyword>
 <keyword>sanctum</keyword>
 <keyword>Asia</keyword>
 <keyword>India</keyword>
 <keyword>Malibalipuram</keyword>
 <keyword>Tamil Nadu</keyword>
 <keyword>night</keyword>
 <keyword>moonlight</keyword>
 <keyword>moon</keyword>
 <keyword>skies</keyword>
 <keyword>sky</keyword>
 <keyword>blue</keyword>
 <instructions>Newsmagazines Out</instructions>
 <dateCreated>2005-01-01</dateCreated>
 <byline>
   <author>Julie Doe</author>
   <authorTitle>Mugwum contract photographer</authorTitle>
 </byline>
 <city>Malibalipuram</city>
 <provinceState>Tamil Nadu</provinceState>
 <location>India</location>
 <transmissionReference>Sacred India</transmissionReference>
 <headline>Shore Temple, Malibalipuram, India</headline>
 <credit>Mugwum Press</credit>
 <source>Julie Doe / Mugwum Press</source>
```

```
<copyright>©2005 Julie Doe / Mugwum Press, all rights
reserved</copyright>
<caption>The Shore Temple of the Seven Pagodas was built
under Narsimha II of the Pallava dynasty between 7th and 8th
century AD and is dedicated to Lord Shiva. It resembles the
structure of the Dharmaraja rath, but its tower rises much
higher (approx. five stories or ~ 60 ft. high) and its stupa
spire is small and slender.</caption>
<captionWriter>Jacques Brown</captionWriter>
</iptcMetadata>
```

If you were to try and create a B*Tree index on the keyword field, you would get an error message as is shown below.

```
SQL> CREATE INDEX iptc_keyword_idx
  2     ON ImagesWithMetadata(extractValue(IPTCMETA,
  3        '/iptcMetadata/keyword',
  4         ' xmlns="http://xmlns.oracle.com/ord/meta/iptc" '
));
CREATE INDEX iptc_keyword_idx
                    *
ERROR at line 1:
ORA-02070: database does not support correlation in this
context
```

In the *inter*Media XMP XML schema, the keyword element is not specified, as the XMP type is quite flexible. However, it is typical for the keyword field to be present. An attempt to create a B*Tree index on this field would also be an error because the schema does not specify a single value for this field.

However, since the XML schema definition indicates that there can only be one <location> element, the following index creation will succeed because it refers to an XML field that can occur only once.

```
CREATE INDEX iptc_location_idx
  ON ImagesWithMetadata(extractValue(IPTCMETA,
    '/iptcMetadata/location',
     ' xmlns="http://xmlns.oracle.com/ord/meta/iptc" ' ));
```

If the XML to be indexed can result in multiple values, the XML DB context or full Oracle Text index can be used.

10.5.1   Oracle Text Indexing

Oracle Text can be used to index XML data. In the following example, a text index is used to create an index on XML data.

```
create index iwnd_context_index on
    ImagesWithMetadata(IPTCMeta)
    indextype is ctxsys.CONTEXT
    PARAMETERS ( 'section group ctxsys.PATH_SECTION_GROUP' )
;
```

This index can now be used to perform a search on IPTC keywords as indicated below.

```
select item_id from ImagesWithMetadata where
contains ( iptcmeta, 'sky INPATH (/iptcMetadata/keyword) ') > 0;
```

Note that when the table is updated, the Oracle Text index must also be updated in another operation. In other words, the change of the Oracle Text index is asynchronous to the update of the indexed table. Oracle Text index updates are often performed on multiple updates rather than individual updates for performance reasons. These performance issues include index fragmentation and processing time. One way to synchronize the index is to call a procedure:

```
begin
    ctx_ddl.sync_index( 'iwnd_path_iptc_idx' );
end;
/
```

Also note that the Oracle Text index should be maintained for peak performance. It is typically necessary to rebuild the index to defragment the index and optimize query performance.

A context index (ctxsys.ctxxpath) is used to find columns that contain a particular xpath. As such, it acts as a primary filter to return only the rows that contain the xpath.

```
create index iwnd_path_iptc_idx
  on imagesWithMetadata( IPTCMETA )
```

```
indextype is ctxsys.ctxxpath;
```

This will allow for index searches such as:

```
select item_id from ImagesWithMetadata where existsNode ( iptcmeta,
        '/iptcMetadata/keyword[ora:contains(text(),"sky")>0]',
        'xmlns:ora="http://xmlns.oracle.com/xdb"
        xmlns="http://xmlns.oracle.com/ord/meta/iptc"')
    > 0;
```

Note that the ctxxpath index is of limited use in cases where the xpath exists in all the indexed columns so its use here is a rather bad example if all of your images have IPTC keyword elements. It is best used for particular xpaths that occur rarely. The ora:contains clause is not evaluated with the index.

10.6 DICOM Metadata

The DICOM standard was created to standardize digital medical information. The information stored in a DICOM file can be images, waveforms (including audio waveforms), video, 3-D volumes, 3-D slices of volumes, and time-variant 3-D volumes. The DICOM standard replaced proprietary binary formats used by various medical equipment manufacturers for most of their medical diagnostic equipment.

Metadata support offered by *inter*Media allows for extraction of metadata from DICOM files. This information is handled in a similar manner to other types of image metadata by *inter*Media.

DICOM images can also be processed using *inter*Media like any other image format. For example, DICOM images can be converted to more Web-friendly formats, like JPEG, for easier perusal on Web pages.

DICOM metadata is stored in a non-XML format within the DICOM image. For *inter*Media, the DICOM metadata is extracted in an XML document form for easier processing. The namespace for this XML format is "http://xmlns.oracle.com/ord/meta/dicomImage."

Creating a table to contain a DICOM image is almost exactly like creating a table for a nonmedical image as is shown in the following example.

```
create table diagnosticImages(id number primary key,
                              desc VARCHAR2(80),
                              DicomMeta XMLType,
```

```
                              image ORDSYS.ORDIMAGE,
                              thumb ORDSYS.ORDIMAGE)
LOB (image.source.localdata) -- store images with 32K chunk
  STORE AS (chunk 32K)
LOB (thumb.source.localdata) -- but the thumbnails with only
16K
  STORE AS (chunk 16K)
-- and bind the XMLType columns to the interMedia metadata
columns
XMLType column metadata
  XMLSCHEMA "http://xmlns.oracle.com/ord/meta/dicomImage"
  ELEMENT "DICOM_IMAGE";
```

The diagnosticsImages table will hold an image, which will include a DICOM image, a description, the DICOM metadata for the image, and a thumbnail of the image. The thumbnail will be converted to JPEG format to view on the Web. We declare the DICOM metadata column as having the *inter*Media DICOM namespace "http://xmlns.oracle.com/ord/meta/ dicomImage" with the root element being DICOM_IMAGE. A procedure to populate a row into this table is given below.

```
create or replace procedure load_dicom_image(id number,
file_name varchar)
as
    img        ORDSYS.ORDImage;
    thmb       ORDSYS.ORDImage;
    ctx        raw(1):=null;
    dicomMetadata XMLTYPE := null;
    thisrowid urowid;
BEGIN

   -- Insert new row into the database
   insert into diagnosticImages (id, DicomMeta, Image, Thumb)
values (
        id,
        null,
        ORDSYS.ORDImage.init(),
        ORDSYS.ORDImage.init())
     returning rowid, image, thumb  into thisrowid, img,
thmb;

   -- Load the image file into the DB
```

```
        img.setsource('FILE', 'DICOMIMAGEDIR', file_name);
        img.import(ctx);

        -- extract DICOM metadata,
        dicomMetadata := img.getDicomMetadata('imageGeneral');
        IF (dicomMetadata IS NULL) THEN
          DBMS_OUTPUT.PUT_LINE('metadata is NULL');
        END IF;

        -- Create thumbnail
        img.processCopy('fileFormat=JFIF maxScale=800 800',
    thmb);

        -- Update the table with the images and metadata
        update diagnosticImages t
            set t.image=img, t.thumb=thmb,
    dicomMeta=dicomMetadata
        where rowid = thisrowid;
        commit;
    END;
    /
```

Note that for now the only type of metadata that can be extracted is the type "imageGeneral."

There is no corresponding putDicomMetadata() method. The reason for this is that the DICOM specification discourages modification of DICOM metadata once the file is created.

10.7 Summary

Image metadata can be used effectively with a database. By using *inter*Media to extract metadata, this information become available to the database. The database XML facilities can be used to manipulate metadata, which then can be inserted into the image.

Extracted metadata can be used in a database index, so that relevant images can be found efficiently. Using XML facilities of the database, fields of interest can be extracted and placed into traditional database columns, that can be indexed, or the XML metadata can be indexed directly.

The amount of metadata within DICOM medical images is extensive. *inter*Media provides support for extraction of this DICOM metadata. This extensive amount of metadata can best be managed with a database.

11

Query Mode

11.1 Introduction

This chapter introduces the way different kinds of multimedia data—audio, image, video, or a combination—can be retrieved from database systems. In this chapter we will first identify the problems in querying multimedia data, and second, study general approaches adopted for dealing with multimedia data particularly by using PL/SQL. With image data it is mainly the semantic nature that is the problem, while video and audio present difficulties in terms of their real-time nature as well. At the end of the chapter the reader will understand how to apply

- Attribute-based retrieval using *inter*Media
- Text-based retrieval using metadata with *inter*Media
- Using object properties in retrieval

In this chapter we shall look at the different approaches taken by *inter*Media technology to address these problems using technical and text-based metadata and the requirements of different application areas. We shall start by applying the technology to the Photo Store application and then go on to systems with more complex requirements.

A key approach is based on extracting information from media objects, attaching this information to the media object, and using it for retrieval from the database. We shall first explain how to do this with a "generic" application such as the Photo Store. Some critics would say that to achieve really effective content-based information retrieval (CBIR) (see Chapter 13) it is also necessary to go further and include specific information in the form of metadata about the domain itself and the semantics of the object.

11.2 Querying Media Data

Interacting with multimedia data is a relatively new possibility. Therefore, it is an area where little is known about users' requirements, such as in what way would users wish to manipulate and change multimedia objects. Unlike traditional databases a key issue is how to present the results of the multimedia query to the user. The result set could vary from a single relational table to a picture gallery or a summary of a number of documents. Many queries will return a set of similar items rather than an exact match so there is the question of how to rank the results of a multimedia query. How can we judge similarity? One solution is to apply methods to estimate the distance of each item in the set from the desired criteria provided by the user. At the same time it is essential that querying the database does not involve unacceptable response times due to the enormous data volumes. With our family Photo Store we may want to answer queries like:

"Show a photo of our grandfather's house and a map of its location"

We will need to consider how a query involving media data can be posed to a DBMS and then how the data is retrieved and subsequently presented. The interrogation of multimedia data raises both opportunities and challenges not present in traditional database systems. For example, using visual information in queries results in different ways of constructing the queries and searching the data, as illustrated in Figure 11.1. This presents the four possible combinations of different query and search modes that could be adopted by a multimedia retrieval system. For example, presenting a query in a linguistic mode such as "Find images of holiday in Mexico" but searching the database using visual attributes (visual mode). A visual attribute of an image is a numerical or logical attribute such as mean intensity or coarseness of texture.

The four combinations of modes can be described as:

Linguistic–Linguistic (LL) operates on the basis of forming a query in linguistic terms, as in SQL, and then searching textual metadata that has been stored in the form of text in order to locate and retrieve the required multimedia information. However, it is clear that the attempt to solve all queries by matching a linguistic form against lin-

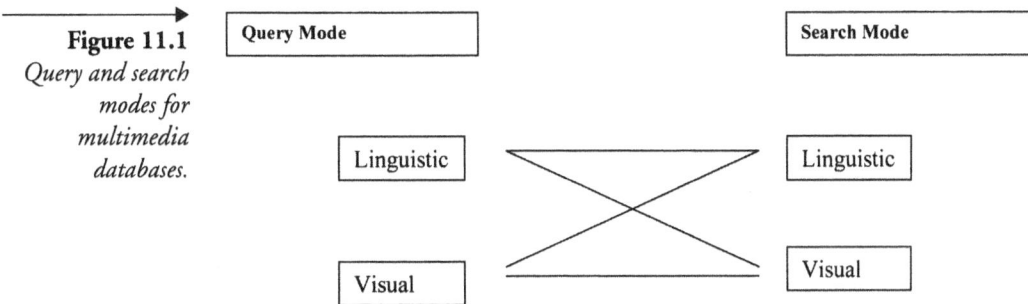

Figure 11.1
Query and search modes for multimedia databases.

guistic identifiers in the form of titles, keywords, and captions offers limited retrieval possibilities.

Visual–Visual (VV) is generally known as retrieval by content. For example, the query is posed in the form of a sketch the user draws, with the underlying assumption, "I want something like this." An alternative to using sketches is to provide the user with a browser based on a small selection of images from the database to use as examples in a query-by-example (QBE) style. These small images are referred to as polyphotos, icon browsers, index images, or thumbnails. A more advanced approach would use a visual thesaurus. For example, NASA developed one of the first visual thesauri to work alongside a text thesaurus for the space domain. Images from the thesaurus could be substituted for textual descriptions of the images in a retrieval system. Approaches to this type of query are explored in Chapter 13.

Visual–Linguistic (VL) provides example images that are then retrieved by linguistic metadata. In this case images are specified by sets of pixels with specific values for color, shape, texture, and geometric relations but indexed by name/title, etc. Queries use a text thesaurus. The image is included in a QBE-style query that places limitations on the variety of information needs that can be expressed by the user. This type of query is explored in Chapter 13.

Linguistic–Visual (LV). In this approach the images are indexed by visual attributes and possibly supplemented by a visual thesaurus. However, the user expresses the query in linguistic form using a standard query language.

Both the VL and LV modes involve the issue of how to create an index by mapping ideas about a subject expressed in different media.

11.3 Attribute-based Retrieval

Attribute-based retrieval (ABR) is a method that uses a set of structured attributes in the same way as traditional DBMS. This method can be particularly effective with text data. However, the method does not make use of the rich content of images to retrieve information. An implementation can easily be achieved by using Oracle *inter*Media itself or combined with other attributes. For example, we created a table for the Photo Store with the following structure.

```
ID                  NOT NULL NUMBER

DESCRIPTION         NOT NULL VARCHAR2(40)

IMAGE               ORDSYS.ORDIMAGE

THUMB               ORDSYS.ORDIMAGE
```

Both the IMAGE and THUMB columns are specified as the ORDImage data type that has a number of useful attributes that can be used for retrieval:

- MIME type
- Height
- Width
- ContentLength
- FileFormat
- CompressionFormat

Within the ORDImage object type there are attributes concerned with the media metadata, for example, file format, MIME type, and compression, which are unlikely on their own to form a basis for attribute-based retrieval.

Often the process of retrieval will be based on searching the metadata using standard SQL and using these results to locate the required data. In these situations Boolean queries are often combined with query-by-example (QBE) methods to provide feedback to narrow the search after the initial Boolean query. In order to carry out a QBE there must be a way to

- Describe (to capture spatial, temporal, and semantic patterns)
- Specify (intuitive and visual metaphors that interact with multimedia)
- Depict (visual metaphors to identify matching patterns)

11.4 How Is Metadata Used in Query Processing?

Before we consider the role of metadata for separate media, it is helpful, particularly when considering design options, to classify metadata and relate this to the three types of information retrieval, as follows:

1. Content independent (i.e., associated with media, e.g., photographer's name) so used in attribute-based retrieval.

2. Content descriptive—used in text-based retrieval.

3. Content dependent (e.g., features of faces from photographs or video operations in a clip) used in content-based retrieval.

In Table 11.1 we give examples of the classes for the different media to clarify the way content-independent, content-descriptive, and content-dependent features are used.

Table 11.1 *Metadata Classes*

Metadata Class	Example	Usage
Content independent	Associated with media (e.g., photographer's name)	Attribute based
Content descriptive	The speakers and topic discussed	Text based
Content dependent	Features of color or texture from photographs or video operations in a clip	Content based

11.5 Using SQL

*inter*Media uses an object-relational approach. This means that the tables we create with *inter*Media object types will have some columns with composite data types with their own attributes and methods. We can include both the attributes and the methods in SQL query statements. The simplest way we are going to query the media is through the metadata.

In Chapter 3 we created a table, photos with image, and thumb columns with data-type ORDImage. The ORDImage object type has several attributes that we could use to query the database:

- MIME type
- contentLength
- fileFormat
- contentFormat
- compressionFormat

These attributes would be accessible by normal SQL functions and could be used for retrieval purposes and for summarizing the content of the database.

When we want to query a column with this data type we need to use a correlation variable (or alias) as follows to retrieve the attributes of the object type.

```
SELECT p.id, p.image.mimetype, p.image.fileformat
FROM   photos p
WHERE p.image.mimetype='image/jpeg';
```

The style used is columnname.object_attribute and this form of attribute specification can appear complex and confusing to the user. We can add substitute headings in SQL to improve usability.

```
SELECT p.id, SUBSTR(p.image.mimetype,1,15) Mime_type,
   SUBSTR(p.image.fileformat,1,15) File_format
FROM   photos p
WHERE p.image.mimetype='image/jpeg'

  ID MIME_TYPE          FILE_FORMAT
---- ---------------    ---------------
4313 image/jpeg         JFIF
4310 image/jpeg         JFIF
4311 image/jpeg         JFIF
```

Similarly, for video object type in the video_ord table we would query as follows:

```
SELECT v.id, v.video.videoDuration, v.video.FrameResolution
FROM   video_ord v;
```

However, we cannot use the ORDImage attributes unless these have stored metadata extracted using the setProperties() method illustrated in Chapter 8. This setProperties() method reads the media data to get the values of the object attributes and then stores them in the object attributes. The method sets the properties for each of the attributes of the media data for which values are available (e.g., compression type, MIME type, etc.), and then for video and audio data populates the comments field of the object with a rich set of format and application properties in XML form, provided that the value of the setComments parameter is TRUE.

If we want to query using an object-type method we will have to provide the IN parameters of the method within the SQL statement. Most of the ORDImage methods do not require IN parameters and can be queried as follows:

```
SELECT  P.image.getCompressionFormat(),
        P.image.getHeight(),
        P.image.getWidth()
FROM photos P
WHERE   P.image.getCompressionFormat() = 'JPEG'
```

Or using column expression substitution we would enter:

```
SELECT    p.id            id,
          p.image.Height  height,
          p.image.Width   width,
          p.image.mimeType mimetype
FROM      photos p
```

However, Oracle recommends using the object-type methods rather than the attributes directly in case there were changes to the internal representation of the ORDImage object type so the first style of query is preferable.

Exactly the same style is used for audio examples:

```
SELECT   t.id              id,
         t.audio.getMimeType() mimetype
   FROM  t.audio_ord t;
```

And for a video query (MimeType Attribute)

```
SELECT t.id               id,
       t. video.getMimeType() mimetype
   FROM   video_ord  t;
```

11.6 Content-based Retrieval

Content-based retrieval (CBR) methods, which we look at in detail in Chapter 13, have been developed to try to overcome some of the limitations and problems of TBR. The idea is that the important details can be extracted from the media by automatic methods, which will be more efficient for data capture and more reliable for retrieval. Retrieval of images by manually assigned keywords is definitely not content-based retrieval. Another more fundamental difference in the three methods is that attribute-based retrieval can be used to address straight forward queries, while the text-based and content-based retrieval address more complex queries known as the semantic gap. CBR implies the ability to search based on the user's association and impression of an image (e.g., sunset at sea). In order for this to be possible a method must exist that defines the semantic quality and similarity of images. This could mean setting up a mapping from the user's ideas and concepts to both the raw image data and the image characteristics.

All three methods summarized in Figure 11.4 involve the use of metadata but the nature of the metadata and its source changes with each method.

Figure 11.2
Retrieval strategies and the techniques employed.

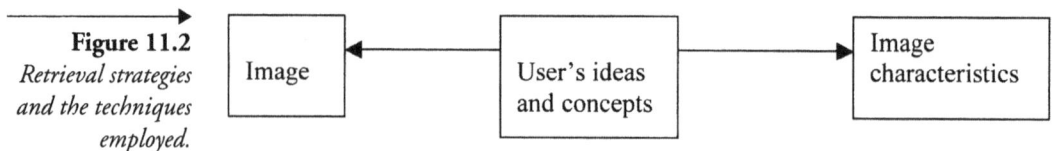

Nature of Retrieval	Techniques Employed
Attribute based	Fixed set of structured attributes, with indexing based on B*Trees and inverted files.
Text based	Text descriptions and structured fields. Indexing by full text (scanning, inversion files).
Content based	Content features automatically extracted, image feature extraction.

11.7 PL/SQL Application Development

In this section we will review how PL/SQL can be used to provide most of the functionality required for a rich-media application. In other words, to perform

- Media download

- Media upload

- Image processing

- Image queries

1. To download media from the database, we need to be able to write to the image directory object:

   ```
   GRANT WRITE ON DIRECTORY PHOTO_DIR TO SCOTT;
   ```

   Then we can compile and execute the following procedure to download an image file into the PHOTO_DIR directory.

   ```
   CREATE or replace PROCEDURE img_export
   AS
       img     ORDSYS.ORDIMAGE;
       ctx     raw(64) :=null;
   BEGIN
     SELECT  image
       INTO  img
       FROM  photos
      WHERE id =4311;
     img.export(ctx, 'FILE', 'PHOTO_DIR', '4311.jpg');
   END;
   ```

2. To upload media into the database means importing media data from the file system into the database tablespaces. The following series of steps are typical:

    ■ Insert a new row into the table, creating new objects by using the init method of the *inter*Media object type.

    ■ Call the import method of the *inter*Media object to bring the data from the file system into the database.

    ■ Call the setProperties() method of the *inter*Media object to determine and populate the attributes of the object.

    ■ Update the table so that the *inter*Media object in the table contains the attribute values extracted in the previous step.

    The PL/SQL code that implements these steps for inserting a new row in the `Family_media` table. The Family_media table is

```
CREATE TABLE Family_media
(  id                        NUMBER,
   description               VARCHAR2(30),
   family_photo              ORDImage,
   family_audio              ORDAudio,
   family_video              ORDVideo)
```

This is shown in the following procedure example:

```
CREATE or replace PROCEDURE family_import
AS
   img ORDImage;
   aud ORDAudio;
   vid ORDVideo;
   ctx RAW(64) := NULL;
BEGIN
   -- Insert a new row into the Family_media table
   DELETE FROM Family_media WHERE id = 3003;
   INSERT INTO Family_media
           (id,
            Family_photo,
            Family_audio,
            Family_video)
   VALUES (3003,
```

```
            ORDImage.init('FILE', 'PHOTO_DIR', 'CATS.jpg'),
            ORDAudio.init('FILE', 'PHOTO_DIR', 'track01.cda'),
            ORDVideo.init('FILE', 'PHOTO_DIR',
               'my_family.mov'))
   RETURNING Family_photo, Family_audio, Family_video
   INTO img, aud, vid;
   -- Bring the media into the database and populate the
   -- attributes
   img.import(ctx);
   -- ORDImage.import also calls ORDImage.setProperties;
   aud.import(ctx);
   aud.setProperties(ctx);
   vid.import(ctx);
   vid.setProperties(ctx);
--Update the table with the properties we have
extracted
   UPDATE Family_media
   SET    Family_photo = img,
          Family_audio = aud,
          Family_video = vid
   WHERE  id = 3003;
   COMMIT;
END;
```

When handling exceptions, PL/SQL uses exception blocks. For example, in PL/SQL, the exception may appear as:

```
BEGIN
<some program logic>
EXCEPTION
     WHEN OTHERS THEN
     <some exception logic
END;
```

One of the main problems will be dealing with unrecognized formats when we want to carry out image-processing methods.

3. To carry out image processing, we know from Chapter 8 that if a procedure tries to use the setProperties() method with an uploaded image (it reads the image data to get the values of the object attributes so it can store them in the appropriate

attributes) and the image format is not recognized, then the `setProperties()` method will fail. To catch this exception and work around this potential problem, the application uses the following exception block.

```
BEGIN
    new_image.setProperties();
EXCEPTION
    WHEN OTHERS THEN
            new_image.contentLength := upload_size;
            new_image.mimeType := upload_mime_type;
END;
```

In the next example, this exception handler sets the MIME type and length of the image. The browser sets a MIME-type header when the file is uploaded. The application can then read this header to set the ORDImage attribute.

If your program tries to process an image in cases when the image format is unknown, then the processCopy() method will always fail. To work around this potential problem, the application uses the following exception block:

```
BEGIN
    new_image.processCopy( 'maxScale=50,50', new_thumb);
EXCEPTION
    WHEN OTHERS THEN
        new_thumb.deleteContent();
        new_thumb.contentLength := 0;
END;
```

The thumbnail image cannot be created so this exception handler deletes the content of the thumbnail image and sets its length to zero.

4.   To query media data, there are two main approaches - to search for keywords to identify an image or search through the image metadata attributes. The following procedure uses a cursor to fetch keyword data that can then be matched with keywords suppied by the user

```
CREATE OR REPLACE PROCEDURE query_img_cursor
IS
CURSOR photos_id IS
 SELECT id, location, description
FROM NEW_PHOTOS;
  v_id   NEW_PHOTOS.ID%TYPE;
  v_loc  NEW_PHOTOS.location%TYPE;
  v_desc NEW_PHOTOS.description%TYPE;
BEGIN
 OPEN photos_id;
--fetch first row, this moves the cursor to the next row
 FETCH photos_id INTO v_id, v_loc, v_desc;
--fetch second row
IF  photos_id%FOUND THEN
FETCH photos_id INTO v_id, v_loc, v_desc;
--the cursor has moved again
ELSE
   CLOSE photos_id;
END IF;
CLOSE photos_id;
END;
```

11.7.1 Developing PL/SQL Web Applications

SQL developers who are familiar with the database can develop Web applications that exclusively use Oracle Application Server and Oracle Database using the PL/SQL development environment. With the PL/SQL development environment, developers can rapidly develop PL/SQL-based Web applications. Developing Web applications using PL/SQL consists of developing one or more PL/SQL packages consisting of sets of stored procedures that interact with Web browsers through HTTP. Stored procedures can be executed in several ways:

- From a hypertext link that calls a stored procedure when it is selected.

- By clicking **Submit** on an HTML form to denote the completion of a task, such as filling out a form supplied on the HTML page.

- By passing parameters to a stored procedure based on user choices from a list.

Information in the stored procedure, such as tagged HTML text, is displayed in the Web browser as a Web page. These dynamic Web pages are generated by the database and are based on the database contents and the input parameters passed into the stored procedure. Using PL/SQL stored procedures is especially efficient and powerful for generating dynamic Web page content. *inter*Media can be employed when media data such as images, audio, video, or combinations of all three are to be uploaded into and retrieved from database tables using the *inter*Media object types and their respective sets of methods.

There are several ways of generating HTML output from PL/SQL:

- Using function calls to generate each HTML tag for output using the PL/SQL Web Toolkit package that is part of Oracle Application Server and Oracle Database.

- Embedding PL/SQL code in Web pages (PL/SQL server pages).

Figure 11.3
*PL/SQL Web
application.*

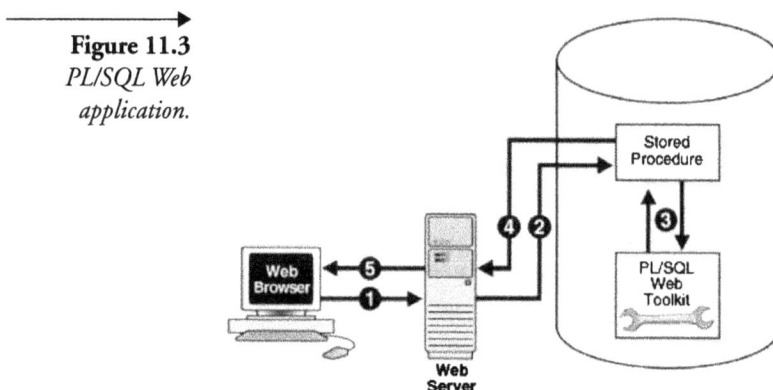

- In Figure 11.3 the following process is shown:
  - A user visits a Web page, follows a hypertext link, or submits data in a form, which causes the browser to send an HTTP request for a URL to an HTTP server.
  - The HTTP server invokes a stored procedure on an Oracle database according to the data encoded in the URL. The data in the URL takes the form of parameters to be passed to the stored procedure.
  - The stored procedure calls subprograms in the PL/SQL Web Toolkit.
  - The subprograms pass the dynamically generated page to the Web server.

The PL/SQL gateway enables a Web browser to invoke a PL/SQL stored procedure through an HTTP listener. The gateway is a platform on which PL/SQL users develop and deploy PL/SQL Web applications. There are several implementations. There is a module called mod_plsql that is a plug-in of Oracle HTTP Server and enables Web browsers to invoke PL/SQL stored procedures. The PL/SQL Web Toolkit is basically a set of packages that enables you to use stored procedures called by mod_plsql at runtime. Oracle HTTP Server is a component of both Oracle Application Server and Oracle Database.

Media upload procedures must first perform an SQL INSERT operation to insert a row of data in the media table so that it also initializes any instances of the respective *inter*Media object columns with an empty BLOB. Next, an SQL SELECT FOR UPDATE operation selects the object columns for update. Finally, an SQL UPDATE operation updates the media objects in their respective columns. This is illustrated in the next procedure, which also outputs the values of the attributes.

```
CREATE or replace PROCEDURE img_upload
AS
    img      ORDSYS.ORDIMAGE;
    ctx      raw(64) :=null;
BEGIN
  INSERT INTO photos(id, image)
  VALUES (4313,ORDSYS.ORDIMAGE.INIT());
      --image column is initalized to empty BLOB
    SELECT p.image INTO img FROM photos p
 WHERE p.id = 4313 FOR UPDATE;
img.importFrom(ctx,'file','PHOTO_DIR','cats.jpg');

  UPDATE  photos SET image=img WHERE id=4313;
 img.setProperties();
 DBMS_OUTPUT.PUT_LINE('Image file format: ' ||
img.getFileformat);
 DBMS_OUTPUT.PUT_LINE('Image Compression: ' ||
img.getCompressionFormat);
 DBMS_OUTPUT.PUT_LINE('Image Content format: ' ||
img.getContentformat);
 DBMS_OUTPUT.PUT_LINE('Image Mime Type: ' ||
img.getMimeType);
 DBMS_OUTPUT.PUT_LINE('Image size: ' ||
img.getContentLength);
```

```
DBMS_OUTPUT.PUT_LINE('Image Height: ' || img.getHeight);
DBMS_OUTPUT.PUT_LINE('Image Width: ' || img.getWidth);
UPDATE  photos p set p.image = img
  WHERE  p.id = 4313;
COMMIT;
END;
```

*inter*Media methods are called to do the following:

- Initialize the object columns with an empty BLOB.

- Set attributes to indicate media data is stored internally in a BLOB.

- Get values of the object attributes and store them in the object attributes.

- When exceptions occur, determine the length of the BLOB content and its MIME type.

Media retrieval operations involve

- Retrieving the object from the database into a local object.

- Checking the cache validity of the object based on its updated time versus that of the HTTP header time.

- Determining where the media object is located: in the database, in a BFILE, or at a URL location; then, getting the media and downloading it for display on an HTML page.

11.7.2   **Optimizing PL/SQL**

There are some routine BLOB operations that will improve the performance of PL/SQL. It is recommended to initialize a persistent LOB to EMPTY rather than NULL. Doing so enables you to obtain a locator for the LOB instance without populating the LOB with data. To set a persistent LOB to EMPTY, use the SQL function EMPTY_BLOB() or EMPTY_CLOB() in the INSERT statement:

```
INSERT INTO a_table VALUES (EMPTY_BLOB());
```

As an alternative, you can use the RETURNING clause to obtain the LOB locator in one operation rather than calling a subsequent SELECT statement.

```
CREATE or replace PROCEDURE img_upload
 AS
    Lob_loc  BLOB;
 BEGIN
    INSERT INTO photo_BLOB(IMAGE) VALUES (EMPTY_BLOB())
    RETURNING IMAGE INTO Lob_loc;
    /* Now use the locator Lob_loc to populate the BLOB with
       data */
 END;
```

In Chapter 3 we reviewed the basic use of OUT and INOUT parameters in PL/SQL procedures and the rules that operate them. If you use OUT or INOUT parameters, PL/SQL adds some performance overhead to ensure correct behavior in case of exceptions (assigning a value to the OUT parameter, then exiting the subprogram because of an unhandled exception, so that the OUT parameter keeps its original value).

If your program does not depend on OUT parameters keeping their values in such situations, you can add the NOCOPY keyword to the parameter declarations, so the parameters are declared OUT NOCOPY or INOUT NOCOPY.

This technique can give significant speedup if you are passing back large amounts of data in OUT parameters, such as collections, big VARCHAR2 values, or LOBS.

This technique also applies to member methods of object types. If these methods modify attributes of the object type, all the attributes are copied when the method ends. To avoid this overhead, you can explicitly declare the first parameter of the member method as SELF INOUT NOCOPY, instead of relying on PL/SQL's implicit declaration SELF INOUT. For information about design considerations for object methods, see *Oracle Database Application Developer's Guide: Object-Relational Features*.

Oracle Database uses two engines to run PL/SQL blocks and subprograms. The PL/SQL engine runs procedural statements, while the SQL engine runs SQL statements. During execution, every SQL statement causes a context switch between the two engines, resulting in performance overhead. Performance can be improved substantially by minimizing the number of context switches required to run a particular block or subprogram.

11.7.3   Make Loops as Efficient as Possible

PL/SQL applications are often built around loops, so it is important to optimize the loop itself and the code inside the loop. For example, the FORALL keyword can improve the performance of INSERT, UPDATE, or DELETE statements that reference collection elements. To issue a series of DML statements, replace loop constructs with FORALL statements.

```
CREATE or replace PROCEDURE image_loop
   TYPE Numlist IS VARRAY (100) OF NUMBER;
   List_Id NUMLIST := NUMLIST(4310,4311,43112,4313);
--
BEGIN

-- Efficient method, using a bulk bind
   FORALL i IN Id.FIRST..Id.LAST    -- bulk-bind the VARRAY
      UPDATE photos SET image = img
      WHERE id= List_Id (i);

-- Slower method, running the UPDATE statements within a
regular loop
   FOR i IN Id.FIRST..Id.LAST LOOP
      UPDATE photos SET image = img
      WHERE id= List_Id (i);
   END LOOP;
END;
```

To loop through a result set and store the values, use the BULK COLLECT clause on the query to bring the query results into memory in one operation. If you need to bring a large quantity of data into local PL/SQL variables, rather than looping through a result set one row at a time, you can use the BULK COLLECT clause. When you query only certain columns, you can store all the results for each column in a separate collection variable. When you query all the columns of a table, you can store the entire result set in a collection of records, which makes it convenient to loop through the results and refer to different columns.

If you have to loop through a result set more than once, or issue other queries as you loop through a result set, you can probably enhance the original query to give you exactly the results you want. Some query operators to explore include UNION, INTERSECT, MINUS, and CONNECT BY.

You can also nest one query inside another (known as a subselect) to do the filtering and sorting in multiple stages. For example, instead of calling a PL/SQL function in the inner WHERE clause (which might call the function once for each row of the table), you can filter the result set to a small set of rows in the inner query, and call the function in the outer query.

PL/SQL stops evaluating a logical expression as soon as the result can be determined. This functionality is known as short-circuit evaluation. Short-circuit evaluation applies to IF statements, CASE statements, and CASE expressions in PL/SQL.

When evaluating multiple conditions separated by AND or OR, put the least expensive ones first. For example, check the values of PL/SQL variables before testing function return values, because PL/SQL might be able to skip calling the functions.

You might need to allocate large VARCHAR2 variables when you are not sure how big an expression result will be. You can actually conserve memory by declaring VARCHAR2 variables with large sizes, such as 32,000, rather than estimating just a little on the high side, such as by specifying 256 or 1,000. PL/SQL has an optimization that makes it easy to avoid overflow problems and still conserve memory. Specify a size of more than 4,000 characters for the VARCHAR2 variable; PL/SQL waits until you assign the variable, then only allocates as much storage as needed.

As you develop larger and larger PL/SQL applications, it becomes more difficult to isolate performance problems. PL/SQL provides a Profiler API to profile runtime behavior and to help you identify performance bottlenecks. PL/SQL also provides a Trace API for tracing the execution of programs on the server. You can use Trace to trace the execution by subprogram or exception.

Once the LOB data is stored in the database, a modified strategy must be used to improve the performance of retrieving and updating the LOB data. The following guidelines should be considered:

- Use the CACHE option on LOBS if the same LOB data is to be accessed frequently by other users since then Oracle places LOB pages in the buffer cache for faster access whereas NOCACHE specifies that LOB values are not brought into the buffer cache.

- Increase the number of buffers if you are going to use the CACHE option.

- Have enough buffers to hold the object. Using a small number of buffers for large objects is not good. Set the DB_CACHE_SIZE parameter to a value that you know will hold the object. DB_CACHE_SIZE is the size in bytes of the cache of standard blocks. To help you specify an optimal cache value, you can use the dynamic DB_CACHE_ADVICE parameter with statistics gathering enabled to predict behavior with different cache sizes through the V$DB_CACHE_ADVICE performance view.

- Ensure that your redo log files are much larger than they usually are; otherwise, you may be waiting for log switches, especially if you are making many updates to your LOB data.

- Ensure that you use a larger page size (DB_BLOCK_SIZE), especially if the majority of the data in the database is LOB data.

The DB_CACHE_SIZE parameter specifies the size of the DEFAULT buffer pool for buffers in bytes. This value is the database buffer value that is displayed when we issue an SQL SHOW SGA statement. Since the value of the DB_BLOCK_SIZE parameter cannot be changed without recreating the database, we can change the value of the DB_CACHE_SIZE parameter instead to control the size of the database buffer cache by using the ALTER SYSTEM...SET clause statement. The DB_CACHE_SIZE parameter is dynamic.

11.8   Server-side SQL

It is possible to embed two different kinds of scripts in HTML pages: client-side scripts and server-side scripts. Client-side scripts are returned as part of the HTML page and are run in the browser. These are mainly used for navigation between HTML pages or data validation carried out on the client side. Server-side scripts, while also embedded in the HTML pages, are run on the server side. They fetch and manipulate data from the database and produce HTML content that is returned as part of the page.

PL/SQL server pages (PSP) are server-side Web pages (in HTML or XML) with embedded PL/SQL scripts marked with special tags. Previously, developers would produce dynamic Web pages by usually writing CGI programs in C or Perl to fetch data and produce the entire Web page within the same program. The development and maintenance of such dynamic pages are costly and time consuming.

Scripting fulfills the demand for rapid development of dynamic Web pages. Small scripts can be embedded in HTML pages without changing their basic HTML identity. The scripts contain the logic to produce the dynamic portions of HTML pages and are run when the pages are requested by the users.

The separation of HTML content from application logic makes script pages easier to develop, debug, and maintain. Figure 11.2 shows how a browser calls the PSP-stored procedure. A PL/SQL gateway receives HTTP requests from an HTTP client, invokes a PL/SQL stored procedure as specified in the URL, and returns the HTTP output to the client. A PL/SQL server page is processed by a PSP compiler, which compiles the page into a PL/SQL stored procedure. When the procedure is run by the gateway, it generates the Web page with dynamic content. PSP is built on one of two existing PL/SQL gateways: PL/SQL cartridge or Oracle Application Server.

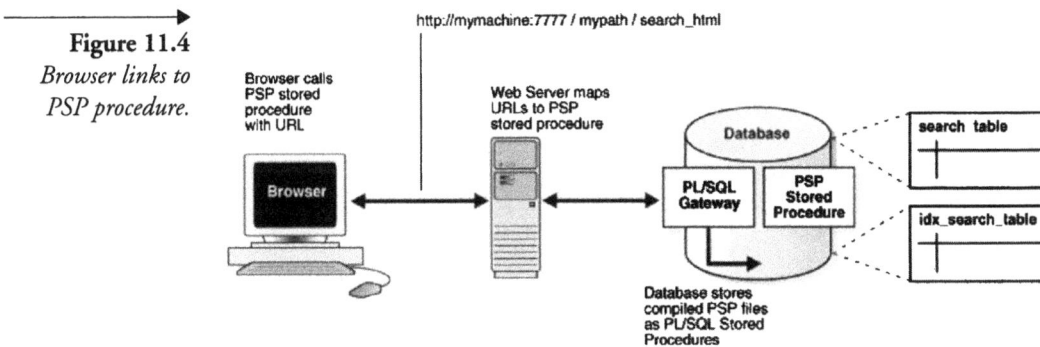

Figure 11.4
Browser links to PSP procedure.

Developing a PSP application has the following requirements:

- Oracle Database (version 8.1.6 or higher)
- Oracle PL/SQL gateway running
- Web server, such as Apache, up and running and correctly configured to send requests to the Oracle Database server

The Web server must be configured to accept client PSP requests as a URL. The Web server forwards these requests to the Oracle Database server and returns server output to the browser. Here is a sample HTML file with PSP to search for matching documents.

```
<%@ plsql procedure="search_html" %>
<%@ plsql parameter="query" default="null" %>
<%! v_results numeric := 0; %>
<html>
<head>
  <title>search_html Search </title>
</head>
<body>
<%
If query is null Then
%>
  <center>
    <form method=post action="search_html">
    <b>Search for: </b>
    <input type=text name="query" size=30> 
    <input type=submit value=Search>
  </center>
<hr>
<%
  Else
%>
   <p>
   <%!
     color varchar2(6) := 'ffffff';
   %>
   <center>
     <form method=post action="search_html">
      <b>Search for:</b>
      <input type=text name="query" size=30
          value="<%= query%>">
      <input type=submit value=Search>
     </form>
   </center>
   <hr>
   <p>
   <%
     -- select statement
    for doc in (
                select /*+ FIRST_ROWS */ rowid, tk, title,
               score(1) scr
                from search_table
```

```
                          where contains(text, query,1) >0
                          order by score(1) desc
                          )
                    loop
                      v_results := v_results + 1;
                      if v_results = 1 then
        %>
                          <center>
                            <table border="0">
                              <tr bgcolor="#6699CC">
                                <th>Score</th>
                                <th>Title</th>
                              </tr>

        <%      end if; %>
                        <tr bgcolor="#<%= color %>">
                          <td> <%= doc.scr %>% </td>
                          <td> <%= doc.title %>
                          [<a href="search_htmlServices.showHTMLDoc?p_id=
                                <%= doc.tk %>">HTML</a>]
                          [<a href="search_htmlServices.showDoc?p_id=
                                <%= doc.tk %>&p_query=
                                      <%=query%>">Highlight</a>]
                          </td>
                        </tr>
        <%
                        if (color = 'ffffff') then
                              color := 'eeeeee';
                            else
                              color := 'ffffff';
                        end if;

            end loop;
          %>
            </table>
          </center>
      <%
        end if;
      %>
      </body></html>
```

11.9 Text-based Retrieval

Text-based retrieval (TBR) methods work by adding annotation, usually brief descriptions combined with some structured data. The disadvantage of text-based systems is that they are very difficult in practice. The following example gives the definition of a table to include audio media.

```
CREATE TABLE audio_example
( id           CHAR(8) PRIMARY KEY,
  description  VARCHAR2(40),
  speakers     VARCHAR2(30),
  speach_text  CLOB,
  audio_data   ORDSYS.ORDAUDIO)
```

In fact ORDSYS.ORDAUDIO contains two attributes already, description (VARCHAR2(4000)) and comments (CLOB), which could be used for ABR and TBR, respectively. We can use TBR by exploiting the DBMS_LOB routines with the CLOB data or use Oracle Text capabilities.

The annotations usually have to be added manually. However, there is a major issue with reliability. Would a typical user be able to come up with the same description of the audio example in the table above as the person doing the annotation? In addition, for images this is a resource-intensive process that is difficult and costly to achieve. Some images, such as abstract art and computer graphics, are very difficult to describe in text. For successful retrieval the user who searches this material must be able to use the same descriptive terms as the annotator. However people may give quite different descriptions of the same image. In addition, if large amounts of descriptive text are involved the retrieval methods become more complicated.

12

inter*Media Application Performance*

12.1 Identify Performance Needs and Goals

One of the first things that is necessary when planning the performance of a system is to identify what the performance needs are. It is also desirable to identify what the performance goals are. It is difficult to reach goals when they do not exist.

Performance does not typically fall into one category, like response time. Performance may be an issue in many other areas of your media database application. Performance goals may include the following issues:

- User response time
- Time to backup the data
- Time to restore operations after a failure
- Amount of time to load data

Depending on your application, it is important to identify strategies to reach your performance goals. For example, a nightly full backup of the database may take too much time. A better strategy may be to do full backups on the weekend and incremental backups during the week.

Defining your performance goals will also allow you to invest your time in the most beneficial manner. Improving performance may entail:

- Hardware changes
- Infrastructure parameter changes (database, operating system, application server, etc.)

- Applications changes

- Process changes (backup methodology, when routine tasks are performed, etc.)

12.2 Tuning the Database

The goal of tuning the system global area (SGA) is to keep the correct amount of data in memory for optimal performance. Too small an SGA could mean excessive disk I/O activity to the database. Too large an SGA could lead to excessive paging and swapping of memory on your system. Since media data is larger than traditional relational data, it may be wise to consider increasing the physical memory so that your *inter*Media application can have a large SGA without increasing swapping and paging that can adversely affect the performance of your system. In general, increasing the default size of the SGA is necessary for *inter*Media applications to perform at their peak.

With Oracle 10g, distribution of SGA memory can be managed automatically. The commonly configured parameters include:

- Shared pool (for PL/SQL and SQL execution)

- Java pool (for Java execution state)

- Large pool (for large allocations such as RMAN backup buffers)

- Buffer cache

- Streams pool

To turn on automatic shared memory management using Enterprise Manager, select the Management tab and then the Memory Parameters link. On the memory parameters page, there is a button to enable automatic shared memory management. For those that want to edit the initialization file to enable automatic shared memory management, the SGA_TARGET initialization parameter is set to a nonzero value and the STATISTICS_LEVEL initialization parameter is set to TYPICAL or ALL. Note if the initialization settings for the pool sizes are not zero, they are considered to be minimum values. These can be set to an initial minimum size for each pool necessary to run your application.

There are too many issues in general performance to cover here, but a good start to tune an Oracle database is to use the automated tuning features built into it. You can use the Automatic Workload Repository (AWR) to collect tuning information, and after a sample workload is performed or simulated, use the Automatic Database Diagnostic Monitor (ADDM) to analyze the information collected by the AWR for possible performance problems with an Oracle database.

One area of note in tuning an Oracle database for *inter*Media is the java_pool_size parameter. Since *inter*Media uses Java for much of its processing, this pool may need to be increased to process large media data.

To turn on AWR, log in as a sysdba user (like sys) into your database Enterprise Manager and select the Administration tab. This will give you the screen shown in Figure 12.1 with the Automatic Workload Repository link.

Figure 12.1
Oracle Enterprise Manager

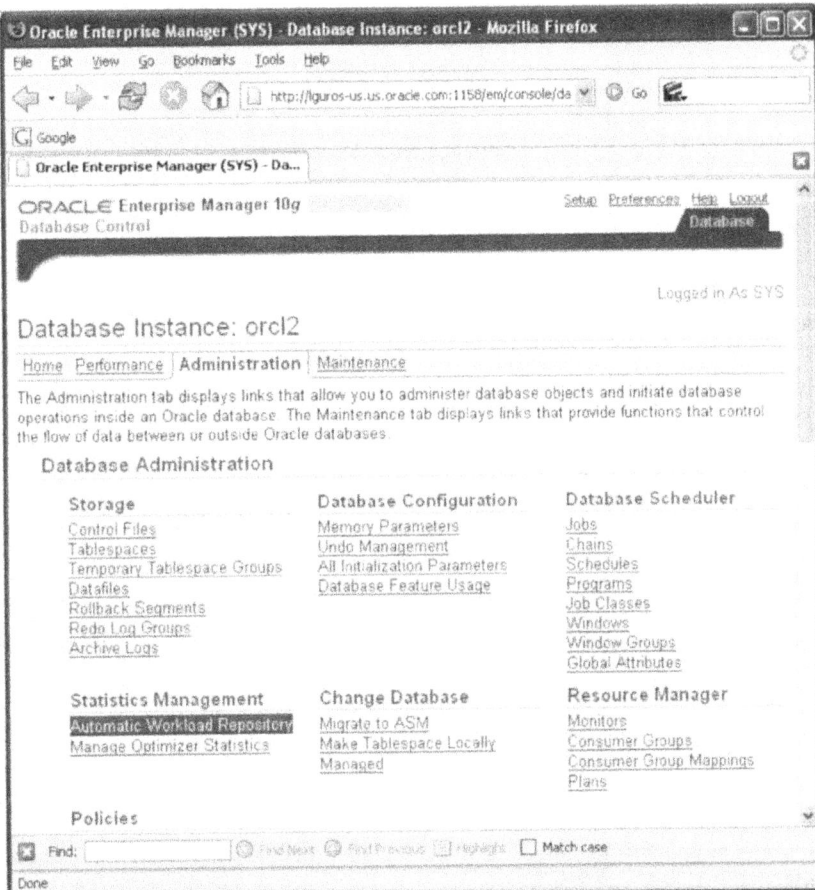

Figure 12.2
*Automatic
Workload
Repository
Configuration*

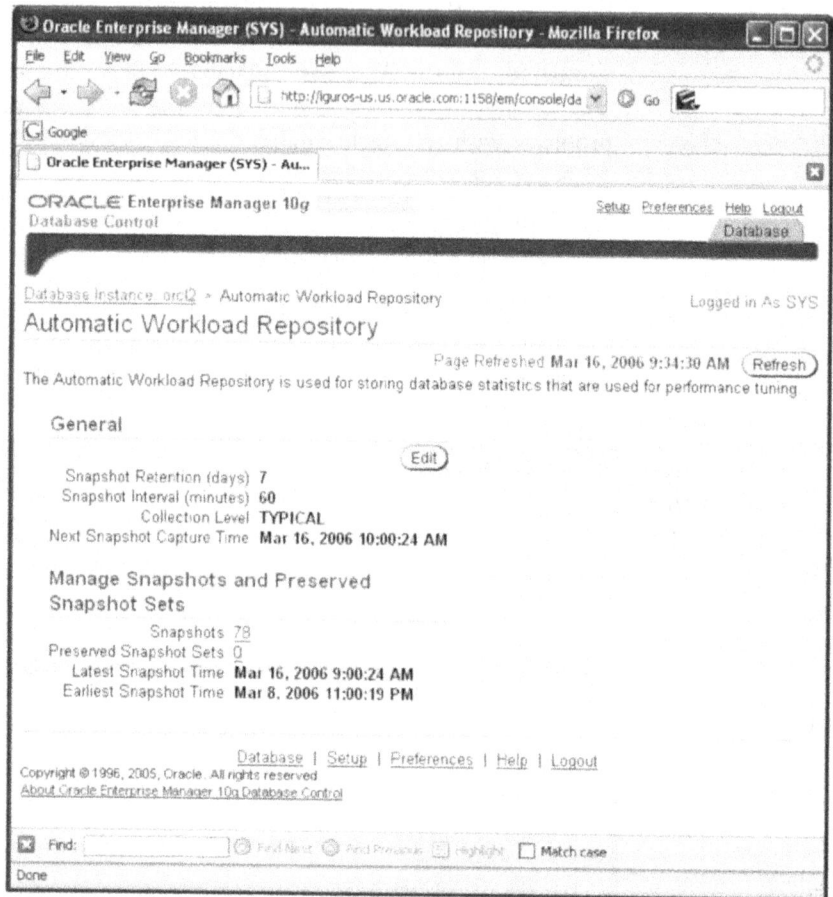

Figure 12.2
Automatic Workload Repository Configuration

On selection of the Automatic Workload Repository link, the screen shown in Figure 12.2 will be displayed.

This screen indicates that database performance data is being collected with Automatic Workload Repository. The main settable parameters are explained below:

- Snapshot Retention. The length of time performance records are retained. Records older than this section are automatically removed.

- Snapshot Interval. The interval at which snapshot records are captured.

- Collection Level. This parameter indicates the level at which records are captured. This parameter can be changed from the initial parameters page, which you can navigate to by clicking on the collection-level setting. This setting can be set to BASIC, TYPICAL, or ALL.

Once Automatic Workload Repository is active, records are saved at every interval. You can also create a snapshot at any time you like, perhaps before and then after a sample workload, with the following PL/SQL:

```
BEGIN DBMS_WORKLOAD_REPOSITORY.CREATE_SNAPSHOT (); END;
    /
```

The retention period indicates how long to save the performance statistics. You will probably want the retention period to include your highest workload time. For example, if you have high system usage once per month at the end of the month, you will likely want to increase the retention period to one month.

Once you have statistics, you then can have them automatically analyzed by the Automatic Database Diagnostic Monitor (ADDM). This monitor will evaluate the statistics gathered by AWR and give specific plain text recommendations on improving performance.

The following is an example ADDM recommendation:

```
FINDING 3: 18% impact (396 seconds)
------------------------------------
The SGA was inadequately sized, causing additional I/O or hard parses.

   RECOMMENDATION 1: DB Configuration, 7% benefit (157 seconds)
      ACTION: Increase the size of the SGA by setting the parameter
         "sga_target" to 345 M.


   ADDITIONAL INFORMATION:
      The value of parameter "sga_target" was "276 M" during the
analysis
      period.


   SYMPTOMS THAT LED TO THE FINDING:
      SYMPTOM: Wait class "User I/O" was consuming significant
database time.
               (21% impact [472 seconds])
```

```
        SYMPTOM: Hard parsing of SQL statements was consuming
significant
                    database time. (17% impact [390 seconds])
```

Some ways to run ADDM reports using Enterprise Manager are:

- On the **database home** page click on the **ADDM Findings** to see the current findings. To see the recommendations for the finding, click on the finding on the findings page.

- On the **database performance** page, click on **Run ADDM Now** to create a new snapshot and run ADDM on the previous to the new snapshot.

- Click on **Advisor Central** under **Related Links**. Click on **ADDM** and select **Run ADDM** to analyze past instance performance. Select the beginning and ending snapshot period. Click **OK** and on the next page click **View Report**.

You can also create ADDM reports from PL/SQL. Since AWR is on by default, it is simple to create a report from PL/SQL if you are more comfortable working this way. To create a report, log into PL/SQL as a SYS-DBA user and run the following PL/SQL script provided with Oracle:

```
SQL> @$ORACLE_HOME/rdbms/admin/addmrpt.sql

Current Instance
~~~~~~~~~~~~~~~~~

  DB Id      DB Name      Inst Num Instance
----------- ------------ -------- ------------
 550525798 ORCL2              1 orcl2


Instances in this Workload Repository schema
~~~~~~~~~~~~~~~~~~~~~~~~~~~~~~~~~~~~~~~~~~~~~~

  DB Id     Inst Num DB Name      Instance     Host
----------- -------- ------------ ------------ ------------
* 550525798        1 ORCL2        orcl2        dbhost

Using  550525798 for database Id
Using           1 for instance number
```

```
Specify the number of days of snapshots to choose from
~~~~~~~~~~~~~~~~~~~~~~~~~~~~~~~~~~~~~~~~~~~~~~~~~~~~~~~~~~~
Entering the number of days (n) will result in the most recent
(n) days of snapshots being listed.  Pressing <return> without
specifying a number lists all completed snapshots.


Listing the last 3 days of Completed Snapshots
                                              Snap
Instance     DB Name       Snap Id   Snap Started    Level
------------ ------------- --------- ------------------- -----
orcl2        ORCL2            3762 14 Mar 2006 00:00     1
                             3763 14 Mar 2006 01:00     1
                             3764 14 Mar 2006 02:00     1
                                :
                                :
                             3809 16 Mar 2006 08:00     1



Specify the Begin and End Snapshot Ids
~~~~~~~~~~~~~~~~~~~~~~~~~~~~~~~~~~~~~~~~~~~
Enter value for begin_snap: 3762
Begin Snapshot Id specified: 3762

Enter value for end_snap: 3809
End   Snapshot Id specified: 3809

Specify the Report Name
~~~~~~~~~~~~~~~~~~~~~~~~~
The default report file name is addmrpt_1_3762_3809.txt.  To use this name,
press <return> to continue, otherwise enter an alternative.

Enter value for report_name:

Using the report name addmrpt_1_3762_3809.txt

Running the ADDM analysis on the specified pair of snapshots ...

Generating the ADDM report for this analysis ...

          DETAILED ADDM REPORT FOR TASK 'TASK_16104' WITH ID 16104
          ----------------------------------------------------------
```

```
             Analysis Period: from 13-MAR-2006 11:41 to 15-MAR-2006 11:00
         Database ID/Instance: 550525798/1
       Database/Instance Names: ORCL2/orcl2
                     Host Name: dbhost
              Database Version: 10.2.0.1.0
                Snapshot Range: from 3762 to 3809
                 Database Time: 2253 seconds
          Average Database Load: 0 active sessions
```

~~~~~~

FINDING 1: 100% impact (2253 seconds)

Significant virtual memory paging was detected on the host operating system.

   RECOMMENDATION 1: Host Configuration, 100% benefit (2253 seconds)
      ACTION: Host operating system was experiencing significant paging but no
         particular root cause could be detected. Investigate processes that
         do not belong to this instance running on the host that are consuming
         significant amount of virtual memory. Also consider adding more
         physical memory to the host.

         :
         :
(More findings and recommendations)
~~~~~~

             ADDITIONAL INFORMATION

Wait class "Application" was not consuming significant database time.
Wait class "Commit" was not consuming significant database time.
Wait class "Configuration" was not consuming significant database time.
Wait class "Network" was not consuming significant database time.
Session connect and disconnect calls were not consuming significant database
time.

The database's maintenance windows were active during 33% of the analysis
period.

The analysis of I/O performance is based on the default assumption that the
average read time for one database block is 8000 micro-seconds.

An explanation of the terminology used in this report is available when you
run the report with the 'ALL' level of detail.

End of Report
Report written to addmrpt_1_3762_3809.txt

Note that ADDM will also give recommendations on other aspects of
your application and the system you are running on. For example, if there is
excessive swaping or paging it will recommend you try and find and eliminate
programs that are not being used. Some example recommendations are:

```
FINDING 1: 100% impact (2253 seconds)
-------------------------------------
Significant virtual memory paging was detected on the host operating system.

   RECOMMENDATION 1: Host Configuration, 100% benefit (2253 seconds)
      ACTION: Host operating system was experiencing significant paging but no
         particular root cause could be detected. Investigate processes that
         do not belong to this instance running on the host that are consuming
         significant amount of virtual memory. Also consider adding more
         physical memory to the host.
```

Another recommendation may relate to the SQL code you are using
(either directly or through a database connection). This recommendation
may look like the following:

```
FINDING 7: 2% impact (157 seconds)
----------------------------------
Time spent on the CPU by the instance was responsible for a substantial part
of database time.

   RECOMMENDATION 1: SQL Tuning, 2% benefit (157 seconds)
      ACTION: Tune the PL/SQL block with SQL_ID "7vd7gcsk3wkzs". Refer to the
         "Tuning PL/SQL Applications" chapter of Oracle's "PL/SQL User's Guide
         and Reference"
         RELEVANT OBJECT: SQL statement with SQL_ID 7vd7gcsk3wkzs
         DECLARE
         thmb ORDImage;
         dicomMD XMLType;
         ctx raw(1) := null;
```

```
BEGIN
load_dicom_image(1, 'SIRONA2.dcm');
SELECT thumb, dicomMeta INTO thmb, dicomMD FROM diagnosticImages
WHERE id = 1;
putMetaToFile(dicomMD, 'DICOMIMAGEDIR', 'dicomMeta.xml');
thmb.export(ctx,'file','DICOMIMAGEDIR','dicomThumb.jpg');
for i in 2..200 loop
load_dicom_image(i, 'SIRONA2.dcm');
SELECT thumb, dicomMeta INTO thmb, dicomMD FROM diagnosticImages
WHERE id = i;
commit;
end loop;
END;
```

With Enterprise Manager there is a link you can click on to view the SQL source that is being called out. You can also see the PL/SQL code in question. Note that this may not be a problem, but you can see what PL/SQL code is being used the most, and can concentrate on that.

12.3　Creating Tables with Media Data

In many cases, if not most cases, the best performance for applications that store the media data in the database (in BLOBS) is achieved when the media data is stored in its own tablespace. First, a tablespace must be created to store the media data. It is best to make this a large tablespace with large extension parameters so that the tablespace is not extended much, if at all, and if it has to be extended, it is done rarely.

From a user connected as SYSDBA, the following example creates such a tablespace:

```
SQL> CREATE TABLESPACE RAWIMG DATAFILE 'images.tbs'
        SIZE 40000M AUTOEXTEND ON NEXT 5000M;
```

Now that a tablespace is created, a normal user can create a table that stores the raw image data into the tablespace.

```
SQL> CREATE TABLE images (imageID INTEGER ,image
ORDSYS.ORDImage)
        LOB (image.source.localData) STORE AS
            (
```

```
     TABLESPACE RAWIMG
     CHUNK 32K
     NOCACHE NOLOGGING
     );
```

In this example, we also specify NOCACHE and NOLOGGING.

The NOCACHE parameter indicates the image should not be cached in the SGA. This is a typical setting for media, unless it is expected that the image will be used frequently.

The NOLOGGING specifies that raw image data should not be stored in the REDO log. This increases performance of inserts, and can increase the performance of bulk loading a table. Note that the lack of REDO logging makes it impossible for the administrator to fully restore the database from the REDO logs after a crash, so you may want to keep a copy of the bulk loaded files or a copy of the tablespace in the case of failure. You can turn on REDO logging after the table is bulk loaded with the following PL/SQL:

```
SQL> ALTER TABLE images MODIFY LOB (image.source.localData)
        ( NOCACHE LOGGING )
```

Another important parameter is the CHUNKSIZE parameter. This should be larger than the default. Clearly, because media data is larger than data that has traditionally been held in a database, it is more efficiently stored, written, and read when the chunksize is larger. Also note that Oracle maintains an index on each chunk of the LOB for random access to the LOB data. The larger the chunk size, the smaller the index overhead.

Other options to consider when creating a table are:

- INITIAL and NEXT parameters. These storage parameters indicate the initial size of the BLOB and how large extents should be. These should be larger than the chunk size. These parameters should be used if you have a relatively uniform media size that you can guess beforehand.

- PCTINCREASE parameter indicates the percent increase a BLOB should extend itself when the BLOB is being filled up piece by piece. This parameter should be set to zero. The default value is 50%, which will increase the BLOB size by 50% on each extension, which is usually too large an extension.

- DISABLE STORAGE IN ROW parameter is used to disable the media from being stored inline within a row. This is almost always advisable as having large BLOB data stored in the row can cause extra overhead in a full table scan. In any case, the largest segment that will be stored inline in a row is 4,000 bytes. Almost all media is larger than this. ENABLE STORAGE IN ROW is the default and should only be accepted if your media data is smaller than 4,000 bytes long.

- MAXEXTENTS sets the maximum number of extents for the BLOB. This should almost always be set to UNLIMITED to prevent fragmentation of the BLOB and to make sure the BLOB can extend itself to the maximum size necessary.

12.4 Distributing the I/O Load

Using a database to store media opens the door to database administration and load balancing techniques. To distribute I/O over a number of disks, so that a single or limited amount of disks does not become a bottleneck, can involve various techniques:

- Striping—distributing a database table I/O over a number of disks

- Automatic storage management (ASM)—automatic management of database storage

Striping is a technique to distribute I/O over a number of disks. This is done by distributing the data among a number of physical disk drives. This can be done by hardware, the operating system, the database, or a combination of any of these. We will concentrate on database striping here.

For example, a database table can be designed to place new records in a table randomly among a set of tablespaces on multiple disks. This will increase the I/O throughput of the database application. The table is partitioned onto a number of tablespaces. In the following example some tablespaces are created as a SYSDBA user.

```
create tablespace mediats1 datafile 'C:\mediats1.tbs' size 10000m;
create tablespace mediats2 datafile 'D:\mediats2.tbs' size 10000m;
create tablespace regts1 datafile 'C:\regts1.tbs' size 10m;
create tablespace regts2 datafile 'D:\regts2.tbs' size 10m;
```

- The mediats tablespaces are to be used to store large images. The regts tablespaces are to be used to store the thumbnail images and the relational data. This can make for less fragmentation of the relational data. If we want, we can also configure the database to be able to use larger block sizes for tablespaces and apply these larger block sizes, up to 32k, to the tablespace.

- Now we can create a table that will be randomly distributed between the tablespaces:

```
CREATE TABLE photosPartitioned
                (id           NUMBER PRIMARY KEY,
                 description VARCHAR2(40) NOT NULL,
                 location    VARCHAR2(40),
                 image       ORDSYS.ORDIMAGE,
                 thumb       ORDSYS.ORDIMAGE)
   LOB (image.source.localdata)
    STORE AS (disable storage in row nocache nologging chunk 32768)
   PARTITION BY HASH (id)
    (PARTITION p1 tablespace regts1
      LOB (image.source.localdata) store as (TABLESPACE mediats1),
     PARTITION p2 tablespace regts2
      LOB (image.source.localdata) store as (TABLESPACE mediats2)
   );
```

This table would now be split between disks C: and D:, and furthermore, the largest BLOBS would be in a separate tablespace from the relational data and thumbnail images.

Another option that is automatic, more flexible, and adapts by itself is automatic storage management (ASM). This will automate the distribution of I/O over a number of physical devices without intervention by a DBA. With ASM, the DBA creates a disk group from the operating system disks, and then database files are automatically created and managed by ASM.

ASM offers more than just striping information. It also provides an option to mirror data to help prevent data loss in the case of a disk failure.

12.5 Load Performance

The loading of data into the database may be a major concern. Consider the bank that needs to store a huge number of check images a day and then make them available for users to securely view them on the Web. In this instance, it may make sense to make use of transportable tablespaces. By using transportable tablespaces, a database that is not online can bulk load check images into a tablespace or tablespace set. When this tablespace or tablespace set is populated, it can simply be copied over to the online database and made part of the online check image table in a matter of seconds. Since this tablespace or tablespace set is populated by time, it is just as easy to remove the tablespace or tablespace set from the table when the amount of time that a check image can be viewed is exceeded. This is much quicker than deleting all the items individually based on the time they were inserted into the database. This tablespace or tablespace set can then be copied to an archive database if desired. An example of using transportable tablespaces is given in Chapter 6. This is an easy way to distribute the loading operation.

As pointed out before in this chapter, bulk loading performance can also be increased by turning off REDO logging when the data is being loaded. Remember that the downside of this is that there is no REDO log, so you may need another strategy, such as making a copy of the loaded tablespace or mirroring, to preserve your data in the case of computer storage failure.

Another way to increase bulk load performance from files is to partition a table among separate tablespaces on separate disks. The data fields can be on different disks as well. The bulk loading can then be done in parallel, with none of the physical disks contending with each other during the load operation for loading media (unless REDO logging is on, in which case there could be some contention for the REDO log).

For a parallel loading example, the following is done in a SYSDBA authorized account:

```
create or replace directory IMG_SRC1 as 'x:\images';
grant read on directory IMG_SRC1 to scott;
create or replace directory IMG_SRC2 as 'y:\images';
grant read on directory IMG_SRC2 to scott;

create tablespace mts1 datafile 'C:\mts1.tbs' size 100000m;
create tablespace mts2 datafile 'D:\mts2.tbs' size 100000m;

create tablespace ts1 datafile 'C:\ts1.tbs' size 100m;
create tablespace ts2 datafile 'D:\ts2.tbs' size 100m;
```

This creates two image source directories on two separate disk drives. It also creates two partitions each on two separate disk drives. On each drive with partitions, one partition is for the relational data and one partition is for the media, both thumbnail and original image in this case.

The stage is now set to create the table in the SCOTT schema:

```
CREATE TABLE photosPart
                (id          NUMBER PRIMARY KEY,
                 description VARCHAR2(40) NOT NULL,
                 location    VARCHAR2(40),
                 image       ORDSYS.ORDIMAGE,
                 thumb       ORDSYS.ORDIMAGE)
  LOB (image.source.localdata)
    STORE AS (disable storage in row nocache nologging chunk 32K)
  LOB (thumb.source.localdata)
    STORE AS (disable storage in row nocache nologging chunk 8K)
  PARTITION BY RANGE(id)
  (PARTITION p1 VALUES LESS THAN (1000000) TABLESPACE ts1
        LOB (image.source.localdata) store as (TABLESPACE mts1)
        LOB (thumb.source.localdata) store as (TABLESPACE mts1),
   PARTITION p2 VALUES LESS THAN (MAXVALUE) TABLESPACE ts2
        LOB (image.source.localdata) store as (TABLESPACE mts2)
        LOB (thumb.source.localdata) store as (TABLESPACE mts2)
  );
```

This table puts the BLOBS into the tablespaces created for the BLOBS, and the relational data in the tablespaces created for the relational data. Also, the table is partitioned by range, so that we can load the partitions on the two physical disks independently.

Now it is possible to load the table in parallel, without contention for one disk drive. Each of the following BEGIN ... END blocks would be performed in separate sessions executing at the same time. In a real application, the loading would load multiple images in each of the two sessions:

```
BEGIN
  load_part_image(1, 'Nice picture', 'Somewhere',
                     'IMG_SRC1', 'loon.jpg');
END;
/
```

```
BEGIN
  load_part_image(1000001, 'Nicer picture', 'Somewhere Else',
                  'IMG_SRC1', 'goldfinch.jpg');
END;
/
```

These same principles can be applied to other loading methodologies, such as using external tables. In this case, there would be multiple external tables whose data is on separate physical disks. A procedure for each external table would be used in separate sessions to load the data into the database.

The data stored or retrieved in *inter*Media BLOBS is typically (almost always) done in a fashion where the entire BLOB is read or written at once (sometimes called check-in check-out), so for the most part considerations on reading and writing pieces of the BLOB do not apply in *inter*Media applications. One noteworthy exception to this is when a streaming server streams an audio or video file from the database. However, since plug-ins for streaming servers are written for you, you may only have to consider these if you write your own streaming server plug-in.

12.6 Performance Tools

As mentioned before in this chapter, your best performance friend is the combination of Automatic Workload Repository (AWR) and Automatic Database Diagnostic Monitor (ADDM). Using these tools, especially in combination with Enterprise Manager, makes it easy to tune your database.

Other tools exist for optimizing PL/SQL code. If it is thought that a particular PL/SQL is taking many resources, as identified by ADDM, this PL/SQL code can be analyzed with the SQL Tuning Advisor.

12.7 Delivery on the Web

After any database issues have been resolved, it may then be time to look at the middle tier or application server. Again, your best friend here is Enterprise Manager.

Note that as in many of the samples in this book, the most efficient delivery of data is data that is not delivered. Make use of the browser cache when possible. This is done by setting an expires tag, Etag tag, or the cache-control max-age directive, like in a media response, and by returning a NOT-MODIFIED HTTP response to an HTTP conditional request.

Another place to look for performance improvements on the Web is by the use of Oracle Cache. The application can control how Oracle Cache, or any other cache mechanism along the HTTP path, handles media by setting the HTTP header cache-control field. The cache-control directives specify how and if the media is cached. This would offload the handling of HTTP responses for media from the HTTP server that the media is delivered from.

12.8 Backup

Storing media in the database greatly simplifies the data for a multimedia system as a consistent backup. In the case of previous implementations, using a combination of database and media files, it is difficult to keep the metadata in the database consistent with the raw data in multimedia data files. In this hybrid system, there must be two backups, one for the database and one for the media files. It could also be near impossible to do a consistent online backup while the system is running.

The database offers a myriad of strategies for backing up data and making this backup consistent and efficient for both full and incremental backups. Recovery Manager (RMAN) is used to make physical backups of a database. Logical backups of a database can be done with Oracle Data Pump. RMAN can be accessed through PL/SQL commands as well as through the Oracle Enterprise Manager GUI.

Some of the database facilities that can be used are:

- Full and incremental backups.
- Backup to disk or tape.
- Applying an incremental backup to a full backup on disk to make a more up-to-date full backup.
- Backup and recovery information can be stored on ASM-managed devices that can be mirrored for data loss protection and striped for better performance.
- Block change tracking (BTC) to keep track of blocks that change so that incremental backups are made much faster.

■ The ability to partition data into transportable tablespaces based on time to allow for backing up tablespace set files directly.

Of course, multimedia information takes much more storage space than traditional data. As with any backup strategy, it should be tested and benchmarked to make sure the performance goals in terms of how long it takes to backup the database and how long it takes to restore a database are met.

12.9 Summary

To get the best performance from your *inter*Media application, it is necessary to consider all aspects of the system. Loading data, backing up data and application performance are potential targets for tuning. It is important to tune the database with *inter*Media in mind, but the other layers such as the application and/or mid-tier layer should be considered.

The database has automated techniques to help tune the database parameters to their optimal values. Tables can be designed to spread I/O over multiple physical disks so that a single physical device does not become a bottleneck.

13

Advanced Queries

13.1 Introduction

The ability to retrieve and manipulate data and obtain information from a rich-media database is, of course, a long-term essential objective for information systems. However, this objective is very challenging. All humans are naturally good at understanding multimedia information, recalling audio and visual images, and linking complex information together. The way in which the human visual system in the brain is able to do this is not well understood although clearly this involves a number of transformations to the data received by the sensory systems in the brain. In contrast, people have to spend years learning how to deal with text, spoken and written. However, text is much easier for computers to deal with because it can be structured to a much greater extent than other media. This is the reason why metadata is very important in media retrieval. Therefore, it is not surprising that achieving content-based retrieval is difficult in practice and requires an effective user interface as well as advanced database capabilities. It also only works for restricted sets of images and with tightly specified requirements.

Oracle *inter*Media provides both a framework to handle the multimedia data objects in Oracle DBMS and a set of tools for content-based image retrieval (CBIR) functionalities. CBIR for video and audio is less well developed. CBIR capabilities can be explored through the StillImage object type introduced in Chapter 3.

13.2 Content-based Image Retrieval in *inter*Media

A primary benefit of using content-based retrieval (CBR) is reduced time and effort required to obtain media-based information but it also allows us to develop new application areas. It is possible to take the simplest approach and annotate the image object with text metadata based on a human being's perception of the image but there are still no standards for developing image descriptions. Photographic images tend not to be self-identifying since the information usually available for text objects, such as title, author, abstract, list of contents, etc., is often not available, although the new digital camera standard will increasingly provide this kind of metadata.

Content-based retrieval is being developed to try to overcome some of these difficulties since very large sets of images are being developed. CBR implies a system with the ability to search based on the user's association of an impression of the media object. Progress in this technology has been limited, especially with audio, but we can still look forward to being able to hum a tune and then obtain from the computer a sample and all the details of the artist, etc. Therefore, for the time being this chapter will focus on image retrieval using the StillImage object type.

The similarity between two images arises because they have similar appearances. This may be the result of several factors, such as color, texture, and orientation. Therefore, one approach is to break down an image into these factors and compare the factors separately.

An image can then be represented by a collection of low-level features, such as color, texture, shape, and spatial relationships (i.e., location information) that can be extracted from the image. These features are then used during query processing to compute the similarity between a sample image provided or selected by a user and the images in a database. The result set consists of a set of similar images rather than a specific result and would require the end user to review and probably refine the output. This is one of the reasons why the design of the user interface is crucial. The system then processes the information contained in image data and creates abstractions of its content in terms of visual attributes.

*inter*Media will support ABR, TBR, and CBR but as we already know these are difficult to achieve. Therefore, the best strategy is usually to combine these approaches in designing an application. We can specify text columns to describe the semantic significance of the image (e.g., that the pictured automobile won a particular award, or that its engine has six or eight cylinders) and use the StillImage object type to permit content-based queries based on intrinsic attributes of the image (for example, how closely its color and shape match a picture of a specific automobile).

When frequent adding and updating of images is needed in massive databases, it is often not practical to require manual entry of all attributes that might be needed for ABR queries, so content-based retrieval provides increased flexibility and practical value. CBIR is also useful in providing the ability to query attributes such as texture or shape that are difficult to represent using text metadata. A *feature* is an attribute derived from transforming the original visual object by using an image analysis algorithm. A feature characterizes a specific property of the image such as its color. Usually a feature is represented by a set of numbers often called a *feature vector.*

The visual query mode (Chapter 11) involves matching the input image to preextracted features of real or idealized objects. Query processing using a visual mode is based on matching a vector of the sample image's features with those of other images in the database. The methods used depend on the type of image. Many query operations deal solely with this abstraction rather than with the image itself. Thus, every image inserted into the database needs to be analyzed first, and a compact representation of its content stored in a feature vector.

The preextracted features can be held in the database using the StillImage object type. The purpose of the feature extraction is to extract a set of numerical features that remove redundancy from the image and reduces its dimension. A well-selected feature set will have useful information that defines the information that discriminated the image from its collection.

The objective is to use very simple computations on low-level features of an image, such as color, to recognize the actual content. These features are used to compute the similarity between a picture selected by a user and the images in a database. Table 13.1 lists some of the features extracted. The

Table 13.1 *Feature Extraction Techniques*

Feature	Main Technique/Measure/Filter	Supported by *inter*Media
Color	Color histogram	Yes
Texture	Luminosity, image intensity	Yes
Shape	Aspect ratio, moments, boundaries	Yes (Not SQL/MM)
Position	Spatial coordinates	Yes
Appearance	Curvature and orientation	Not yet

most commonly used features for CBIR are shape, color, and texture.

These object types offer the database designer an alternative to defining image-related attributes in columns separate from the image. The database designer can create a specialized composite data type that combines an

SI.StillImage object and the appropriate text, numeric, and date attributes. Oracle *inter*Media not only allows the media data, like images, to be stored in the database table, but also allows the features of the images to be stored inside the database table as well.

For example, the feature vector of an image can be extracted by segmenting the image into regions based on color. Each region can be associated with color, texture, and shape information. One way to improve its retrieval is to crop images so that background noise is removed and the object of interest occupies the main part of the image.

Figure 13.1
*Image with
corresponding
color histogram.*

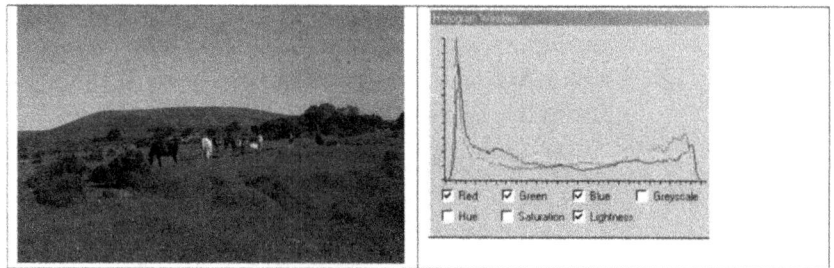

It is useful to consider the following visual attributes:

- **Color** represents the distribution of colors within the entire image. This distribution represents the amounts of each color. Each image added to the collection is analyzed to compute a *color histogram* (see Figure 13.1) that reflects the proportion of pixels of each basic color (red, green, blue) within the image. The color histogram for each image is then stored in the database. The user would not query the database by specifying the desired proportion of each color (e.g., 75% green and 25% red), rather the user submits an example image from which an image signature containing its color histogram is also calculated. The matching process then retrieves a set of images whose color attributes most closely match those of the query. The color attribute based on the histogram alone is independent of many imaging conditions, such as orientation of a scene or relative position of particular scene elements. However, problems could result because image colors depend on the lighting condition (shown in Figure 13.1). Small variations in lighting can lead to indexing problems. Color and position attributes specified together reflect the color distributions and where they occur in the image.

- **Location** represents the positions of the shape components, color, and texture components. For example, the color blue could be expected to be located in the top half of a landscape image. A certain texture could be located in the bottom right corner of the image. Using spatial location is one of the oldest image retrieval methods and is an essential aspect of geographical information systems and biological systems. However, to exploit this method the image collections must contain objects in defined spatial relationships with each other.

- **Texture** represents the low-level patterns and textures within the image, such as graininess or smoothness. Unlike shape, texture is very sensitive to features that appear with great frequency in the image. The ability to match on texture similarity can often distinguish between areas of images with similar color (such as sky and sea, or leaves and grass). The method uses pixel intensity values that result from the reflection of light from illuminated surfaces or the transmission of light through translucent media. This variation is the result of the nature of the illumination and the topography of the surface. The two-dimensional arrangement of the intensities defines the visual texture of the image. A variety of techniques have been used for measuring texture similarity based on statistical analysis. Essentially, these calculate and compare the relative brightness of selected *pairs* of pixels from the query image to the other images, each in turn. From these it is possible to calculate measures of image texture, such as the degree of *directionality* and *regularity*, or *periodicity*. This process is proposed for comparing iris images to identify people for security purposes.

- **Shape** represents the shapes that appear in the image, as determined by color-based segmentation techniques. A shape is characterized by a region of uniform color. The ability to retrieve by shape involves giving the shape of an object a quantitative description that can be used to match other images. Unlike texture, shape is a fairly well-defined concept, and there is considerable evidence that in the brain natural objects are primarily recognized by their shape. The process involves computing a number of features characteristic of an object's shape that are independent of its size or orientation. These features are then computed for every object identified within each stored image. Shape and location specified together compare the location of the shapes in the images. The SQL/MM StillImage standard does not support image retrieval based on shape.

13.3   Retrieval Process—Precision and Recall

Images in the database can be retrieved using the visual–visual mode queries by matching them with a comparison image. The comparison image can be any image inside or outside the current database, a sketch drawn by the user, an algorithmically generated image, and so forth. The comparison is not based on an exact match as in the case of SQL traditional data types. Instead the similarity of the images is evaluated for each of the three visual attributes (color, location, texture). A very difficult issue in image retrieval using visual mode is determining the relevance of each image in a result set to the query image. Ideally, the process would not miss any relevant images and not return any irrelevant ones. The quality of the retrieval process in terms of text retrieval is well established and can be measured in terms of two metrics, namely *recall* and *precision*. Recall is a measure of how well the retrieval engine performs in finding relevant objects. The recall of a system is defined as how much of the information that ideally could have been retrieved or extracted by the system was in fact retrieved or extracted by the system.

Precision is a measure of how well the engine performs in not returning irrelevant images. If every image is relevant the precision is 100%. The precision of a system is defined as how much of the information that ideally could have been retrieved or extracted by the system belongs to the information that should have been retrieved or extracted by the system. The retrieval engine must balance recall against precision. High precision means few unwanted media objects are retrieved, while low recall means many relevant objects are missed.

We can measure the similarity for each visual attribute of an image by calculating the **score** or ***distance*** between the two images with respect to that attribute. It is convenient to define the score to range from 0.00 (no difference) to 100.0 (maximum possible difference). Thus, the more similar two images are with respect to a particular visual attribute, the *smaller* the score will be for that attribute.

As an example of how distance could be used, assume that the dots in Figure 13.2 represent scores for three images with respect to two visual attributes, such as color and texture, plotted along the x-axis and y-axis of a graph. Suppose the user specifies Image 1 as the example and we want to locate similar images (recall) that are as close as possible to the sample image (precision). For matching, Image 1 is the comparison image, and Images 2 and 3 are each being compared with Image 1. We can see that Images 2 and 3 are both roughly equidistant from Image 1, but with respect to the color attribute plotted on the x-axis, the distance between Image 1 and Image 2 is relatively small (e.g., 15), whereas the distance between Image 1 and Image 3 is much greater (e.g., 50). If the color attribute is given more weight, then the fact that the two distance values differ by a great deal will probably be very important in determining whether or not Image 2 and Image 3 match Image 1. However, if color is minimized and the texture attribute is emphasized instead, then Image 3 will match Image 1 better than Image 2 matches Image 1.

Figure 13.2
*Similarity over
visual attributes.*

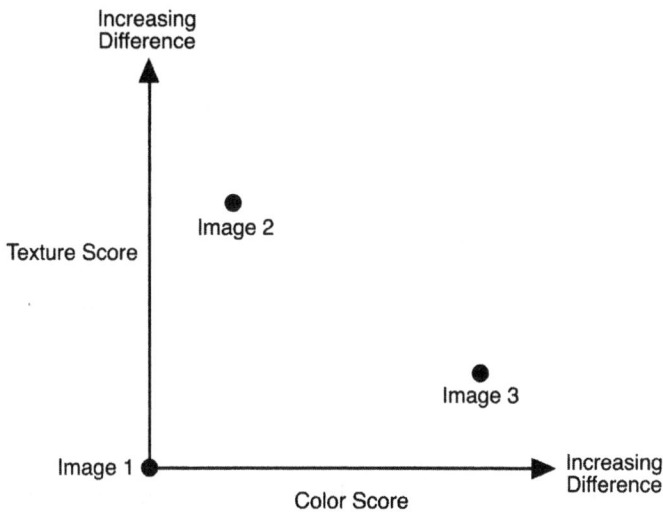

If we measured the distance just between Image 1 and Image 2 on three visual attributes we would get the result shown in Table 13.2. In this theoretical example, the two images are most similar with respect to texture (distance = 5) and most different with respect to positional color (distance = 50).

Table 13.2 *Distances for Visual Attributes between Image 1 and Image 2, Figure 13.3*

Visual Attribute	Distance
Color	15
Texture	5
Positional Color	50

In Figure 13.3 there are two very different images but we can see that some areas of color and texture in both images are similar by viewing the histograms.

Figure 13.3
*Images and color
histograms.*

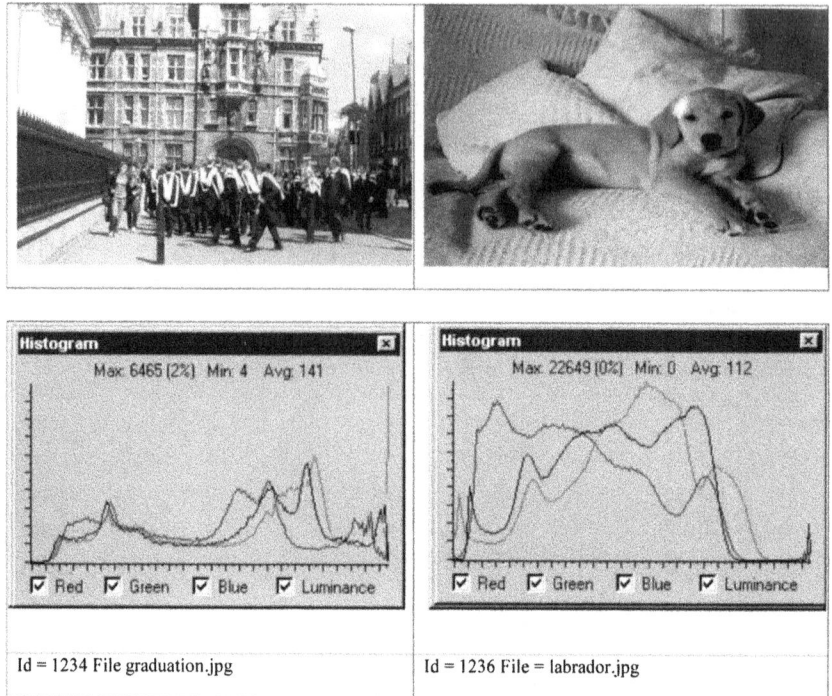

The result of using the different visual attributes as the basis for comparison is shown in Table 13.3. Looking at the distance score we can see that the images are considered most similar in terms of texture but most different in terms of color. The table gives information about the distance when the visual attributes are given different weightings. Before we consider how these results were obtained we need to deal with the concept of *weightings*.

Table 13.3   *Distances for Visual Attributes between Images 1234 and 1236*

Visual Attribute	Weightings Used	Distance
Color	1.0,0,0,0	26.9861
Texture	0,1.0,0,0	14.8712
Positional Color	0.1,0,0,1.0	18.7703

Each **weight** value reflects how sensitive the matching process for a given attribute should be to the degree of similarity or dissimilarity between two images. For example, if we want color to be completely ignored in matching, we would assign a weight of 0.0 to color; in this case, any similarity or difference between the color of the two images is totally irrelevant in matching. In Table 13.3 the value for texture is 14.8712 where color is set at 0.0. On the other hand, if color is extremely important, we would assign it a weight greater than any of the other attributes; this will cause any similarity or dissimilarity between the two images with respect to color to contribute greatly to whether or not the two images match, so a value of 26.9861 is shown in Table 13.3. These results suggest the images are closest in terms of texture and furthest apart in terms of position.

When all attributes were set at 0.25 or 1.0 (i.e., equal weighting) the score (i.e., similarity) of the two images in Figure 13.3 is 23.2217. How have these similarity values been derived?

Assume that for the matching process, the following weights have been assigned to each visual attribute:

- Color = 0.7

- Texture = 0.2

- Position = 0.1

The weights are supplied in the range of 0.0 to 1.0. Within this range, a weight of 1.0 indicates the strongest emphasis, and a weight of 0.0 means the attribute should be ignored. The values you supply are automatically normalized such that the weights total 1.0, still maintaining the ratios supplied. In this example, the weights specified meant that normalization was not necessary.

The following formula is used to calculate the weighted sum of the distances, which is used to determine the degree of similarity between two images:

```
weighted_sum =   color_weight    * color_distance +
                 texture_weight  * texture_distance +
                 position_weight   * position_distance
```

The degree of similarity between two images in this case is computed as:

```
0.7* color_distance + 0.2* texture_distance +
0.1* position_distance
```

Suppose we obtain distance scores of 15 for color, 5 for texture, and 50 for position, then using these values, the overall distance can be calculated as:

$$(0.7*15 + 0.2*5 + 0.1*50) = (10.5 + 1.0 + 5.0) = 16.5$$

To illustrate the effect of different weights in this case, assume that the weights for color and shape were reversed. In this case, the degree of similarity between two images is computed as:

0.1*color_distance + 0.2*texture_distance + 0.7*position_distance

That is:

$$(0.1*15 + 0.2*5 + 0.7*50) = (1.5 + 1.0 + 35.0) = 37.5$$

In this second case, the images are considered to be less similar than in the first case, because the overall score (37.5) is greater than in the first case (16.5).

13.4 Using SQL/MM StillImage for CBIR

The SI_StillImage object types form a complex interrelated group that exploit many of the features of object-relational database theory. The SI_StillImage object type can be used to store actual image data together with standard image metadata, such as height, width, format, etc. There are six object types that represent image features that could be used for CBIR:

- Color types:
  - Color
  - Average Color
  - Color Histogram
  - Positional Color
- Texture

In addition, there is an object type, SI_FeatureList, that represents an image as a composite feature based on the above with associated feature weights.

There are three object types that represent image features that could be used for CBIR object types for the color values, the average color feature, and the color histogram. As you can imagine this abundance of object types makes CBIR complex (see Table 13.4).

Table 13.4 *Object Types for CBIR*

Object Type	Purpose
SI_AverageColor	Describes the average color of an image. The image is divided into *n* samples, the R,G,B values of the samples are summed and divided by the number of samples
SI_Color	Encapsulates color values of an image in terms of its R,G,B values as integers in range 0 to 255
SI_ColorHistogram	Describes relative frequencies of image colors in terms of arrays of colors of object-type SI_Color, and their frequencies in range 0 to 100
SI_Texture	Describes texture of an image in terms of coarseness, contrast, and directionality
SI_PositionalColor	Describes an image in terms of most significant colors in relation to position within an image
SI_FeatureList	Describes an image as a composite feature based on SI_AverageColor, SI_ColorHistogram, SI_Texture, and SI_PositionalColor, and their associated weights

A public synonym has been created for each StillImage object type so that we do not need to specify the ORDSYS schema name when we use these object types in SQL procedures and functions, for example, SI_MKAvgClr(). In addition, there is a set of views accessible to the public that give useful information about these object types. It makes good sense to check these out before deciding to employ the SI_StillImage object types for CBIR.

- SI_IMAGE_FORMAT—gives a list of image formats supported by the type

- SI_IMAGE_FORMAT_CONVERSIONS—gives a list of source formats supported by the image conversion operations and the corresponding target formats

- SI_IMAGE_FORMAT_FEATURES—gives a list of the image format and the CBIR features that are supported by the format (e.g., SI_TEXTURE)

- SI_THUMBNAIL_FORMAT—gives a list of image formats from which thumbnail images can be derived that are supported by the type

In Chapter 3 we introduced the following table:

```
CREATE TABLE photos_SI
(id            NUMBER PRIMARY KEY,
              description VARCHAR2(40) NOT NULL,
              location    VARCHAR2(40),
              image       SI_StillImage,
              thumb       SI_StillImage)
```

The SI_StillImage has a number of methods that are useful for image processing that we can illustrate with this table.

SI_ClearFeatures() should be used when we know we do not want to do image matching as clearing the image features can improve performance for other operations because the image features, such as color histograms and texture, are synchronized with changes to the image.

SI_InitFeatures() is a related method that extracts image features and caches them in the SI_StillImage object. The method only needs to be called once as afterward every time an image is processed, new image features will be automatically extracted.

SI_RetainFeatures checks whether the features have been extracted.

SI_Content() returns the BLOB stored in the content_SI attribute of the SI_StillImage object.

```
CREATE OR REPLACE PROCEDURE still_content
AS
myimage  SI_StillImage;
photo    BLOB;
BEGIN
   SELECT image INTO myimage FROM photos_SI
   WHERE id = 1235;
   photo := myimage.SI_Content;
END;
```

SI_SetContent() updates the content of an SI_StillImage object as well as setting the value of its attributes (content_SI, contentLength, height_SI, width_SI).

```
CREATE OR REPLACE PROCEDURE still_setcontent
AS
   Newlob  blob;
   fils    BFILE := BFILENAME('PHOTO_DIR','raven.bmp');
   myimage    SI_StillImage;
BEGIN
--use temporary BLOB
   DBMS_LOB.CREATETEMPORARY(newlob, TRUE);
   DBMS_LOB.fileopen(fils, DBMS_LOB.file_readonly);
   DBMS_LOB.LOADFROMFILE(newlob, fils,
DBMS_LOB.GETLENGTH(fils));
   DBMS_LOB.FILECLOSE(fils);
--select row for update
 SELECT image INTO myimage FROM photos_SI
 WHERE id = 1235 FOR UPDATE;
                 myimage.SI_SetContent(newlob);
--update table
    UPDATE photos_si SET
 Image = myimage WHERE id = 1235;
   DBMS_LOB.FREETEMPORARY(newlob);
   COMMIT;
END;
```

13.4.1 Image Matching

We can use the object types set out in Table 13.4 in image-matching operations. For color, when using SI_AverageColor object type, there are two specialized methods available:

- SI_AverageColor(sourceimage)—derives an SI_AverageColor value.

- SI_Score(sourceimage)—determines the score of a specified image when compared with an SI_AverageColor object and returns a value between 0, identical images, and 100, no match. Note that this method will return NULL if the value of the image.SI_Content was NULL.

The next procedure illustrates the use of the SI_AverageColor() method

```
CREATE OR REPLACE PROCEDURE still_averageColor
AS
myimage      SI_StillImage;
myAvgColor   SI_AverageColor;

BEGIN
    SELECT image INTO myimage FROM photos_SI
    WHERE id = 1235;
    myAvgColor := NEW SI_AverageColor(myimage);
END;
```

We have an SI_AverageColor object as a result of executing the procedure but we need to add some statements to get the score from matching two images:

```
CREATE OR REPLACE PROCEDURE match_averageColor
AS
score        DOUBLE PRECISION;
myimage      SI_StillImage;
other_image  SI_StillImage;
myAvgColor   SI_AverageColor;

BEGIN
   SELECT image INTO myimage FROM photos_SI
   WHERE id = 1234;
   myAvgColor := NEW SI_AverageColor(myimage);
SELECT image INTO other_image FROM photos_SI
   WHERE id = 1235;
   Score := myAvgColor.SI_Score(other_image);
   DBMS_OUTPUT.PUT_LINE('Score is ' || score);
END;
```

This time when we compare the same images as before (the raven and the robin) using the color histograms we get a slightly different result:

```
SQL> execute score_ColorHistogram;
Score is 31.173184375
```

We can use this with a .bmp file format but not with .psp because the average color feature cannot then be determined. A list of supported file formats can be found in the *inter*Media Reference Manual in Table B-1.

13.4.2 For Color Matching—Using SI_ColorHistogram Object Type

Using the color histogram should give a more reliable result than just using average color values. This object type has two attributes:

- SI_ColorsList as an array of colors (check SI_VALUES view for maximum size)

- SI_FrequenciesList as an array of color frequencies

However, it is recommended to use the methods rather than the attributes of this object type. We can use the SI_ColorHistogram(image) method to generate a color histogram for the image specified, provided the image is on the supported list. First we need to alter the photos_SI table to add a column to hold the color histogram when it's been generated.

```
ALTER TABLE photos_SI ADD(COLOR_HISTOGRAM SI_ColorHistogram);

CREATE OR REPLACE PROCEDURE store_ColorHistogram
AS
myimage      SI_StillImage;
myColorHist SI_ColorHistogram;
BEGIN
 SELECT image INTO myimage FROM photos_SI
 WHERE id = 1235 FOR UPDATE;
 myColorHist:= NEW SI_ColorHistogram(myimage);
 UPDATE photos_SI SET color_histogram = myColorHist
WHERE id = 1235;
COMMIT;
DBMS_OUTPUT.PUT_LINE('Update completed');
END;
```

Now that we have the color histogram of the image we can use this in matching using another object method called SI_Score(image) from the SI_ColorHistogram object type. This will compare two color histograms and return a value between 0, identical, and 100, no match. Note that this method will return NULL if the value of the image.SI_Content is NULL. We can also use SI_ScoreByClrHstgr() as an SQL function that accepts a color histogram object as the argument.

```
CREATE OR REPLACE PROCEDURE score_ColorHistogram
AS
myimage         SI_StillImage;
myColorHist     SI_ColorHistogram;
other_image     SI_StillImage;
score           DOUBLE PRECISION;
BEGIN
 SELECT image INTO myimage FROM photos_SI
 WHERE id = 1236;
 myColorHist:= NEW SI_ColorHistogram(myimage);
SELECT image INTO other_image FROM photos_SI
 WHERE id = 1235;
myColorHist := NEW SI_ColorHistogram(myimage);
score := SI_ScoreByClrHstgr(myColorHist,other_image);
DBMS_OUTPUT.PUT_LINE('Score is' || score);
END;
```

This time when we compare the same images as before (the raven and the robin) using the color histograms we get a slightly different result:

```
SQL> execute score_ColorHistogram;
Score is31.173184375
```

We can also use this method with color histogram data that has already been stored in the attributes of the image as is illustrated in the next procedure.

```
CREATE OR REPLACE PROCEDURE match_ColorHistogram
AS
myimage         SI_StillImage;
myColorHist     SI_ColorHistogram;
other_image     SI_StillImage;
score           DOUBLE PRECISION;
BEGIN
 SELECT color_histogram INTO myColorHist FROM photos_SI
 WHERE id = 1235;
```

```
SELECT image INTO other_image FROM photos_SI
 WHERE id = 1236;
score := SI_ScoreByClrHstgr(myColorHist,other_image);
DBMS_OUTPUT.PUT_LINE('Score is '|| score);
END;


SQL> execute match_ColorHistogram;
Score is 31.173184375
```

The score can range from 0 to 100. A value of 0 means that the color histogram of the specified image and the SI_ColorHistogram object instance are identical. A NULL value is returned if any one of the following is true:

- The value of the SI_ColorHistogram object instance is NULL.

- The value of the specified image is NULL.

- The value of image.SI_Content is NULL.

- The value of the color histogram feature is not supported for the format of the specified image.

But if it executes without generating a score? The score is NULL.

As we may want to use the other features and store them, we can modify the photos_SI table to add columns to hold the four feature types as follows:

```
ALTER TABLE photos_SI ADD (average_color    SI_AverageColor,
                Positional_Color SI_PositionalColor,
                Texture          SI_Texture,
                Feature_List     SI_FeatureList);
```

The facility that is most related to the ORDImageSignature object type is SI_FeatureList. This specifies an object containing up to four of the basic features and associated weights. The weight specifies the importance of the feature during image matching. Each weight can have a value between 0.0 and 1.0, where 0.0 indicates the feature should not be considered. Thus, the object type has four attributes corresponding to average color, color histogram, texture, and positional color each with a DOUBLE PRECISION weight. However, we usually use the object methods rather than the attributes. There is a constructor method called SI_FeatureList() with an equivalent SQL function called SI_MKFtrList() with a list of input parameters for the four features and weights that can be used as follows:

```
CREATE OR REPLACE PROCEDURE Still_features
AS
myimage          SI_StillImage;
myColorHist      SI_ColorHistogram; -- WEIGHTING 0.35
myAvgColor       SI_AverageColor; -- WEIGHTING 0.25
myPosColor       SI_PositionalColor; -- WEIGHTING 0.10
myTexture        SI_Texture; -- WEIGHTING 0.50
myFeatures       SI_FeatureList;
other_image      SI_StillImage;

BEGIN
    SELECT image INTO myimage FROM photos_SI
    WHERE id = 1235 FOR UPDATE;
    myColorHist :=SI_ColorHistogram(myimage);
myAvgColor := SI_AverageColor(myimage);
myPosColor := SI_PositionalColor(myimage);
myTexture  := SI_Texture(myimage);
myFeatures := NEW SI_FeatureList(myAvgColor, 0.25,
myColorHist, 0.35, myPosColor, 0.10,
myTexture, 0.50);

UPDATE photos_SI SET feature_list = myFeatures
    WHERE id = 1235;
COMMIT;
END;
```

If we want to use the SQL function we would change the myFeatures assignment statement to

```
myFeatures := SI_MkFtrList(myAvgColor, 0.25,
myColorHist, 0.35, myPosColor, 0.10, myTexture, 0.50)
```

For image matching we would use the SI_Score() method for the SI_FeatureList. This operator determines and returns the score of a specified image compared with a given SI_FeatureList value. The lower the returned score value, the better the image is characterized by the

SI_FeatureList object used for scoring the image. The return score value is computed as follows.

Let n be the number of non-NULL feature attributes of the FeatureList object to which you are applying the method. For i ranging from 1 to n, let f_i be the feature attribute and W_i be the value of the corresponding feature weight. The result is the sum of f_i.SI_Score(image) * W_i divided by the sum of W_i. The process by which the score value is determined can also be described by the following expression:

$$\frac{\sum_{i=1}^{n} f_i.\text{SI SCORE(image)} \cdot W_i}{\sum_{i=1}^{n} W_i}$$

A DOUBLE PRECISION value between 0 and 100 is returned. A value of 0 means that the image is identical to the FeatureList object. A value of 100 means that the image is completely different from the FeatureList object.

```
CREATE OR REPLACE PROCEDURE Score_features
AS
myimage      SI_StillImage;
myFeatures   SI_FeatureList;
score        DOUBLE PRECISION;

BEGIN
    SELECT feature_list INTO myfeatures FROM photos_SI
    WHERE id = 1235;
SELECT image INTO myimage FROM photos_SI
    WHERE id = 1235;
Score := myFeatures.SI_Score(myimage);
DBMS_OUTPUT.PUT_LINE( 'Score is ' || score);
END;

SQL> execute Score_features;
Score is 0
```

Internal helper types are created in the ORDSYS schema and do not have public synonyms. The internal helper types are the following.

colorsList

The syntax for this internal helper type is:

```
CREATE OR REPLACE TYPE colorsList AS VARRAY(100) OF SI_Color;
```

This internal helper type is used to specify the SI_ColorsList attribute of the SI_ColorHistogram object type as described.

colorFrequenciesList

The syntax for this internal helper type is:

```
CREATE OR REPLACE TYPE colorFrequenciesList AS VARRAY(100) OF
DOUBLE PRECISION;
```

This internal helper type is used to specify the SI_FrequenciesList attribute of the SI_ColorHistogram object type as described.

colorPositions

The syntax for this internal helper type is:

```
CREATE OR REPLACE TYPE colorPositions AS VARRAY(9) OF
SI_Color;
```

This internal helper type is used to specify the SI_ColorPositions attribute of the SI_PositionalColor object type as described.

textureEncoding

The syntax for this internal helper type is:

```
CREATE OR REPLACE TYPE textureEncoding AS VARRAY(5) of DOUBLE
PRECISION;
```

This internal helper type is used to specify the SI_TextureEncoding attribute of the SI_Texture object type as described.

13.5 Summary

The rich semantic nature of multimedia data creates difficulties for information retrieval that require the application of advanced techniques. Although queries can be carried out based on attributes and text annotation, the goal is to achieve content-based retrieval. In this chapter we introduced several techniques that can be used to support multimedia queries.

In present-day image applications the main process involved is to identify various features (color, texture, shape, etc.) of all the images in the database and to use these features to classify the images into groups. This has led to the development of a framework for image retrieval that we have seen several examples of in the practical exercises. It can be summarized as follows.

1. Index images by their content while avoiding the segmentation and recognition issues. Several attributes such as color, texture, shape, and appearance can be associated with image content.

2. Apply operators to extract features that measure statistical properties of the selected attribute.

3. Compile features into representations of images. An image is replaced by its feature representation (e.g., color histogram) for the purposes of retrieval.

4. Retrieve in a query-by-example fashion. A user selects an image as a query and its representation is compared with those in the collection to obtain a ranked list of images.

14

Streaming Audio and Video

14.1 Introduction

Streaming is used to deliver, and simultaneously view, time-based media. Time-based media includes video and audio. Other kinds of presentations include play lists of audio or video, or perhaps image slide shows expressed in a markup language that specifies when they should be displayed.

The alternative to streaming media is download and play. In this style of playing time-based media, the media file is first downloaded and then played. This is suitable for media of short duration and/or small size. For long media, the user would not want to wait 10 minutes for download before watching a 10-minute video. Streaming allows the user to view the media while it is being downloaded.

Streaming media on a personal computer can be viewed in the following manners:

- From a streaming media player such as RealPlayer, Windows Media Player, Quicktime, or others.
- From a browser plug-in based on a plug-in associated with a dedicated streaming media player or a Java applet.

Streaming media players can either be invoked by the user who supplies a location for the data, either a local file or a location over the network using various streaming protocols, or by an anchor tag that is associated with the media type in the browser. The user experience would then be that he or she would click on a hyperlink in a Web page and the media player would open in another window and start playing the media.

If the streaming media is to be displayed within a Web page plug-in, a metafile is necessary. This metafile indicates what media will be played, rather than the data itself. The metafile is necessary because a browser plug-in will download the file specified. So, if the media was specified in the plug-in, the media would be downloaded obviating the desired streaming effect.

For Internet Explorer, an ActiveX Control may be used instead of a plug-in. This will not work with other browsers, such as the Firefox browser, but there are techniques to have the browser use the ActiveX control in Internet Explorer, and a browser plug-in in other browsers.

Streaming media can also be viewed on wireless devices. Most popular streaming players have been ported to work on various mobile phones. Streaming to mobile phones typically uses the same servers used to stream media over the Internet, but because of the smaller screen, and lower connection bandwidth, the media itself is typically geared to the mobile device.

When using *inter*Media with either RealServer or Microsoft Media Server, the source of data is an Oracle database procedure. Combining streaming media with the power of the database allows the endpoint of data to be either a discrete presentation or something more abstract, like the most popular song of the day, a random video, or anything else that can be created dynamically.

14.2 Microsoft Media Services

14.2.1 Background

As we have seen before, *inter*Media supports streaming data directly from the database to the client. The client media player itself is unaware that the media is being delivered from the database.

Microsoft Media Services supports formats that include:

- Windows Media Video (.wmv)
- Windows Media Audio (.wma)
- Advanced Systems Format (.asf)
- MP3 (.mp3)
- SMIL-based play list (a limited subset of SMIL) (.wsx)

It should be noted that the Advanced Systems Format is a binary format that can contain other media and delivers it in a coordinated (or synchronized) manner. This should not be confused with a Microsoft ASX file that is an XML-formatted script that is a metafile used to coordinate the delivery of media from the client player side and is typically delivered from an HTTP Web server.

The Windows Media Player supports a much wider number of formats than Windows Media Services. These other supported formats are typically delivered with an HTTP server. For example, synchronized media presentations, in the form of markup tags, can be delivered by an HTTP Web server.

For Windows Media Services, static synchronized presentations can be put together by a presentation GUI and embedded within a single ASF file.

The Windows Media Player supports HTML pages. These Web pages can themselves contain media presentations that use the Windows Media Player ActiveX control plug-in.

To coordinate the delivery of media from a Microsoft Media Services server the choices are:

- Advanced Systems Format (ASF)
- SMIL-based play list—limited to playing a list of Windows media files in sequence

To coordinate media from the client side, the choices are:
- ASX metafiles
- XHTML+TIME SMIL profile within Internet Explorer

In addition to the above formats, time-based captioning can be added to a streaming presentation with a synchronized accessible media interchange (SAMI) file that is similar to SMIL or XHTML+TIME, but limited to captioning as it is designed for captioning media. As with the SMIL implementations, SAMI can be used to add captioning to a video or audio in different languages based on the settings of the language of the client Windows system.

Windows media presentations, like slide shows, are typically a mix of XHTML+TIME delivered from a Web server, and streaming audio or video from Microsoft Media Services. To view presentations using HTML+TIME within the Windows Media Player, the media player must include a Web page.

14.2.2 Integration with Oracle

Integration of Windows Media Services and Oracle is accomplished with the *inter*Media data source plug-in for Windows Media Services (Figure 14.1). This plug-in allows the creation of mount points then publishing points (the first part of a path in a URL) with the *inter*Media plug-in.

Figure 14.1
Microsoft Windows Media Services with Oracle interMedia

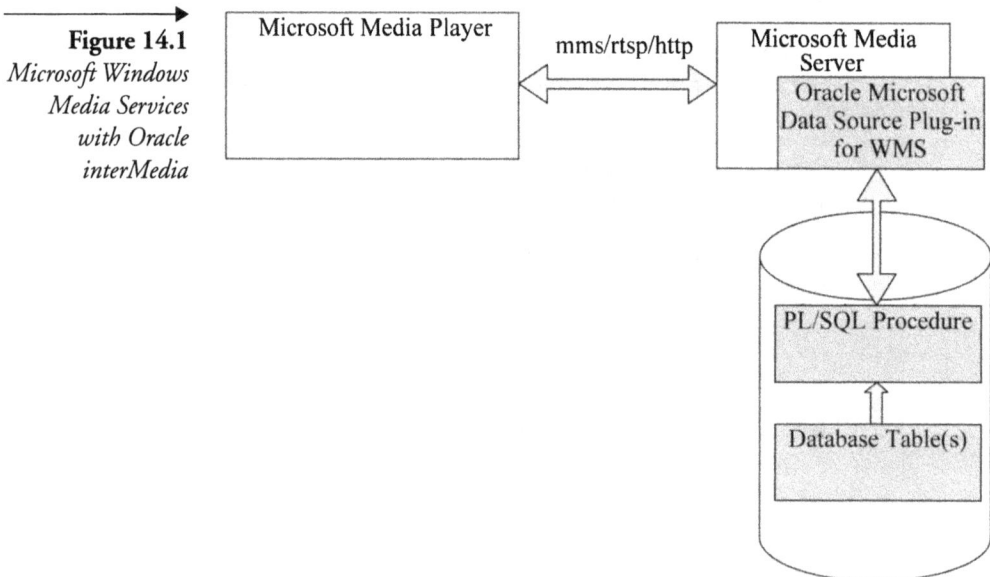

The Microsoft streaming server can stream Windows media audio and video, JPEG, or MP3 files. Play lists are also recognized and can be represented as a directory, in which all the files in the directory are played, or in SMIL or WSX formats. Other formats could be added with plug-ins from third-party providers. Other formats that are supported by the Microsoft Media Player can be encapsulated in a Windows media file.

The Oracle plug-in will stream any format that can be streamed from the Microsoft streaming server. However, if the data is not in WMF, a pseudo–file name with the extension used by the requested format must be used (more on this later).

14.2.3 Creating a Mount Point

After installation of the Oracle *inter*Media data source plug-in for WMS, the creation of a mount point is done through the Microsoft Media Services management GUI. When you click on the "Show All Plug-in Categories" checkbox, the "Data Source" category appears in the category list. Selecting the Data Source category shows a screen similar to Figure 14.2.

Figure 14.2
Selecting the Oracle
interMedia
Custom Data
Source

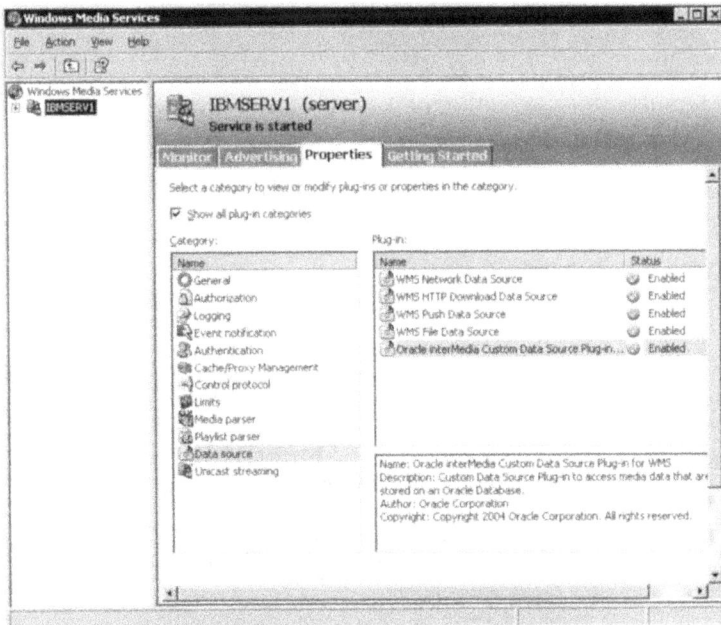

The *inter*Media plug-in is enabled by right clicking the plug-in and selecting "Enable" from the list of options. Double clicking on the *inter*Media plug-in results in the window in Figure 14.3 being displayed.

Initially, no mount points are defined. When the Add or Properties button is pressed, the dialog in Figure 14.4 allows the user to define or change a mount point.

14.2.4 Creating a Publishing Point

After a mount point has been defined, a publishing point must be created. To start this process, "Publishing Point" is selected from the navigation menu on the left of the Microsoft Media Services administration screen. You must choose the advanced option when adding an *inter*Media publish-

Figure 14.3
Data Source
Plug-in
Mount Points

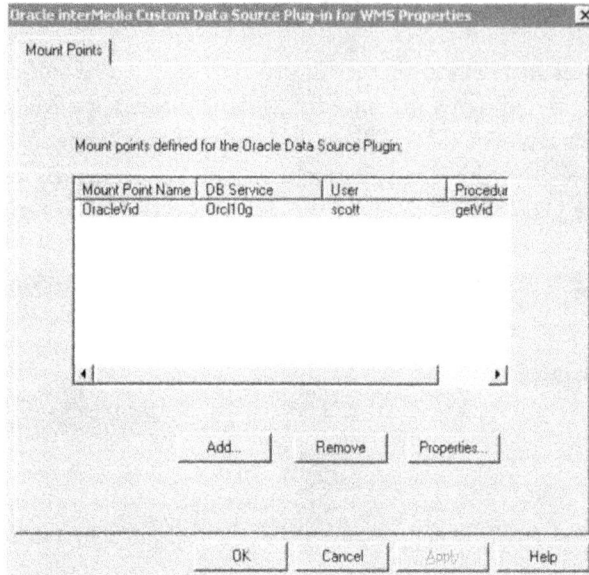

Figure 14.4
Adding an
interMedia
Data Source
Mount Point

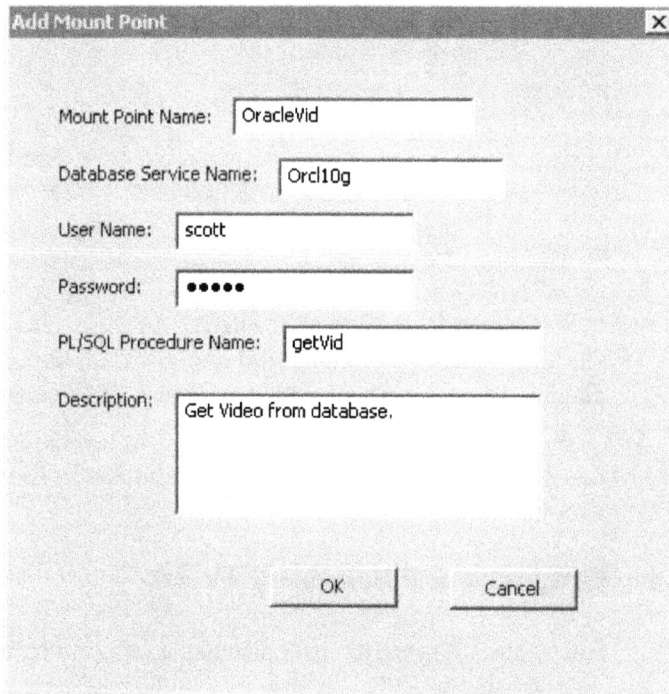

ing point. Figure 14.5 shows a publishing point being defined on an *inter-*
Media mount point.

Figure 14.5
*Adding an
interMedia
Publishing Point*

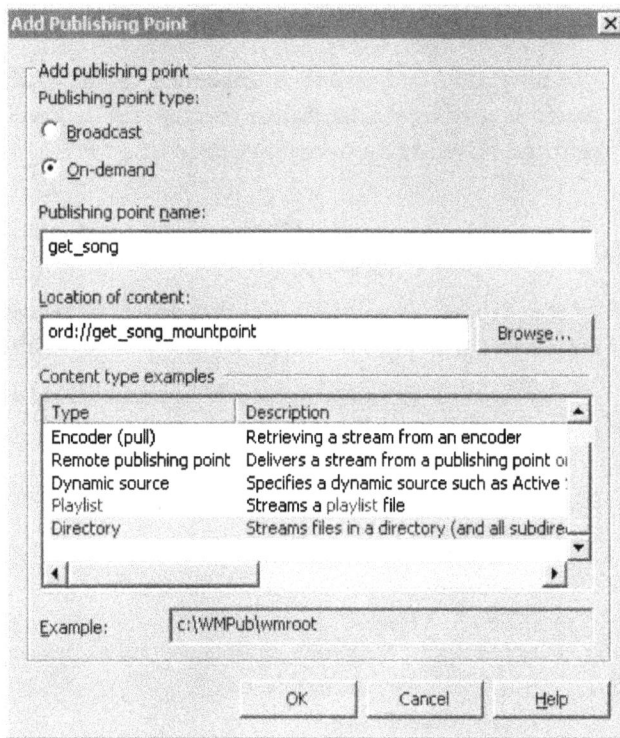

If at any time an error occurs, for example, when connecting to the database while defining a publishing point, look at Windows event viewer for the error.

Now that a publishing point is defined, you can use a media PL/SQL procedure to select or compose the media (as in a text-based SMIL play list).

14.2.5   File Types Supported by the *inter*Media MMS Data Source Plug-in

Files delivered by the *inter*Media data source plug-in are, by default, Windows media files. Other MIME types can be used, but only if the requesting URL has an appropriate file extension. This is because the data source plug-in interface for MMS does not use the MIME type passed back from the database procedure. However, it should be programmed for compatibility with procedures written for the Real/Helix server, and since in the future the use of the MIME type in MMS may be supported.

For example, if a procedure has one input field, and the data referenced by the key is in MP3 format, the following URL will not work:

```
mms://mediaserver/orclPubPoint/1
```

However, if a filename is appended to the URL, which will not be passed or used by the database procedure, the data will be successfully delivered and played as the following example:

```
mms://mediaserver/orclPubPoint/1/dummy.mp3
```

Since many of the Web pages that deliver or expose streaming media are created dynamically, this is typically not a large problem to solve.

For creating appropriate file extensions for MMS-served files in a Web page, a function like the following can be used:

```
--
-- Return an appropriate file extension for a mime type
--
create or replace
function get_file_ext_from_mime(mime in varchar2)
        return varchar2 as
    ext varchar2(8) := '';
    typ varchar2(20);
    pos integer;
begin
    pos := instr(mime, '/');
    if pos != 0 then
        ext := substr(mime, pos + 1);
        typ := substr(mime, 1, pos - 1);
    end if;
    if typ = 'audio' and ext = 'mpeg' then
        ext := 'mp3';
    end if;
    -- Skip x-ms part.
    pos := instr(ext, 'x-ms-');
    if pos != 0 then
        ext := substr(ext, pos + 5);
    end if;

    return ext;
end;
/
```

14.3   Real/Helix Server

14.3.1   Background

The Real/Helix servers can stream just about any kind of data you like. The infrastructure is such that plug-ins can be added to stream just about any data format. These include:

- Video formats
- Audio formats
- Image formats
- Streaming text formats
- SMIL

In general, the only time that an HTTP server is typically necessary is to deliver a metafile. The Real/Helix server includes HTTP services that can also generate needed metafiles (.ram and .rpm) using its ramgen facility. Ramgen takes parameters from the passed URL and constructs a ram or rpm file from these contents. These metafiles can include a list of media to play in sequence, but typically only include one item. As with the Microsoft Media Services, you can use your favorite Web application environment to deliver or construct metafiles. Unlike HTML+TIME, a SMIL presentation is interpreted by the player, and not the browser.

14.3.2   Integration with Oracle

Integration with Oracle is accomplished with a Real/Helix server file system plug-in. Using administration functions, or a text editor, a mount point is defined to access a database procedure through the plug-in. The plug-in connects to the database and returns the contents and MIME type of data from the database procedure. See Figure 14.6.

The kind of data delivered to the Real/Helix server by the Oracle procedure is only limited by what the streaming server is configured to handle. This includes script files like SMIL, RealText, and RealPix, as well as media binary data like images, audio, and video.

The database procedure can return anything from a discrete piece of media, like the image in row 1, or something more abstract, like the most

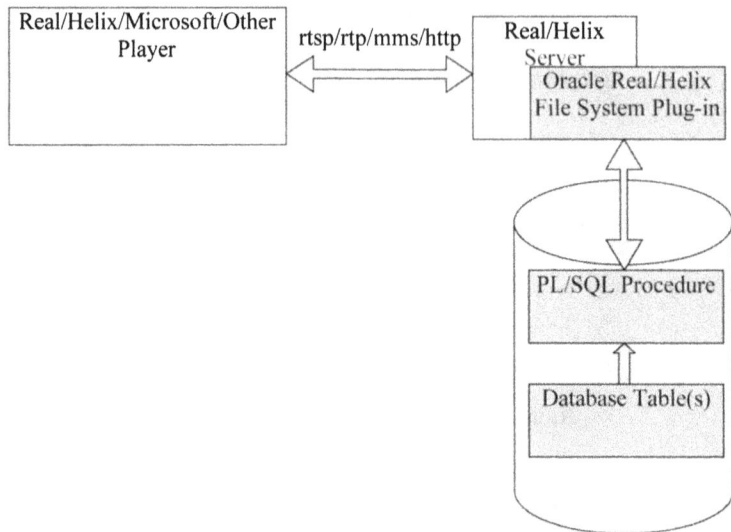

Figure 14.6
Real/Helix with
Oracle interMedia

viewed video to a SMIL presentation that includes elements based on any programmable selection criteria.

Note that it is possible to use the HTTP file system plug-in that comes with Real/Helix server to obtain streaming media from the database. As you know, *inter*Media data can be served from a URL. The disadvantage to this is it adds another level of indirection and would, in theory, add more overhead.

14.3.3 Creating a Mount Point

A Real/Helix server mount point defines the initial URL path for the streaming data URL. In the following example, it defines <PATH>.

```
RTSP://<SERVER>:<PORT>/<PATH>/.....
```

The rest of the URL is the file portion of the URL that can be used by procedures to pass parameters to the procedure.

The mount point can be created with the Real/Helix server management page, or it can be edited directly into the Real/Helix XML configuration file.

After installation, the Oracle Real/Helix configuration screen looks like Figure 14.7.

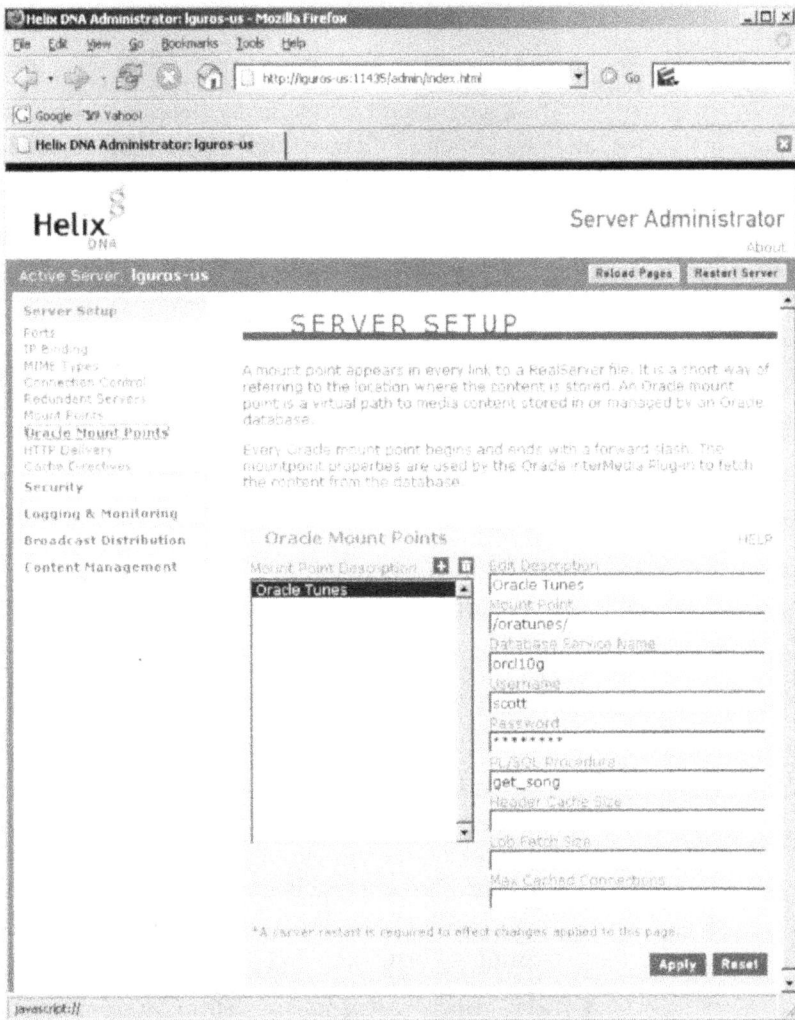

Figure 14.7
*Creating an
interMedia Mount
Point for
Real/Helix Server*

The above mount point results in the following XML section inserted into the Real/Helix configuration file in the `<List Name="FSMount">` section.

```
<List Name="Oracle Tunes">
    <Var Database="orcl10g"/>
    <Var MountPoint="/oratunes/"/>
    <Var Password="dGlnZXI="/>
    <Var ShortName="pn-oracle"/>
    <Var SQL="get_song"/>
```

```
                <Var Username="scott"/>
        </List>
```

If we were to add values for the "Header Cache Size," "Lob Fetch Size," and "Max Cached Connections" parameters, the configuration would look like the following sample.

```
<List Name="Oracle Tunes">
        <Var Database="orcl10g"/>
        <Var MountPoint="/oratunes/"/>
        <Var Password="dGlnZXI="/>
        <Var ShortName="pn-oracle"/>
        <Var SQL="get_song"/>
        <Var Username="scott"/>
        <Var HeaderCacheSize=î2048î/>
        <Var LobFetchSize=î32768î/>
        <Var MaxCachedConnections=î1î/>
</List>
```

The extra optional parameters are:

- The *header cache size* parameter controls how many bytes from the beginning of the file are cached in order to satisfy frequent requests for bytes located in the file header. The minimum value is 512 bytes, the maximum is 8,192 bytes, and the default value is 2,048 bytes. Up to three times the size of the header cache can be allocated per streaming file request.

- The *lob fetch size* parameter controls how much data is retrieved from the database whenever new data is required. Fetching larger chunks of data in fewer requests is more efficient than fetching smaller chunks using more requests. The fetched data is cached in the plug-in to satisfy subsequent requests. The minimum value is 8,192 bytes and the maximum and default values are 32,768 bytes. Up to three times the size of the lob fetch size parameter can be allocated per streaming file request.

- The *max cached connections* parameter controls the maximum number of connections to the Oracle database that will be maintained during periods of inactivity. A cached connection is used to decrease the time required to begin streaming a new request. The minimum value is 0, the maximum value is 10, and the default value is 1.

14.4   Creating an *inter*Media Streaming Server Plug-in Procedure

The database procedures for either the Real/Helix server or the Microsoft streaming server are the same. The only thing to be aware of is that they may or may not support the same data MIME types.

As you can see from the configurations, an Oracle *inter*Media streaming server mount point specifies a PL/SQL procedure. This is the procedure that is invoked. The procedure should have a call signature of the form:

```
<PROCEDURE_NAME>(<INPUT_PARAM1> in <TYPE>,    (optional)
                 <INPUT_PARAM2> in <TYPE>,    (optional)
                      :    :    :   :    :
                 <INPUT_PARAMn> in VARCHAR2,  (optional)
                 MIMETYPE out VARCHAR2        (required)
                 DATA out BLOB or BFILE,      (required)
                 )
```

The <TYPE> parameter should be VARCHAR2, NUMBER, or integer. If you want to use other types, it is recommended that the input is converted to the type you need, for example, with the TO_DATE function in PL/SQL if you need to query with a DATE or DATE range. Below is an example of a somewhat generalized procedure.

```
create or replace
procedure getMedia(tbl IN VARCHAR2,
                   col IN VARCHAR2,
                   keycol IN VARCHAR2,
                   key IN VARCHAR2,
                   mimetype OUT VARCHAR2,
                   data OUT BLOB)
is
begin
   EXECUTE IMMEDIATE
     'SELECT t.'|| col || '.getMimeType(),' ||
           't.'|| col || '.getContent()' ||
```

```
        ' INTO :mime, :blob' ||
        ' FROM ' || tbl || ' t ' ||
        ' WHERE t.' || keycol || ' = ''' || key || ''''
      INTO mimetype, data;
  end;
  /
```

The above procedure would take a URL of the following form:

```
rtsp://<SERVER>:<PORT>/<MOUNTPOINT>/<TABLE>/<COLUMN>/
<KEYCOL>/<KEY>
```

For example, for a mount point called dbpoint with a table name vidtbl with two columns and an ID of type INTEGER and VIDEO of type ORDVideo, the following URL would return the video in column 1 in this table for the user specified in the mount point:

```
rtsp://yourserver/dbpoint/vidtbl/video/id/1
```

This will play the implied video in the database defined by dbpoint mount point, in the vidtbl table from the video column where the ID column is one.

These procedures can return any data that is supported by a Real/Helix server and the format plug-ins that are installed. Along with binary formats, this returned data can also include text formats like SMIL, RealText, and RealPix. When returning text formats, it is advisable to cast the text into a known character set when being placed into the BLOB.

For example, the following procedure will return a play list for all the songs by a particular band in the songs table, or a particular audio depending on the "type."

```
procedure PlayList(type IN VARCHAR2,
                   key IN VARCHAR2,
                   mimetype OUT VARCHAR2,
                   data OUT BLOB)
is
  s VARCHAR2(4096);
  tempBLOB BLOB;
  bad_type exception;
```

```
        CURSOR band_cursor IS
            select id from songs where band = key;
    begin
      if (UPPER(type) = 'SMIL') then
        s := '<smil
             xmlns="http://www.w3.org/2001/SMIL20/Language">
             <body><seq>';
        FOR row_rec in band_cursor
        LOOP
          s := s || '
            <audio src="../audio/' || row_rec.id || '" />';
        END LOOP;
        s := s || '</seq></body></smil>';
        DBMS_LOB.CREATETEMPORARY( tempBLOB, TRUE,
                                  DBMS_LOB.SESSION );
        DBMS_LOB.WRITEAPPEND(tempBLOB, length(s),
            utl_raw.cast_to_raw(convert(s,'WE8ISO8859P1')));
        data := tempBlob;
        mimetype := 'application/smil';
      elsif (UPPER(type) = 'AUDIO') then
        select t.audio.getContent(), t.audio.getMimetype()
          into data, mimetype
          from songs t where t.id = key;
      else
        raise bad_type;
      end if;
    end;
    /
```

What should be noted, as highlighted, is that when returning a character-based script, it should be cast to a character set recognized by the media server. This procedure will use a URL similar to the following for a play list:

```
rtsp://server.com/oracleMountPoint/smil/The%20Loonies
```

The playlist will play all the songs from a particular band in the songs table.

For a particular audio:

```
rtsp://server.com/oracleMountPoint/audio/3
```

14.5 Summary

*inter*Media supports streaming technologies from both Microsoft and Real/Helix with a custom plug-in.

Alternatively, it is possible to support these servers by providing a URL that represents streaming data stored in a database. The server would refer to the URL, and an application, perhaps a servlet, would query the database for the streaming data and deliver it to the streaming server, via HTTP, for delivery to the streaming client.

Other streaming technologies can be supported by writing a custom plug-in, or by using the alternative approach.

Appendix

Where to get more information

The main page for information on *inter*Media can be found at the following location on the web:

```
http://www.oracle.com/technology/products/intermedia/
index.html
```

*inter*Media documentation including the interMedia Reference, *inter*Media User's Guide, *inter*Media Java Classes API Reference and *inter*Media Java Classes for Servlets and JSP API Reference can be found at:

```
http://www.oracle.com/technology/documentation/
database10gR2.html
```

The documentation from the Oracle 10g database documentation set that pertains to *inter*Media can also be found at:

```
http://www.oracle.com/technology/documentation/
intermedia.html
```

*inter*Media sample code can be found at:

```
http://www.oracle.com/technology/sample_code/products/
intermedia/index.html
```

*inter*Media training can be found at:

```
http://www.oracle.com/technology/products/intermedia/
training/index.html
```

*inter*Media downloadable software (plugins, drives, libraries, wizards, etc) can be found at

```
http://www.oracle.com/technology/software/products/
intermedia/index.html
```

The *inter*Media discussion forum, where you can ask questions or search other user questions can be found at:

```
http://www.oracle.com/technology/discussionforums/
intermedia.html
```

Information on Jdeveloper and other Oracle java technologies can be found at:

```
http://www.oracle.com/technology/tech/java/index.html
```

Information on the Java Media Framework (JMF) API can be found at:

```
http://www.oracle.com/technology/tech/java/index.html
```

Information of the Java Advanced Imaging (JAI) API can be found at:

```
http://java.sun.com/products/java-media/jai/
```

Information on C# and Microsoft Studio can be found at:

```
http://msdn.microsoft.com/vcsharp/
```

Information on PHP can be found at:

```
http://www.php.net/
```

Information on using Oracle with PHP can be found at:

```
http://www.oracle.com/technology/tech/php/index.html
```

For information added after the release of the documentation, refer to the online README.txt file under your <ORACLE_HOME> directory. Depending on your operating system, this file may be in:

```
<ORACLE_HOME>/ord/im/admin/README.txt  (Unix and Linux)
<ORACLE_HOME>\ord\im\admin\README.txt (Windows)
```

Index

3GP standards, 41

Analog-to-digital converter (ADC), 12
Apache HTTP Server, 230
Apache module for Oracle distributed
    authoring and versioning. *See* OraDAV
Apache Web server, 125
    configuration files, loading, 148
    PHP use, 125
Application development, 225–27
    J2EE/ADF, 311–72
    PL/SQL, 405–16
    PSP, 417
    Web, 409–12
Application Development Framework (ADF),
        311, 312–23
    business services layer, 312
    controller component creation, 316–23
    controller layer, 312
    defined, 311
    domain classes, 313
    Integration Package, 313
    *inter*Media integration, 312
    layers, 312
    model component creation, 313–16
    model layer, 312
    run-time framework, 313
    view component creation, 316–23
    view layer, 312

Application performance, 421–38
    backup, 437–38
    database tuning, 422–30
    delivery on Web, 436–37
    goals, 421–22
    I/O load distribution, 432–33
    load, 433–36
    needs, 421
    table creation, 430–32
    tools, 436
Application planning, 213–58
    architecture definition, 227–40
    data modeling, 235–40
    prototyping, 240–52
    requirements gathering, 215–27
    requirements refinement, 252–53
    test infrastructure, 253–57
    *See also inter*Media
Architecture(s)
    alternative, 232–34
    applications, 228
    client-server, 231–32
    defining, 227–34
    elements, 227
    technical, 230–31
    three-tier, 232
    Zachman's enterprise, 228, 229–30
    See also Application planning
ASF file format, 68
Aspirational needs, 216

.aspx file, 112, 118
Attribute-based retrieval (ABR), 400–401
    defined, 400
    *inter*Media support, 440
    QBE, 400–401
    queries, 440–41
    techniques, 405
Attributes
    application, extracting, 291
    color, 442
    defined, 260
    image, 296
    ISO/IEC 11179, 44
    ORDImage, 262, 402
    retrieving, 338
    SI_StillImage type, 296–97, 299
Audio, 37
    exception type and, 199
    loading, 198–99
    loading, from local files, 192–94
    metadata, reading, 284
    nonstreaming, 37
    playing from database, 140
    streaming, 37–38
    See also Images; Video
Automatic Database Diagnostic Monitor
        (ADDM), 423
    defined, 425
    example recommendation, 425–26
    recommendations, 429
    reports, creating, 426
    reports, run methods, 426
Automatic Workload Repository (AWR), 423
    configuration, 424
    link, 424
    log, 423
    parameters, 424–25

Backups, 437–38
    full, 437

    incremental, 207, 437
Bandwidth, 19
BFILENAME() function, 58
BFILES, 50
    database access, 52
    defined, 51
    disadvantages, 53–54, 58
    manipulating, 57
    using, 51–54
Binary large objects. *See* BLOBS
Bitmap index, 380
Bitmaps, 15
Blob class, 167
BLOBS
    columns, 162
    copying file to, 177
    data storage/retrieval, 436
    data type, 5, 50
    disadvantage, 58
    input parameter setting, 177
    inserting in database, 129
    OCCI object, 170
    operation failure, 162
    streams, 168
    in tablespaces, 435
    thumbnail, copying from, 179–80
Block change tracking (BTC), 437
BMPF image format, 263
Browse.jsp, 322
Browsers
    media handling, 87–88
    ODP.NET media delivery from, 118–25
    ODP.NET media delivery to, 112–18
    PHP media delivery from, 129–32
    PHP media delivery to, 125–29
    plug-ins, 89–90
B*Tree index, 380
Built-in data types, 260
Business component, 314–16
    creating, 315–16
    initialization, 315

C#
information on, 478
with ODP.NET, 172–80
Caching
firewalls, 129
HTTP, 90–92
servers, 129
CHARACTER data type, 260
CheckProperties() method, 341, 343, 346
CIE_XYZ color-space, 30
Classes
object types and, 259
UML, 237, 261
See also Java classes
CLASSPATH, 159–60
setting on command line, 160
setting with JDeveloper, 160
ClearLocal() method, 339
Client-server architecture, 231–32
CLOB data types, 50, 388
CloseSource() method, 339
CMYK, 31
comparison, 32
defined, 31
Code Wizard, 100
Color, 29–34
attribute, 442
CIE_XYZ color-space, 30
CMYK, 31
gamut, 33
histograms, 446
histograms comparison, 453–54
HSB, 31–32
matching, 453–58
model comparison, 32–34
RGB, 30–31
RYB, 32
types, 448
Comparison methods, 293
Compression, 22–29
algorithms, 23

decompression and, 23
issues, 22
lossless, 23
lossy, 23
LZW, 24
objectives, 23
Computer graphics metafile (CGM), 24–25
Constructor methods, SI_StillImage, 298–99
Content-based information retrieval (CBIR), 397
features, 441
object types, 448–49
SI_StillImage for, 448–58
Content-based retrieval (CBR), 404–5
benefit, 439
defined, 404
in *inter*Media, 439–43
searches, 404
techniques, 405
Context parameter, 335
Contrast correction, 18
Contrast operator, 274
Control Data Corporation (CDC), 12
Copy() method, 341
CREATE TABLE statement, 84
Cropping, 17
Cut verb, 272

Database definition language (DDL), 334
Database Management System (DBMS), 24
Databases
connection, creating, 314
copying between with Data Pump, 206
in data security, 5
design stereotypes, 238
digital media, value proposition, 4–5
extracting thumbnails from, 170–71
image placement into, 154–55
ISAM, 4
media object update, 338–39

playing audio from, 140
preparation, 153–54
tuning, 422–30
Data modeling, 235–40
Data Pump, 206–7
   in data transfer, 206
   file creation, 206
   use, 206
Data requirements, 217
DBMS_LOB package, 299–301
   LOADFROMFILE routine, 300, 301
   routines, 299–300
   use, 299
Decompression, 23
DeleteContent() method, 339
Delivery, 18–22
   application performance, 436–37
   HTTP, 87–92
   media, with JSPs, 352–55
   media, with servlets, 356–61
   ODP.NET, from browser, 118–25
   ODP.NET, to browser, 112–18
   PHP, from browser, 129–32
   PHP, to browser, 125–29
   streaming server, 133–39
DICOM standard, 281
   image metadata, 373, 393–95
   images, 393, 394
   specification, 395
Dictionary method, 23–24
Digital images. *See* Images
Digital imaging and communications in
   medicine (DICOM), 47
Digital media
   challenge, 3
   elements, 1
   infrastructure for, 6
   management, 4
   storage, 3–4
   use popularity, 1–2
   uses, 1–2, 2

   See also Media; Multimedia
Digital media databases
   infrastructure, 6
   rich, 10
   value proposition, 4–5
   See also Databases
Dithering, 18
Documentation
   *inter*Media, 477
   Java classes, 160–61
Document tables
   creation, 103–5
   defined, 103
DOUBLE PRECISION, 455, 457
Dublin Core metadata standards, 85
DUCE session, 251, 252
   objective, 251
   use comments, 252
Dynamic range, 16
Dynamic systems design method (DSDM),
   241

EmbedAudio tag, 324
Embedded metadata, 43
EmbedImage tag, 324
EmbedVideo tag, 324
Encoding rules, 281
Endpoints
   OraDAV, 148, 149–50
   servlet, 320
Enterprise Manager, 422
   illustrated, 423
   running ADDM reports with, 426
   SQL source view, 430
Environmental requirements, 217–18
EPS file format, 15, 25
Etags, 129
EvaluateScore() method, 350
Exception blocks, 407, 408
EXIF

defined, 45
focus, 374
Exporting thumbnails, 156–57
Export() method, 339
Extensible metadata platform. *See* XMP
External tables, 203–7
  dropping, 205
  loading, 201
  technology, 203
  using, 203–5
  See also Tables
Extracting
  application attributes, 291
  features, 441
  image metadata, 380–83
  metadata, 43
  thumbnails, 170–71
Extreme programming (XP), 224

Feature extraction techniques, 441
Feature vector, 441
File formats, 9
  list, 14–15
  unrecognized, 195–200
  video, 37
  See also specific formats
Files
  image row, populating from, 167–70
  local, loading media from, 192–94
  putting images in, 185–88
  supported by *inter*Media data source plug-in, 467–68
  uploading images from, 162–63
Forms, loading, 210–11
Forms Wizard, 106, 107
  accessing, 106
  illustrated, 108
Functional needs, 216
Functional requirements, 217
Functional understandability, 256

Function-based indexes, 388
Function methods, 293

Gamma
  defined, 18
  operator, 271
GenerateSignature() method, 351
GetAllAttributes() method, 288, 343, 346
GetAttribute() method, 343, 346
GetAudioDuration() method, 343
GetBFILE() method, 339
GetBitRate() method, 346
GetComments() method, 343, 346, 349
GetCompressionFormat() method, 341
GetCompressionType() method, 343, 346
GetContentFormat() method, 341, 343, 346
GetContentInLob() method, 343, 346, 349
GetContentLength() method, 339, 343, 346, 349
GetContent() method, 339
GetDataInByteArray() method, 339
GetDataInFile() method, 165, 339
GetDataInStream() method, 340
GetDescription() method, 343, 346
GetDicomMetadata() method, 281
GetEncoding() method, 343, 346
GetFormat() method, 340
GetFrameRate() method, 346
GetFrameResolution() method, 346
GetHeight() method, 341, 346
GetMetadata() method, 275–77, 281, 379
  defined, 275
  function, 275–78
  image metadata extraction with, 381
  input parameter, 276
GetMimeType() method, 340
GetNamespace() method, 276
GetNumberOfChannels() method, 343
GetNumberOfColors() method, 347
GetNumberOfFrames() method, 347

GetORADataFactory() method, 340, 351
GetRootElement() method, 380
GetSamplingRate() method, 344
GetSourceLocation() method, 340
GetSource() method, 340
GetSourceName() method, 340
GetSourceType() method, 340
GetUpdateTime() method, 340
GetVideoDuration() method, 347
GetWidth() method, 341, 347
GIF file format, 14
    defined, 25
    images, 143
Grid technology, 233

High-fidelity prototypes, 245–52
    advantages/disadvantages, 246
    characteristics, 246
    defined, 245
    interactivity, 245
    interface evaluation methods, 249–50
    See also Prototypes
Horizontal prototyping
    defined, 242
    illustrated, 243
    See also Prototypes
HSB system, 31–32
    comparison, 33
    defined, 32
HTML, 87, 88
HTTP
    caching, 90–92
    classes, 92, 93–100
    data, loading, 210–11
    defined, 87
    delivery, 87–92
    form load, 210–11
    header fields, 92
    loading media from, 194–95
    proxies, 90

request/response, 93
response message, 101
response packet, 89
servers, 92
uploading media over, 362

ICC/ICM profiles, 31
Image metadata, 43–45, 274–81
    DICOM, 373, 393–95
    extracting, 380–83
    format, 45–47
    indexing, 387–93
    information, selecting from XML data
        types, 382
    insert extraction capabilities, 375
    inserting, 374, 384–87
    summary, 395–96
    support, 373–96
    See also Metadata
Image processing, 155–56, 267
    SI_StillImage methods, 305–8
    verbs, 268–70
    within database, 271–74
Images
    attribute specification, 296
    bitmap, 15
    color histograms and, 446
    data, 11–12
    data, downloading from tables, 165–66
    DICOM, 393, 394
    distance between, 444
    formatting, 267
    GIF, 143
    grayscale, 15
    matching, 451–53
    media, adaptation, 140–43
    placement into database, 154–55
    properties, retrieving, 164
    properties, setting, 183
    putting in file, 185–88

RAW, 28
row, populating, 175–78
row, populating from file, 167–70
score between, 444
static, 142
uploading, from files to tables, 162–63
visual attributes, 442–43
WBMP, 143
See also Audio; Video
Impdp, 206–7
ImportData() method, 342, 344, 347, 349
ImportFrom() method, 282–83, 286, 287, 291, 342, 344, 347, 349
Import() method, 155, 192
Incremental backups, 207
Indexed sequential access method (ISAM), 4
Indexes
    Bitmap, 388
    B*Tree, 388
    context, 392
    function-based, 388
    image metadata, 387–93
    Oracle Text, 392–93
    text-based, 388
    XML data, 389
    XMLType, 387
Information and communication technology (ICT), 11
Information systems (IS)
    complexity, 214
    questions, 214–15
INIT() methods, 62, 68, 264, 294
INSERT statement, 285
INTEGER data type, 260
Integrated development environment (IDE), 311
*Inter*Media
    ABR support, 440
    ADF Integration Package, 313
    application development, 225–27
    application performance, 421–38

application planning, 213–58
ASF file format support, 68
Code Wizard, 100
content-based image retrieval in, 439–43
data exposure, 147–48
data source plug-in, 464
data types, 49, 63
discussion forum, 478
documentation, 477
downloadable software, 478
HTTP classes, 93–100
image data manipulation, 64–67
information on, 477
JAI I/O classes, 180
Java advanced imaging APIs, 180–89
Java classes for servlets, 351–72
Java Client, 158
Java proxy classes, 157–66, 334–51
JSP tag library, 105, 324–34
metadata and, 65
new formats supported, 67–68
in object type creation, 83–86
object types, 60
OracleAS Portal, 105–10
OraDAV driver, 143–50
PL/SQL wizard, 101, 103
sample code, 477
schema definition, 377–78
storage, 49–86
TBR support, 440
TIFF decoder, 29
TIFF support, 28
training, 477–78
type attributes, 66–67
using, 59–78
XMP XML schema, 391
Internal helper types, 457–58
    colorFrequenciesList, 458
    colorList, 458
    colorPositions, 458
    defined, 457

textureEncoding, 458
Interpolation, 17
I/O load distribution, 432–33
IPTC-IIM, 45
IsLocal() method, 340
ISO/IEC 11179 attributes, 44
IsSimilar() method, 351

J2EE
    application development, 311–72
    IDEs, 311
    model-view-controller (MVC), 311, 312
    technologies, 311
Java Advanced Imaging (JAI)
    clients, 181
    database row creation, 181–85
    example steps, 181
    image encoding, 183
    image input, 184
    image scaling, 184
    includes, 181
    information on, 478
    *inter*Media APIs, 180–89
    I/O classes, 180
    output stream, 183
    PlanarImage, 186
    sample, running, 188–89
    scaled image storage, 184–85
Java classes, 157–66
    documentation, 160–61
    for JSP, 329
    media upload, for servlets, 361–72
    proxy, 334–51
    for servlets, 329
Java Client, 158
Java Media Framework (JMF), 232
    information on, 478
    thick client use, 232
Java Server Faces (JSF), 311
    controller, 316

JSP creation, 317–18
JSP form fields, 319
wizard, 316
Java Server Pages (JSP), 311
    Editor, 318
    form design, 320
    form fields, 319
    Java classes for, 329
    media delivery with, 352–55
    source code, 321
    See also JSP tag library
JDBC
    connection, creating, 161–62, 335–36
    connectivity, 95
    drivers, 161
    extension classes, 159
    interface, 231
JDeveloper, 311
    development lifecycle development, 247–
        48
    information on, 478
    library selection, 161
    RAD tools, 254
    setting CLASSPATH with, 160
    UI debugger, 254
    UML modelers, 248
JLabel, 338
JPEG2000 file format, 14
    defined, 26
    features, 26–27
JPEG file format, 14
    defined, 25–26
    thumbnails, 155–56
JPEG-Progressive, 26
JSP tag library, 105, 324–34
    defined, 324
    media retrieval tags, 324
    platform deployment, 324
    retrieving multimedia data with, 324–29
    uploading multimedia data with, 329–34
    See also Java Server Pages (JSP)

JSP/UIX, 312

Large object data types. *See* LOB data types
Layers, 18
Linguistic-Linguistic (LL) mode, 398–99
Linguistic-Visual (LV) mode, 399
LoadDataFromByteArray() method, 340
LoadDataFromFile() method, 340
LoadDataFromInputStream() method, 340
Loading media, 191–212
    external tables, 203–7
    HTTP forms, 210–11
    from HTTP source, 194–95
    from local files, 192–94
    PL/SQL, 191–201
    SQL*Loader, 201–3
    thick client, 211–12
    transportable tablespaces, 207–10
Load performance, 433–36
LOB data types, 50
    columns, disabling logging, 200
    locators, 51
    manipulating, 57
    Oracle 10g, 52
    summary, 52–53
    using, 50–51
Location understandability, 256
Logging
    disabling, 200
    REDO, 431, 433
Logos
    painting into thumbnail, 187
    putting on images, 185–88
Loops
    efficiency, 414–16
    through result set, 414
Lossless compression, 23
Lossy compression, 23
Low-fidelity prototypes, 243–45

Media
    browser handling of, 87–88
    compression, 22–29
    delivery, 18–22
    delivery, with JSPs, 352–55
    delivery, with servlets, 356–61
    loading, 191–212
    objects, 259–63
    in object types, 259–310
    real-time, 34–41
    resolution, 15–18
    target, 192
    types, value proposition, 5–6
    unrecognized formats, 195–200
Media upload
    classes, 361–72
    into database, 406
    with OrdHttpUploadFormData, 370–71
    with OrdMultipartFilter, 371–72
    over HTTP, 362
MediaURL tag, 324
Metadata
    associating with rich-media objects, 226
    audio, reading, 284
    classes, 401
    defined, 9
    DICOM, 393–95
    embedded, 43
    examples, 10
    extracting, 43
    generating, 42–43
    image, 43–45, 274–81
    image, format, 45–47
    image, support, 373–96
    indexes, 3–4
    insert extraction capabilities, 375
    insertion, 374
    *inter*Media and, 65
    multimedia, 9–10
    in query processing, 401
    schemas, 375–80

setting explicitly, 197–98
setting manually, 196
type determination, 276–77
uses, 42
XML types, 375
Methods, 290–96
    common, 339–41
    comparison, 293
    data manipulation, 265
    defined, 260
    function, 293
    image processing, 305–8
    ORDAudio, 281–84
    ORDImage, 73, 263–81
    OrdImageSignature, 350–51
    ORDSource, 261
    ORDVideo, 284–90
    SI_StillImage, 297–305
    See also specific methods
Microsoft Media Services, 136–39, 462–68
    background, 462–64
    configuration, 137
    delivery of media, 463
    format support, 462
    integration with Oracle, 464
    *inter*Media plug-in, 136
    mount point creation, 465
    procedure parameter, 137
    publishing point, 138–39
    publishing point creation, 465–67
MIME
    defined, 19
    header field, 262
    RFC, 19
    standard flexibility, 21
MIME types, 5, 19–22, 134–35, 467
    arbitrary types, 88–89
    default, 169
    default, setting, 174–75
    elements, 20
    gathering, 195

major type, 20
minor type, 20
obtaining, 178
plug-ins, 21–22
setting, 36
support, 20
Mirror operator, 271
Mobile XML, 140
Model component
    business, 314–16
    creating, 313–16
    project, naming, 313
Model-view-controller (MVC), 311, 312
Mod_plsql, 100–105
    defined, 100
    HTTP requests and, 101
    procedures, 101
Monitors, dynamic range, 16
MoSCoW rules, 252, 253
Mount points
    creating, Microsoft Media Services, 465,
        466
    creating, Real/Helix server, 470–73
    data source plug-in, 466
    Oracle *inter*Media streaming server, 473
MPEG-1, 38
MPEG-2, 38, 67
MPEG-4, 38, 67
MPEG-7, 38–40
    defined, 38
    implementations, 40
    standard definition, 39
    terms, 39–40
MPEG-21, 40
Multi Channel Server, 140
Multimedia
    basics, 7–47
    challenges, 8
    defined, 9
    file formats, 9
    metadata, 9–10

operations, 13–14
Web, 9
Multimedia data, 8–9
    acquisition, 12–13
    querying, 398–99
    retrieving with JSP tag library, 324–29
    storing, 56
    table creation with, 430–32
    transformation, 13–29
    uploading with JSP tag library, 329–34
Multipurpose Internet mail extension. *See*
        MIME type

NESTED TABLE type, 237
Network place
    adding, 149–50
    name specification, 149, 150
NULL value, 455
Nyquist theorem, 19

Object-relational approach, 58–59
Objects
    case sensitive names, 154
    empty, 201
    media, 259–63
    media, updating, 338–39
    ORDImage, 158
    proxy, 337–38
    references, 310
    row, 310
    transparency, 312
Object tables, 309–10
    creating, 309
    defined, 309
    object references, 310
    OID, 310
    rows, 309–10
    See also Tables
Object types

classes and, 259
components, 59
created, disadvantage, 85–86
creating, 83–86
defined, 58
*inter*Media, 60, 295
media in, 259–310
methods, 260
properties extracted from, 266
SQL/MM, 79–80
use advantage, 73
ODP.NET, 110–25
    application prerequisite, 111
    applications for the Web, 112
    .aspx file, 112, 118
    AutoCommit setting, 175
    connection creation, 173
    C# using, 172–80
    image row population, 175–78
    media delivery from browser, 118–25
    media delivery to browser, 112–18
    object references, 172
    row insertion commands, 173–75
    thumbnail extraction, 178–80
    Visual Studio preparation, 172
Open grid services architecture (OGSA), 234
OpenSource() method, 344, 347, 349
Operability metrics, 257
Oracle Callable Interface (OCI), 166
Oracle C++ Call Interface (OCCI), 166–71
    AutoCommit setting, 167
    Blob class, 167
    BLOB object, 170
    connection creation, 167
    defined, 166
    image row population, 167–70
    includes, 166
    namespaces, 166
    Stream class, 167
    thumbnail extraction, 170–71
Oracle Database Enterprise Edition, 207

Oracle Data Provider for .NET. *See*
    ODP.NET
Oracle HTTP Server, 230, 232, 233
Oracle Portal, 105–10
    CREATE DATABASE provider, 107
    created form, 109
    form, using, 110
    *inter*Media support, 105
    providers, 106
    report illustration, 112
    Report Wizard, 108, 111
OraclePreparedStatement class, 159
OracleResultSet class, 159
Oracle Technology Network website, 234
Oracle Text, indexing, 392–93
Oracle Wireless, 139–43
    defined, 139
    media image adaptation, 140–43
    static images and, 142
OraDAV, 143–50
    containers, 144, 145
    defined, 143
    driver, 143, 144
    endpoint definition, 148
    endpoint use, 149–50
    installing in ORDSYS, 144–48
    media exposure steps, 144
    module, 143
ORDAudio, 60, 64, 74–75
    attributes, 281–82
    INIT() method, 282
    in Java programs, 159
    methods, 281–84
    noncommon methods, 343–45
    object initialization, 74
    setProperties() method support, 67, 75
    wrapper methods, 261
ORDDoc, 64
    attributes, 290
    defined, 60, 76
    in Java programs, 159

methods, 290–96
noncommon methods, 345, 349–50
purpose, 290
setProperties() method support, 67, 76
wrapper methods, 261
OrdHttpJspResponseHandler, 352, 353
OrdHttpResponseHandler, 351
OrdHttpUploadFile, 352, 363
OrdHttpUploadFormData, 352
    defined, 352
    media upload using, 370–71
    parsing with, 363
ORDImage, 46, 47, 60, 64, 68–69
    attributes, 262, 402
    defined, 157–58
    initialization methods, 68
    INIT() method, 294
    Java object, 158, 159
    in Java programs, 159
    methods, 73, 263–81
    methods, invoking, 263–64
    noncommon methods, 341
    object in database table, 158
    object initialization, 69
    ORDSYS object, 158, 159
    wrapper methods, 261
OrdImageSignature
    defined, 350
    methods, 350–51
    object population, 350
OrdMultipartFilter, 352
    defined, 352
    media upload using, 371–72
    use steps, 372
OrdMultipartWrapper, 352
ORDSource
    attributes, 61
    defined, 60
    methods, 261
    object embedding, 62
    object methods, 61

ORDSourceExceptions, 287
ORDVideo, 60, 64, 77–78
    attributes, 285
    importFrom() method, 286
    Init() method, 285
    in Java programs, 159
    methods, 284–90
    noncommon methods, 345, 346–48
    setProperties() method support, 67, 285
    wrapper methods, 261

Peer-based SOA (PSOA), 234
Performance tools, 436
Photo Store, 397
PHP, 125–32
    application development prerequisite, 125
    defined, 125
    information on, 478
    media delivery from browser to database,
        129–32
    media delivery to browser, 125–29
    objects, handling, 125
Physical accessibility, 257
Physical needs, 216
PICT file format, 15, 27
PICTIVE, 243
    materials, 244
    sessions, 245
    strongest use, 245
Pixels
    history of, 11–12
    resolution and, 16
PL/SQL, 153–57
    anonymous block, 167
    application development, 405–16
    code, embedding, 410
    development environment, 409
    exception blocks, 407, 408
    Gateway, 232–34, 411
    HTML output generation, 410

loading from HTTP source, 194–95
loading from local files, 192–94
loading from user written source, 195
loading media, 191–201
loading method performance, 200–201
loop efficiency, 414–16
optimizing, 412–13
precompiled procedures, 132
subprograms, 413
unrecognized formats, 195–200
Web application development, 409–12
Web Toolkit, 410, 411
wizard, 101, 103
PL/SQL procedures
    INOUT parameter, 413
    matching documents search, 417–20
    metadata extraction, 275
    moving data to media table, 204–5
    OUT parameter, 413
    putMetadata() method demonstration,
        278–80
    for uploading images, 154
PL/SQL server pages (PSP), 233, 416
    application development, 417
    browser links to, 417
    compiler, 417
    defined, 416
PL/SQL stored procedures
    defined, 70
    execution, 293, 409
    IN, 70
    INOUT, 70, 71
    OUT, 70, 71
    parameters, 70
    using, 70–74
Plug-ins
    browser, 89–90
    interMedia data source, 464
    Microsoft Streaming Services, 136
    Real/Helix server, 133
PNG file format, 14

"Principle of triangulation," 223
ProcessAudioCommand() method, 284, 344
ProcessCopy() method, 164, 265, 266
    defined, 342
    failure, 408
    operations, 266–67
    process() method versus, 267
    verbs used with, 270–71
Process() method, 265, 266
    defined, 342
    operations, 266–67
    processCopy() method versus, 267
    verbs used with, 270–71
ProcessSourceCommand() method, 344, 347,
        349
ProcessVideoCommand() method, 347
Progressive download, 35
Property Inspector, 248
Prototypes, 240–52
    build and test stage, 250
    defined, 242
    high-fidelity, 245–52
    interface evaluation methods, 249–50
    low-fidelity, 243–45
    problems, 249
    reasons for, 240–42
    strategies, 242
    See also Application planning
Proxy classes, 334–51
    database table for, 334
    JDBC connection, 335–36
    media rows, creating, 336–37
    preparing to use, 335–39
    SQL Select statement, executing, 337–38
    use actions, 335
    using, 338
PSD file format, 27
Publishing points, 138–39
    creating, 465–67
    illustrated, 467
PutMetadata() method, 277–81

demonstration, 278–80
    string parameter, 281
    XML data, 277

Quality in use
    defined, 254
    metrics, 255–56
    See also Test infrastructure
Quantize verb, 273–74
Queries, 397–420
    ABR, 440–41
    advanced, 439–59
    media data, 408
    nesting, 415
    processing, metadata use, 401
Query-by-example (QBE), 400–401
    defined, 400
    requirements, 401
Quicktime, 41

RAW images, 28
ReadFromSource() method, 344, 347, 349
Real/Helix server, 133–36, 469–73
    background, 469
    database procedures for, 473
    header cache size parameter, 472
    integration with Oracle, 469–70
    lob fetch size parameter, 472
    max cached connections parameter, 472–
        73
    MIME type, 134–35
    mount point creation, 470–73
    plug-in, 133
    streaming, 469
    See also Streaming
RealMedia, 41
Real-time media, 34–41
    3GP standards, 41
    audio, 37

availability, 38–41
streaming, 37–38
video, 34–37
Real-Time Streaming Protocol (RTSP), 41
Red, green, and blue (RGB), 17, 30–31
comparison, 32
defined, 31
REDO logs, 431, 434
Relational approach, 55–58
Report Wizard, 108, 111
Requirements gathering, 215–27
bias possibility, 221
costs, 221
data, 217
density of information, 221
environmental, 217–18
functional, 217
objectives, 221
objectivity /subjectivity, 221
"principle of triangulation," 223
reliability of information, 221
richness of information, 221
scenarios, 223–25
stories and, 225
techniques for rich-media applications,
222–23
tools and techniques, 220–27
usability, 218–20
user, 218
as user needs, 215–16
See also Application planning
Requirements refinement, 252–53
Resampling. *See* Interpolation
Resolution, 15–18
color depth, 17
image channels, 17
pixel count, 15
pixels and, 16
spatial, 16
Resource Description Framework (RDF), 45,
46

Resources, 477–78
Response time, 257
Retrieval process, 444–48
Rotate operator, 271
ROWIDs, 182, 183, 201
Rows
adding, from remote database, 207
inserting, 168, 182
insertion commands, 173–75
media, creating, 336–37
objects, 310
object table, 309–10
populating, 175–78
scanning through, 202
worked-on, referencing, 201
See also Tables
RPIX file format, 28, 263
RYB color system, 32, 33

Scenarios, 223–25
elements, 223–24
uses, 224
Schemas
defining, 235–40
metadata, 375–80
XML, 46, 274
SELECT statement, 72, 151
Selfish invocation style, 294
Server-side SQL, 416–19
Servlets, 92–93
Java classes for, 351–72
media delivery with, 356–61
media upload classes for, 361–72
SetAudioDuration() method, 344
SetBitRate() method, 347
SetComments() method, 287, 344, 347, 349
SetCompressionFormat() method, 342
SetCompressionType() method, 344, 347
SetContentFormat() method, 342
SetContentLength() method, 342

SetDescription() method, 344, 348
SetEncoding() method, 344, 348
SetFormat() method, 341
SetFrameRate() method, 348
SetFrameResolution() method, 348
SetHeight() method, 342, 348
SetKnownAttributes() method, 345
SetLocal() method, 341
SetMimeType() method, 192, 341
SetNumberOfChannels() method, 345
SetNumberOfColors() method, 348
SetNumberOfFrames() method, 348
SetProperties() method, 192, 264
    audio metadata, 284
    defined, 342, 345, 348, 349
    empty parameter list, 294
    obj variable, 265
    overhead, 196
    populating metadata with, 169
    support, 67, 75, 76
SetSampleSize method, 345
SetSamplingRate() method, 345
SetSource() method, 341
SetUpdateTime() method, 341
SetVideoDuration() method, 348
SetWidth() method, 342, 348
Shapes, 443
SI_AverageColor() method, 449, 451, 452
SI_AverageColor type, 79
SI_ClearFeatures() method, 305, 450
    function, 305, 306
    unsupported image formats and, 306
SI_Color, 449
SI_ColorHistogram type, 80, 449, 453–58
    attributes, 453
    defined, 80
SI_Content() method, 450
SI_FeatureList type, 80, 449, 456
SI_InitFeatures() method, 305, 450
    calling, 305–6
    function, 305

SI_MkAvgClr(), 298
SI_MkFtrList(), 456
SI_MkStillImageI(), 304–5
SI_PositionalColor type, 80, 449
SI_RetainFeatures() method, 450
SI_Score() method, 451, 453
SI_SetContent() method, 451
SI_StillImage type, 81, 296–308
    attributes, 296–97
    attributes, initializing, 299, 301–2
    for CBIR, 448–58
    constructor methods, 298–99
    content, explicitFormat, 301–3
    content, explicitFormat, height, width,
        303–4
    contentLength_SI, 296
    content_SI, 296
    data attributes, 82
    DBMS_LOB package, 299–301
    format_SI, 296
    height_SI, 296
    image processing methods, 305–8
    methods, 297–305
    objects, 260
    SI_MkStillImageI() function, 304–5
    structure, 296
    for table columns, 298
    width_SI, 297
SI_Texture type, 80, 449
SI_Thumbnail() method, 305
    function, 305
    use, 307
Spatial resolution, 16
SQL
    query statements, 402
    server-side, 416–19
    source view, 430
    UPDATE operation, 411
    using, 401–4
SQL:1999, 236, 238
    attribute specification, 296

stereotypes, 239–40
user-defined data types, 260
SQL*Loader, 201–3
    advantage, 201
    control file, 201–2
    invoking, 202
    loading over network, 201
SQL/MM, 78–83
    defined, 78
    as multipart standard, 79
    object types, 79–80
    revised version, 81–82
Streaming, 461–76
    alternatives, 461
    audio, 37–38
    defined, 35
    media players, 461
    with Microsoft Media Services, 136–39,
        462–68
    with Real/Helix server, 133–36, 469–73
    server delivery, 133–39
    summary, 476
    use, 461
    video, 37–38
    viewing, 461
    viewing on wireless devices, 462
Synchronized accessible media interchange
        (SAMI), 463
System global area (SGA), 422

Table partitions, 207
    adding, 208
    exchanging, 210
    moving, 209
Tables
    column data type, 298
    creating, with media data, 430–32
    DICOM image, 393
    DISABLE STORAGE IN ROW
        parameter, 432

downloading image data from, 165
external, 203–7
external, loading, 201
heterogeneous data, 291
for historical archiving, 208
INITIAL parameter, 431
inserting rows, 168
MAXEXTENTS, 432
NEXT parameter, 431
object, 309–10
ORDImage object in, 158
PCTINCREASE parameter, 431
row IDs, 168
target, 210
uploading images from files to, 162–63
Tablespaces
    BLOBS in, 435
    defined, 207
    transportable, 207–10
    writable, 210
Team evidence analysis (TEA) session, 253
Technical architecture, 230
Test infrastructure, 253–57
    external quality, 254
    internal quality, 254
    quality in use, 254, 255–56
    testing process, 255
    See also Application planning
Text-based indexes, 388
Text-based retrieval, 420
    annotations, 420
    defined, 420
    interMedia support, 440
    techniques, 405
Textures, 443
Thick clients
    advantages, 211–12
    loading, 211–12
Throughput time, 257
Thumbnails
    creating, 155–56, 164–65

creating, from SI_StillImage object, 308
default size, 307
extracting from database, 170–71, 178–80
getting, 185–88
obtaining, in file, 156–57
painting logos into, 187
updating, 156
TIFF file format, 15
defined, 28
support, 28–29
Transfer syntax, 281
Transportable tablespaces, 207–10
creating, 208
defined, 207
moving data with, 207, 209
self-contained tablespaces, 207
using, 207–8
writable, 210
See also Tablespaces
TrimSource() method, 345, 348, 350
Tuning, 422–30
automatic, 422–23
goal, 422
SGA, 422
See also Application performance

UI debugger, 254
UML, 236
advantage, 235
class attributes, 237
classes, 261
conceptual schema, 237
graphical representation, 235
specific logical schema, 237
Universal preservation format (UPF), 43
UPDATE statement, 72, 275, 287
Uploading
images from files to tables, 162–63
media from browser, 363
media over HTTP, 362

multimedia data with JSP tag library, 329–34
Usability
goals, 218
metrics, 255
planning, 240–41
poor design, 240
Usability requirements, 218–20
case study, 218–20
defined, 218
See also Requirements gathering
User-centered design (UCD), 215
User-defined data types, 260
User needs, 215–16
aspirational, 216
defined, 215
functional, 216
physical, 216
See also Requirements
User requirements, 218
User stories, 225

VARRAY collection type, 237
Vector graphics
defined, 10
image advantages, 24
Verbs
cut, 272
gamma processing, 271
image processing, 268–70
with processCopy() method, 270–71
processing, effects, 272
with process() method, 270–71
quantize, 273–74
Vertical prototyping
defined, 242
illustrated, 243
See also Prototypes
Video, 34–37
audiovisual feature extraction, 34

data attributes, 289
from database, 135
delivery, 35
download, 35
exception type and, 199
file formats, 37
loading, 198–99
loading, from local source, 192–94
progressive download, 35
streaming, 35
on Web page, 136
See also Audio; Images
Video Studio, preparing for ODP.NET, 172
Visual attributes, 442–43
color, 442
distances, 444, 445, 446
location, 443
shape, 443
similarity over, 445
texture, 443
weights, 446, 447
Visual-Linguistic (VL) mode, 399
Visual Studio .NET, prerequisites for Oracle
with, 172
Visual-Visual (VV) mode, 399

WBMP format
defined, 29
images, 143
WebDAV
configuration file, 148
container, browsing, 150
defined, 231
server, 149
as standard extension, 231
Web forms, loading, 210–11

Web services, 233–34
Windows Media format, 41
Windows Media Player, format support, 463
WriteToSource() method, 345, 348, 350

XHTML/XForms, 140
XML
data storage, 376
data types, 382
storing in CLOB, 388
XML DB, 375
annotations, 378
Developers Guide, 380
structured storage, 380
XML documents, 46–47, 379
schema-based, 47
structure, 379
XML schemas, 274
available, 46
in DTD format, 375
metadata, 46
registration, 375
storage, 379
XMP, 391
XMLType, 375, 376
indexing, 387
structured, 387–88
unstructured, 380
XMP
defined, 46
packets, 277
XML schema, 391

Zachman's enterprise, 228, 229–30

www.ingramcontent.com/pod-product-compliance
Lightning Source LLC
Chambersburg PA
CBHW080117220326
41598CB00032B/4874